I HEAR THAT THE COMIC VERSION OF "DEATH NOTE" WILL FIRST HIT
JAPANESE BOOKSTORES ON APRIL 2, 2004.

SNOWMELT FLOWS INTO STREAMS
AND BELOW THE DANCING PETALS OF CHERRY BLOSSOMS
STIRRED UP BY THE SPRING WIND
FIRST GRADERS, BRIGHTLY COLORED WITH THEIR SHINY LEATHER
BACKPACKS
HOLD HANDS AND STEP OUT TOWARD HOPE ON THE GREEN.

-TSUGUMI OHBA

Tsugumi Ohba
Born in Tokyo.
Hobby: Collecting teacups
Day and night, develops manga plots
while holding knees on a chair.

Takeshi Obata was born in 1969 in Niigata, and is the
artist of the wildly popular SHONEN JUMP title **Hikaru
no Go**, which won the 2003 Tezuka Shinsei "New Hope"
award and the Shogakukan Manga award. Obata is also
the artist of **Arabian Majin Bokentan Lamp Lamp,
Ayatsuri Sakon** and **Cyborg Jichan G**.

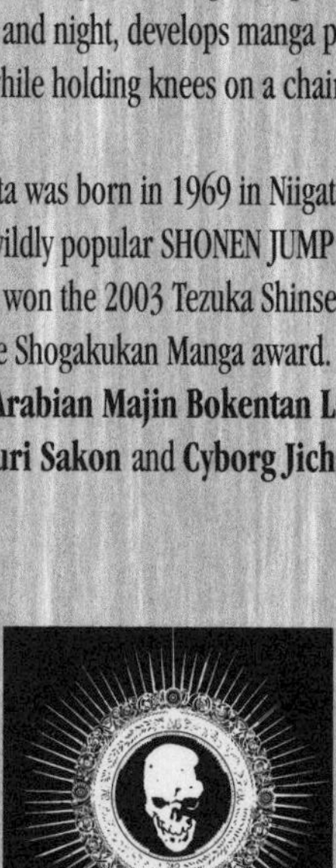

DEATH NOTE VOL 1
SHONEN JUMP ADVANCED Manga Edition

STORY BY TSUGUMI OHBA
ART BY TAKESHI OBATA

Translation & Adaptation/Pookie Rolf
Consultant/Alexis Kirsch
Touch-up Art & Lettering/Gia Cam Luc
Design/Sean Lee
Editor/Pancha Diaz

Printed in the U.S.A.

Published by VIZ Media, LLC
P.O. Box 77010
San Francisco, CA 94107

29
First printing, September 2005
Twenty-ninth printing, August 2016

PARENTAL ADVISORY
DEATH NOTE is rated T+ for Older Teen and is recom-
mended for ages 16 and up. It contains fantasy violence.

ratings.viz.com

SHONEN JUMP ADVANCED MANGA

DEATH NOTE

デスノート

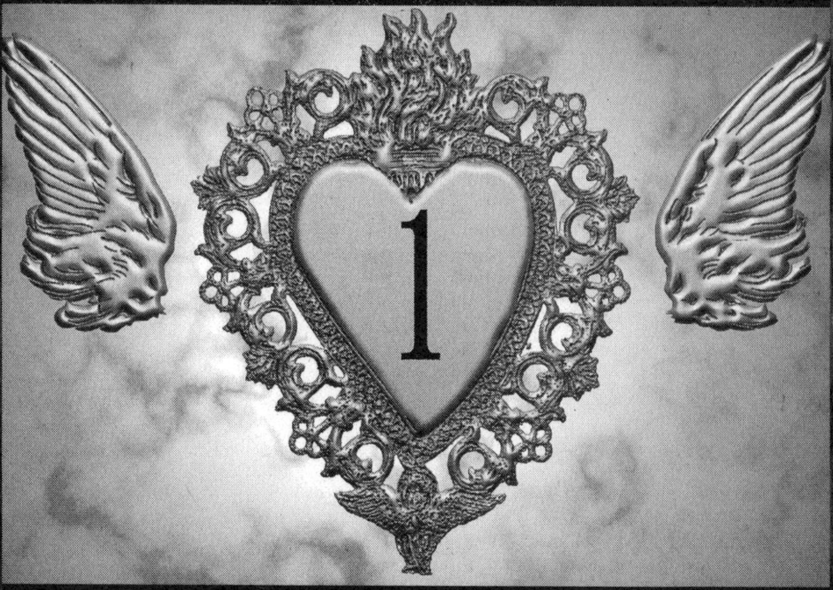
1

Vol. 1

Boredom

Story by Tsugumi Ohba
Art by Takeshi Obata

DEATH NOTE
Vol. 1

CONTENTS

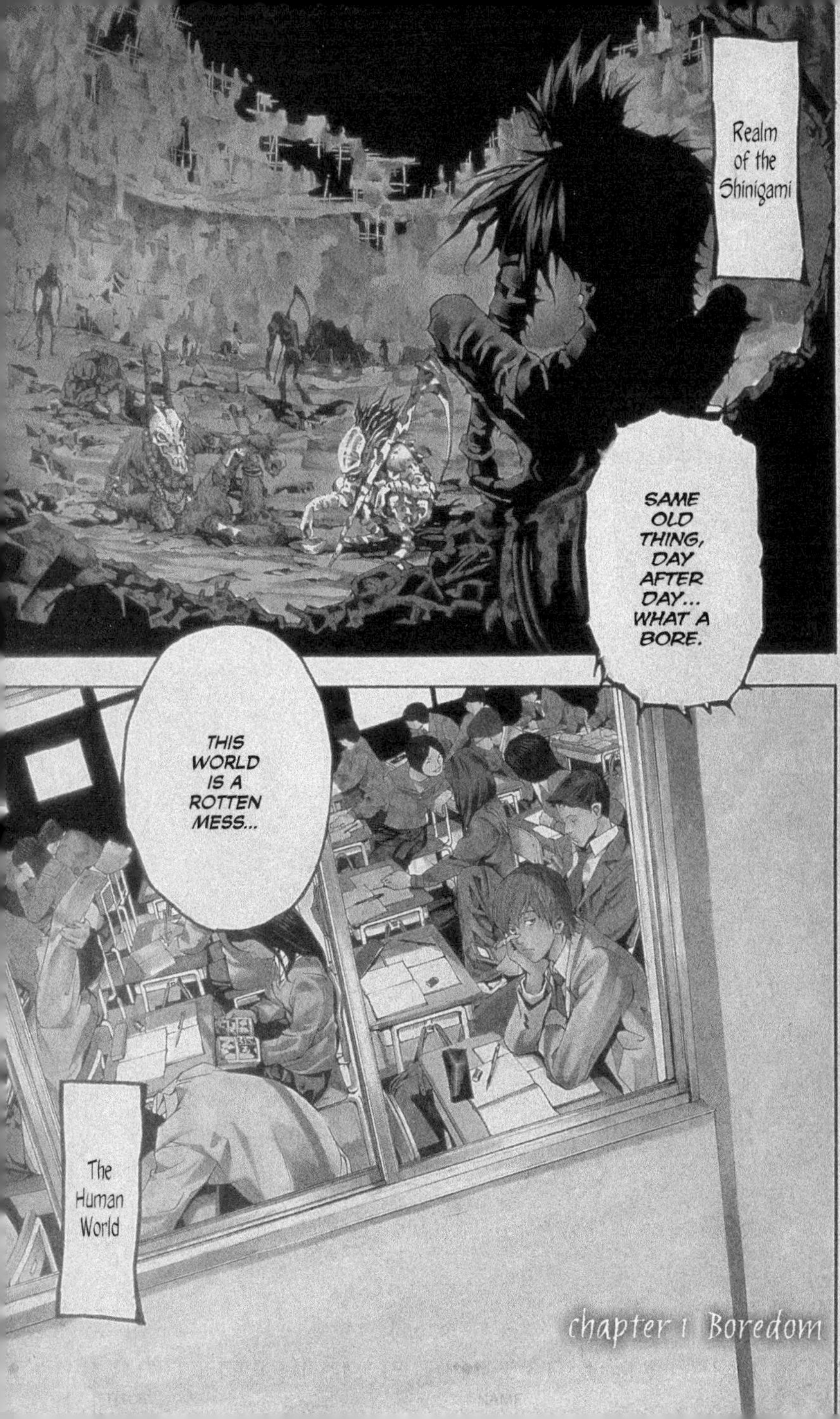
Realm of the Shinigami
SAME OLD THING, DAY AFTER DAY... WHAT A BORE.
THIS WORLD IS A ROTTEN MESS...
The Human World
chapter 1 Boredom

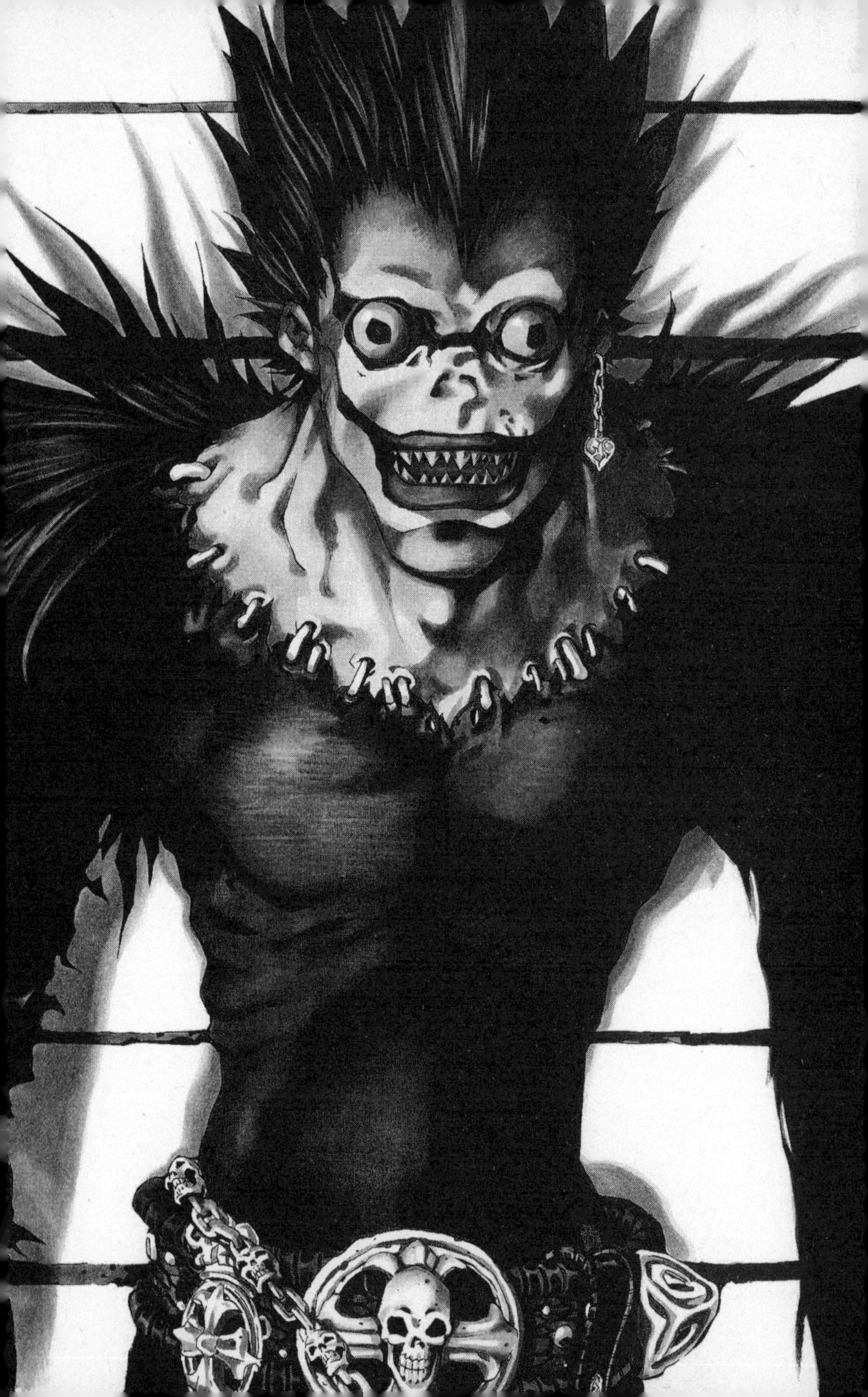

chapter 1 Boredom

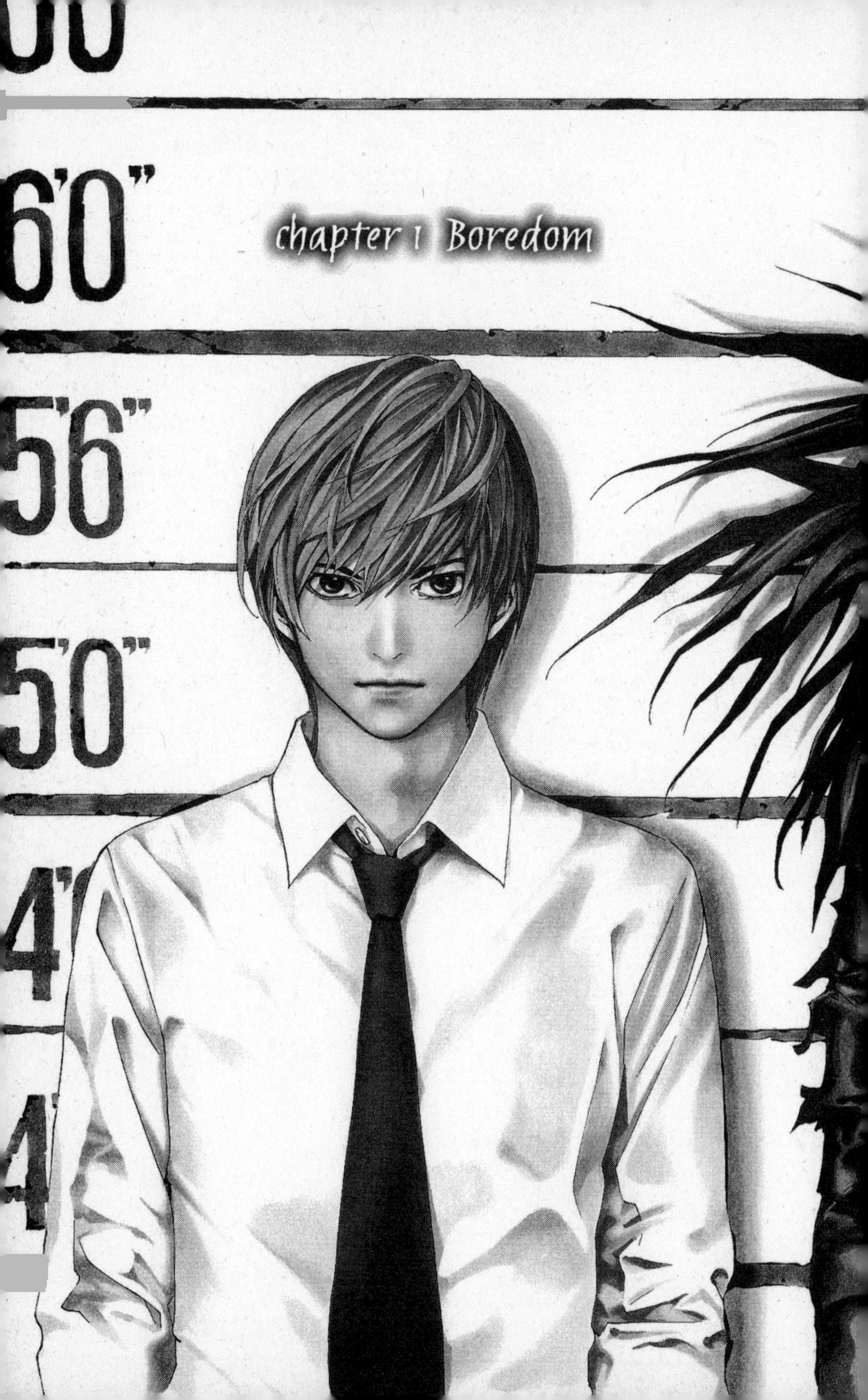
6'0"
5'6"
5'0"

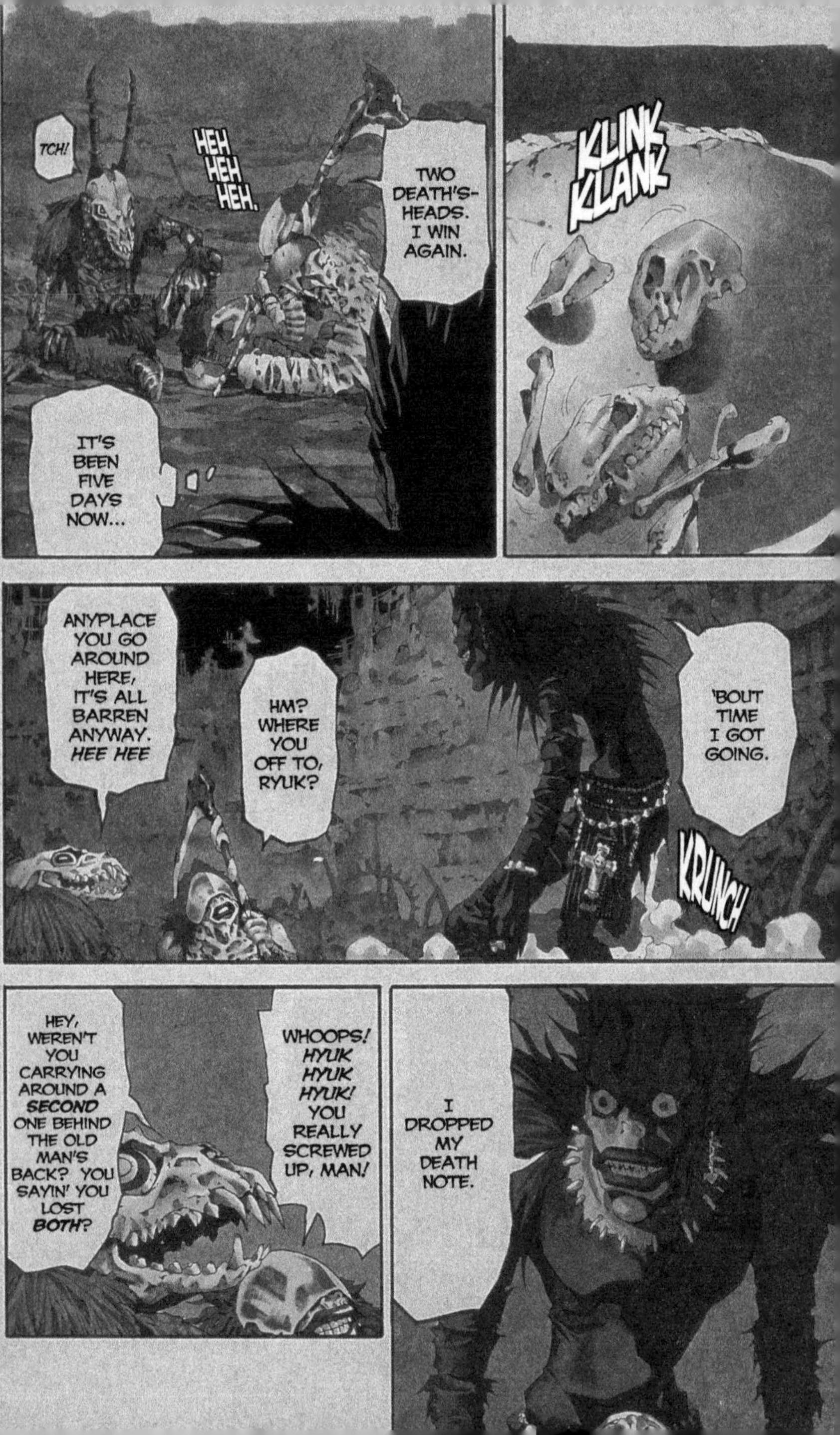
KLINK KLANK
TWO DEATH'S-HEADS. I WIN AGAIN.
HEH HEH HEH.
TCH!
IT'S BEEN FIVE DAYS NOW...
'BOUT TIME I GOT GOING.
KRUNCH
HM? WHERE YOU OFF TO, RYUK?
ANYPLACE YOU GO AROUND HERE, IT'S ALL BARREN ANYWAY. HEE HEE
I DROPPED MY DEATH NOTE.
WHOOPS! HYUK HYUK HYUK! YOU REALLY SCREWED UP, MAN!
HEY, WEREN'T YOU CARRYING AROUND A SECOND ONE BEHIND THE OLD MAN'S BACK? YOU SAYIN' YOU LOST BOTH?

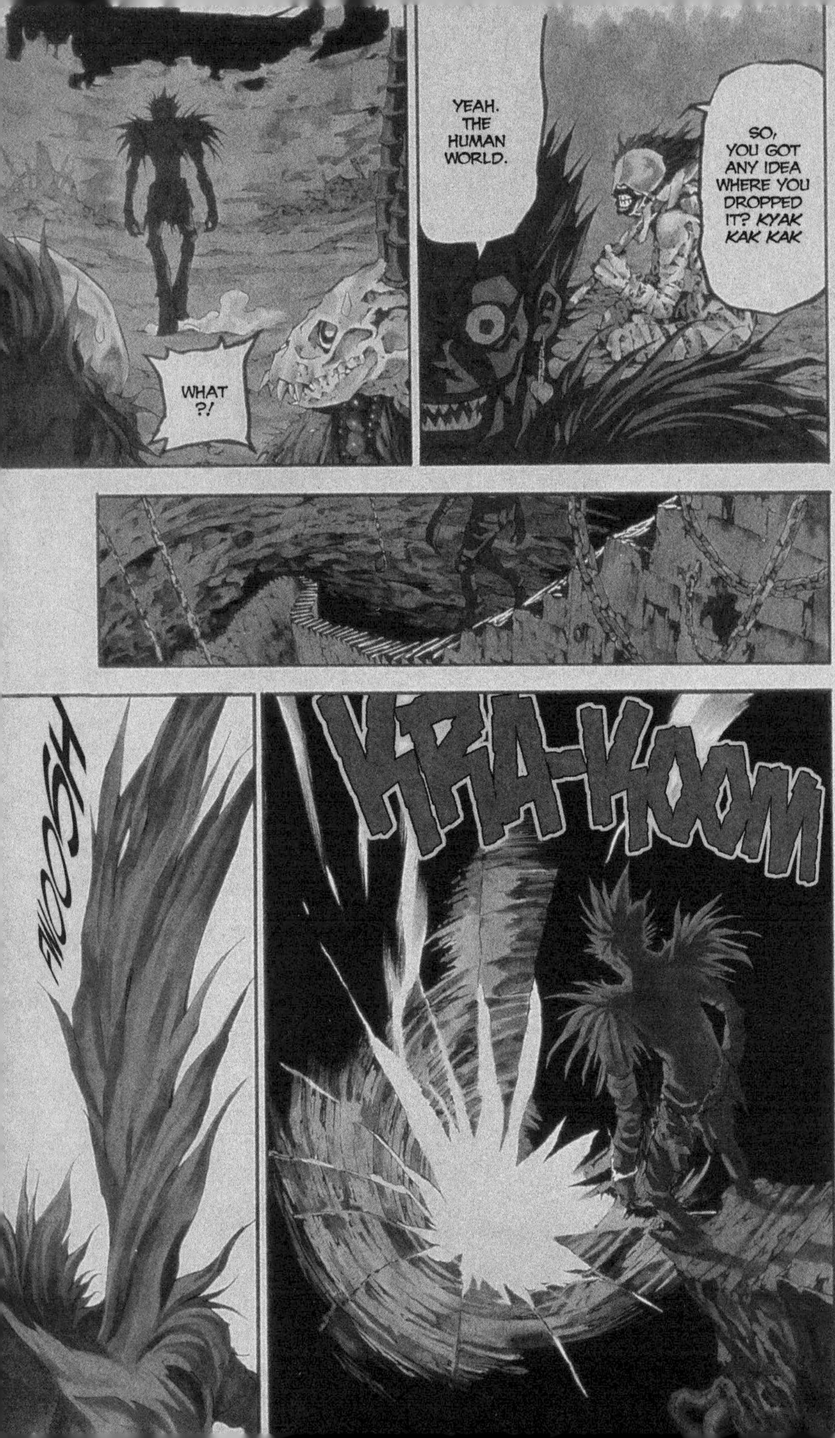
SO, YOU GOT ANY IDEA WHERE YOU DROPPED IT? KYAK KAK KAK
YEAH. THE HUMAN WORLD.
WHAT ?!
KRA-KOOM
WHOOSH

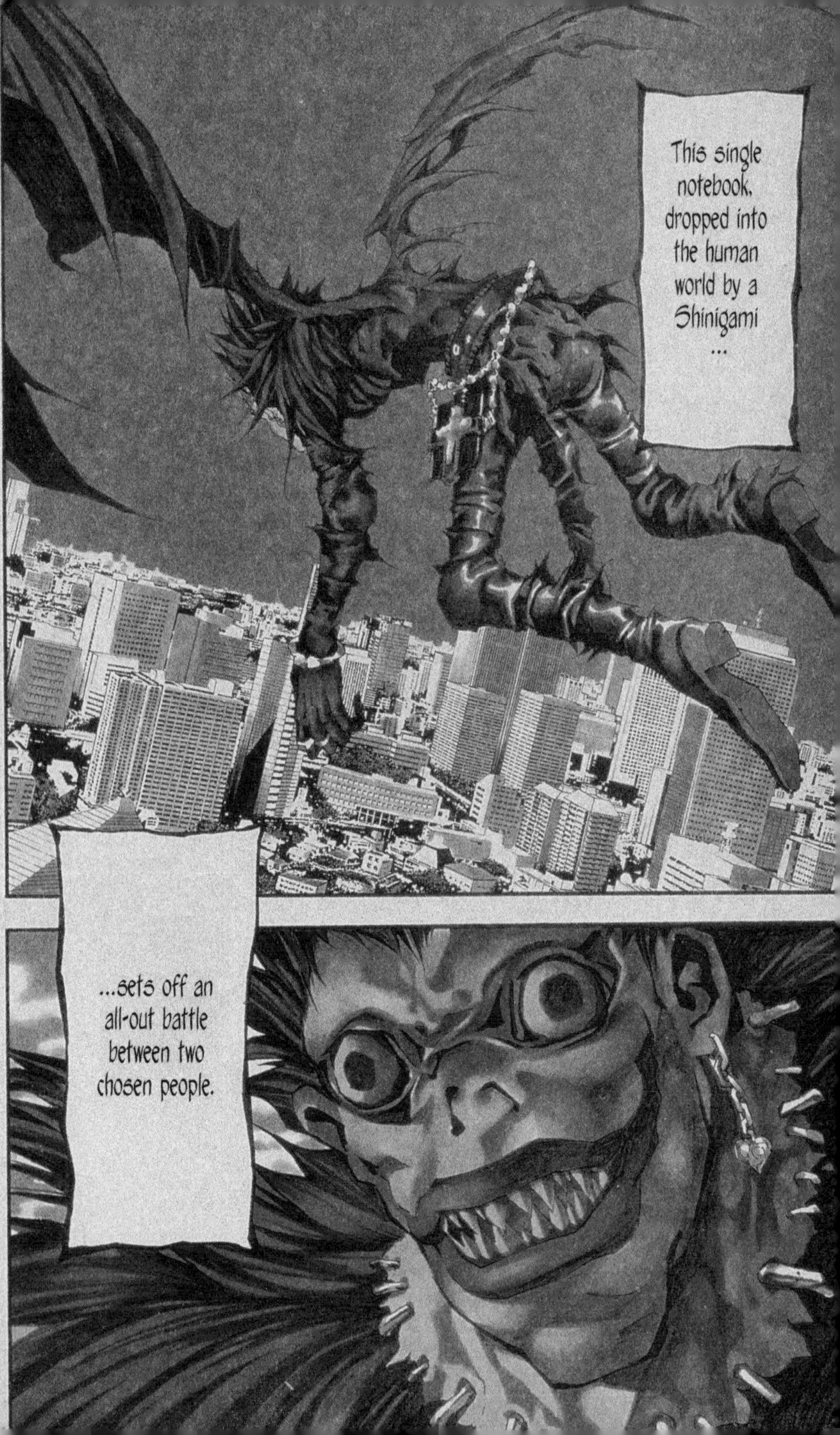
This single notebook, dropped into the human world by a Shinigami ...
...sets off an all-out battle between two chosen people.

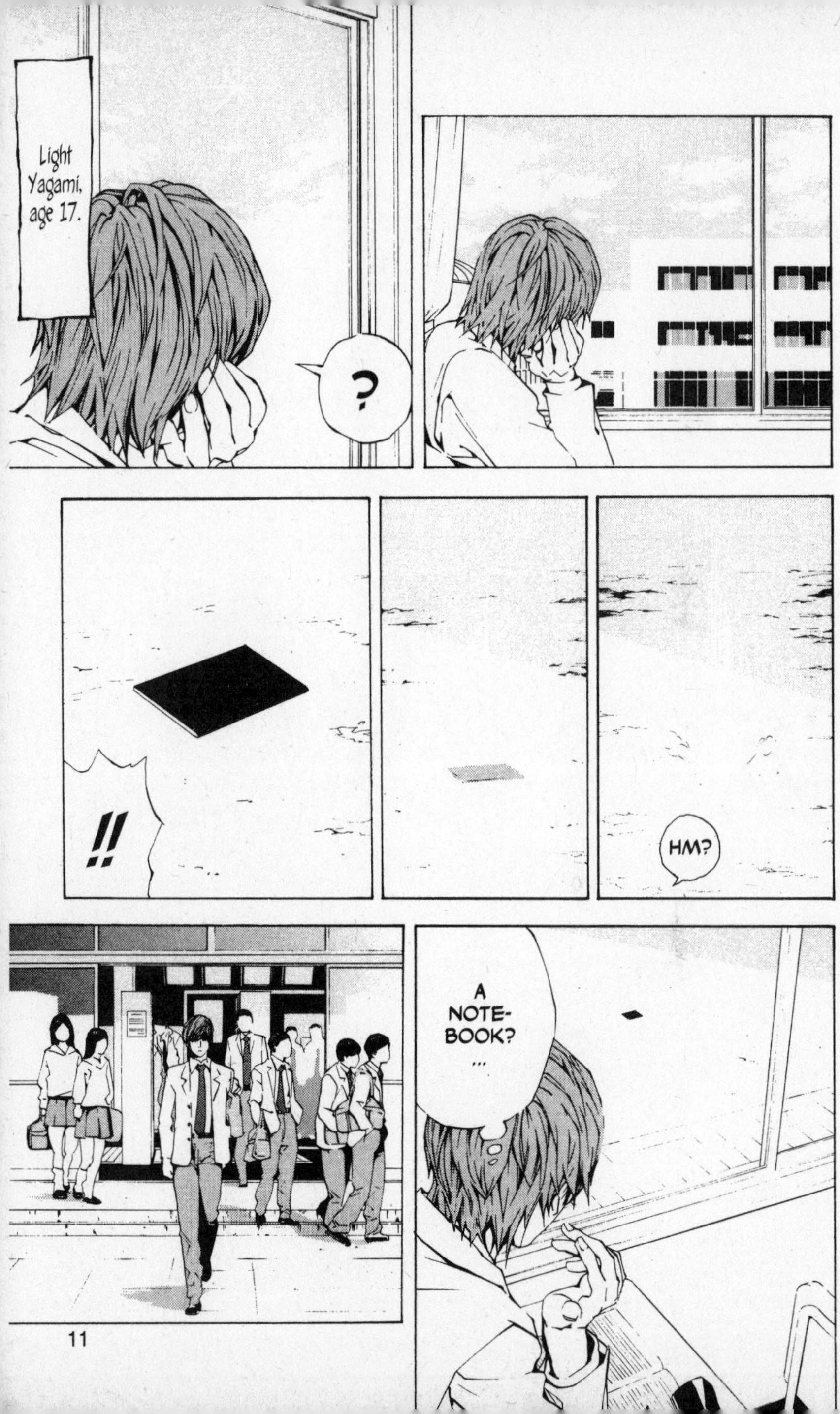
Light Yagami, age 17.
?
HM?
!!
A NOTE-BOOK? ...

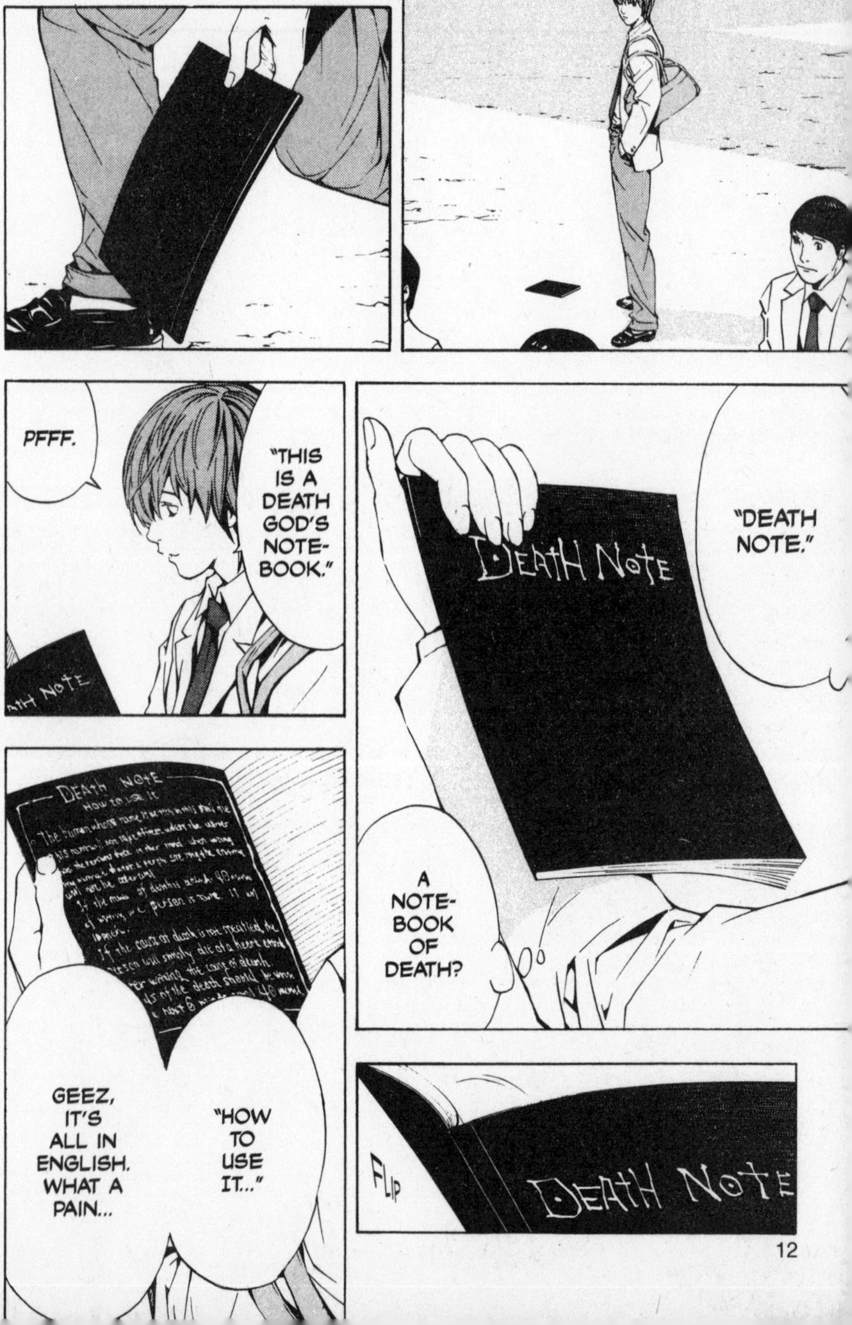
"DEATH NOTE."
DEATH NOTE
A NOTEBOOK OF DEATH?
FLIP
DEATH NOTE
"THIS IS A DEATH GOD'S NOTEBOOK."
PFFF.
DEATH NOTE
HOW TO USE IT
"HOW TO USE IT..."
GEEZ, IT'S ALL IN ENGLISH. WHAT A PAIN...

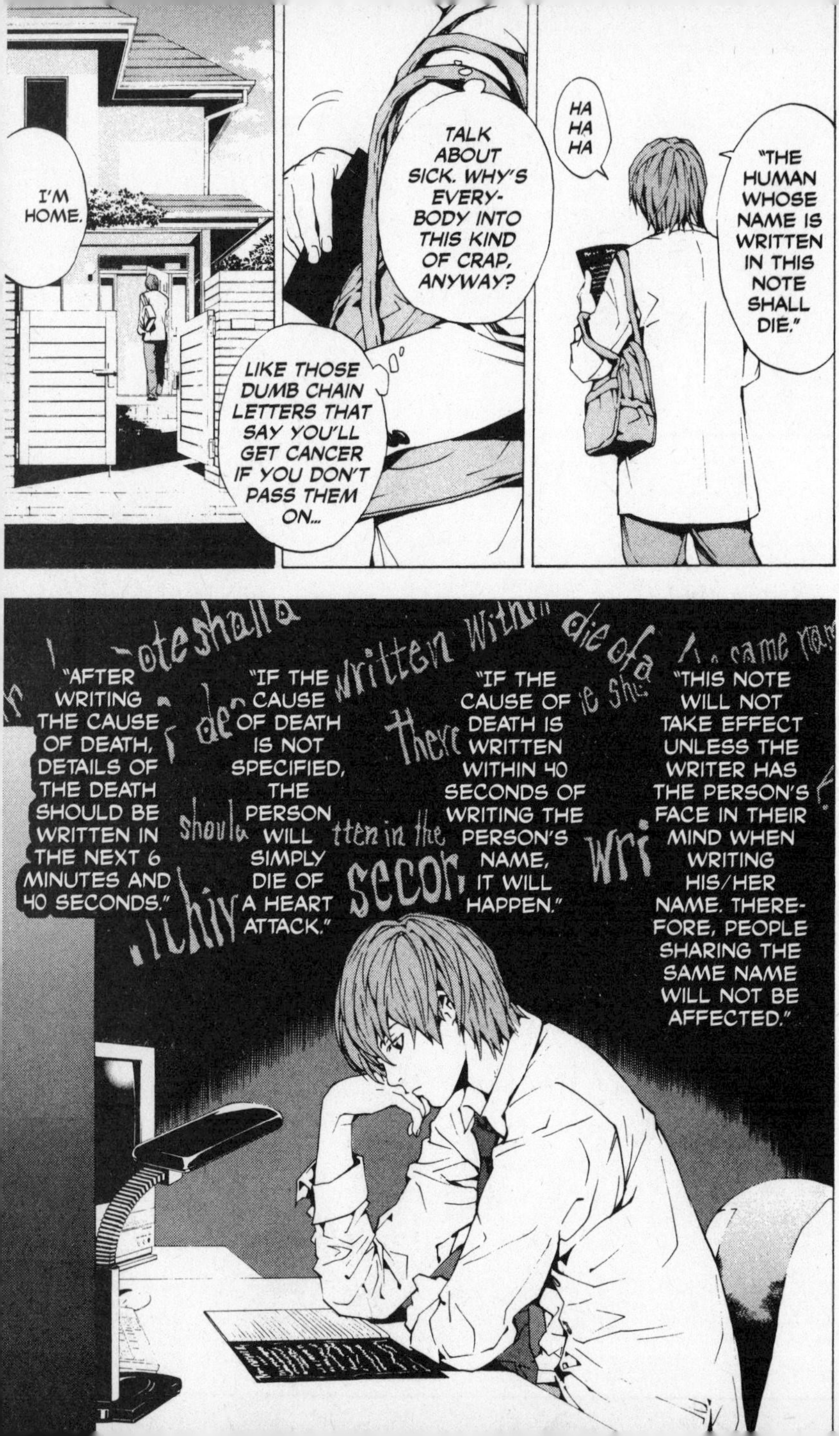
"THE HUMAN WHOSE NAME IS WRITTEN IN THIS NOTE SHALL DIE."
HA HA HA
TALK ABOUT SICK. WHY'S EVERY-BODY INTO THIS KIND OF CRAP, ANYWAY?
LIKE THOSE DUMB CHAIN LETTERS THAT SAY YOU'LL GET CANCER IF YOU DON'T PASS THEM ON...
I'M HOME.
"THIS NOTE WILL NOT TAKE EFFECT UNLESS THE WRITER HAS THE PERSON'S FACE IN THEIR MIND WHEN WRITING HIS/HER NAME. THERE-FORE, PEOPLE SHARING THE SAME NAME WILL NOT BE AFFECTED."
"IF THE CAUSE OF DEATH IS WRITTEN WITHIN 40 SECONDS OF WRITING THE PERSON'S NAME, IT WILL HAPPEN."
"IF THE CAUSE OF DEATH IS NOT SPECIFIED, THE PERSON WILL SIMPLY DIE OF A HEART ATTACK."
"AFTER WRITING THE CAUSE OF DEATH, DETAILS OF THE DEATH SHOULD BE WRITTEN IN THE NEXT 6 MINUTES AND 40 SECONDS."

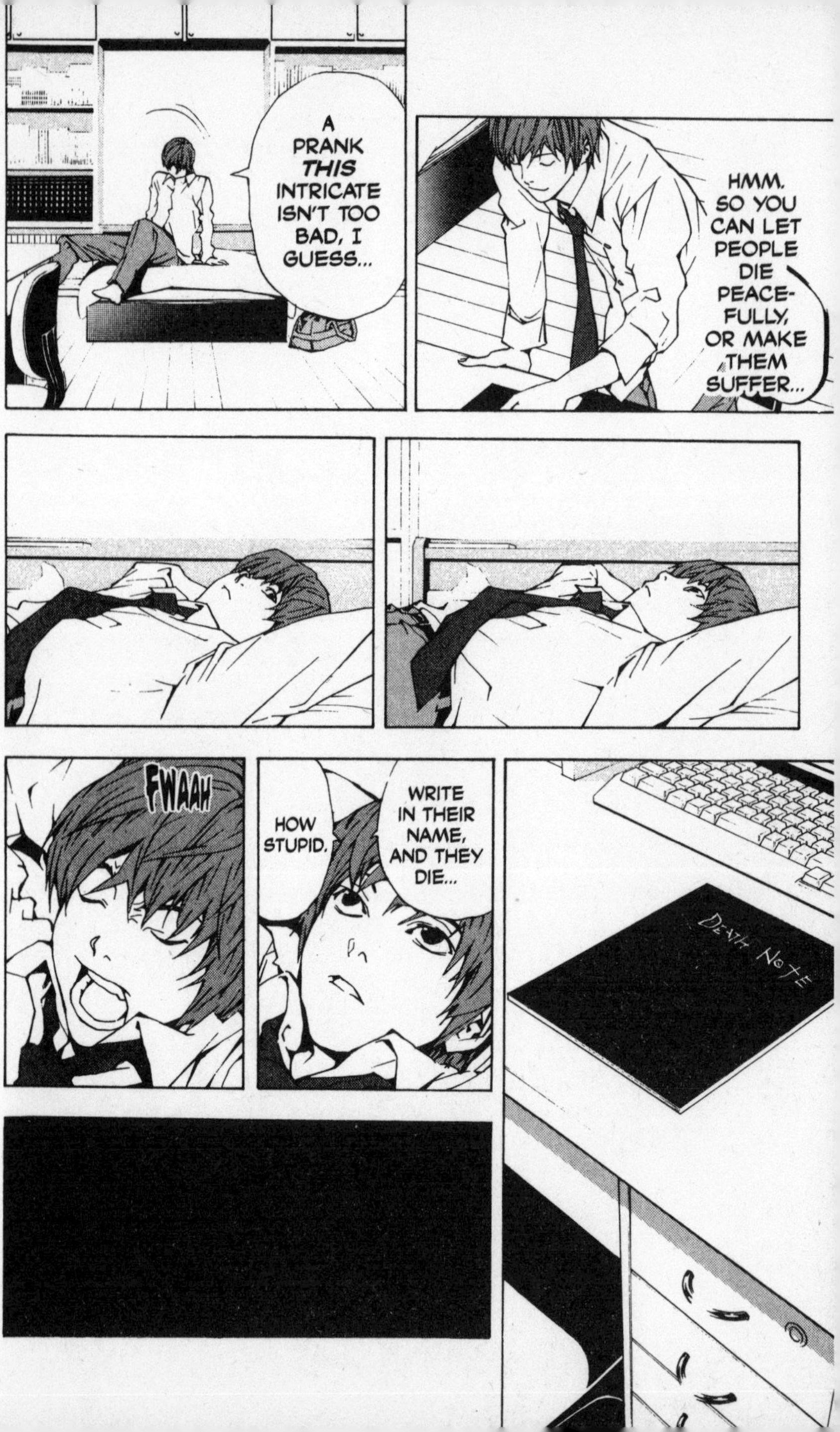
HMM. SO YOU CAN LET PEOPLE DIE PEACEFULLY, OR MAKE THEM SUFFER...
A PRANK *THIS* INTRICATE ISN'T TOO BAD, I GUESS...
DEATH NOTE
WRITE IN THEIR NAME, AND THEY DIE...
HOW STUPID.
FWAAH

READ THIS WAY

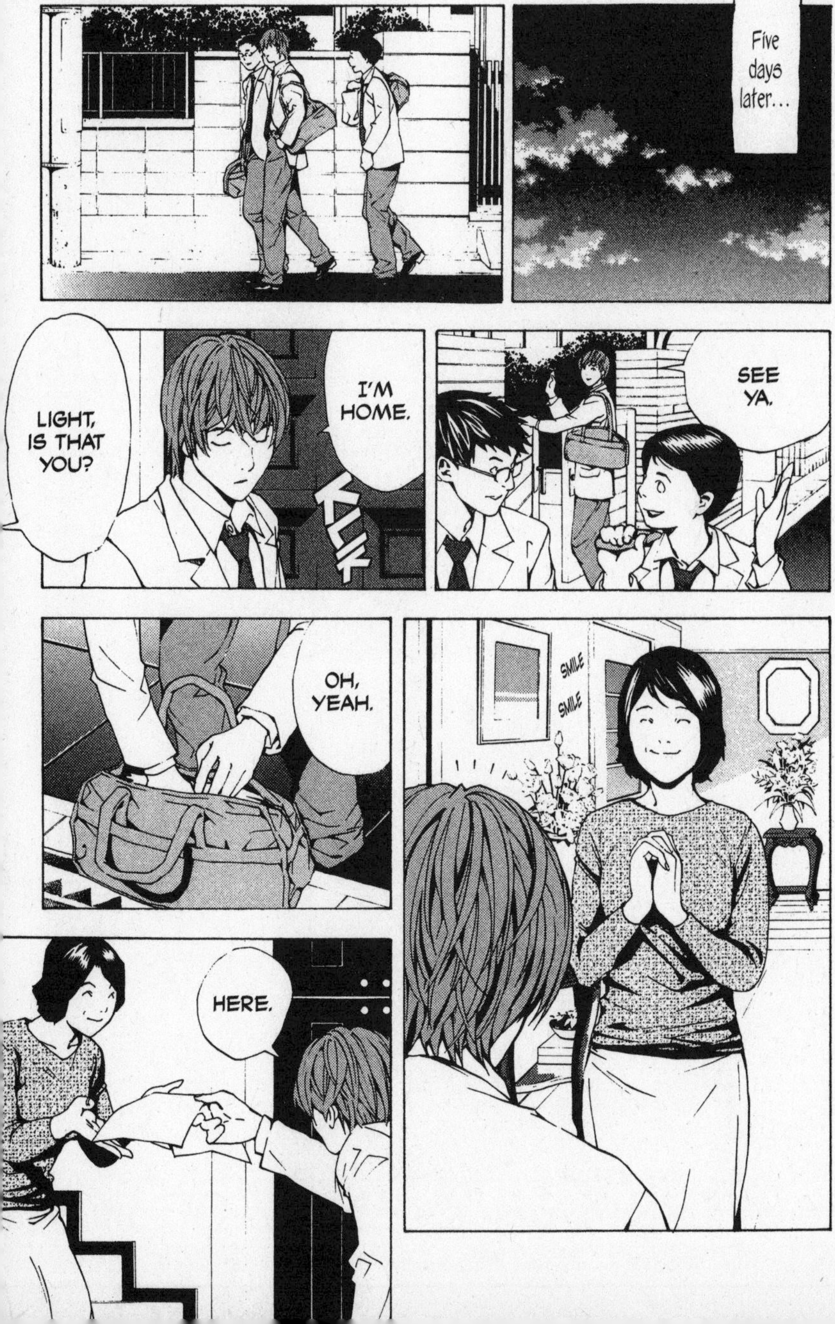
Five days later...
SEE YA.
I'M HOME.
KLIK
LIGHT, IS THAT YOU?
SMILE
SMILE
OH, YEAH.
HERE.

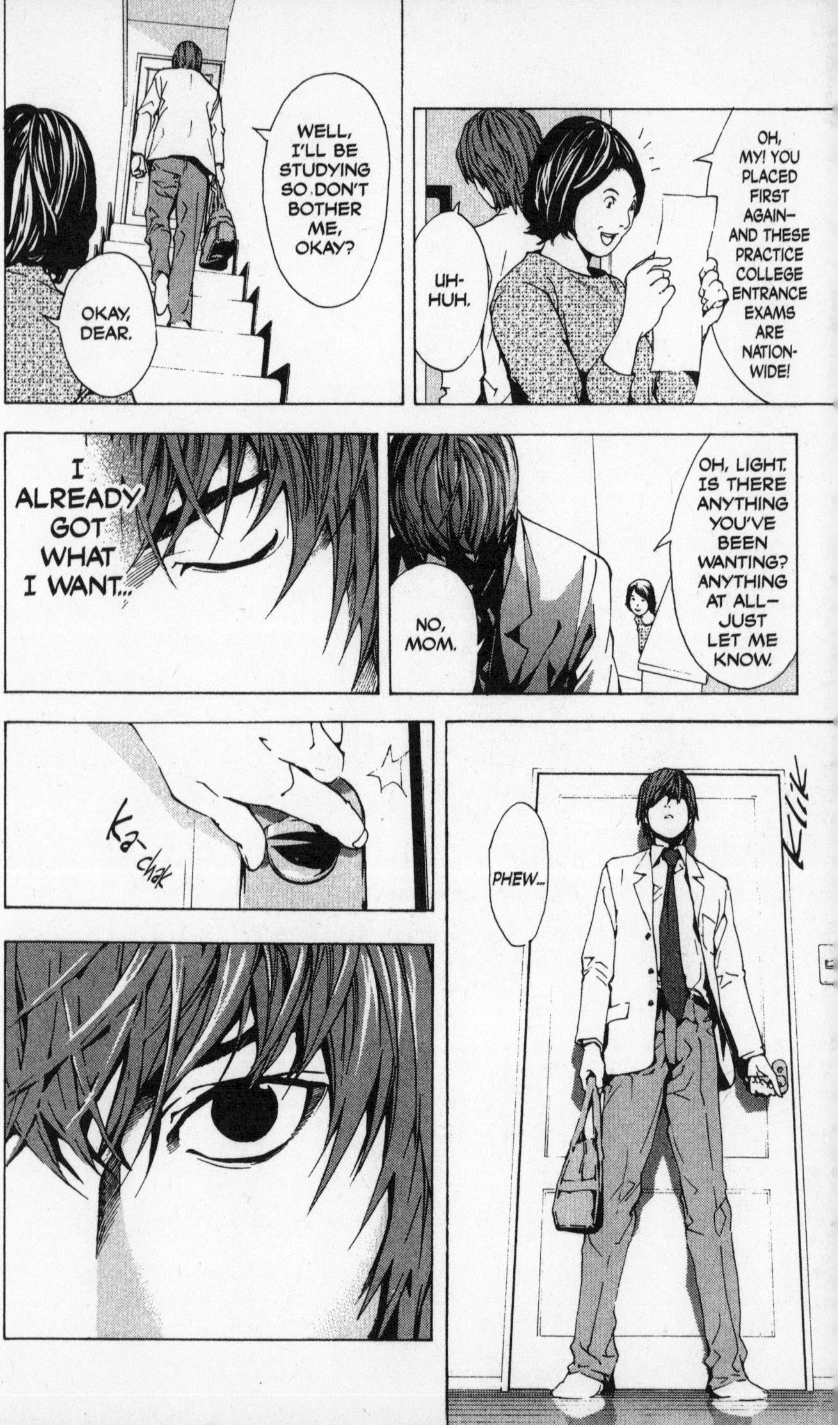

OH, MY! YOU PLACED FIRST AGAIN—AND THESE PRACTICE COLLEGE ENTRANCE EXAMS ARE NATION-WIDE!
UH-HUH.
WELL, I'LL BE STUDYING SO DON'T BOTHER ME, OKAY?
OKAY, DEAR.
OH, LIGHT. IS THERE ANYTHING YOU'VE BEEN WANTING? ANYTHING AT ALL—JUST LET ME KNOW.
NO, MOM.
I ALREADY GOT WHAT I WANT...
Klik
PHEW...
Ka-chak

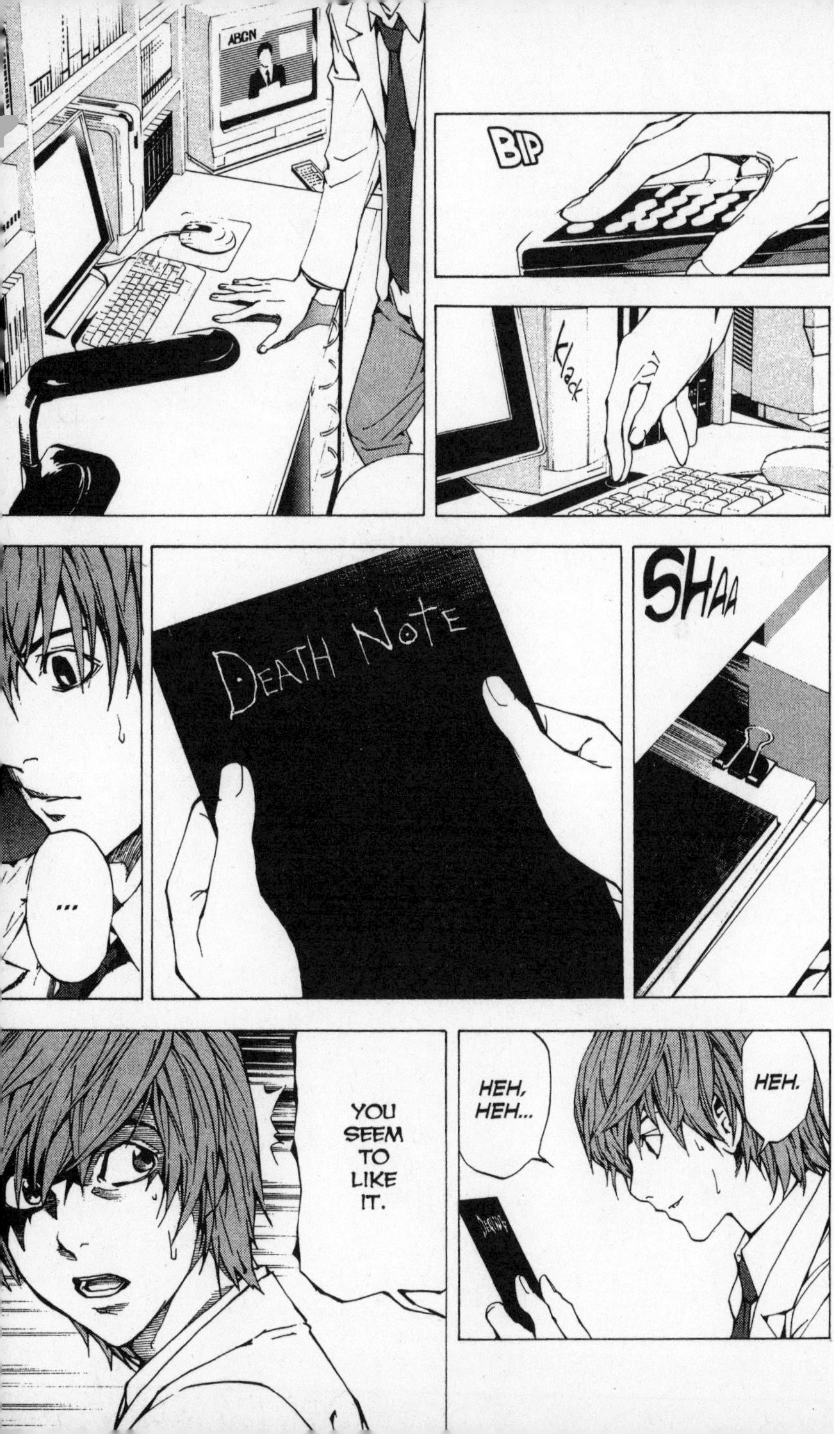
BIP
klack
ABCN
SHAA
DEATH NOTE
...
HEH.
HEH, HEH...
YOU SEEM TO LIKE IT.

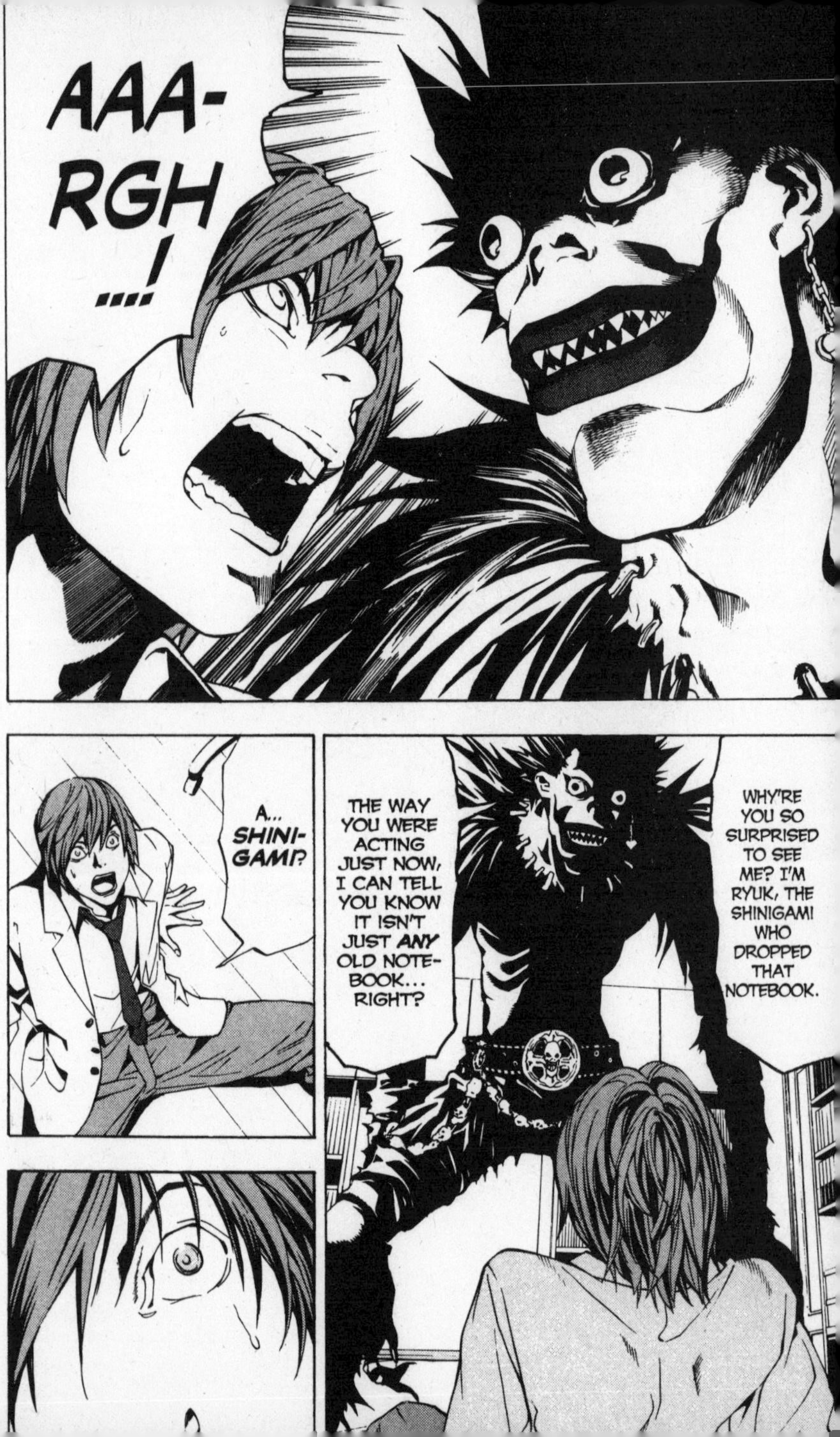
AAA-RGH ....!
WHY'RE YOU SO SURPRISED TO SEE ME? I'M RYUK, THE SHINIGAMI WHO DROPPED THAT NOTEBOOK.
THE WAY YOU WERE ACTING JUST NOW, I CAN TELL YOU KNOW IT ISN'T JUST ANY OLD NOTEBOOK... RIGHT?
A... SHINIGAMI!?

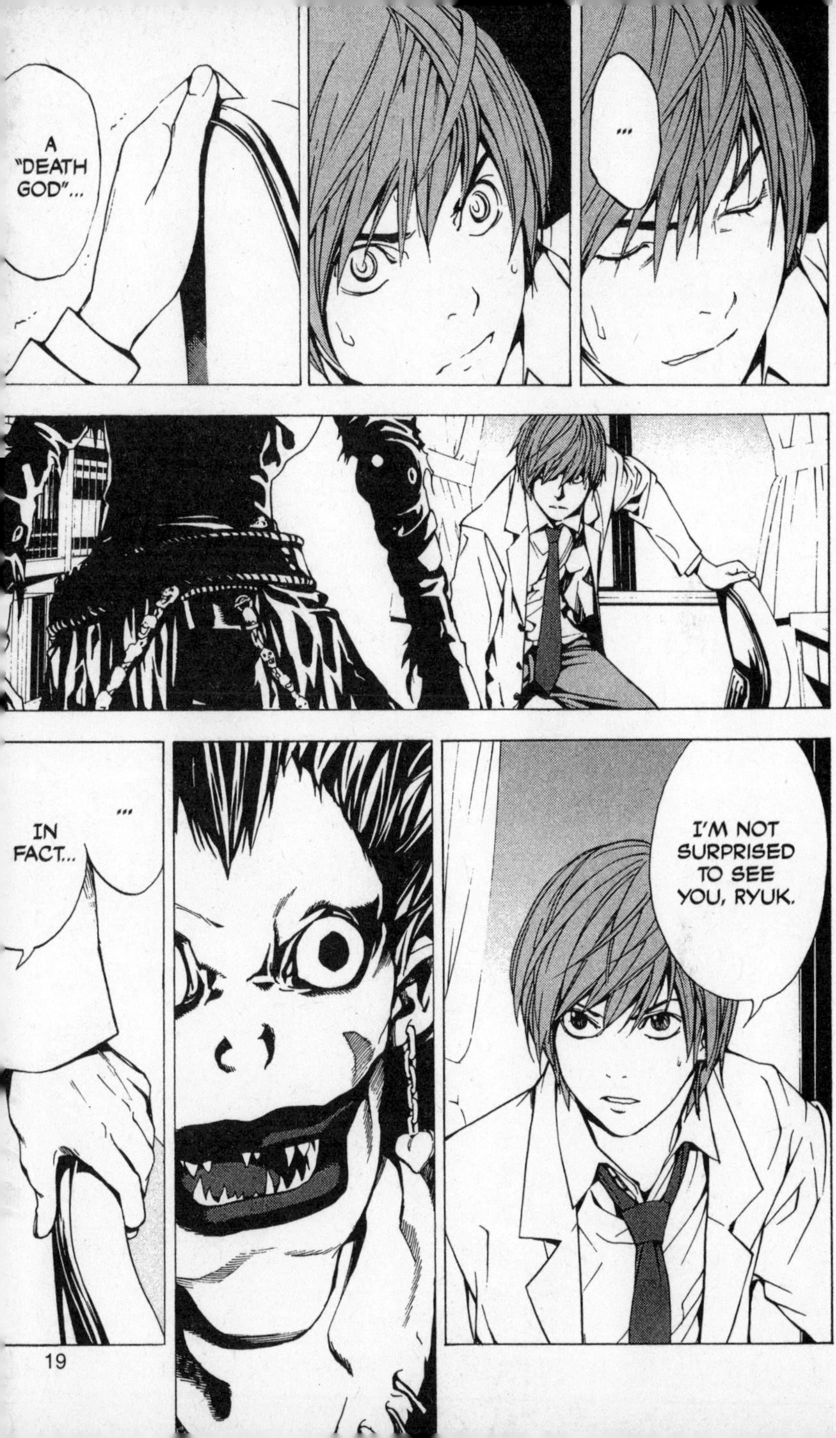
...
A "DEATH GOD"...
I'M NOT SURPRISED TO SEE YOU, RYUK.
... IN FACT...

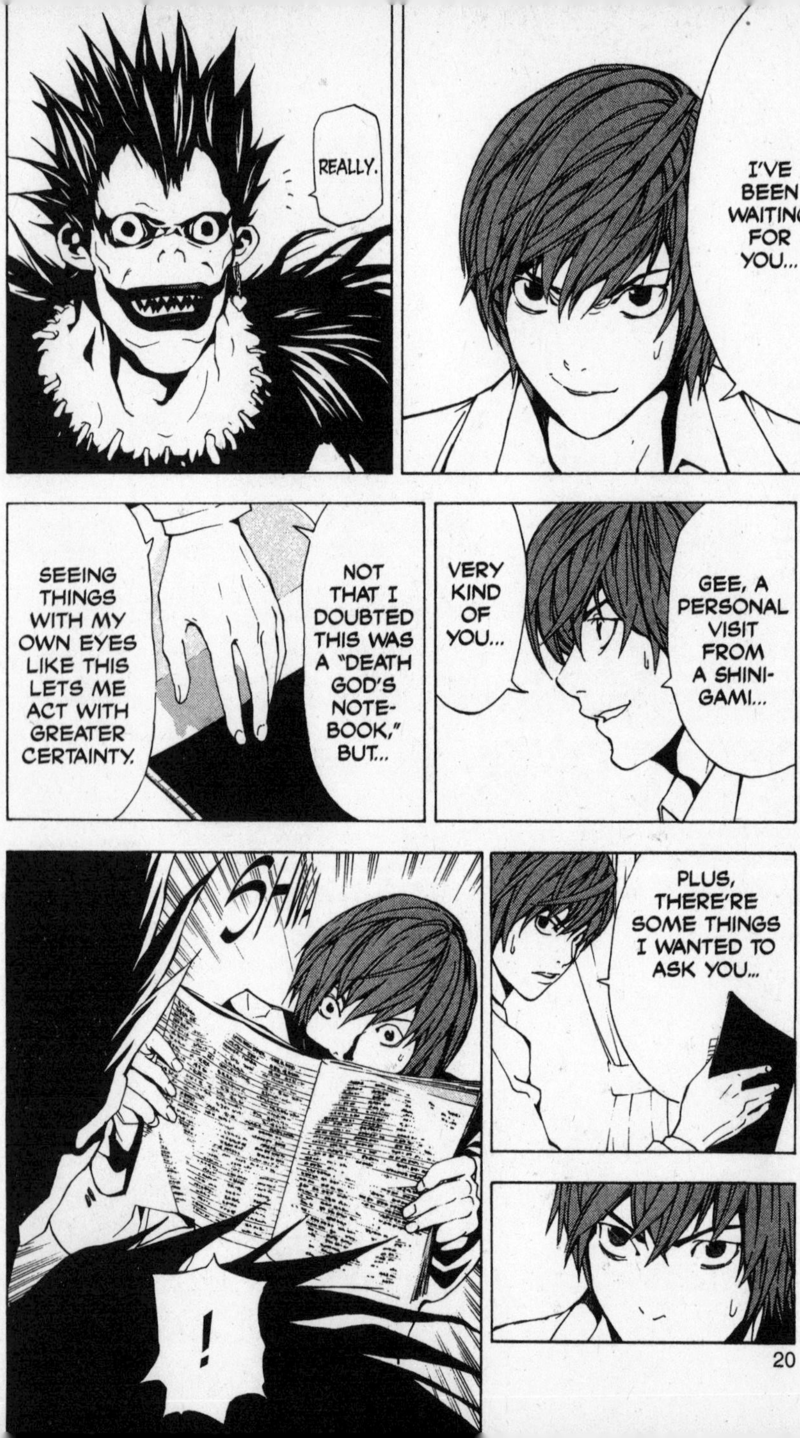
I'VE BEEN WAITING FOR YOU...
REALLY.
GEE, A PERSONAL VISIT FROM A SHINI-GAMI...
VERY KIND OF YOU...
NOT THAT I DOUBTED THIS WAS A "DEATH GOD'S NOTE-BOOK," BUT...
SEEING THINGS WITH MY OWN EYES LIKE THIS LETS ME ACT WITH GREATER CERTAINTY.
PLUS, THERE'RE SOME THINGS I WANTED TO ASK YOU...
SH
!

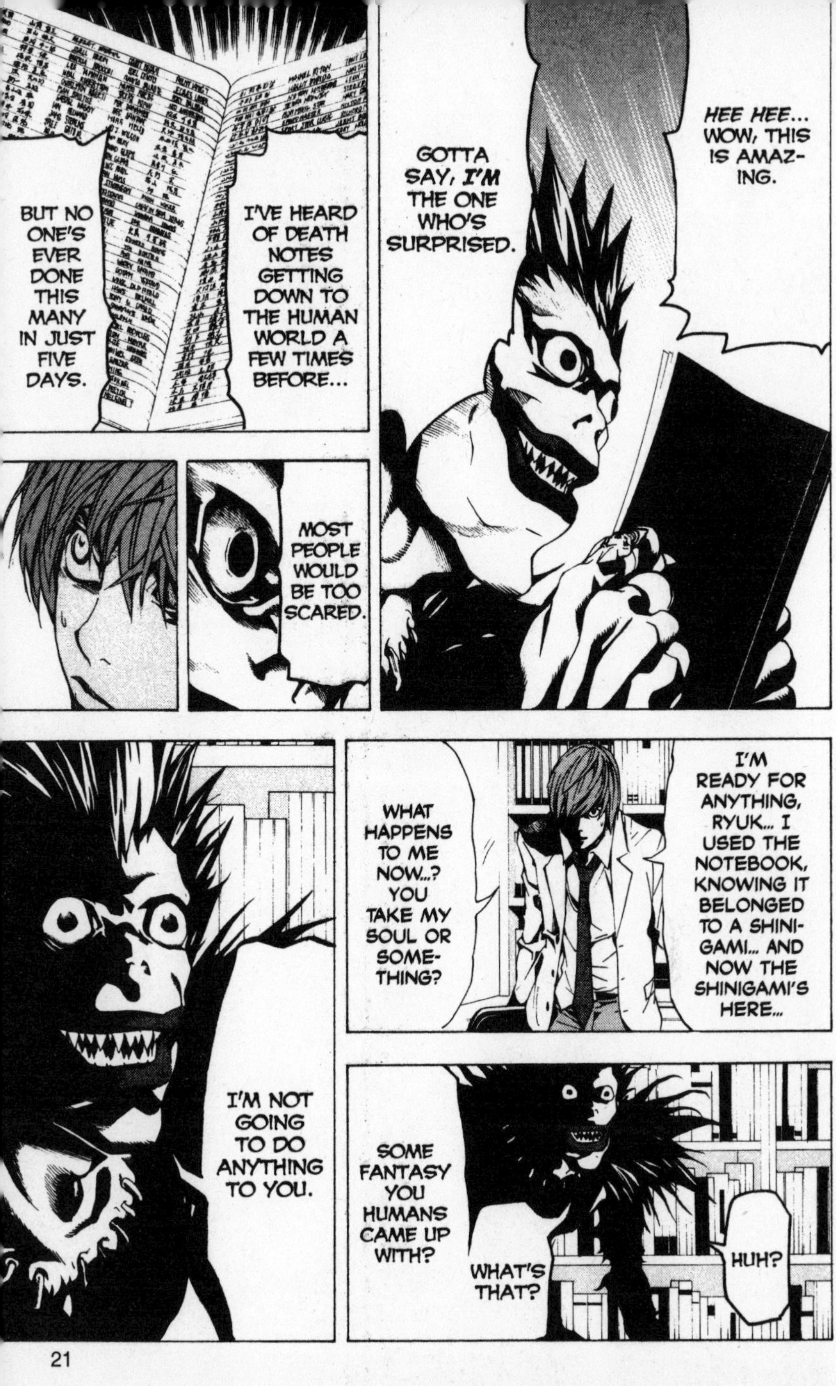
HEE HEE... WOW, THIS IS AMAZING.
GOTTA SAY, I'M THE ONE WHO'S SURPRISED.
I'VE HEARD OF DEATH NOTES GETTING DOWN TO THE HUMAN WORLD A FEW TIMES BEFORE...
BUT NO ONE'S EVER DONE THIS MANY IN JUST FIVE DAYS.
MOST PEOPLE WOULD BE TOO SCARED.
I'M READY FOR ANYTHING, RYUK... I USED THE NOTEBOOK, KNOWING IT BELONGED TO A SHINIGAMI... AND NOW THE SHINIGAMI'S HERE...
WHAT HAPPENS TO ME NOW...? YOU TAKE MY SOUL OR SOMETHING?
HUH?
WHAT'S THAT?
SOME FANTASY YOU HUMANS CAME UP WITH?
I'M NOT GOING TO DO ANYTHING TO YOU.

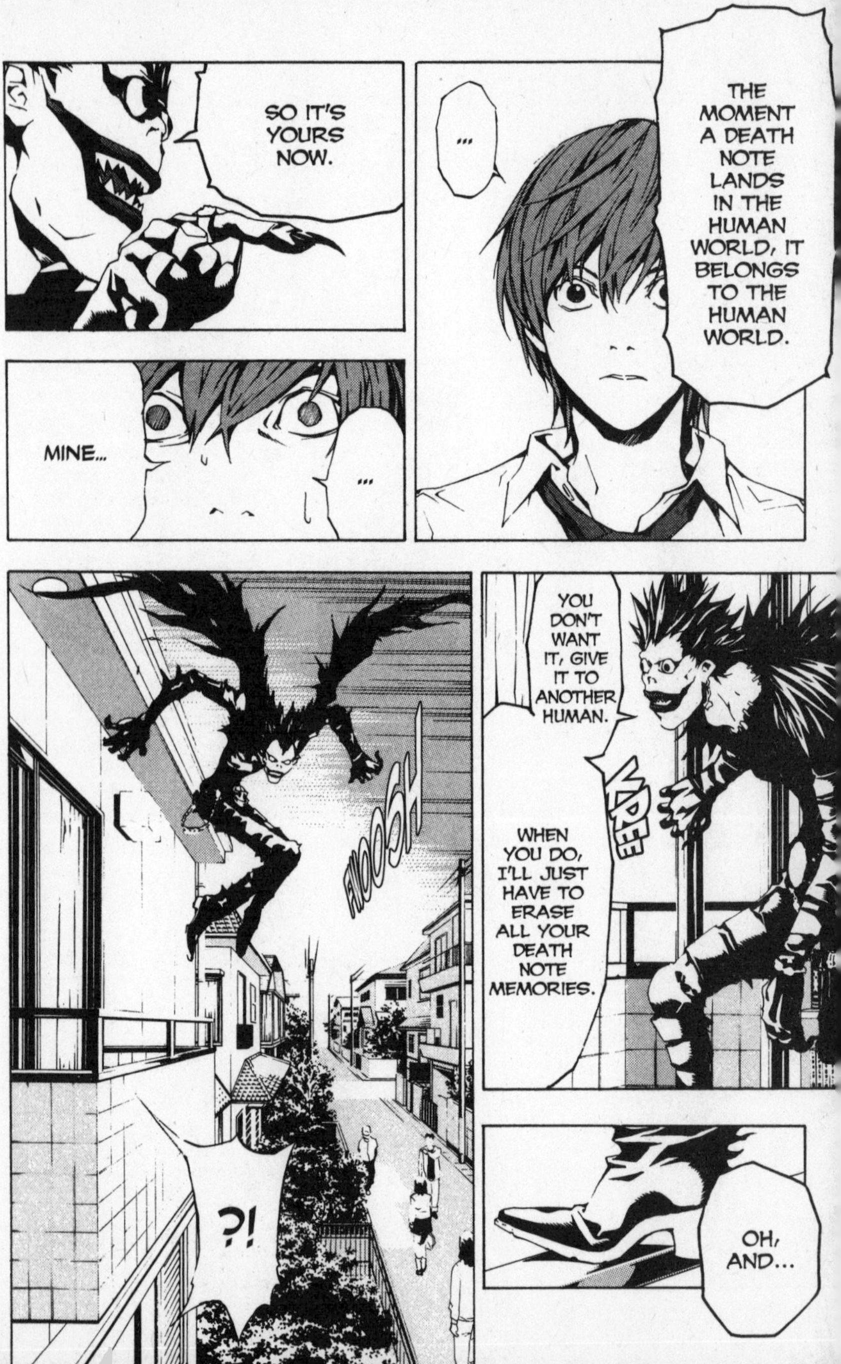
THE MOMENT A DEATH NOTE LANDS IN THE HUMAN WORLD, IT BELONGS TO THE HUMAN WORLD.
...
SO IT'S YOURS NOW.
MINE...
...
YOU DON'T WANT IT, GIVE IT TO ANOTHER HUMAN.
VREE
WHEN YOU DO, I'LL JUST HAVE TO ERASE ALL YOUR DEATH NOTE MEMORIES.
OH, AND...
FWOOSH
?!

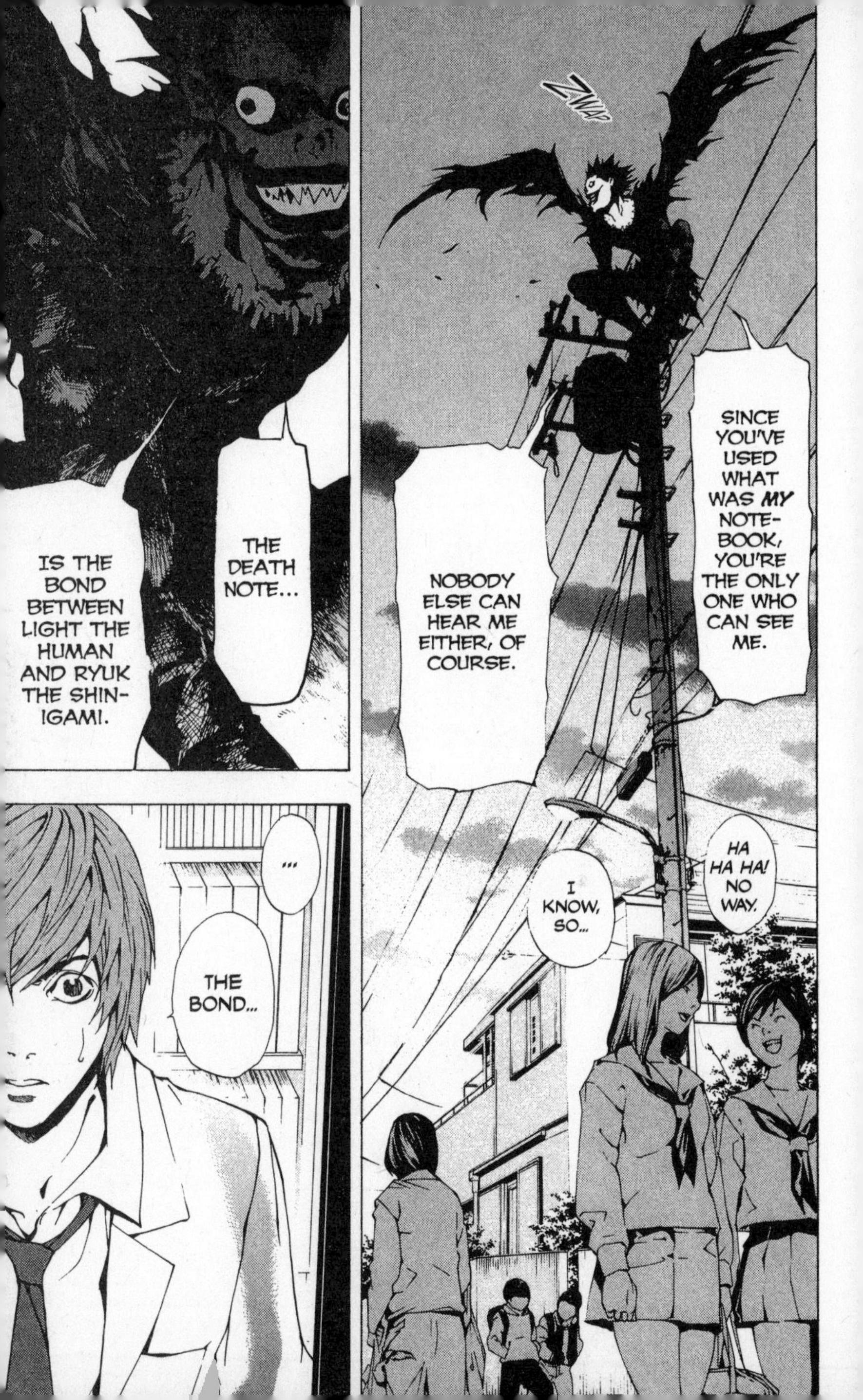
ZWAP
SINCE YOU'VE USED WHAT WAS *MY* NOTE-BOOK, YOU'RE THE ONLY ONE WHO CAN SEE ME.
NOBODY ELSE CAN HEAR ME EITHER, OF COURSE.
HA HA HA! NO WAY.
I KNOW, SO...
THE DEATH NOTE...
IS THE BOND BETWEEN LIGHT THE HUMAN AND RYUK THE SHIN-IGAMI.
...
THE BOND...

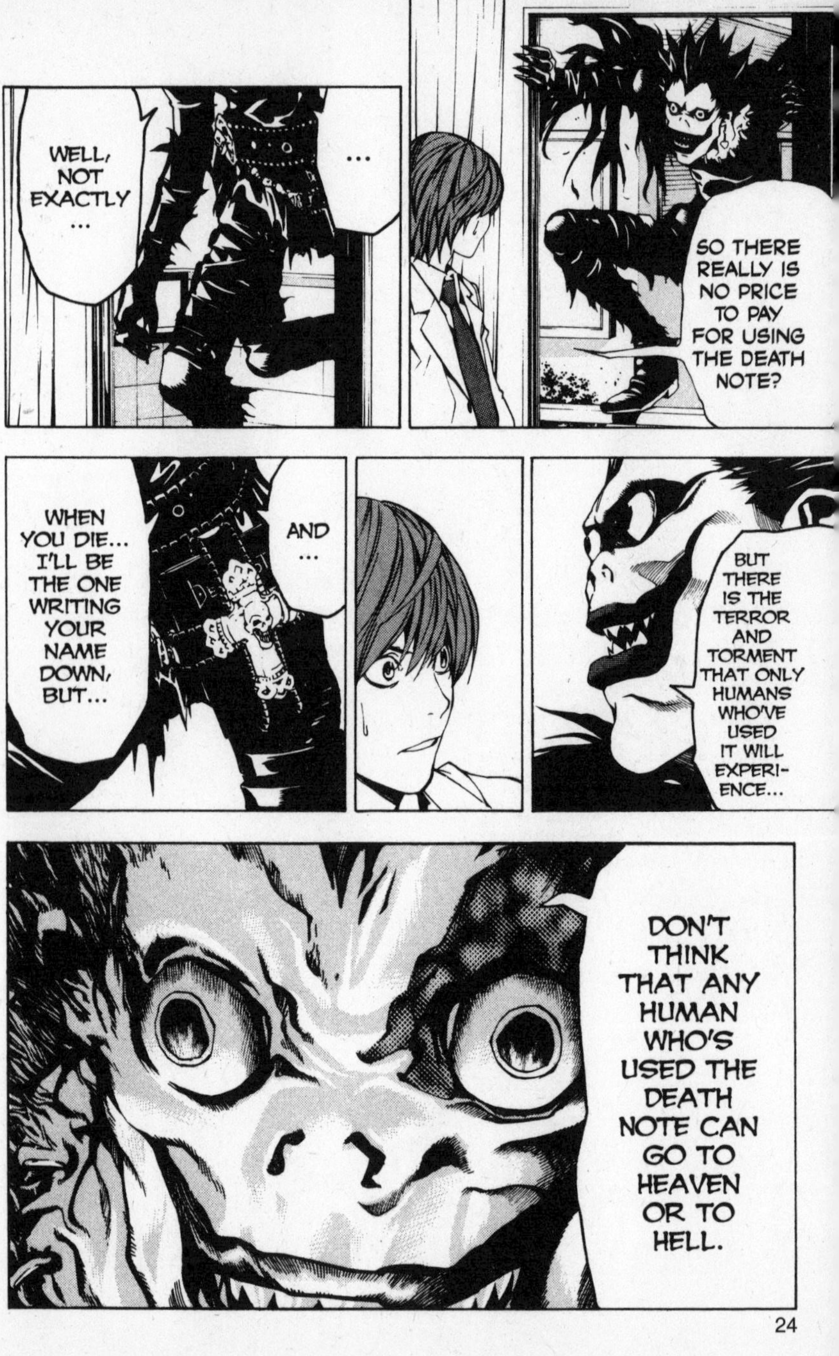
SO THERE REALLY IS NO PRICE TO PAY FOR USING THE DEATH NOTE?
...
WELL, NOT EXACTLY ...
BUT THERE IS THE TERROR AND TORMENT THAT ONLY HUMANS WHO'VE USED IT WILL EXPERIENCE...
AND ...
WHEN YOU DIE... I'LL BE THE ONE WRITING YOUR NAME DOWN, BUT...
DON'T THINK THAT ANY HUMAN WHO'S USED THE DEATH NOTE CAN GO TO HEAVEN OR TO HELL.

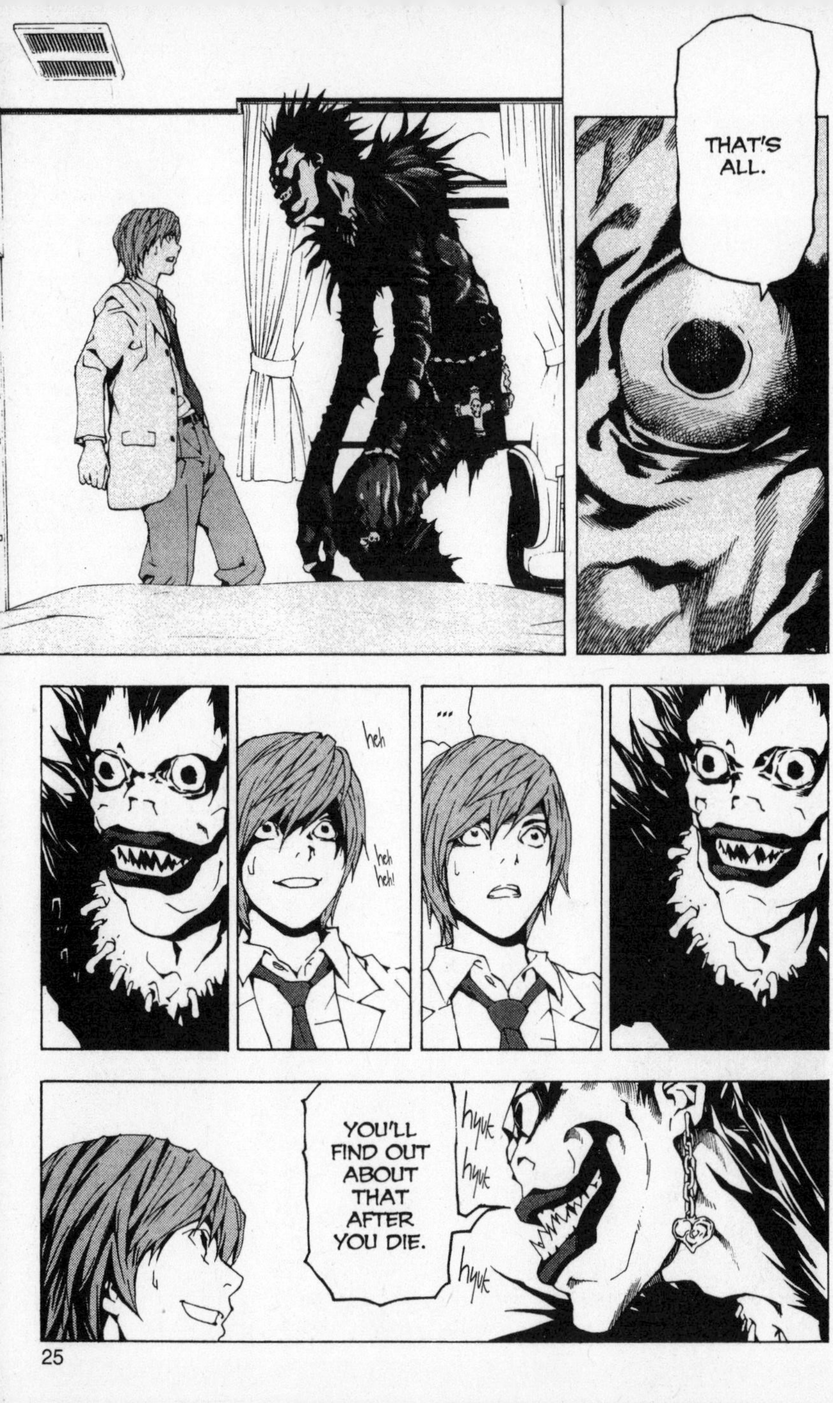
THAT'S ALL.
...
heh
heh heh!
hyuk hyuk
YOU'LL FIND OUT ABOUT THAT AFTER YOU DIE.
hyuk

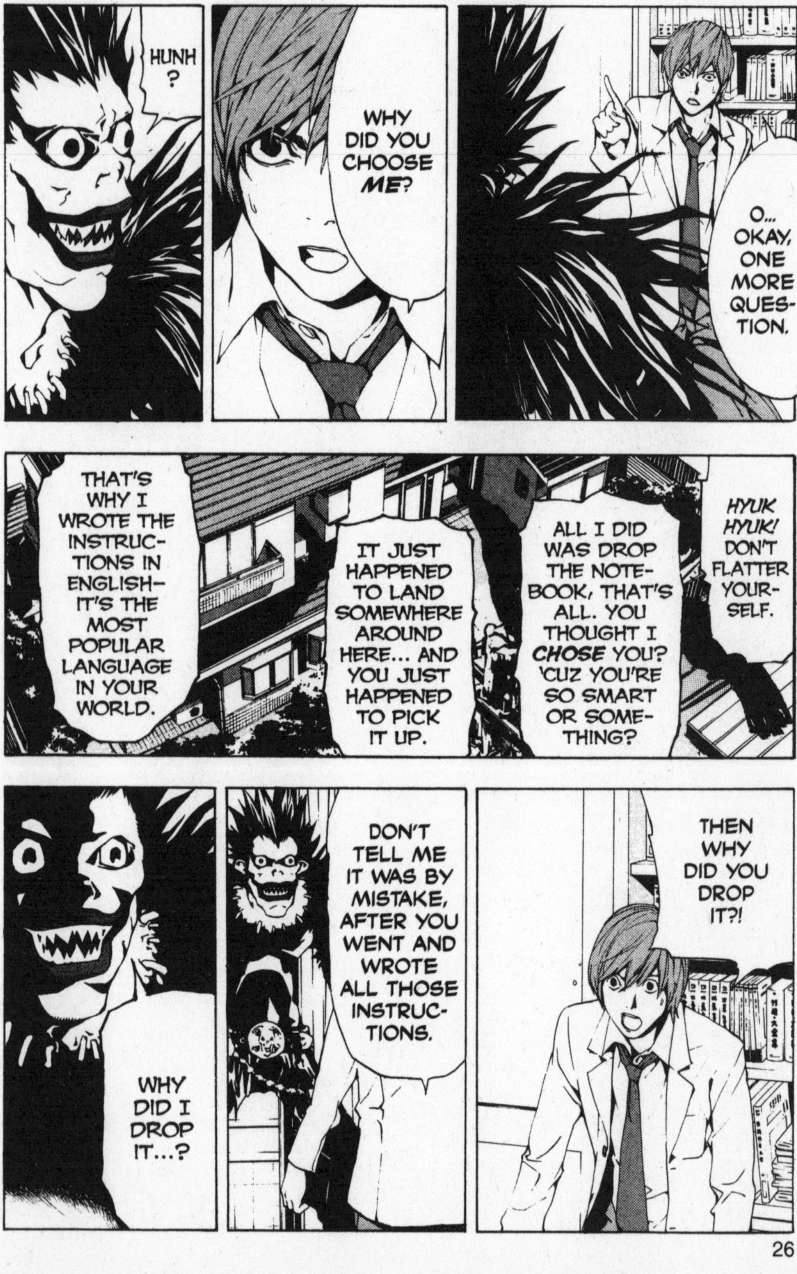
O... OKAY, ONE MORE QUES-TION.
WHY DID YOU CHOOSE *ME*?
HUNH ?
HYUK HYUK! DON'T FLATTER YOUR-SELF.
ALL I DID WAS DROP THE NOTE-BOOK, THAT'S ALL. YOU THOUGHT I *CHOSE* YOU? 'CUZ YOU'RE SO SMART OR SOME-THING?
IT JUST HAPPENED TO LAND SOMEWHERE AROUND HERE... AND YOU JUST HAPPENED TO PICK IT UP.
THAT'S WHY I WROTE THE INSTRUC-TIONS IN ENGLISH-IT'S THE MOST POPULAR LANGUAGE IN YOUR WORLD.
THEN WHY DID YOU DROP IT?!
DON'T TELL ME IT WAS BY MISTAKE, AFTER YOU WENT AND WROTE ALL THOSE INSTRUC-TIONS.
WHY DID I DROP IT...?

READ THIS WAY

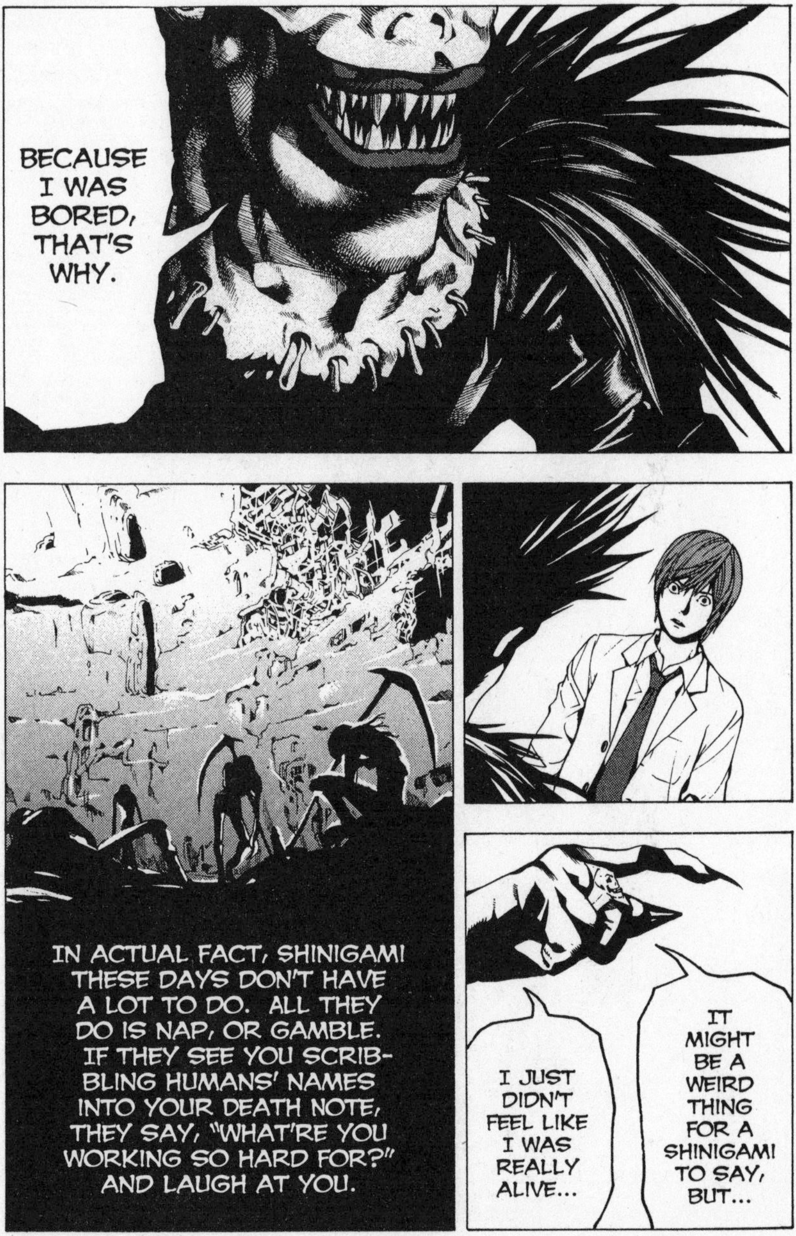
BECAUSE I WAS BORED, THAT'S WHY.
IT MIGHT BE A WEIRD THING FOR A SHINIGAMI TO SAY, BUT...
I JUST DIDN'T FEEL LIKE I WAS REALLY ALIVE...
IN ACTUAL FACT, SHINIGAMI THESE DAYS DON'T HAVE A LOT TO DO. ALL THEY DO IS NAP, OR GAMBLE. IF THEY SEE YOU SCRIB-BLING HUMANS' NAMES INTO YOUR DEATH NOTE, THEY SAY, "WHAT'RE YOU WORKING SO HARD FOR?" AND LAUGH AT YOU.

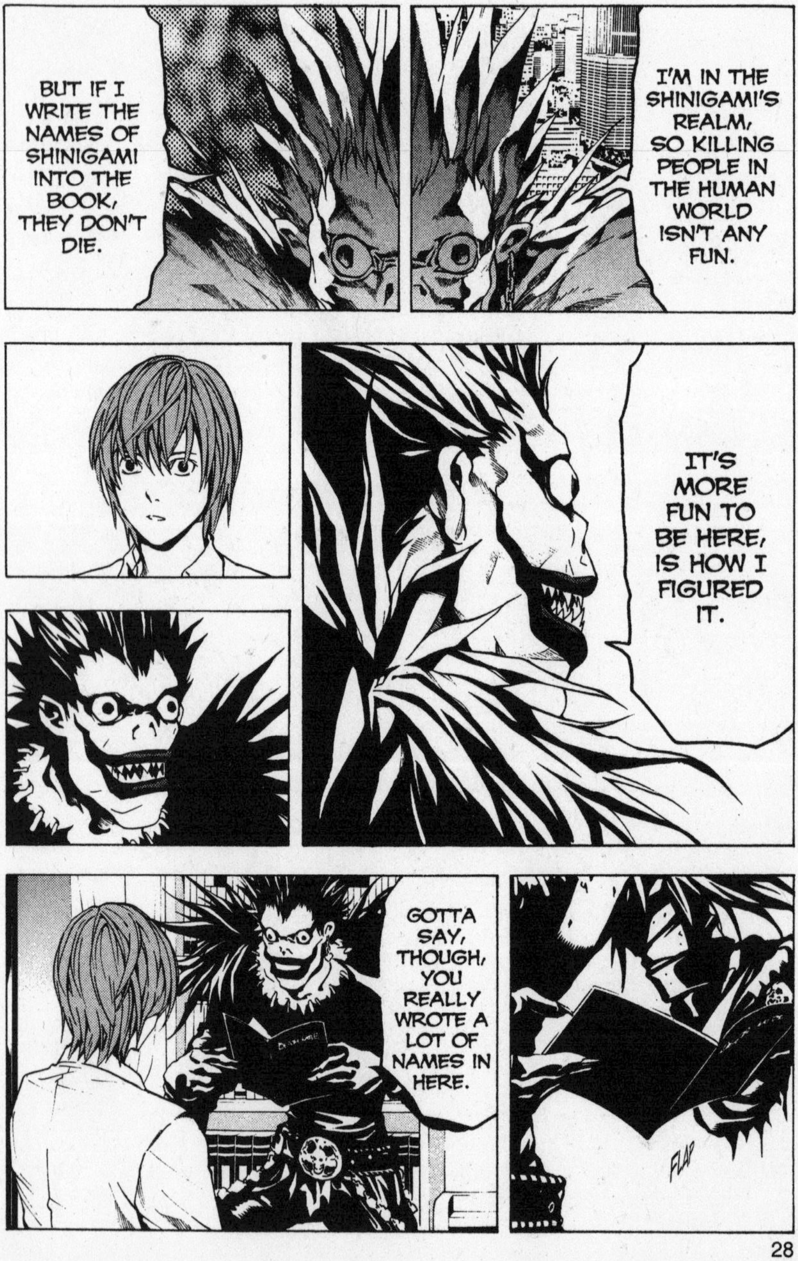
I'M IN THE SHINIGAMI'S REALM, SO KILLING PEOPLE IN THE HUMAN WORLD ISN'T ANY FUN.
BUT IF I WRITE THE NAMES OF SHINIGAMI INTO THE BOOK, THEY DON'T DIE.
IT'S MORE FUN TO BE HERE, IS HOW I FIGURED IT.
FLAP
GOTTA SAY, THOUGH, YOU REALLY WROTE A LOT OF NAMES IN HERE.

READ THIS WAY

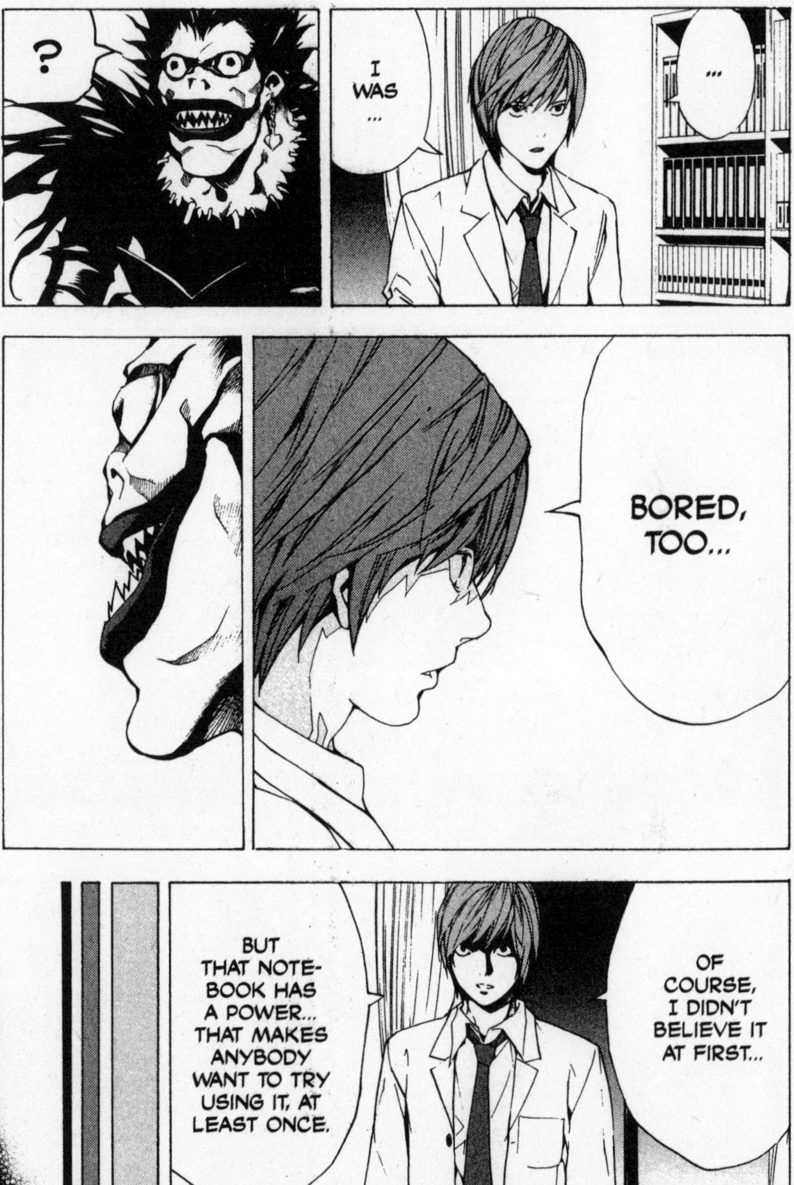
...
I WAS ...
?
BORED, TOO...
OF COURSE, I DIDN'T BELIEVE IT AT FIRST...
BUT THAT NOTE-BOOK HAS A POWER... THAT MAKES ANYBODY WANT TO TRY USING IT, AT LEAST ONCE.

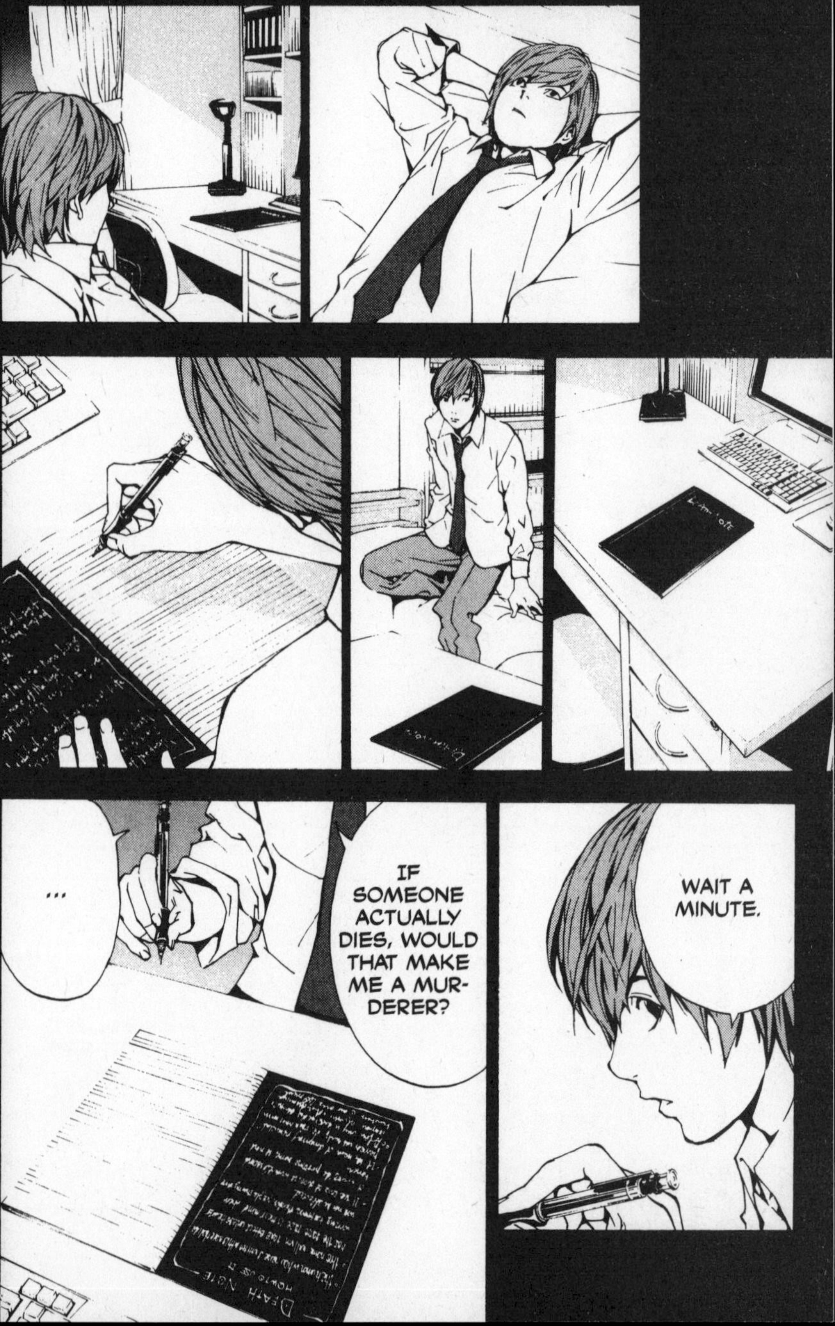
WAIT A MINUTE.
IF SOMEONE ACTUALLY DIES, WOULD THAT MAKE ME A MURDERER?
...

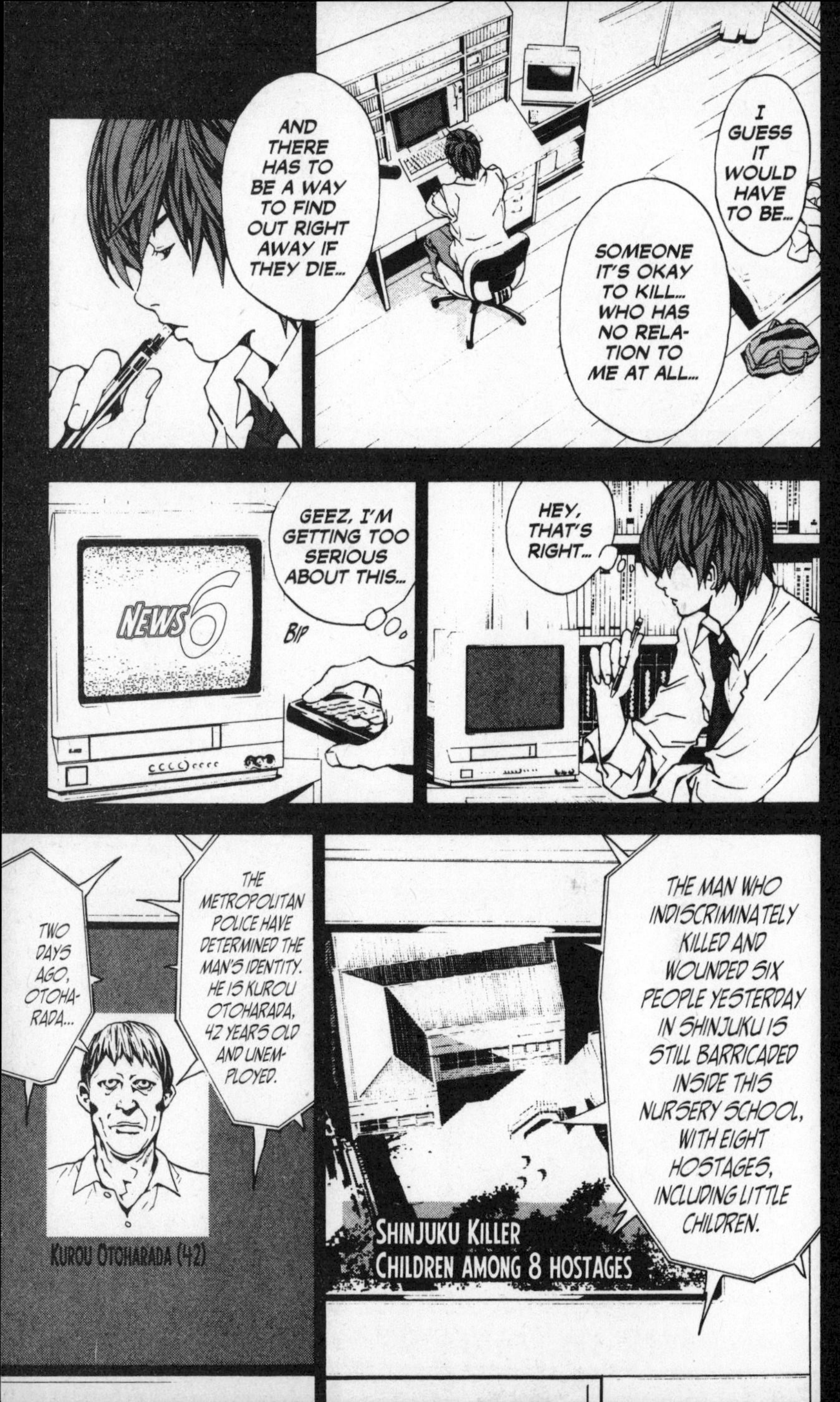
I GUESS IT WOULD HAVE TO BE...
SOMEONE IT'S OKAY TO KILL... WHO HAS NO RELATION TO ME AT ALL...
AND THERE HAS TO BE A WAY TO FIND OUT RIGHT AWAY IF THEY DIE...
HEY, THAT'S RIGHT...
GEEZ, I'M GETTING TOO SERIOUS ABOUT THIS...
NEWS 6
BIP
THE MAN WHO INDISCRIMINATELY KILLED AND WOUNDED SIX PEOPLE YESTERDAY IN SHINJUKU IS STILL BARRICADED INSIDE THIS NURSERY SCHOOL, WITH EIGHT HOSTAGES, INCLUDING LITTLE CHILDREN.
SHINJUKU KILLER
CHILDREN AMONG 8 HOSTAGES
THE METROPOLITAN POLICE HAVE DETERMINED THE MAN'S IDENTITY. HE IS KUROU OTOHARADA, 42 YEARS OLD AND UNEMPLOYED.
TWO DAYS AGO, OTOHARADA...
KUROU OTOHARADA (42)

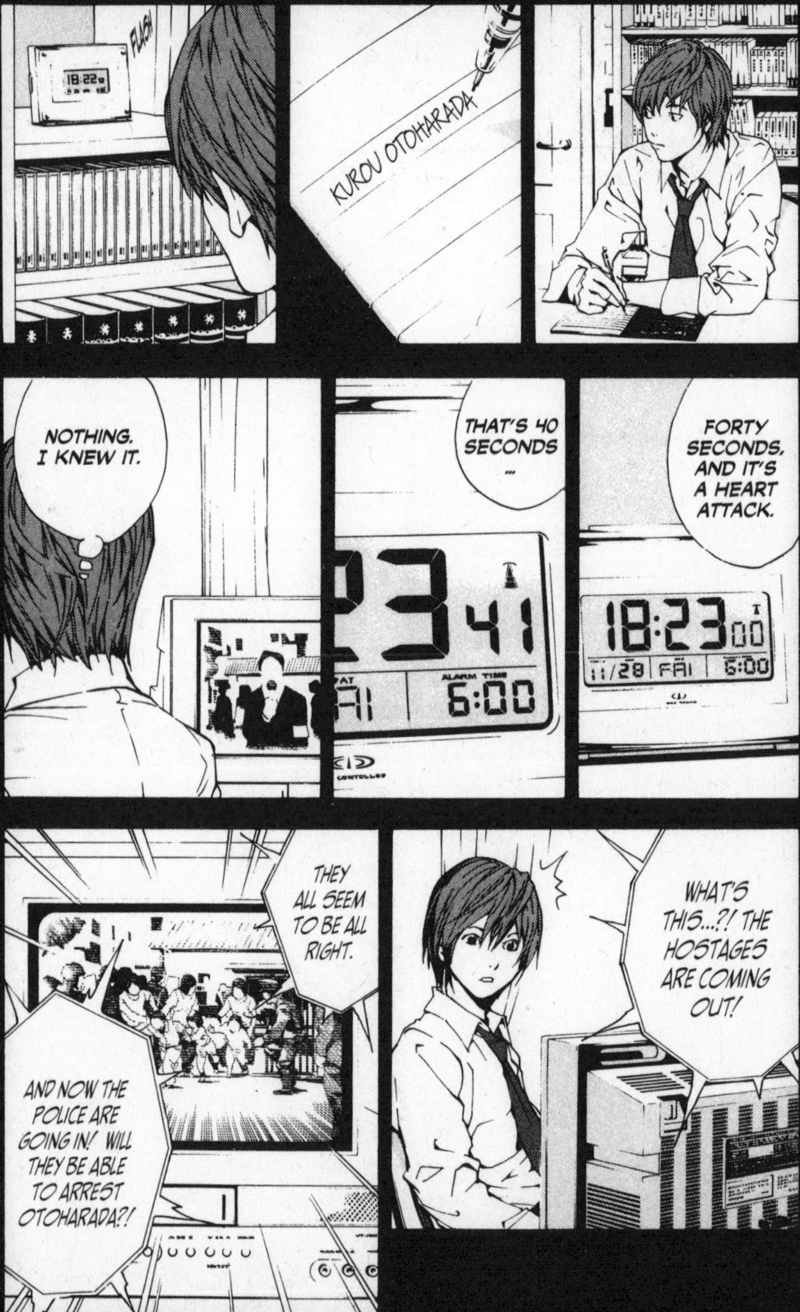
KUROU OTOHARADA
FLASH
FORTY SECONDS, AND IT'S A HEART ATTACK.
THAT'S 40 SECONDS ...
NOTHING. I KNEW IT.
WHAT'S THIS...?! THE HOSTAGES ARE COMING OUT!
THEY ALL SEEM TO BE ALL RIGHT.
AND NOW THE POLICE ARE GOING IN! WILL THEY BE ABLE TO ARREST OTOHARADA?!

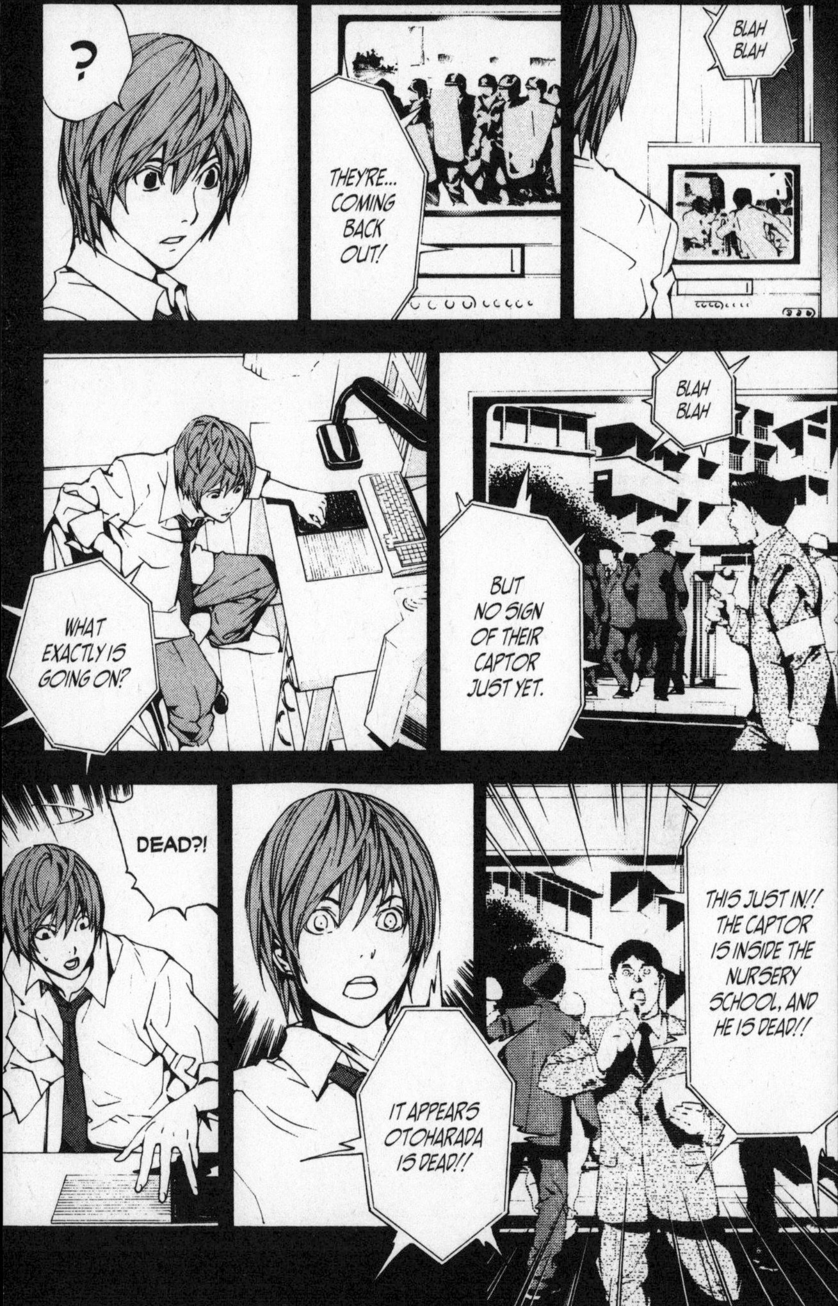
BLAH BLAH
THEY'RE... COMING BACK OUT!
?
BLAH BLAH
BUT NO SIGN OF THEIR CAPTOR JUST YET.
WHAT EXACTLY IS GOING ON?
THIS JUST IN!! THE CAPTOR IS INSIDE THE NURSERY SCHOOL, AND HE IS DEAD!!
IT APPEARS OTOHARADA IS DEAD!!
DEAD?!

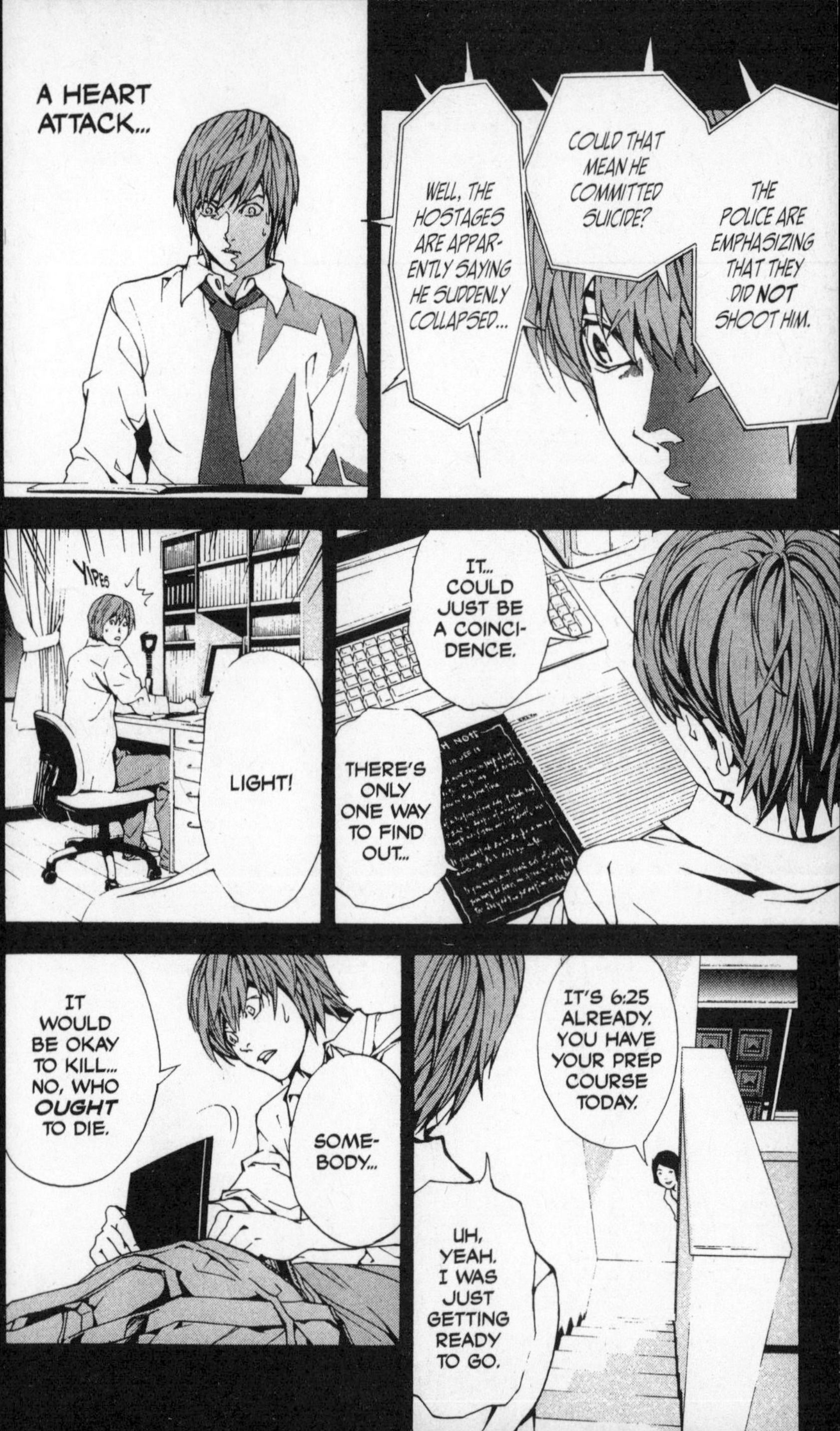
THE POLICE ARE EMPHASIZING THAT THEY DID **NOT** SHOOT HIM.
COULD THAT MEAN HE COMMITTED SUICIDE?
WELL, THE HOSTAGES ARE APPARENTLY SAYING HE SUDDENLY COLLAPSED...
A HEART ATTACK...
IT... COULD JUST BE A COINCIDENCE.
THERE'S ONLY ONE WAY TO FIND OUT...
YIPES
LIGHT!
IT'S 6:25 ALREADY. YOU HAVE YOUR PREP COURSE TODAY.
UH, YEAH. I WAS JUST GETTING READY TO GO.
SOMEBODY...
IT WOULD BE OKAY TO KILL... NO, WHO ***OUGHT*** TO DIE.

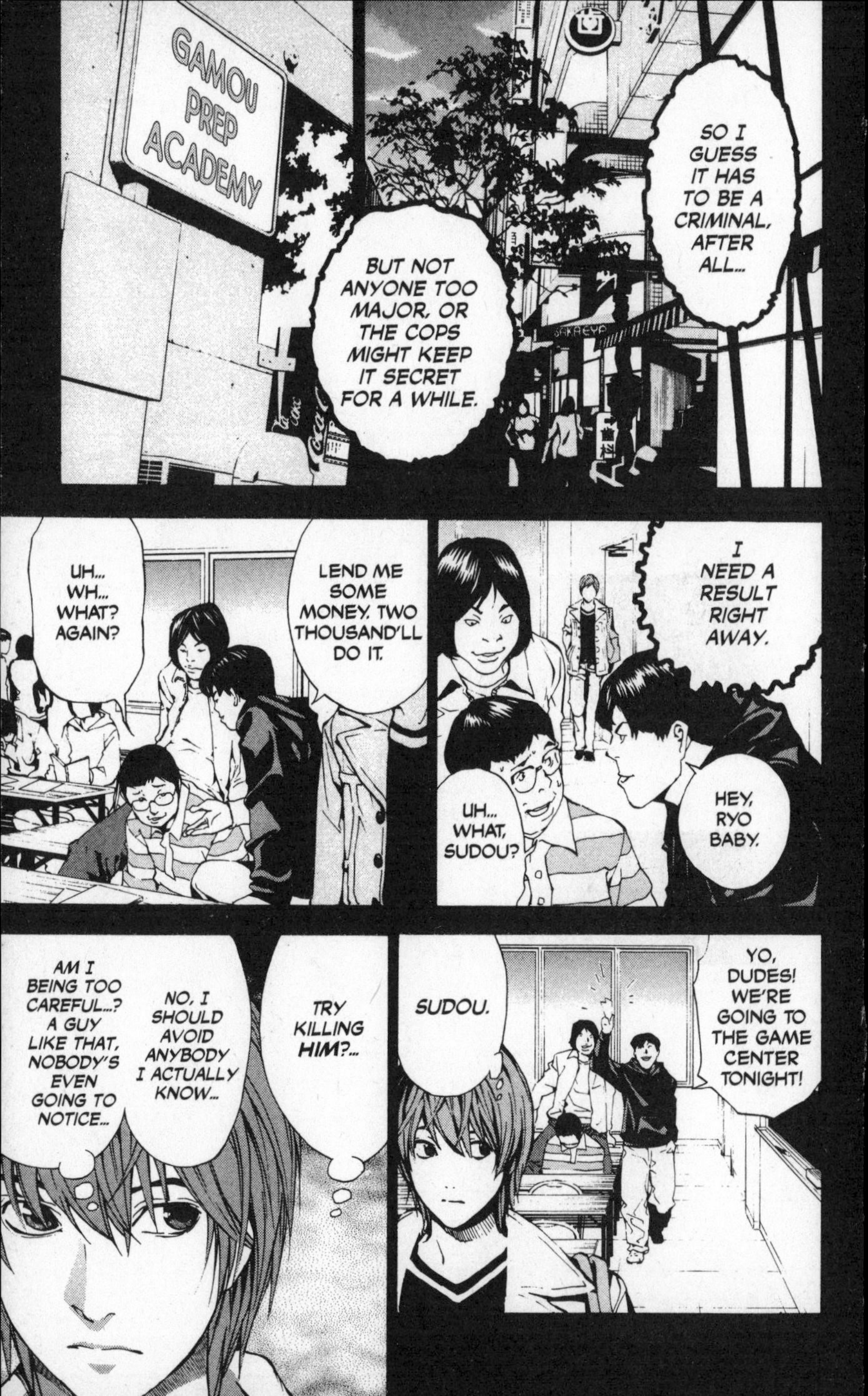
SO I GUESS IT HAS TO BE A CRIMINAL, AFTER ALL...
BUT NOT ANYONE TOO MAJOR, OR THE COPS MIGHT KEEP IT SECRET FOR A WHILE.
GAMOU PREP ACADEMY
SAKAEYA
I NEED A RESULT RIGHT AWAY.
HEY, RYO BABY.
UH... WHAT, SUDOU?
LEND ME SOME MONEY. TWO THOUSAND'LL DO IT.
UH... WH... WHAT? AGAIN?
YO, DUDES! WE'RE GOING TO THE GAME CENTER TONIGHT!
SUDOU.
TRY KILLING *HIM*?...
NO, I SHOULD AVOID ANYBODY I ACTUALLY KNOW...
AM I BEING TOO CAREFUL...? A GUY LIKE THAT, NOBODY'S EVEN GOING TO NOTICE...

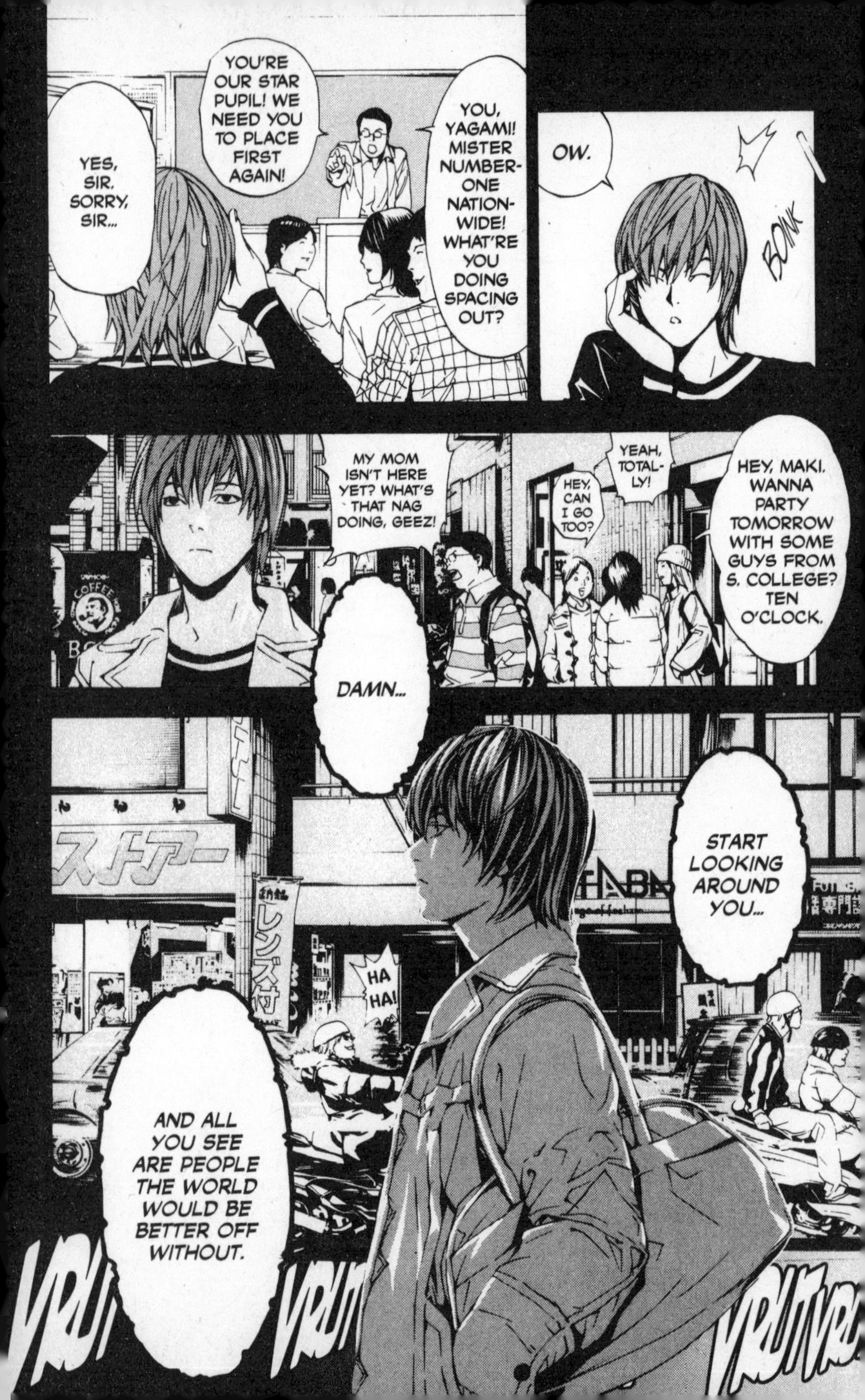
OW.
BOINK
YOU, YAGAMI! MISTER NUMBER-ONE NATION-WIDE! WHAT'RE YOU DOING SPACING OUT?
YOU'RE OUR STAR PUPIL! WE NEED YOU TO PLACE FIRST AGAIN!
YES, SIR. SORRY, SIR...
HEY, MAKI. WANNA PARTY TOMORROW WITH SOME GUYS FROM S. COLLEGE? TEN O'CLOCK.
YEAH, TOTAL-LY!
HEY, CAN I GO TOO?
MY MOM ISN'T HERE YET? WHAT'S THAT NAG DOING, GEEZ!
DAMN...
START LOOKING AROUND YOU...
HA HA!
AND ALL YOU SEE ARE PEOPLE THE WORLD WOULD BE BETTER OFF WITHOUT.

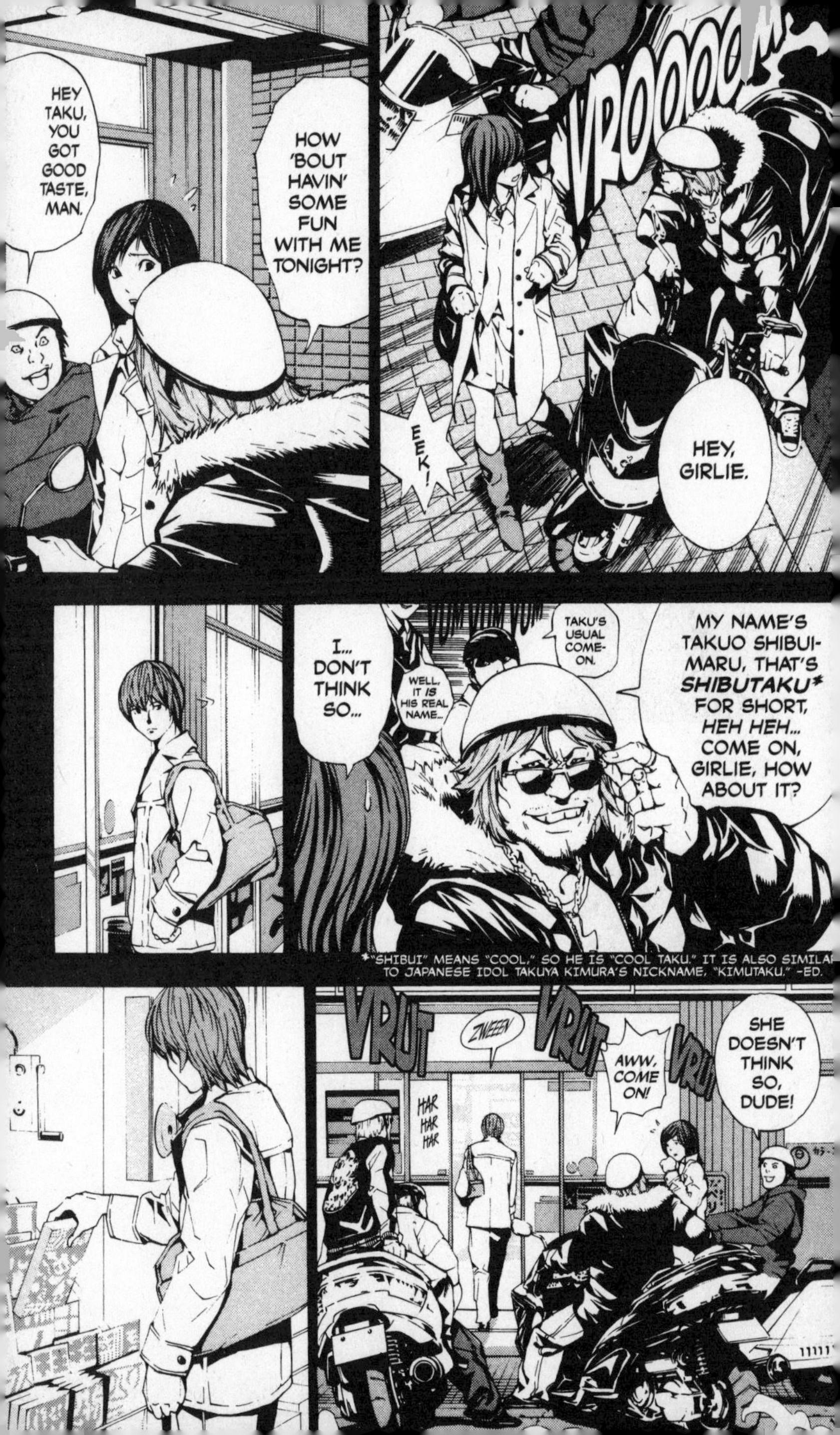
VROOOOM!!
EEK!
HEY, GIRLIE.
HOW 'BOUT HAVIN' SOME FUN WITH ME TONIGHT?
HEY TAKU, YOU GOT GOOD TASTE, MAN.
VUM VUM VUM
MY NAME'S TAKUO SHIBUI-MARU, THAT'S *SHIBUTAKU** FOR SHORT, *HEH HEH*... COME ON, GIRLIE, HOW ABOUT IT?
TAKU'S USUAL COME-ON.
WELL, IT *IS* HIS REAL NAME...
I... DON'T THINK SO...
SHE DOESN'T THINK SO, DUDE!
VRUT
VRUT
VRUT
AWW, COME ON!
ZWEEEN
HAR HAR HAR

*"SHIBUI" MEANS "COOL," SO HE IS "COOL TAKU." IT IS ALSO SIMILAR TO JAPANESE IDOL TAKUYA KIMURA'S NICKNAME, "KIMUTAKU." -ED.

KUROU OTOHARADA.

TAKUO SHIBUIMARU. TRAFFIC ACCIDENT
TAKUOH SHIBUIMARU. TRAFFIC ACCIDENT
TAKUO SIBUIMARU. TRAFFIC ACCIDENT
TAKUOH SIBUIMARU. TRAFFIC ACCIDE
TAKUO SHIBUYIMARU. TRAFFIC ACCI
TAKUOH SHIBUYIMARU. TRAF

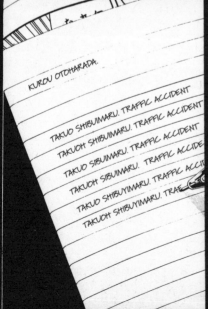

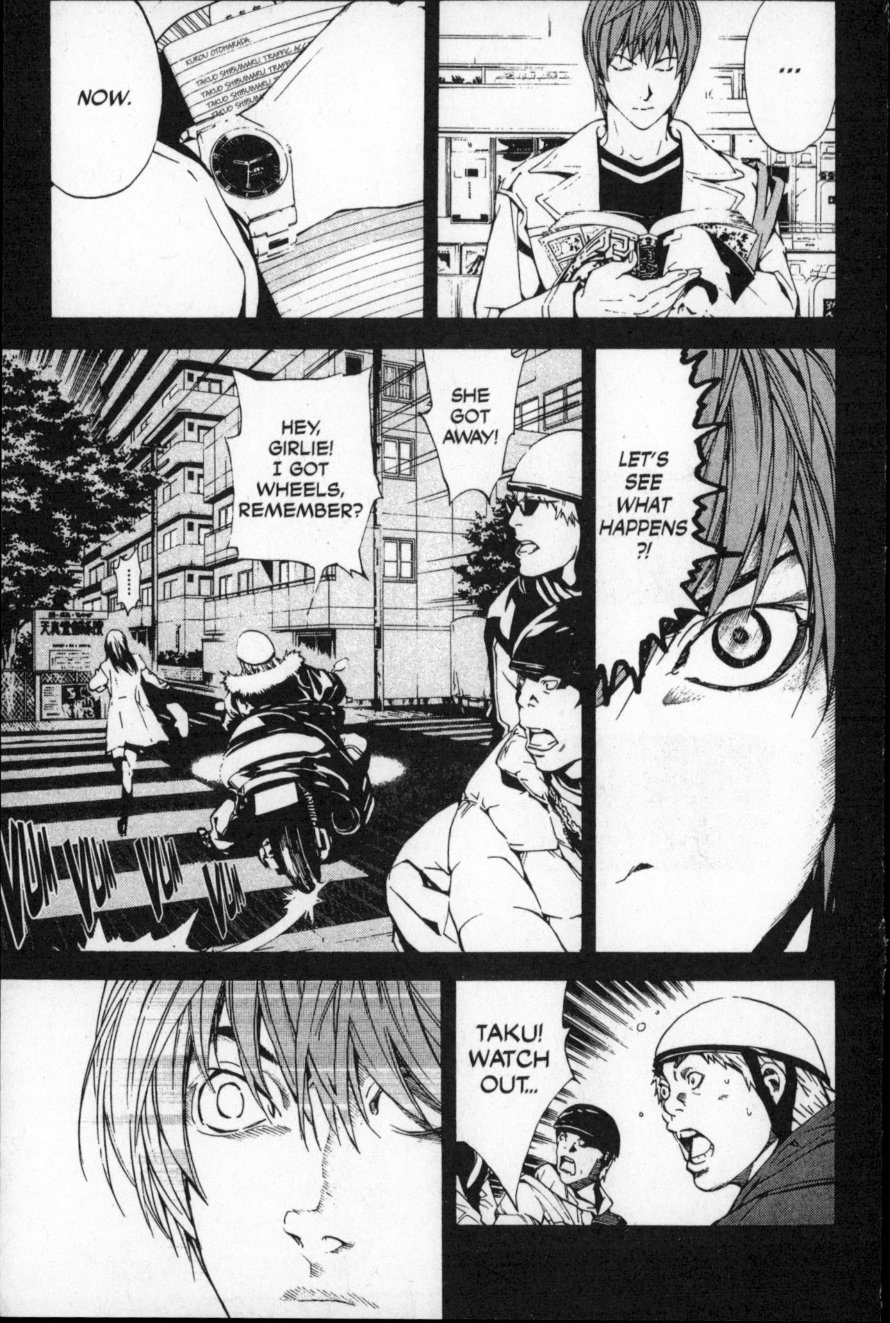
...
NOW.
LET'S SEE WHAT HAPPENS?!
SHE GOT AWAY!
HEY, GIRLIE! I GOT WHEELS, REMEMBER?
VUN VUN VUN VUN
TAKU! WATCH OUT...

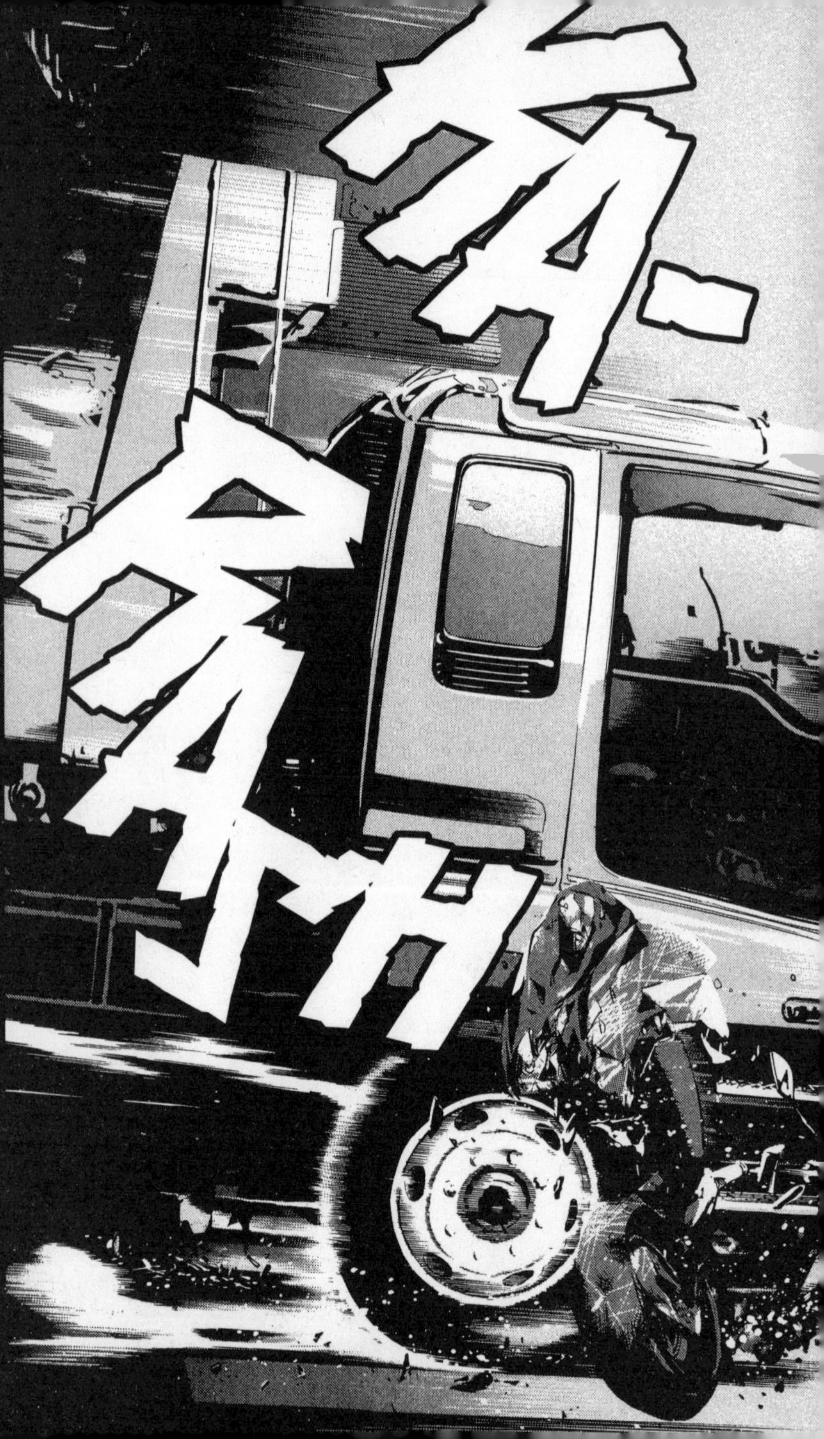

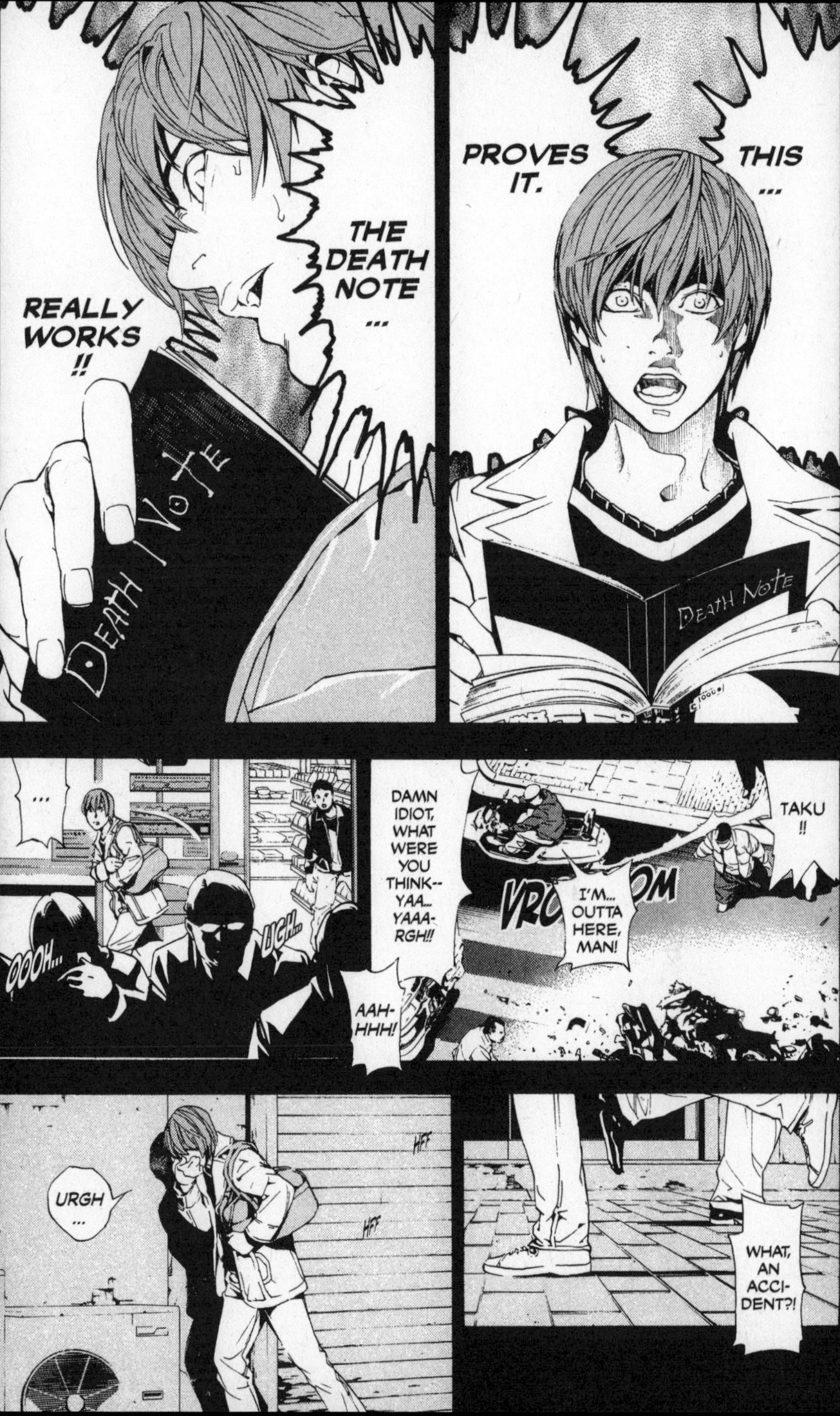
THIS ...
PROVES IT.
DEATH NOTE
THE DEATH NOTE ...
REALLY WORKS !!
DEATH NOTE
TAKU !!
I'M... OUTTA HERE, MAN!
DAMN IDIOT, WHAT WERE YOU THINK-- YAA... YAAA-RGH!!
AAH-HHH!
...
UGH...
OOOH...
WHAT, AN ACCI-DENT?!
HFF
URGH ...
HFF

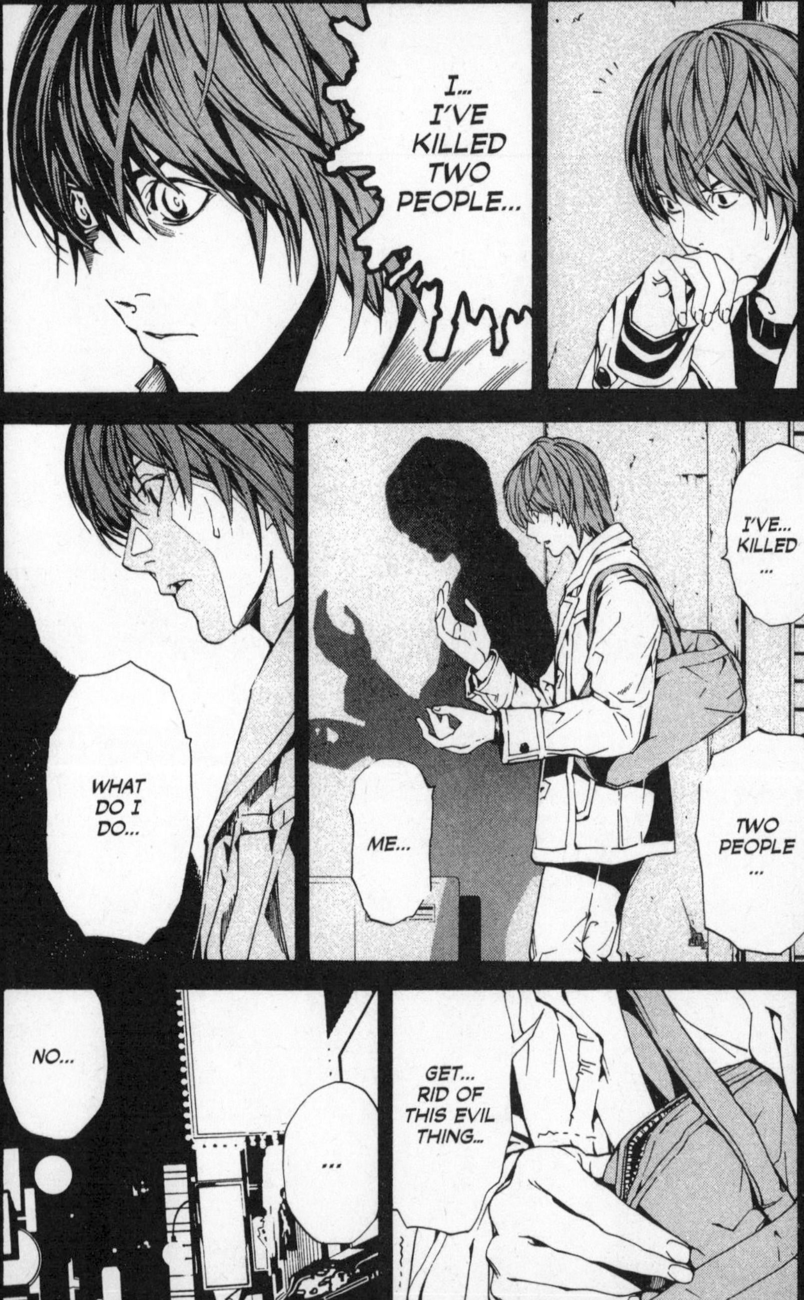
I... I'VE KILLED TWO PEOPLE...
I'VE... KILLED ...
TWO PEOPLE ...
ME...
WHAT DO I DO...
GET... RID OF THIS EVIL THING...
...
NO...

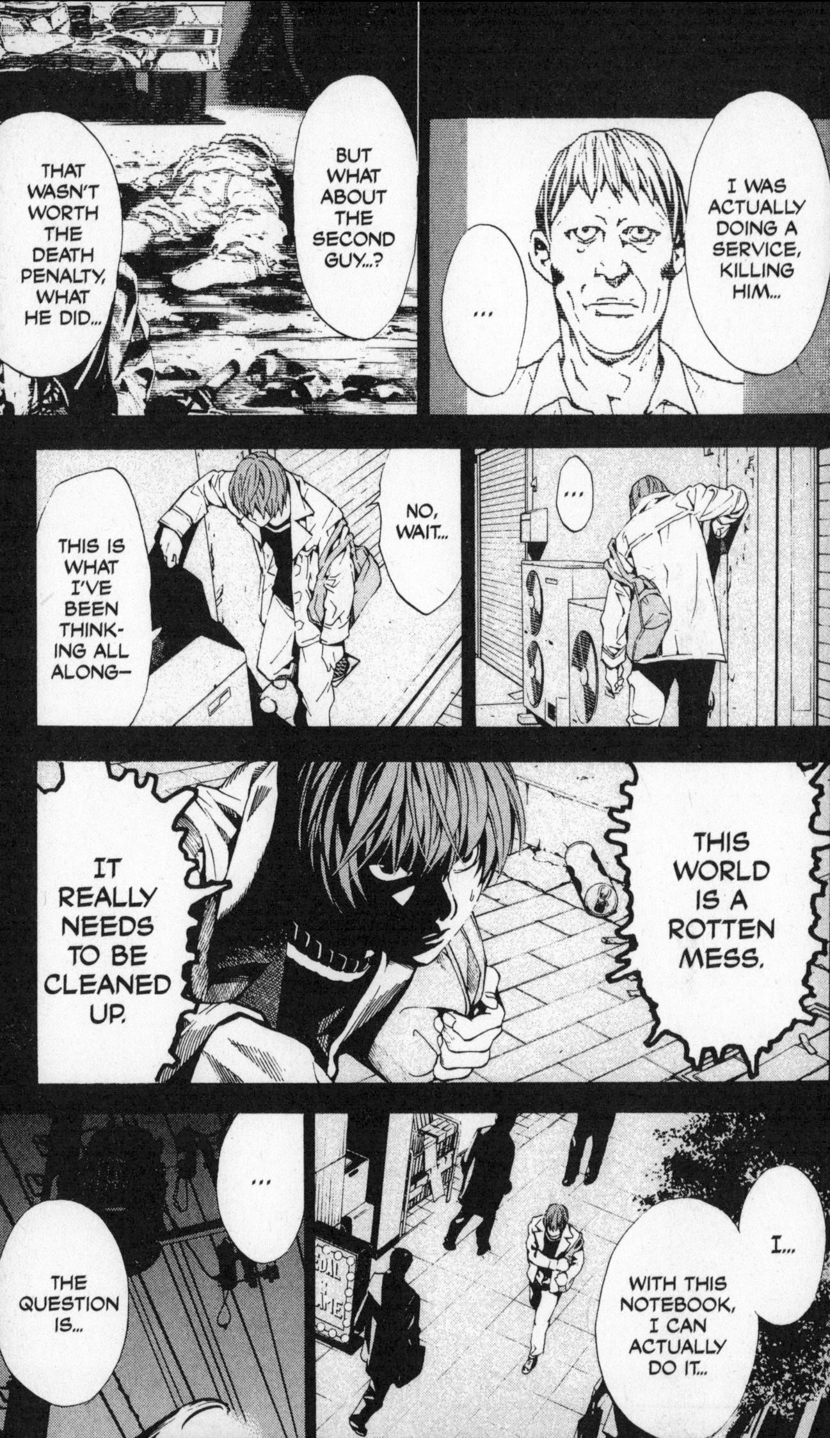
I WAS ACTUALLY DOING A SERVICE, KILLING HIM...
...
BUT WHAT ABOUT THE SECOND GUY...?
THAT WASN'T WORTH THE DEATH PENALTY, WHAT HE DID...
...
NO, WAIT...
THIS IS WHAT I'VE BEEN THINKING ALL ALONG—
THIS WORLD IS A ROTTEN MESS.
IT REALLY NEEDS TO BE CLEANED UP.
I...
WITH THIS NOTEBOOK, I CAN ACTUALLY DO IT...
...
THE QUESTION IS...

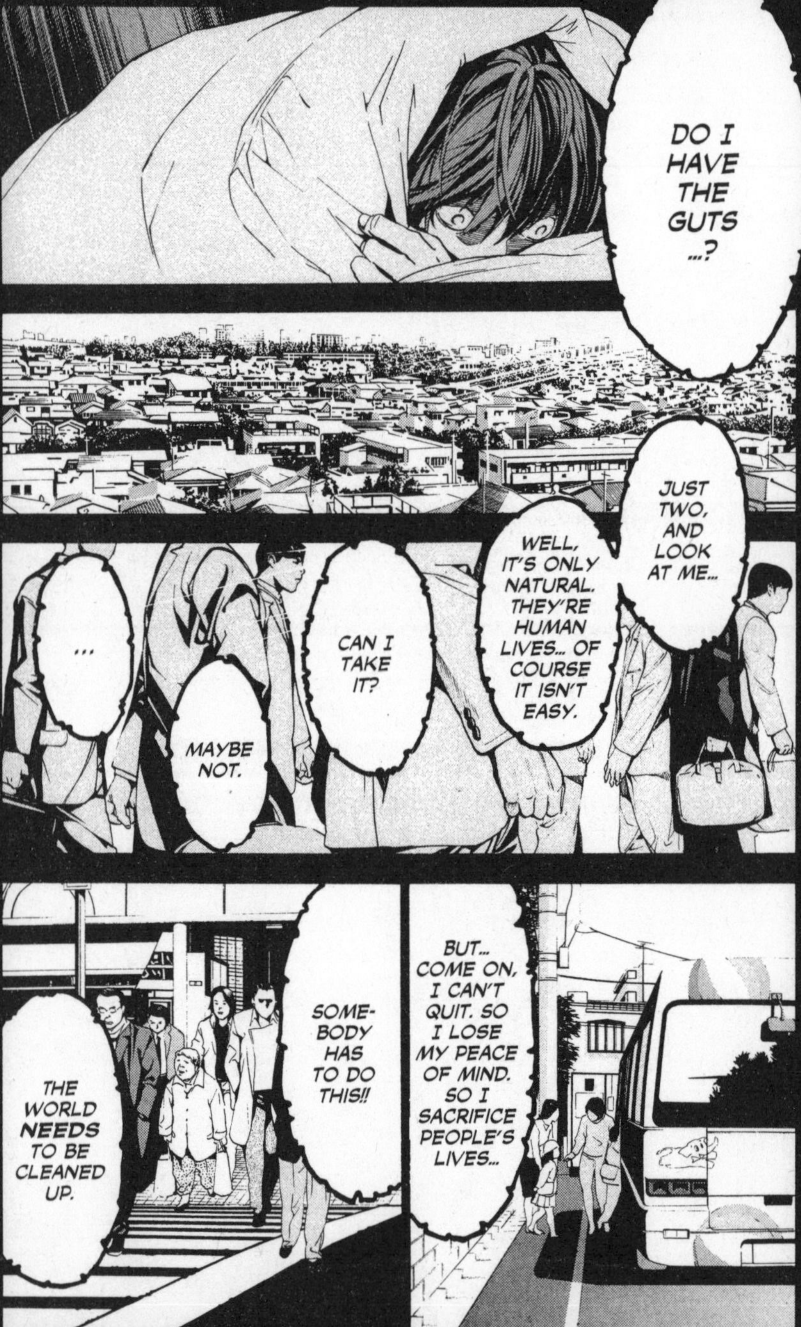
DO I HAVE THE GUTS ...?
JUST TWO, AND LOOK AT ME...
WELL, IT'S ONLY NATURAL. THEY'RE HUMAN LIVES... OF COURSE IT ISN'T EASY.
CAN I TAKE IT?
MAYBE NOT.
...
BUT... COME ON, I CAN'T QUIT. SO I LOSE MY PEACE OF MIND. SO I SACRIFICE PEOPLE'S LIVES...
SOME-BODY HAS TO DO THIS!!
THE WORLD **NEEDS** TO BE CLEANED UP.

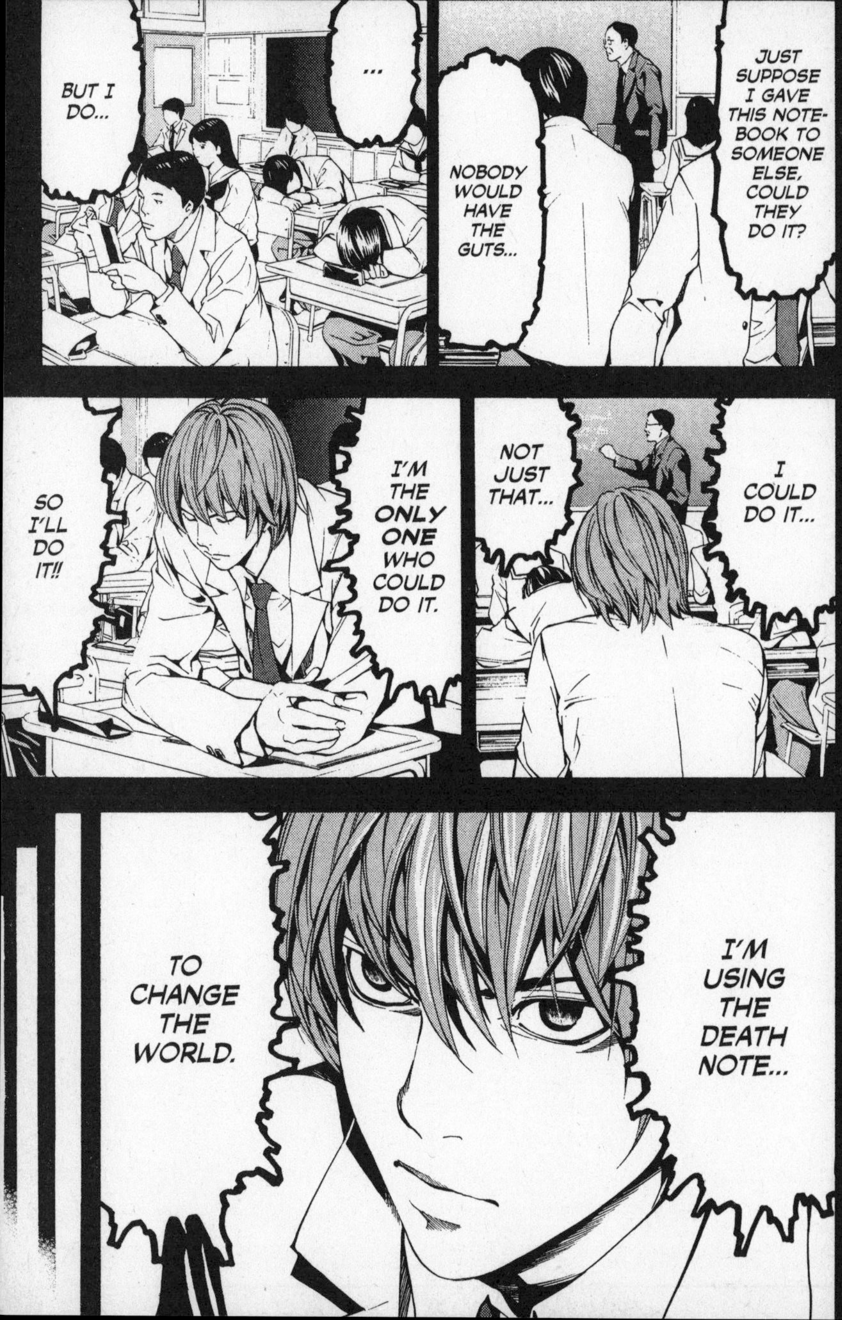
JUST SUPPOSE I GAVE THIS NOTE-BOOK TO SOMEONE ELSE, COULD THEY DO IT?
NOBODY WOULD HAVE THE GUTS...
...
BUT I DO...
I COULD DO IT...
NOT JUST THAT...
I'M THE ONLY ONE WHO COULD DO IT.
SO I'LL DO IT!!
I'M USING THE DEATH NOTE...
TO CHANGE THE WORLD.

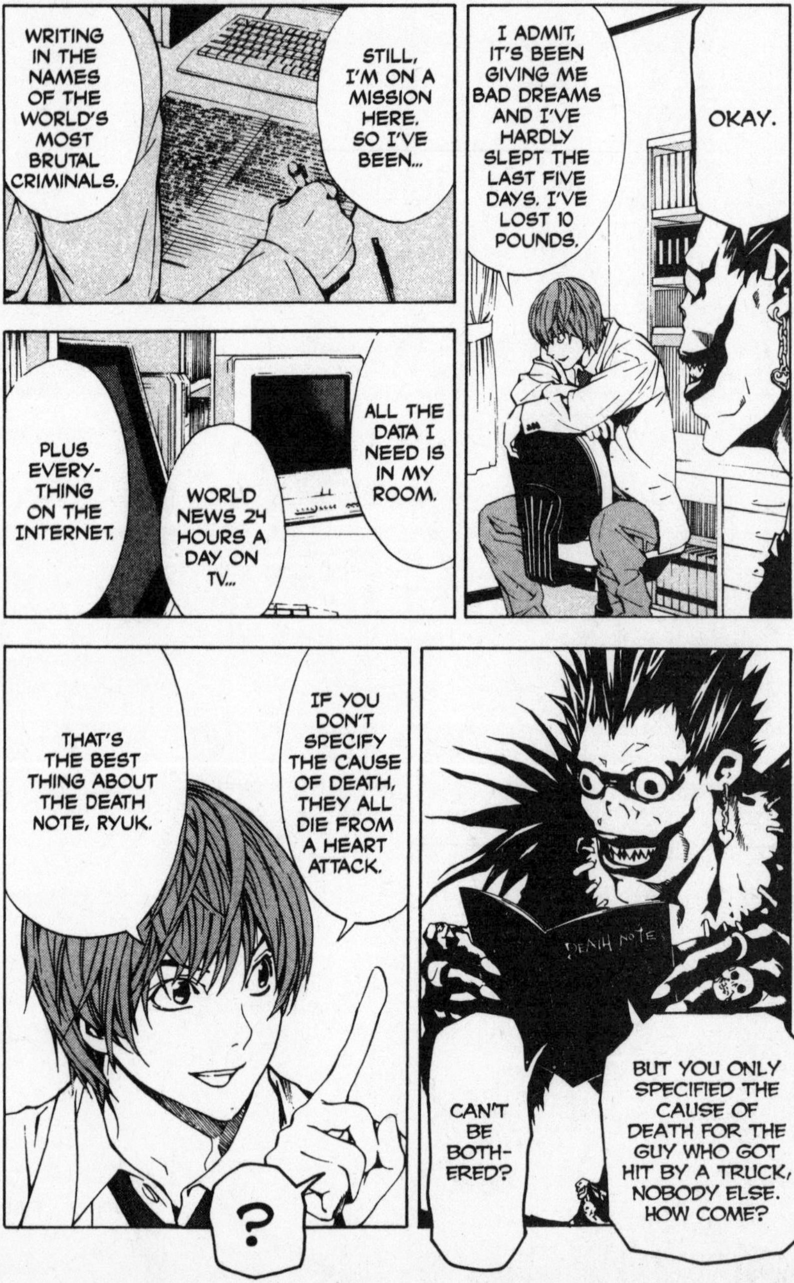
OKAY.
I ADMIT, IT'S BEEN GIVING ME BAD DREAMS AND I'VE HARDLY SLEPT THE LAST FIVE DAYS. I'VE LOST 10 POUNDS.
STILL, I'M ON A MISSION HERE. SO I'VE BEEN...
WRITING IN THE NAMES OF THE WORLD'S MOST BRUTAL CRIMINALS.
ALL THE DATA I NEED IS IN MY ROOM.
WORLD NEWS 24 HOURS A DAY ON TV...
PLUS EVERY-THING ON THE INTERNET.
BUT YOU ONLY SPECIFIED THE CAUSE OF DEATH FOR THE GUY WHO GOT HIT BY A TRUCK, NOBODY ELSE. HOW COME?
CAN'T BE BOTH-ERED?
DEATH NOTE
IF YOU DON'T SPECIFY THE CAUSE OF DEATH, THEY ALL DIE FROM A HEART ATTACK.
THAT'S THE BEST THING ABOUT THE DEATH NOTE, RYUK.
?

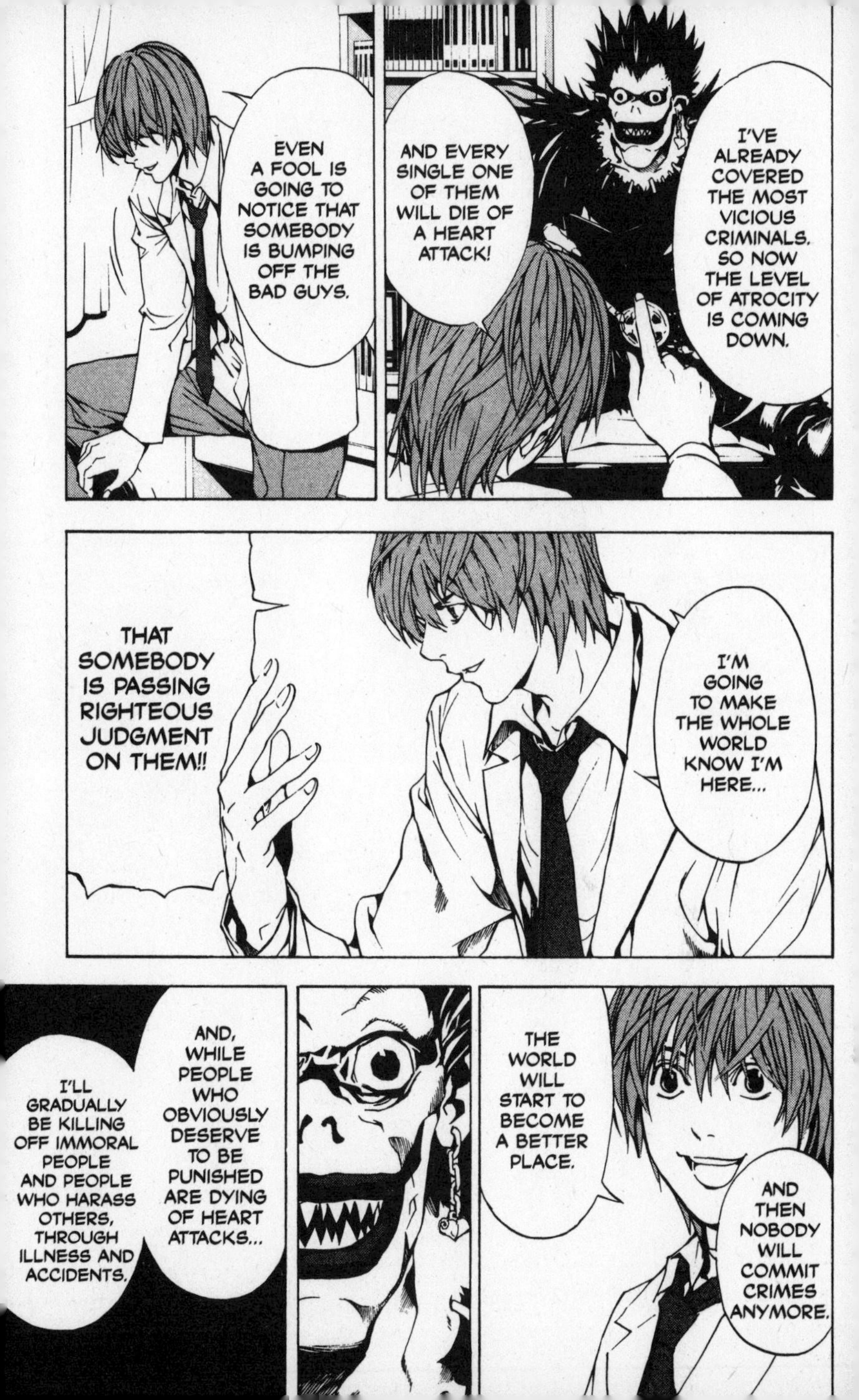
I'VE ALREADY COVERED THE MOST VICIOUS CRIMINALS. SO NOW THE LEVEL OF ATROCITY IS COMING DOWN.
AND EVERY SINGLE ONE OF THEM WILL DIE OF A HEART ATTACK!
EVEN A FOOL IS GOING TO NOTICE THAT SOMEBODY IS BUMPING OFF THE BAD GUYS.
I'M GOING TO MAKE THE WHOLE WORLD KNOW I'M HERE...
THAT SOMEBODY IS PASSING RIGHTEOUS JUDGMENT ON THEM!!
THE WORLD WILL START TO BECOME A BETTER PLACE.
AND THEN NOBODY WILL COMMIT CRIMES ANYMORE.
AND, WHILE PEOPLE WHO OBVIOUSLY DESERVE TO BE PUNISHED ARE DYING OF HEART ATTACKS...
I'LL GRADUALLY BE KILLING OFF IMMORAL PEOPLE AND PEOPLE WHO HARASS OTHERS, THROUGH ILLNESS AND ACCIDENTS.

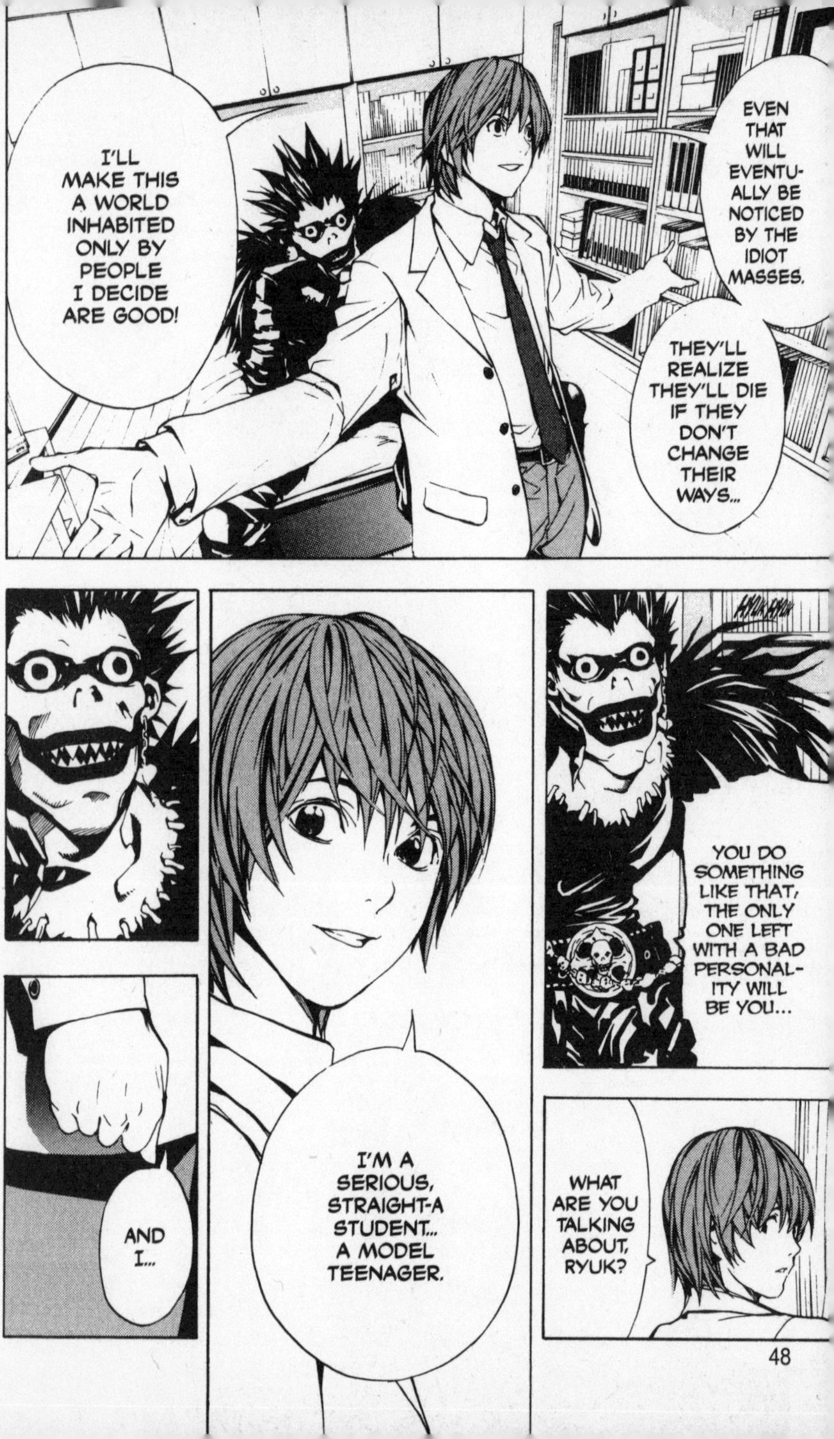
EVEN THAT WILL EVENTUALLY BE NOTICED BY THE IDIOT MASSES.
THEY'LL REALIZE THEY'LL DIE IF THEY DON'T CHANGE THEIR WAYS...
I'LL MAKE THIS A WORLD INHABITED ONLY BY PEOPLE I DECIDE ARE GOOD!
HYUK HYUK
YOU DO SOMETHING LIKE THAT, THE ONLY ONE LEFT WITH A BAD PERSONALITY WILL BE YOU...
WHAT ARE YOU TALKING ABOUT, RYUK?
AND I...
I'M A SERIOUS, STRAIGHT-A STUDENT... A MODEL TEENAGER.

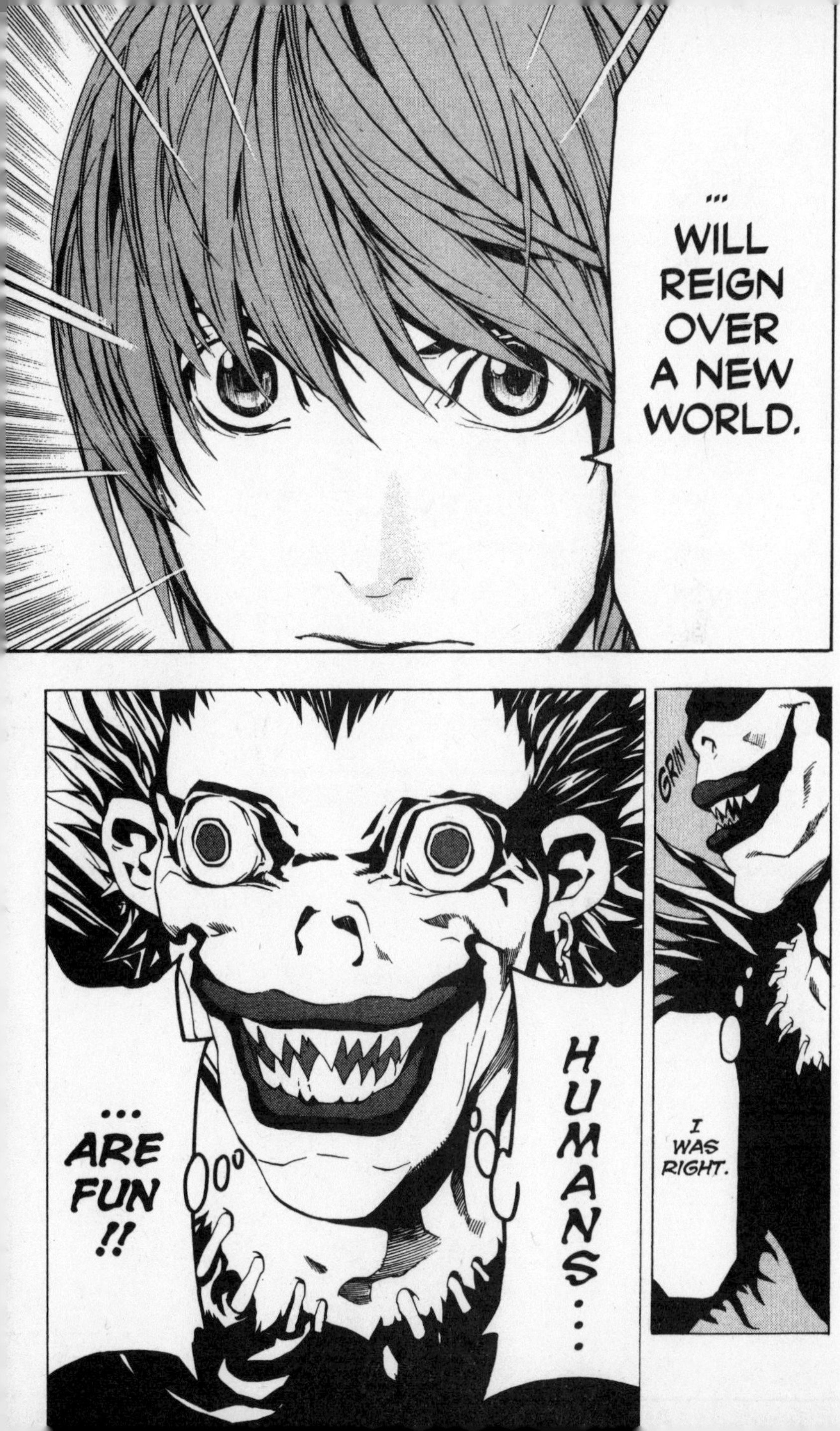
... WILL REIGN OVER A NEW WORLD.
GRIN
I WAS RIGHT.
HUMANS...
... ARE FUN !!

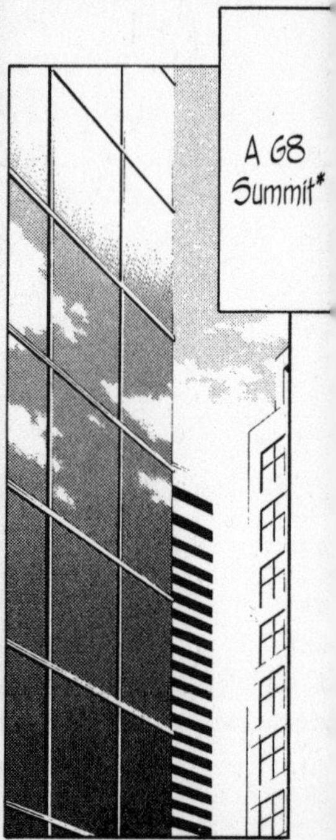
A G8 Summit*
*G8 STANDS FOR GROUP OF EIGHT, WHICH IS MADE UP OF THE WORLD'S LEADING NATIONS.

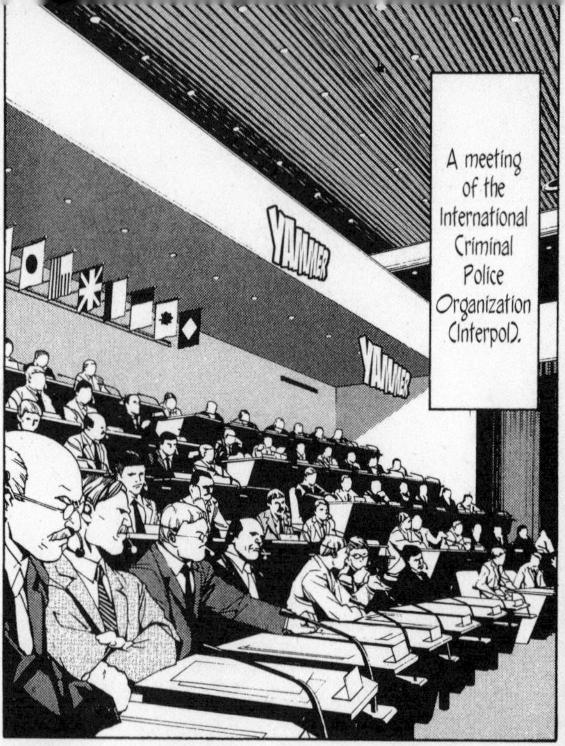
A meeting of the International Criminal Police Organization (Interpol).
YAMMER
YAMMER

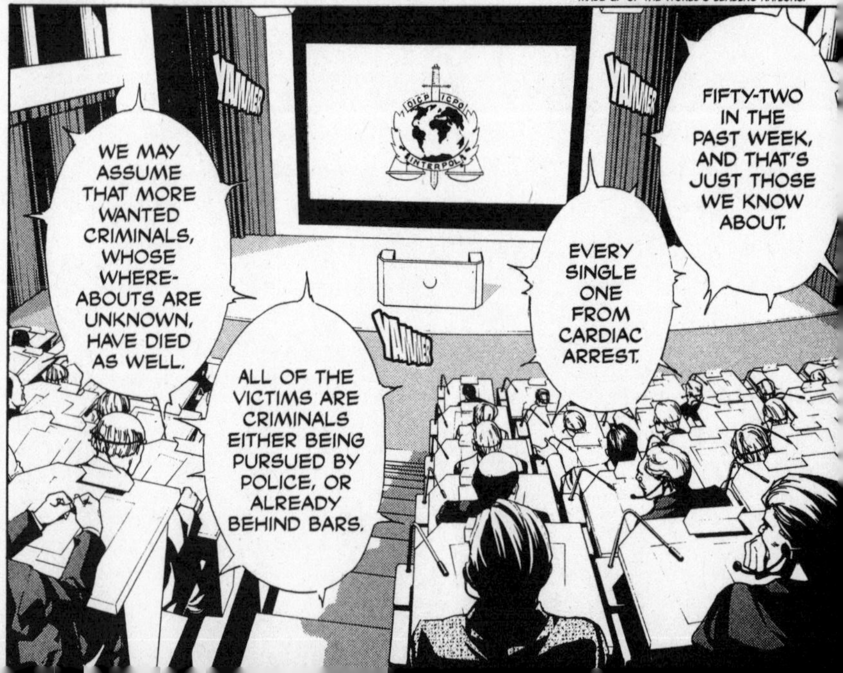
YAMMER
FIFTY-TWO IN THE PAST WEEK, AND THAT'S JUST THOSE WE KNOW ABOUT.
EVERY SINGLE ONE FROM CARDIAC ARREST.
YAMMER
YAMMER
ALL OF THE VICTIMS ARE CRIMINALS EITHER BEING PURSUED BY POLICE, OR ALREADY BEHIND BARS.
WE MAY ASSUME THAT MORE WANTED CRIMINALS, WHOSE WHERE-ABOUTS ARE UNKNOWN, HAVE DIED AS WELL.

READ THIS WAY

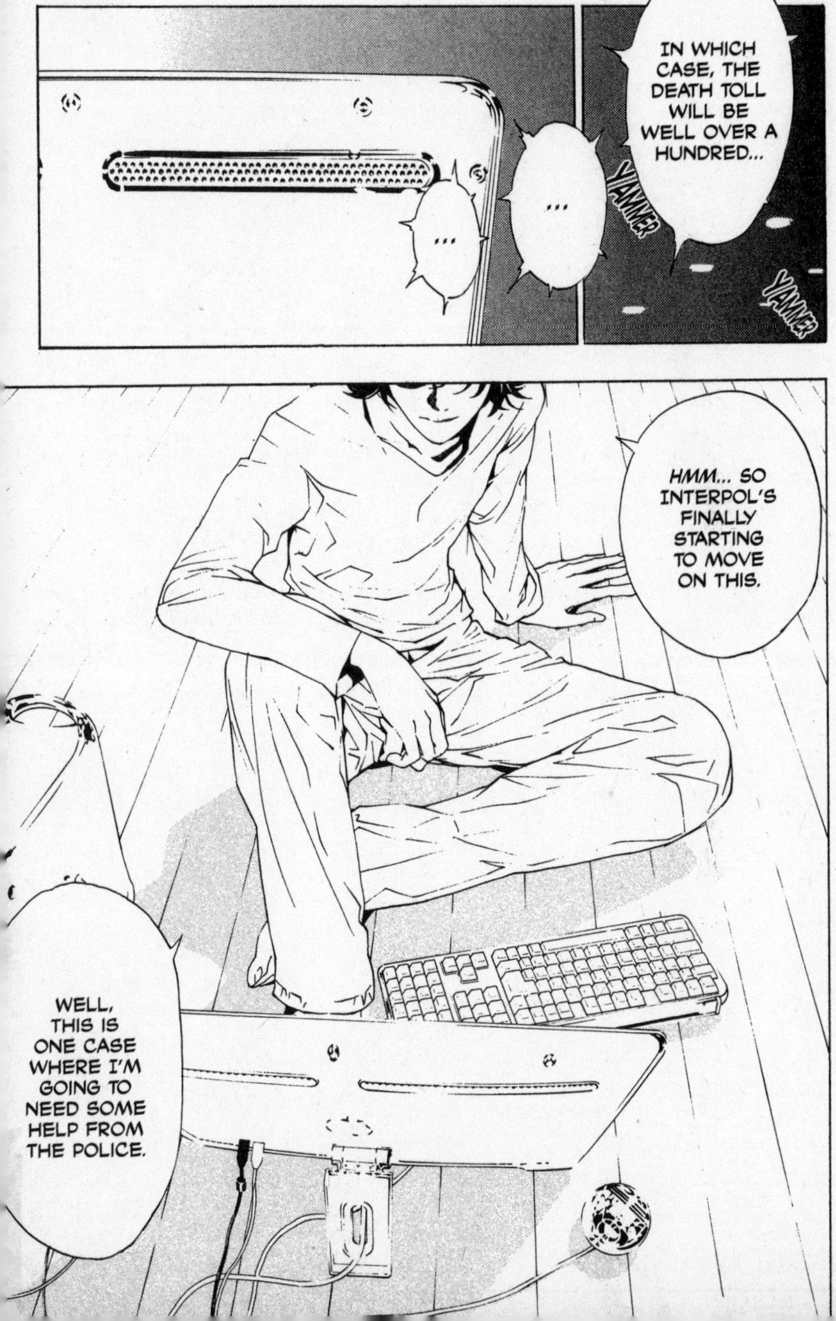
IN WHICH CASE, THE DEATH TOLL WILL BE WELL OVER A HUNDRED...
YAMMER
YAMMER
...
...
HMM... SO INTERPOL'S FINALLY STARTING TO MOVE ON THIS.
WELL, THIS IS ONE CASE WHERE I'M GOING TO NEED SOME HELP FROM THE POLICE.

DEATH NOTE
How to use it
I

○ The human whose name is written in this note shall die.

このノートに名前を書かれた人間は死ぬ。

○ This note will not take effect unless the writer has the person's face in their mind when writing his/her name. Therefore, people sharing the same name will not be affected.

書く人物の顔が頭に入っていないと効果はない。
ゆえに同姓同名の人物に一遍に効果は得られない。

○ If the cause of death is written within 40 seconds of writing the person's name, it will happen.

名前の後に人間界単位で40秒以内に死因を書くと、その通りになる。

○ If the cause of death is not specified, the person will simply die of a heart attack.

死因を書かなければ全てが心臓麻痺となる。

○ After writing the cause of death, details of the death should be written in the next 6 minutes and 40 seconds.

死因を書くと更に6分40秒、詳しい死の状況を記載する時間が与えられる。

chapter 2 L

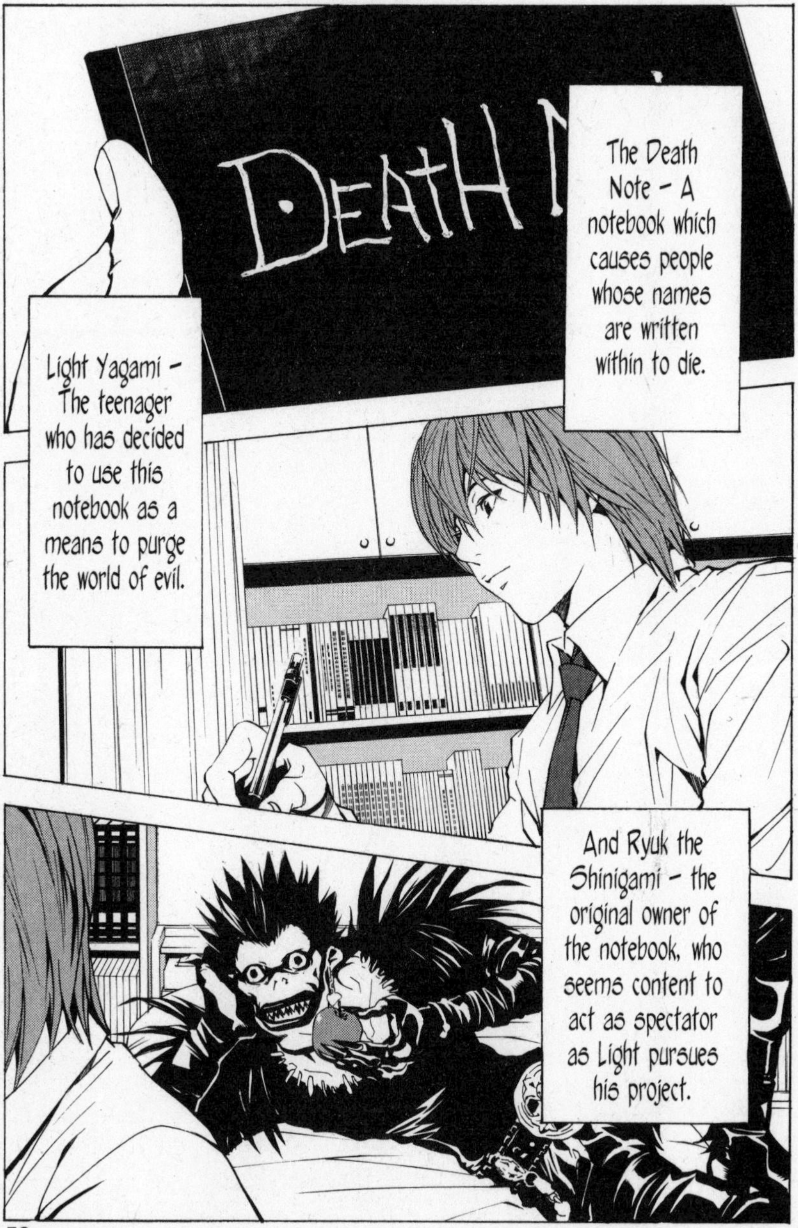
The Death Note - A notebook which causes people whose names are written within to die.
Light Yagami - The teenager who has decided to use this notebook as a means to purge the world of evil.
And Ryuk the Shinigami - the original owner of the notebook, who seems content to act as spectator as Light pursues his project.

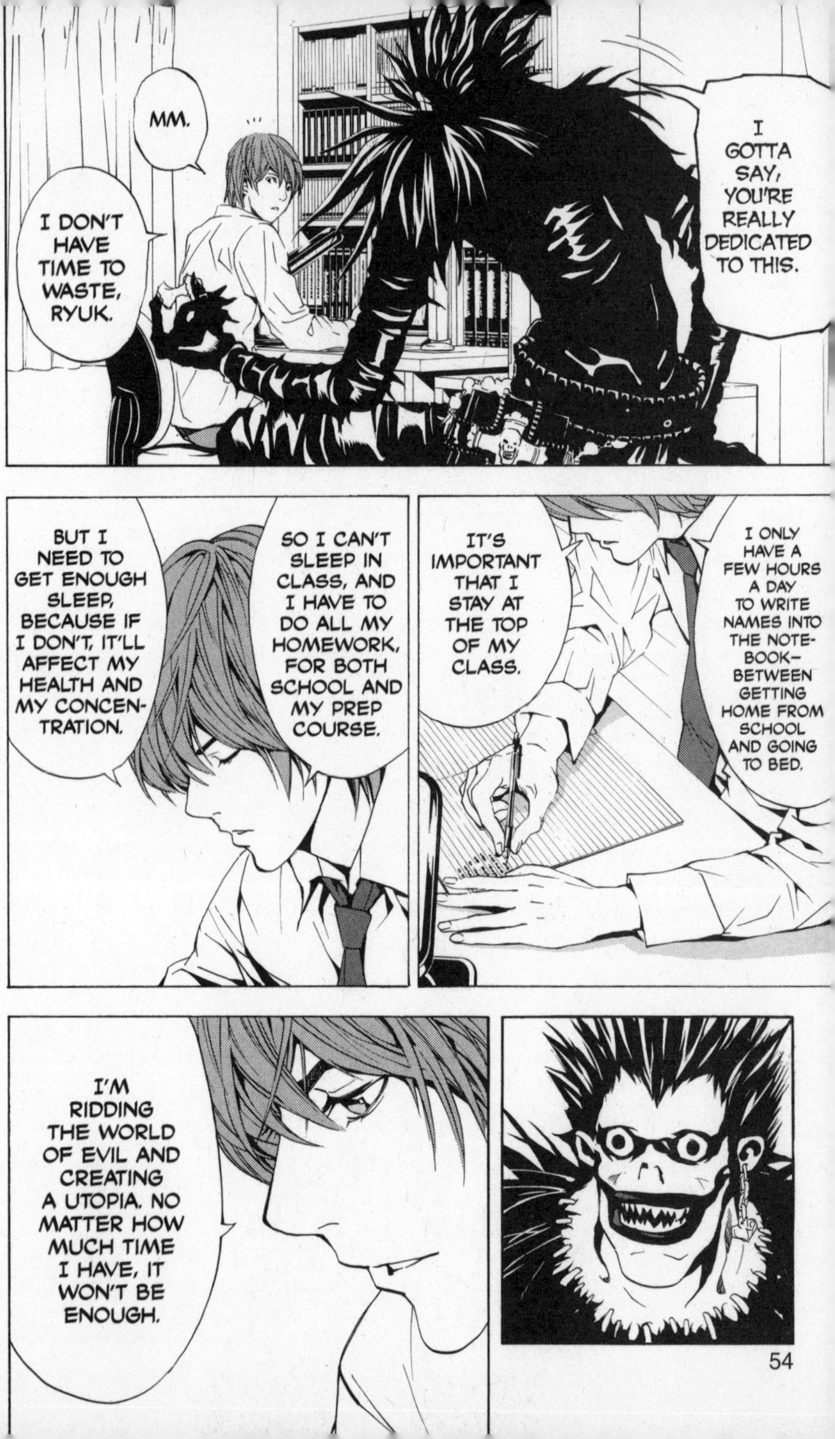
I GOTTA SAY, YOU'RE REALLY DEDICATED TO THIS.
MM.
I DON'T HAVE TIME TO WASTE, RYUK.
I ONLY HAVE A FEW HOURS A DAY TO WRITE NAMES INTO THE NOTE-BOOK—BETWEEN GETTING HOME FROM SCHOOL AND GOING TO BED.
IT'S IMPORTANT THAT I STAY AT THE TOP OF MY CLASS.
SO I CAN'T SLEEP IN CLASS, AND I HAVE TO DO ALL MY HOMEWORK, FOR BOTH SCHOOL AND MY PREP COURSE.
BUT I NEED TO GET ENOUGH SLEEP, BECAUSE IF I DON'T, IT'LL AFFECT MY HEALTH AND MY CONCEN-TRATION.
I'M RIDDING THE WORLD OF EVIL AND CREATING A UTOPIA. NO MATTER HOW MUCH TIME I HAVE, IT WON'T BE ENOUGH.

chapter 2 L

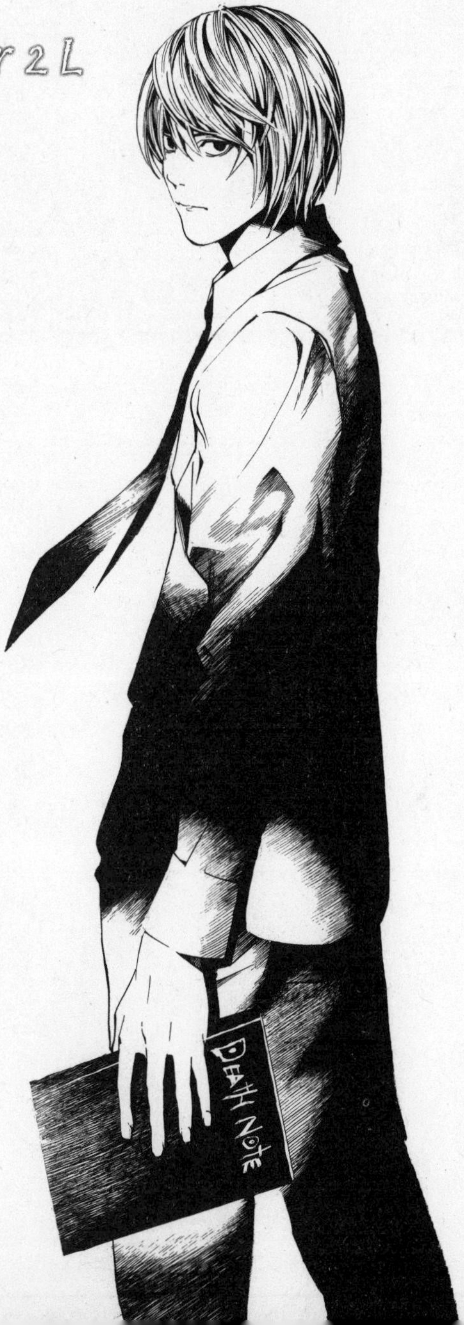
DEATH NOTE

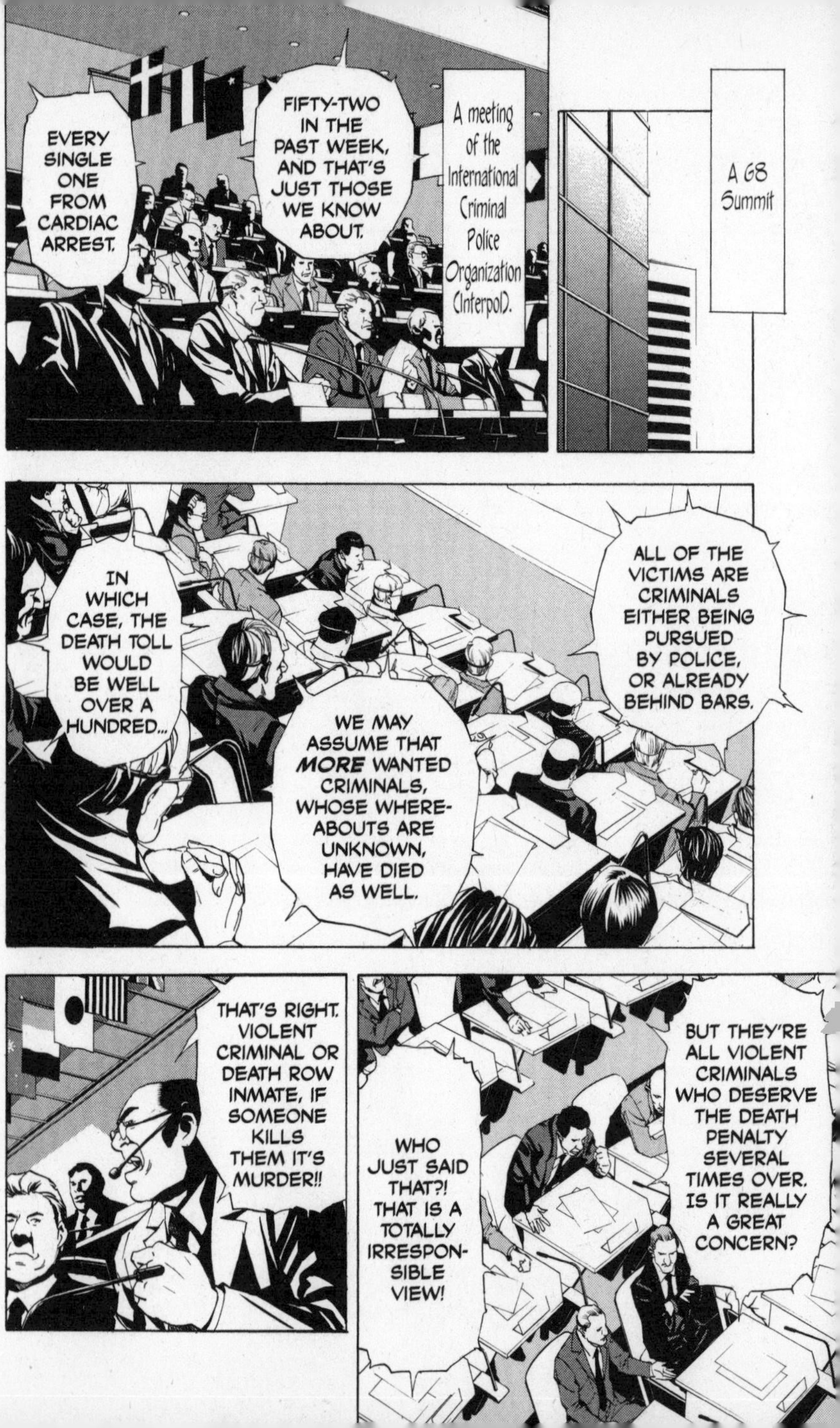
A G8 Summit
A meeting of the International Criminal Police Organization (Interpol).
FIFTY-TWO IN THE PAST WEEK, AND THAT'S JUST THOSE WE KNOW ABOUT.
EVERY SINGLE ONE FROM CARDIAC ARREST.
ALL OF THE VICTIMS ARE CRIMINALS EITHER BEING PURSUED BY POLICE, OR ALREADY BEHIND BARS.
WE MAY ASSUME THAT *MORE* WANTED CRIMINALS, WHOSE WHEREABOUTS ARE UNKNOWN, HAVE DIED AS WELL.
IN WHICH CASE, THE DEATH TOLL WOULD BE WELL OVER A HUNDRED...
BUT THEY'RE ALL VIOLENT CRIMINALS WHO DESERVE THE DEATH PENALTY SEVERAL TIMES OVER. IS IT REALLY A GREAT CONCERN?
WHO JUST SAID THAT?! THAT IS A TOTALLY IRRESPONSIBLE VIEW!
THAT'S RIGHT. VIOLENT CRIMINAL OR DEATH ROW INMATE, IF SOMEONE KILLS THEM IT'S MURDER!!

READ THIS WAY

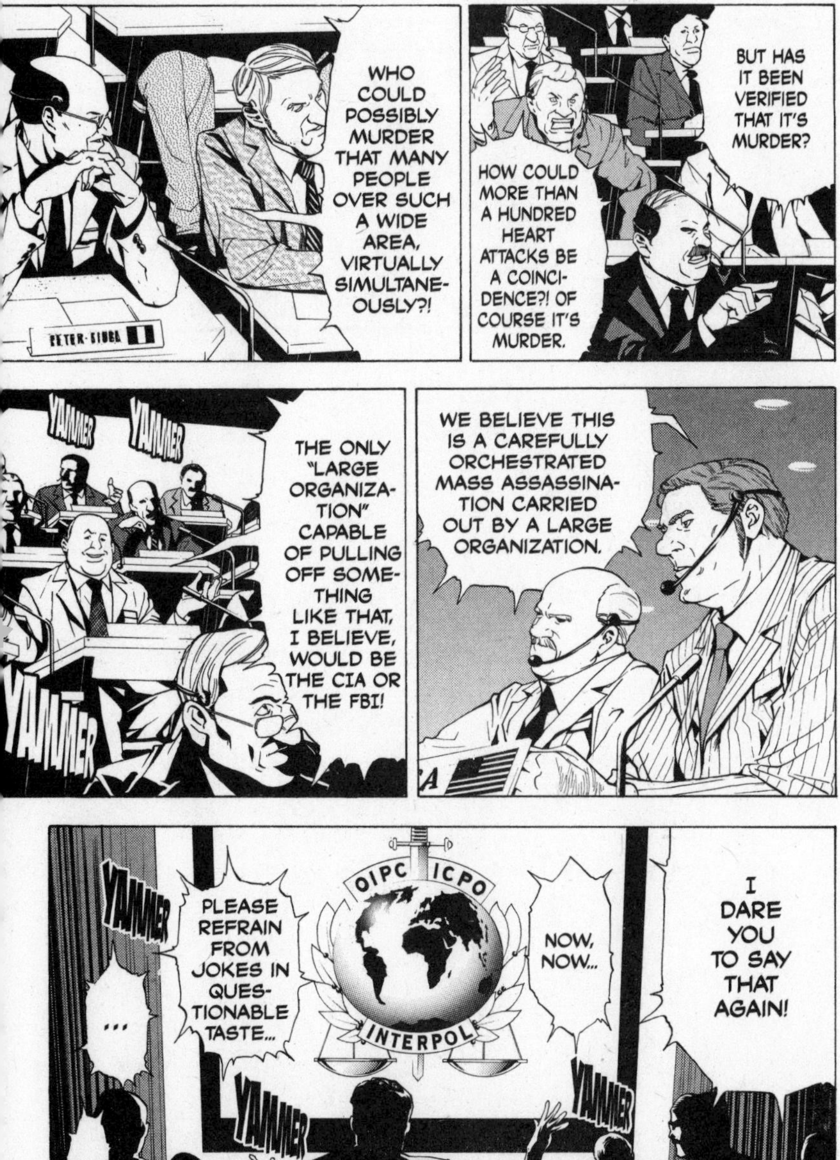
BUT HAS IT BEEN VERIFIED THAT IT'S MURDER?
HOW COULD MORE THAN A HUNDRED HEART ATTACKS BE A COINCIDENCE?! OF COURSE IT'S MURDER.
WHO COULD POSSIBLY MURDER THAT MANY PEOPLE OVER SUCH A WIDE AREA, VIRTUALLY SIMULTANEOUSLY?!
WE BELIEVE THIS IS A CAREFULLY ORCHESTRATED MASS ASSASSINATION CARRIED OUT BY A LARGE ORGANIZATION.
YAMMER
YAMMER
THE ONLY "LARGE ORGANIZATION" CAPABLE OF PULLING OFF SOMETHING LIKE THAT, I BELIEVE, WOULD BE THE CIA OR THE FBI!
YAMMER
I DARE YOU TO SAY THAT AGAIN!
NOW, NOW...
YAMMER
OIPC ICPO
INTERPOL
PLEASE REFRAIN FROM JOKES IN QUESTIONABLE TASTE...
YAMMER
YAMMER
...
...

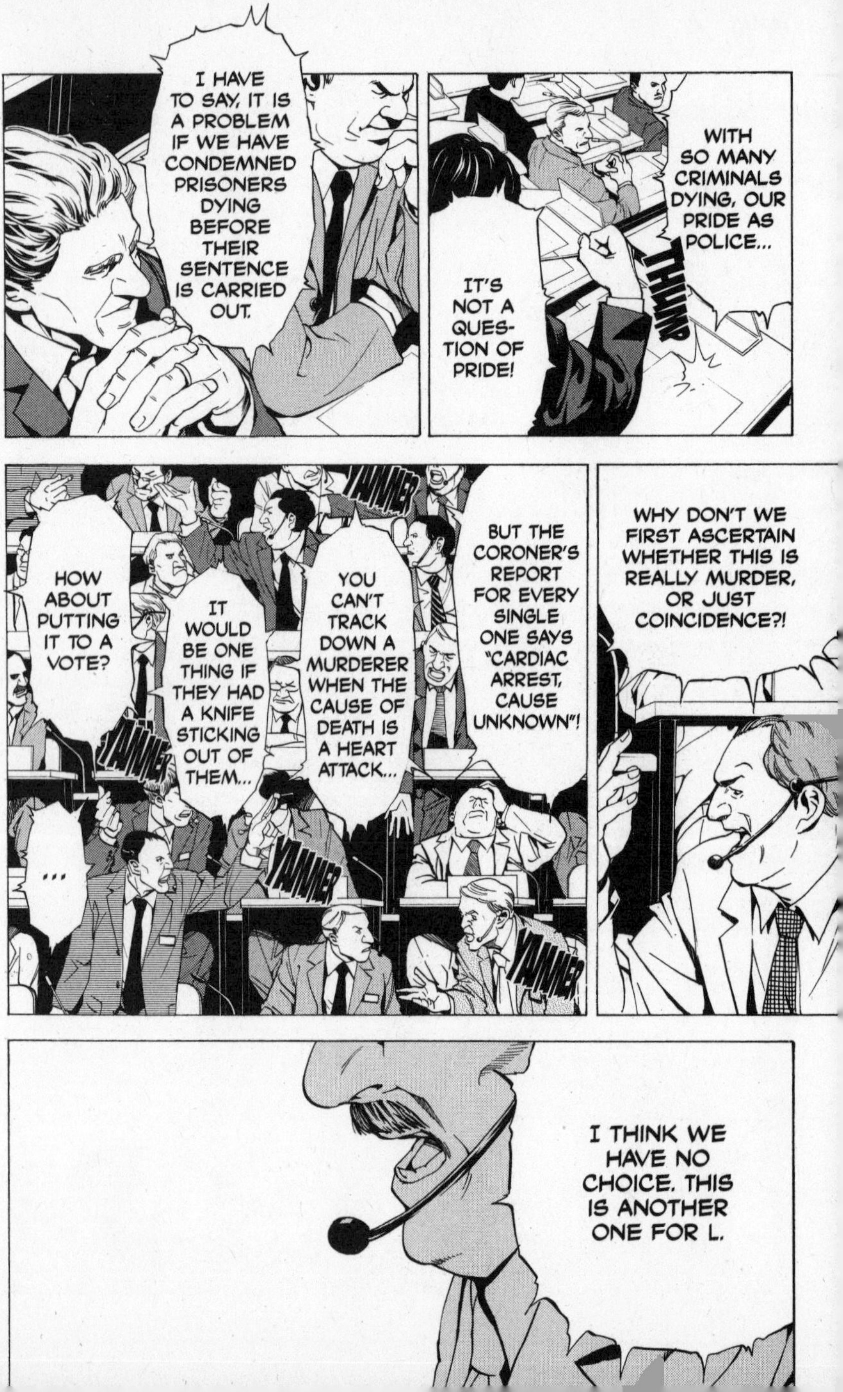

WITH SO MANY CRIMINALS DYING, OUR PRIDE AS POLICE...
THUMP
IT'S NOT A QUESTION OF PRIDE!
I HAVE TO SAY, IT IS A PROBLEM IF WE HAVE CONDEMNED PRISONERS DYING BEFORE THEIR SENTENCE IS CARRIED OUT.
WHY DON'T WE FIRST ASCERTAIN WHETHER THIS IS REALLY MURDER, OR JUST COINCIDENCE?!
YAMMER
BUT THE CORONER'S REPORT FOR EVERY SINGLE ONE SAYS "CARDIAC ARREST, CAUSE UNKNOWN"!
YOU CAN'T TRACK DOWN A MURDERER WHEN THE CAUSE OF DEATH IS A HEART ATTACK...
IT WOULD BE ONE THING IF THEY HAD A KNIFE STICKING OUT OF THEM...
HOW ABOUT PUTTING IT TO A VOTE?
YAMMER
YAMMER
...
YAMMER
I THINK WE HAVE NO CHOICE. THIS IS ANOTHER ONE FOR L.

READ THIS WAY

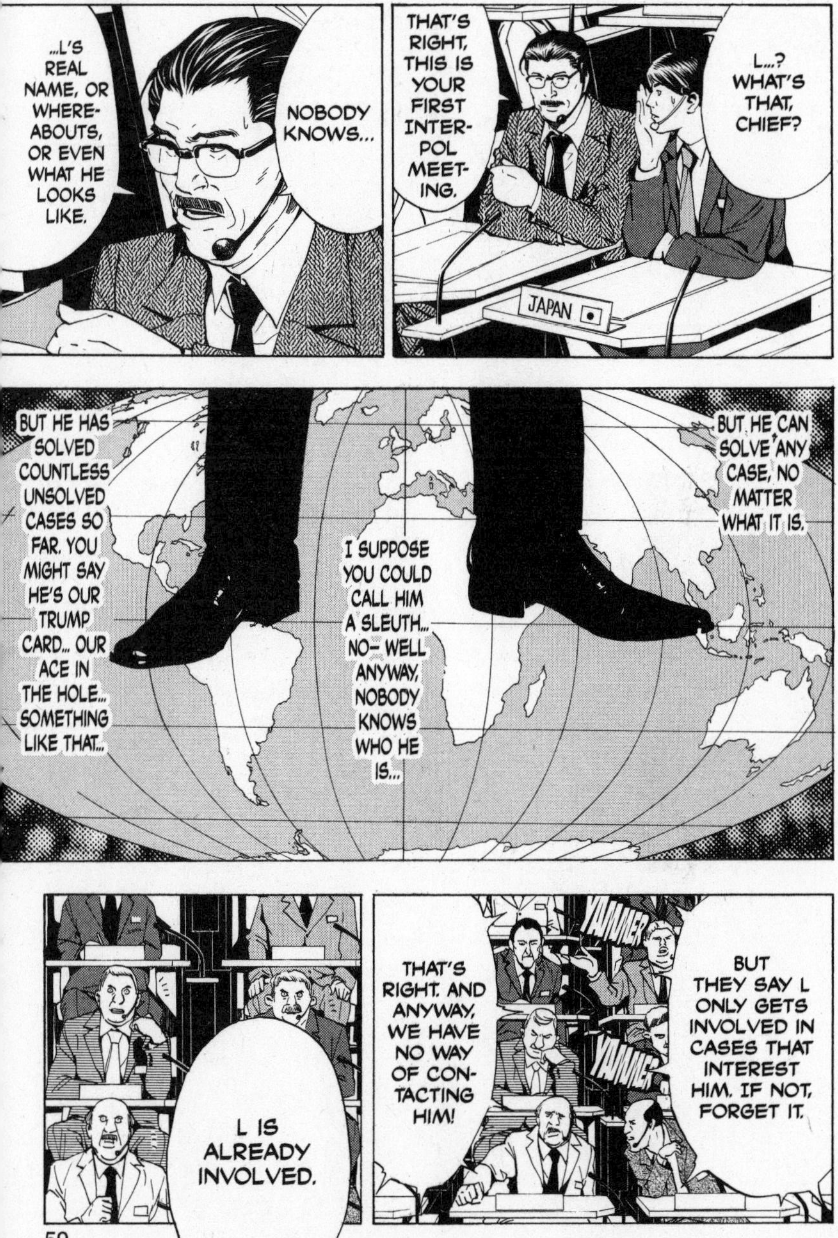
L...? WHAT'S THAT, CHIEF?
THAT'S RIGHT, THIS IS YOUR FIRST INTER-POL MEET-ING.
JAPAN
NOBODY KNOWS...
...L'S REAL NAME, OR WHERE-ABOUTS, OR EVEN WHAT HE LOOKS LIKE.
BUT HE CAN SOLVE ANY CASE, NO MATTER WHAT IT IS.
I SUPPOSE YOU COULD CALL HIM A SLEUTH... NO-- WELL ANYWAY, NOBODY KNOWS WHO HE IS...
BUT HE HAS SOLVED COUNTLESS UNSOLVED CASES SO FAR. YOU MIGHT SAY HE'S OUR TRUMP CARD... OUR ACE IN THE HOLE... SOMETHING LIKE THAT...
BUT THEY SAY L ONLY GETS INVOLVED IN CASES THAT INTEREST HIM. IF NOT, FORGET IT.
YAMMER
THAT'S RIGHT. AND ANYWAY, WE HAVE NO WAY OF CON-TACTING HIM!
YAMMER
L IS ALREADY INVOLVED.

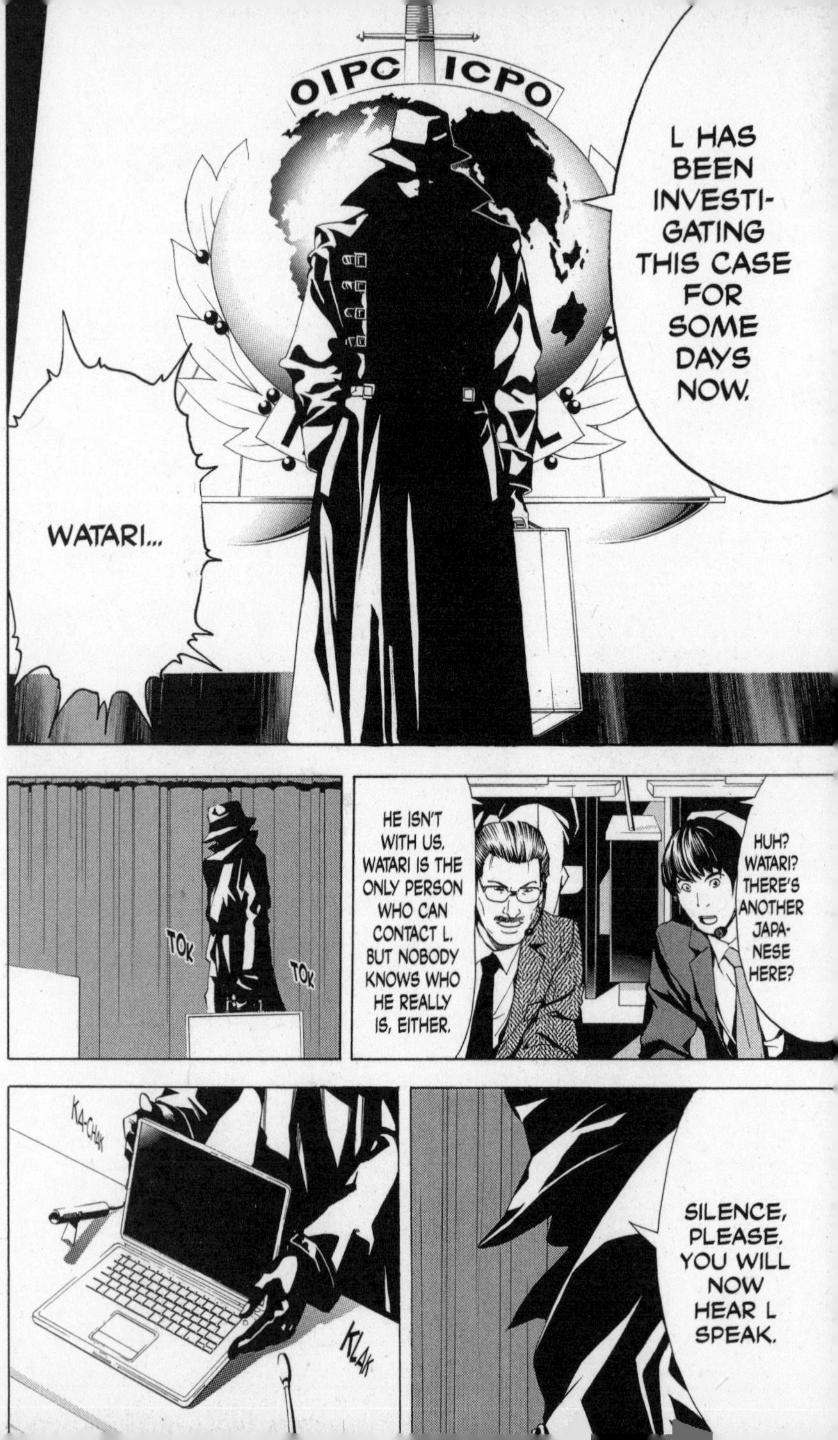
OIPC ICPO
L HAS BEEN INVESTIGATING THIS CASE FOR SOME DAYS NOW.
WATARI...
HUH? WATARI? THERE'S ANOTHER JAPANESE HERE?
HE ISN'T WITH US. WATARI IS THE ONLY PERSON WHO CAN CONTACT L. BUT NOBODY KNOWS WHO HE REALLY IS, EITHER.
TOK
TOK
SILENCE, PLEASE. YOU WILL NOW HEAR L SPEAK.
KA-CHAK
KLAK

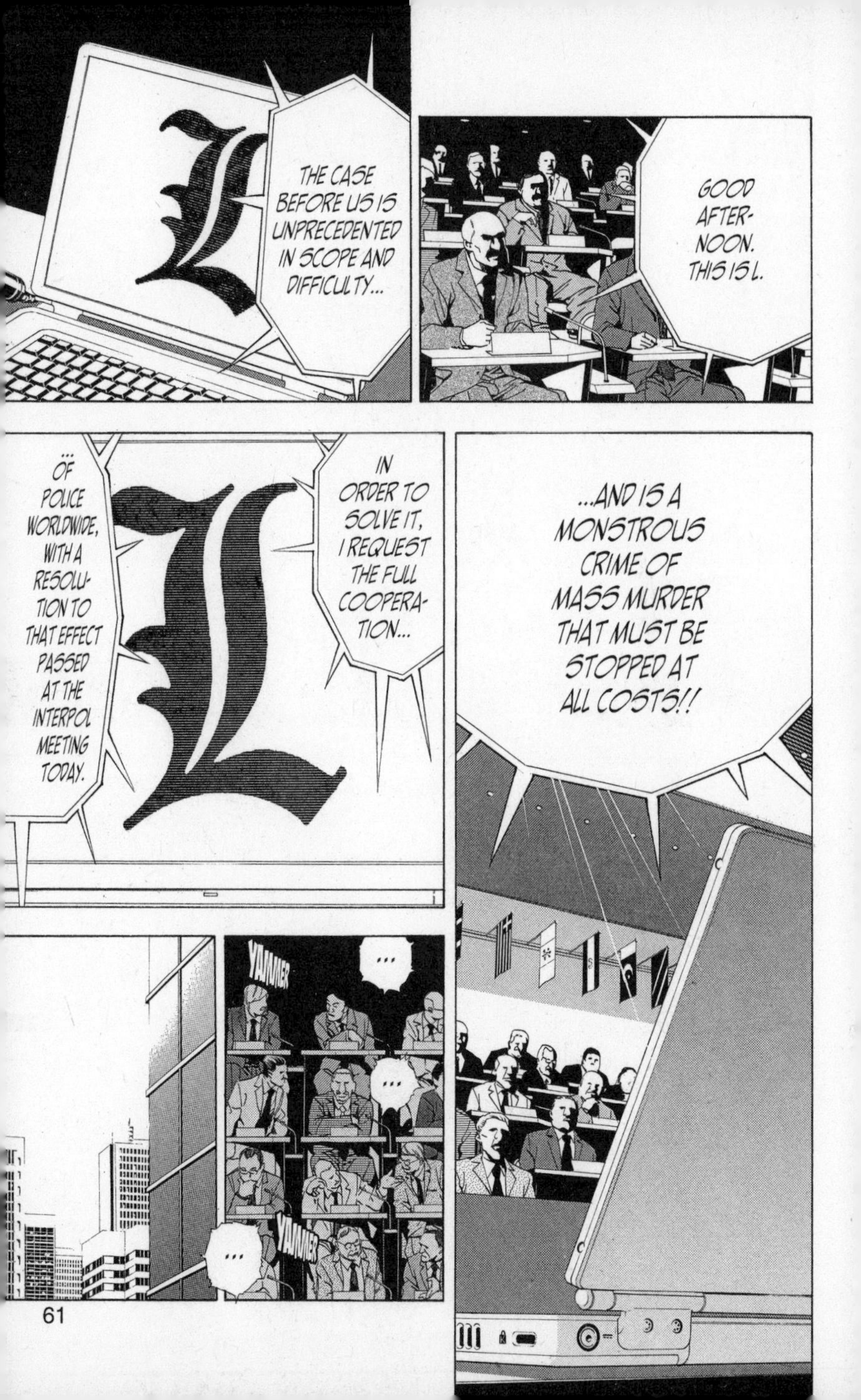
GOOD AFTER-NOON. THIS IS L.
THE CASE BEFORE US IS UNPRECEDENTED IN SCOPE AND DIFFICULTY...
...AND IS A MONSTROUS CRIME OF MASS MURDER THAT MUST BE STOPPED AT ALL COSTS!!
IN ORDER TO SOLVE IT, I REQUEST THE FULL COOPERA-TION...
...OF POLICE WORLDWIDE, WITH A RESOLU-TION TO THAT EFFECT PASSED AT THE INTERPOL MEETING TODAY.
YAMMER
...
...
YAMMER
...

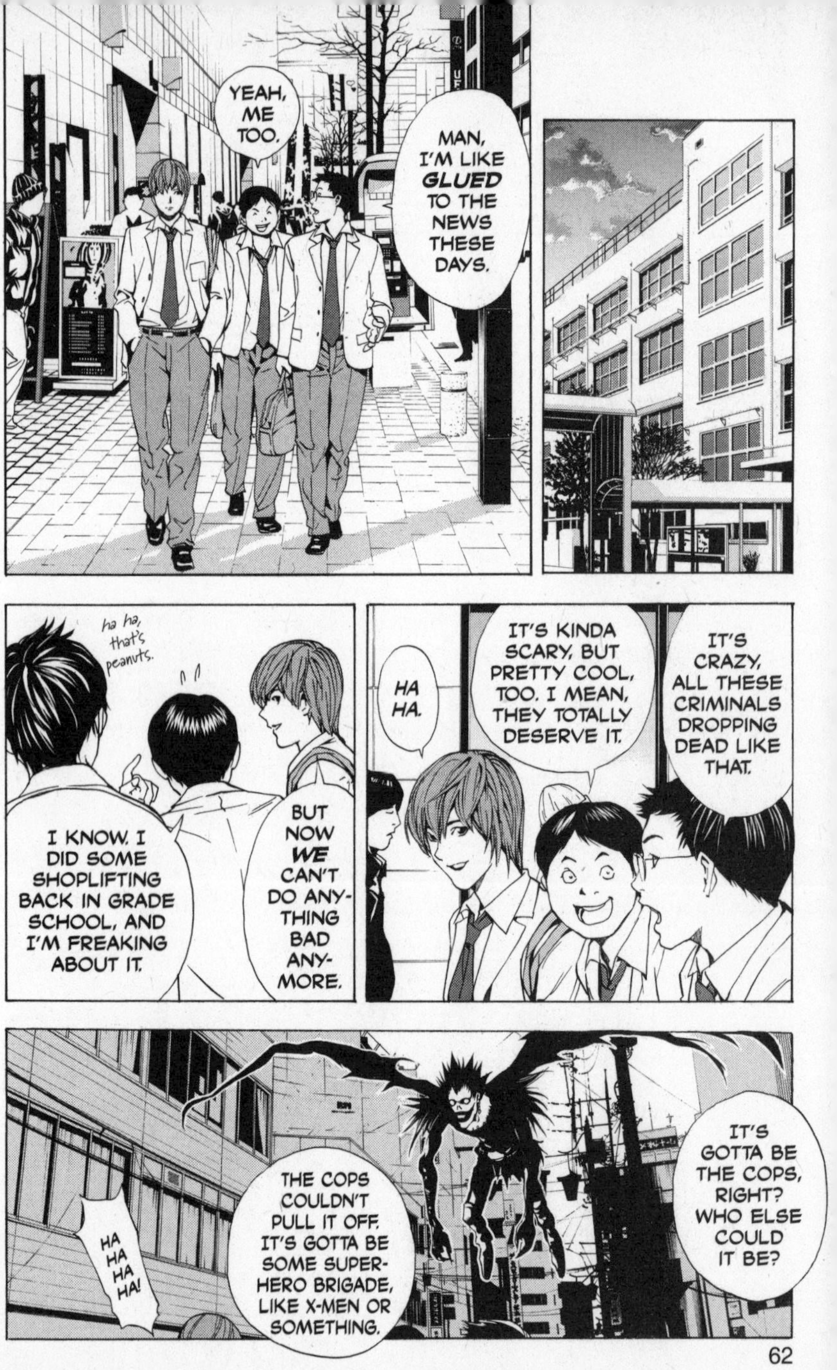
MAN, I'M LIKE **GLUED** TO THE NEWS THESE DAYS.
YEAH, ME TOO.
IT'S CRAZY, ALL THESE CRIMINALS DROPPING DEAD LIKE THAT.
IT'S KINDA SCARY, BUT PRETTY COOL, TOO. I MEAN, THEY TOTALLY DESERVE IT.
HA HA.
BUT NOW **WE** CAN'T DO ANYTHING BAD ANYMORE.
I KNOW. I DID SOME SHOPLIFTING BACK IN GRADE SCHOOL, AND I'M FREAKING ABOUT IT.
ha ha, that's peanuts.
IT'S GOTTA BE THE COPS, RIGHT? WHO ELSE COULD IT BE?
THE COPS COULDN'T PULL IT OFF. IT'S GOTTA BE SOME SUPER-HERO BRIGADE, LIKE X-MEN OR SOMETHING.
HA HA HA HA!

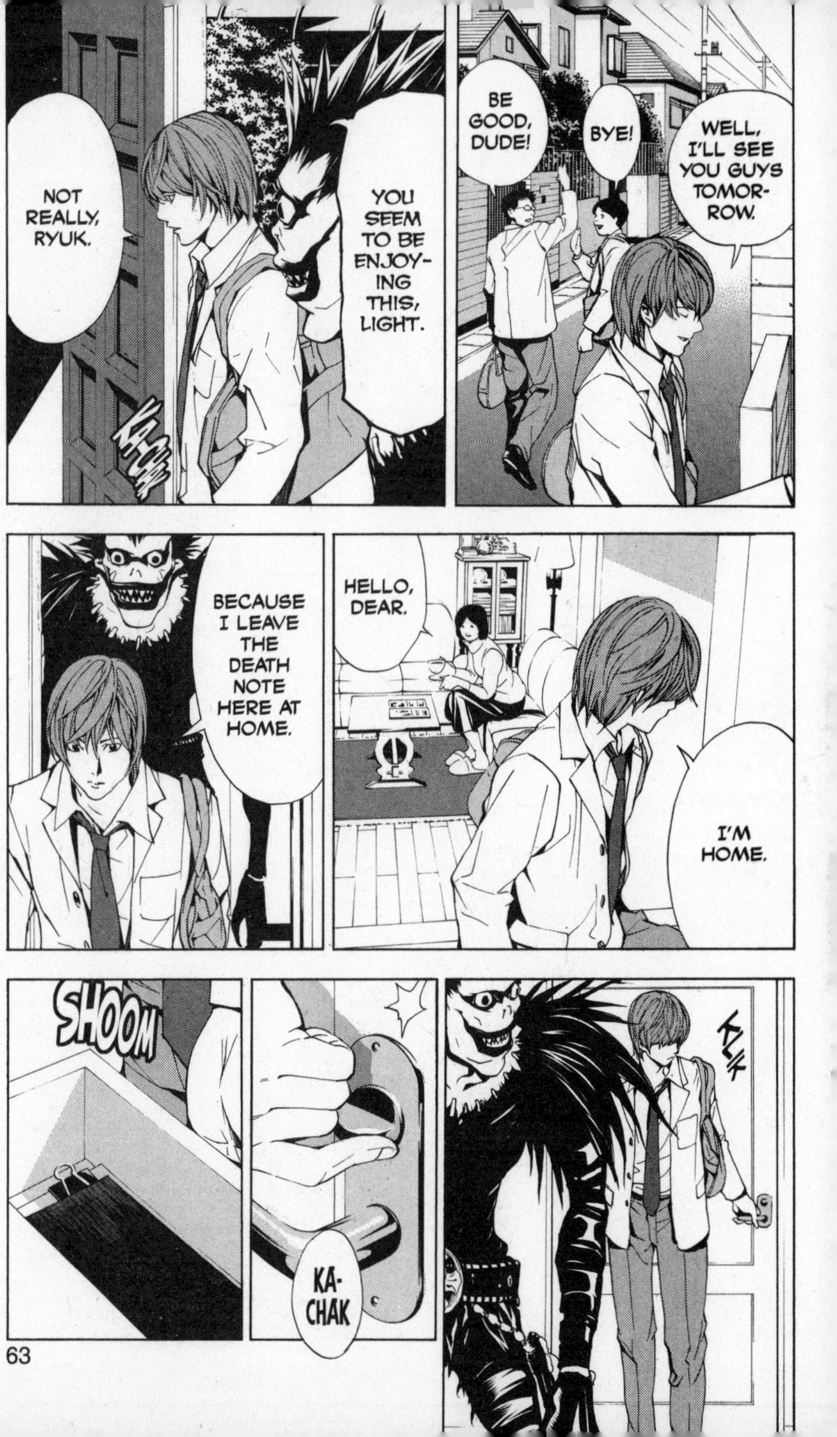
WELL, I'LL SEE YOU GUYS TOMORROW.
BYE!
BE GOOD, DUDE!
YOU SEEM TO BE ENJOYING THIS, LIGHT.
NOT REALLY, RYUK.
KACHAK
I'M HOME.
HELLO, DEAR.
BECAUSE I LEAVE THE DEATH NOTE HERE AT HOME.
KLIK
KA-CHAK
SHOOM

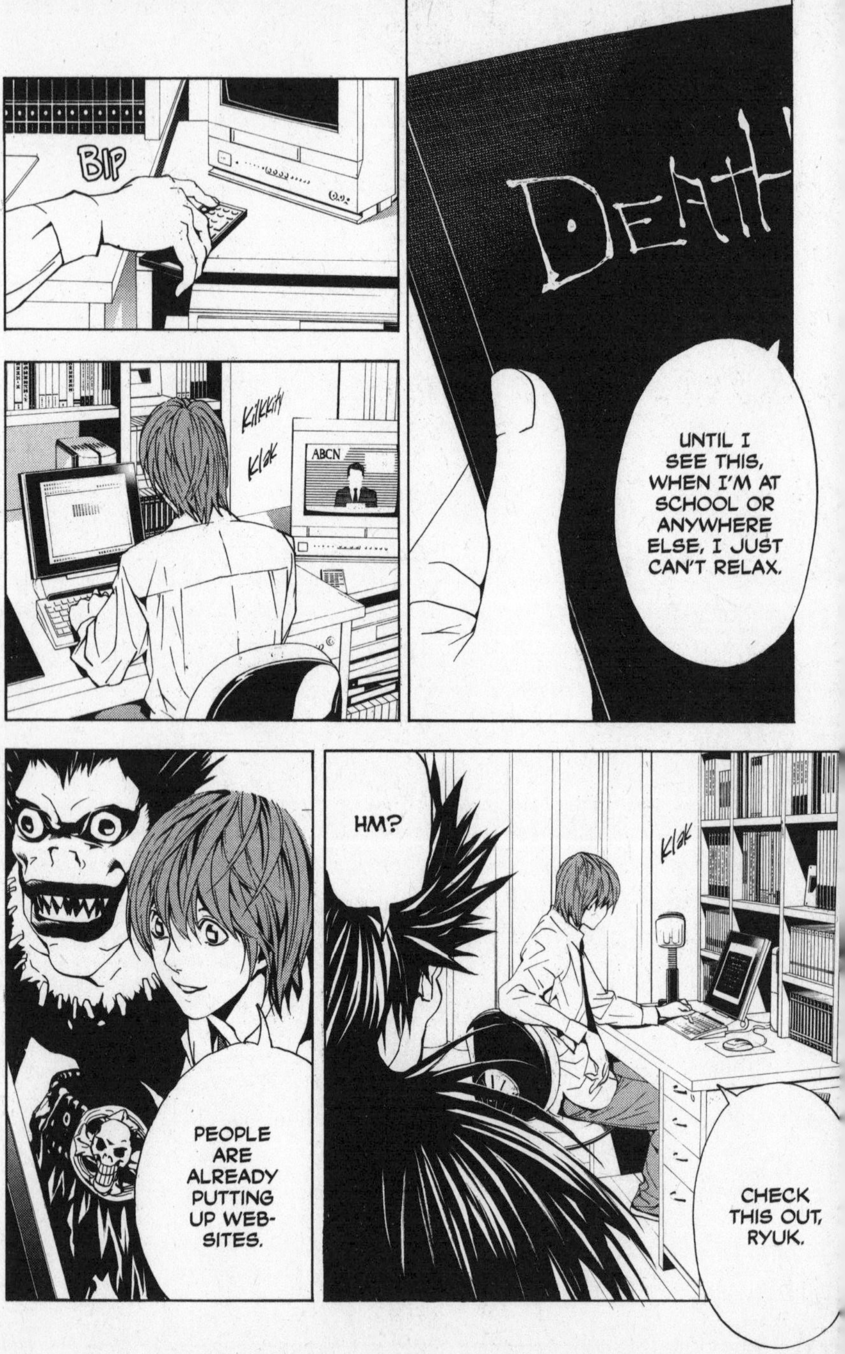
DEATH
UNTIL I SEE THIS, WHEN I'M AT SCHOOL OR ANYWHERE ELSE, I JUST CAN'T RELAX.
BIP
KIKKITY
KLAK
ABCN
KLAK
CHECK THIS OUT, RYUK.
HM?
PEOPLE ARE ALREADY PUTTING UP WEB-SITES.

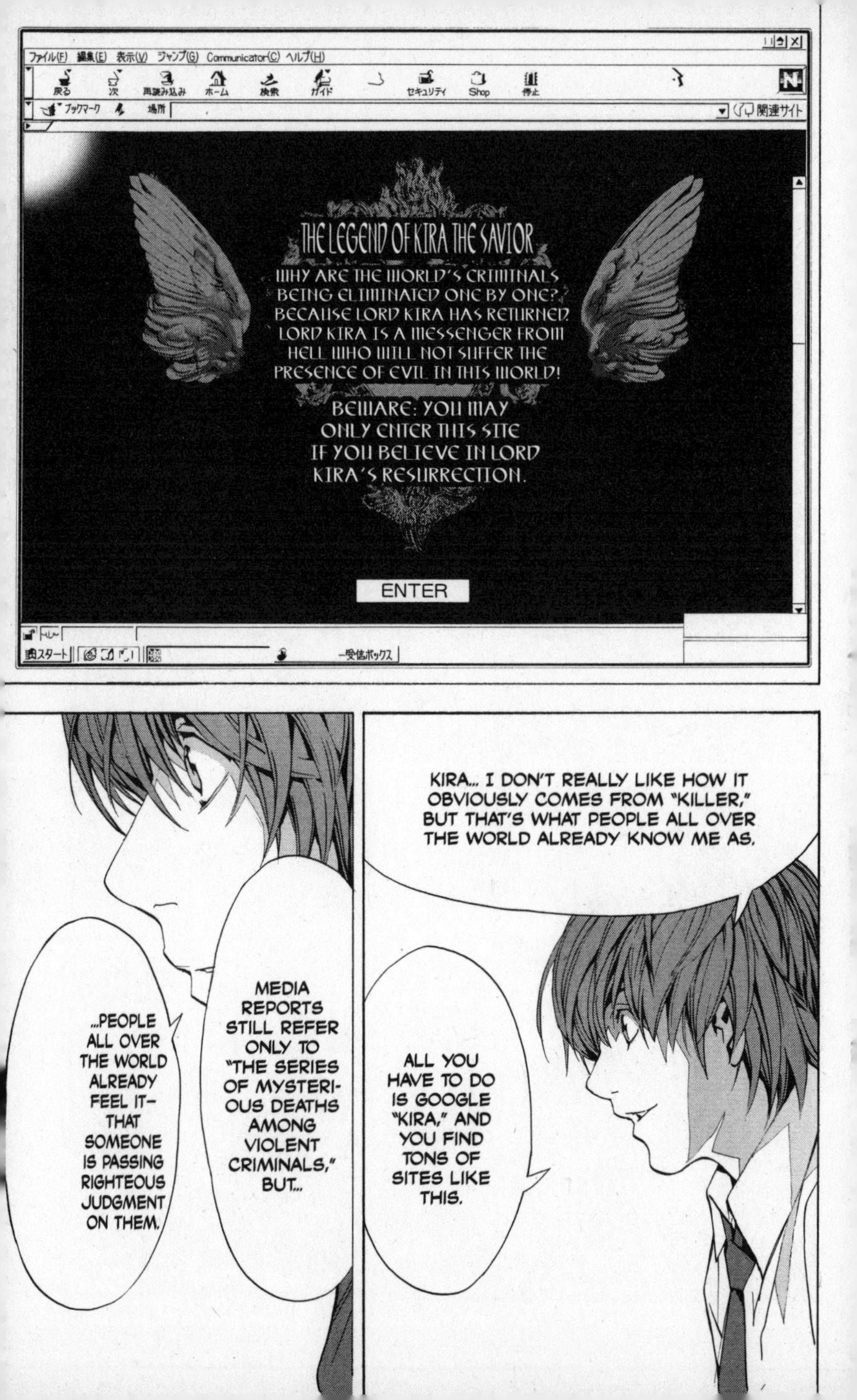

ファイル(F) 編集(E) 表示(V) ジャンプ(G) Communicator(C) ヘルプ(H)
戻る 次 再読み込み ホーム 検索 ガイド セキュリティ Shop 停止
ブックマーク 場所 関連サイト
THE LEGEND OF KIRA THE SAVIOR
WHY ARE THE WORLD'S CRIMINALS BEING ELIMINATED ONE BY ONE? BECAUSE LORD KIRA HAS RETURNED. LORD KIRA IS A MESSENGER FROM HELL WHO WILL NOT SUFFER THE PRESENCE OF EVIL IN THIS WORLD!
BEWARE: YOU MAY ONLY ENTER THIS SITE IF YOU BELIEVE IN LORD KIRA'S RESURRECTION.
ENTER
スタート 受信ボックス
KIRA... I DON'T REALLY LIKE HOW IT OBVIOUSLY COMES FROM "KILLER," BUT THAT'S WHAT PEOPLE ALL OVER THE WORLD ALREADY KNOW ME AS.
ALL YOU HAVE TO DO IS GOOGLE "KIRA," AND YOU FIND TONS OF SITES LIKE THIS.
MEDIA REPORTS STILL REFER ONLY TO "THE SERIES OF MYSTERIOUS DEATHS AMONG VIOLENT CRIMINALS," BUT...
...PEOPLE ALL OVER THE WORLD ALREADY FEEL IT—THAT SOMEONE IS PASSING RIGHTEOUS JUDGMENT ON THEM.

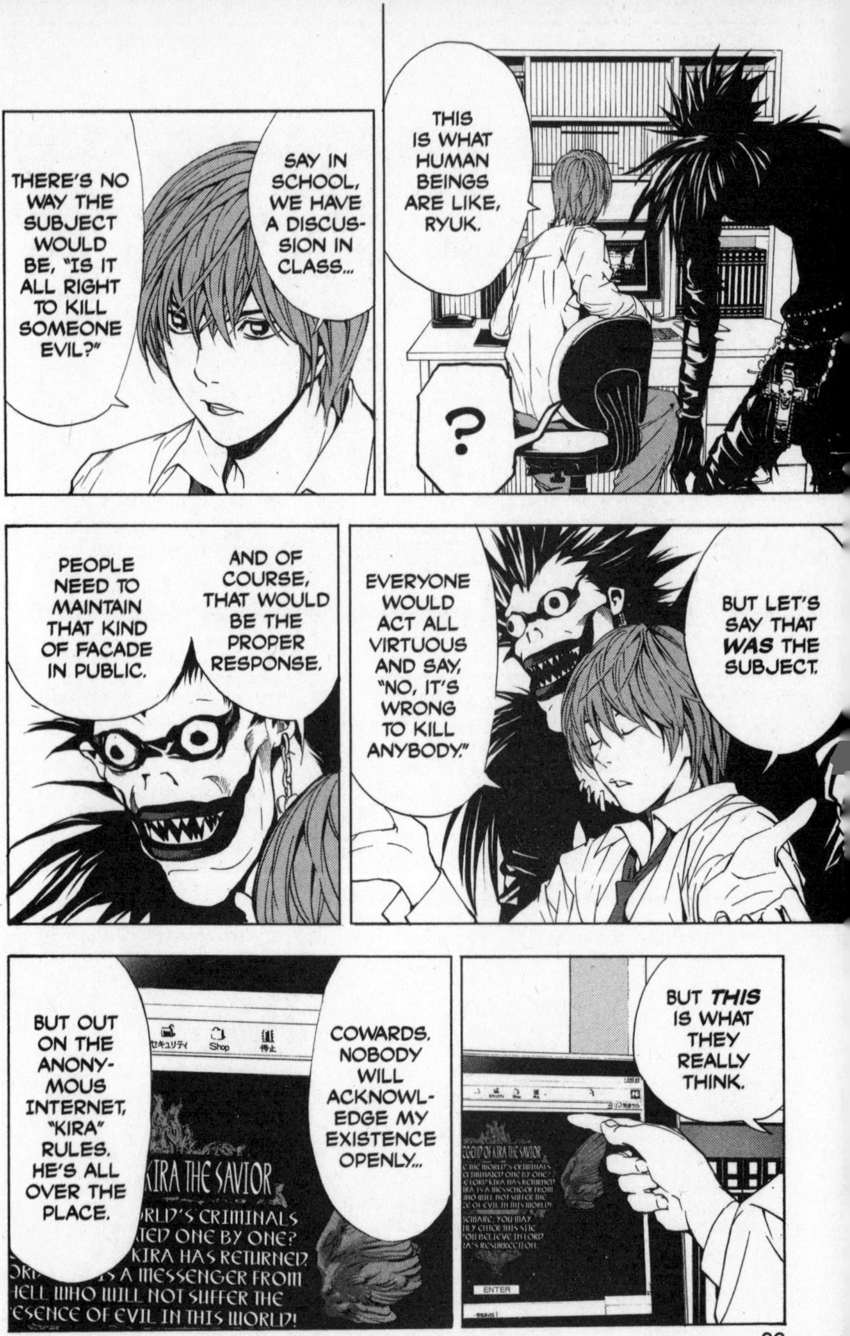
THIS IS WHAT HUMAN BEINGS ARE LIKE, RYUK.
?
SAY IN SCHOOL, WE HAVE A DISCUSSION IN CLASS...
THERE'S NO WAY THE SUBJECT WOULD BE, "IS IT ALL RIGHT TO KILL SOMEONE EVIL?"
BUT LET'S SAY THAT *WAS* THE SUBJECT.
EVERYONE WOULD ACT ALL VIRTUOUS AND SAY, "NO, IT'S WRONG TO KILL ANYBODY."
AND OF COURSE, THAT WOULD BE THE PROPER RESPONSE.
PEOPLE NEED TO MAINTAIN THAT KIND OF FACADE IN PUBLIC.
BUT *THIS* IS WHAT THEY REALLY THINK.
ENTER
COWARDS. NOBODY WILL ACKNOWLEDGE MY EXISTENCE OPENLY...
BUT OUT ON THE ANONYMOUS INTERNET, "KIRA" RULES. HE'S ALL OVER THE PLACE.
Shop
KIRA THE SAVIOR

READ THIS WAY

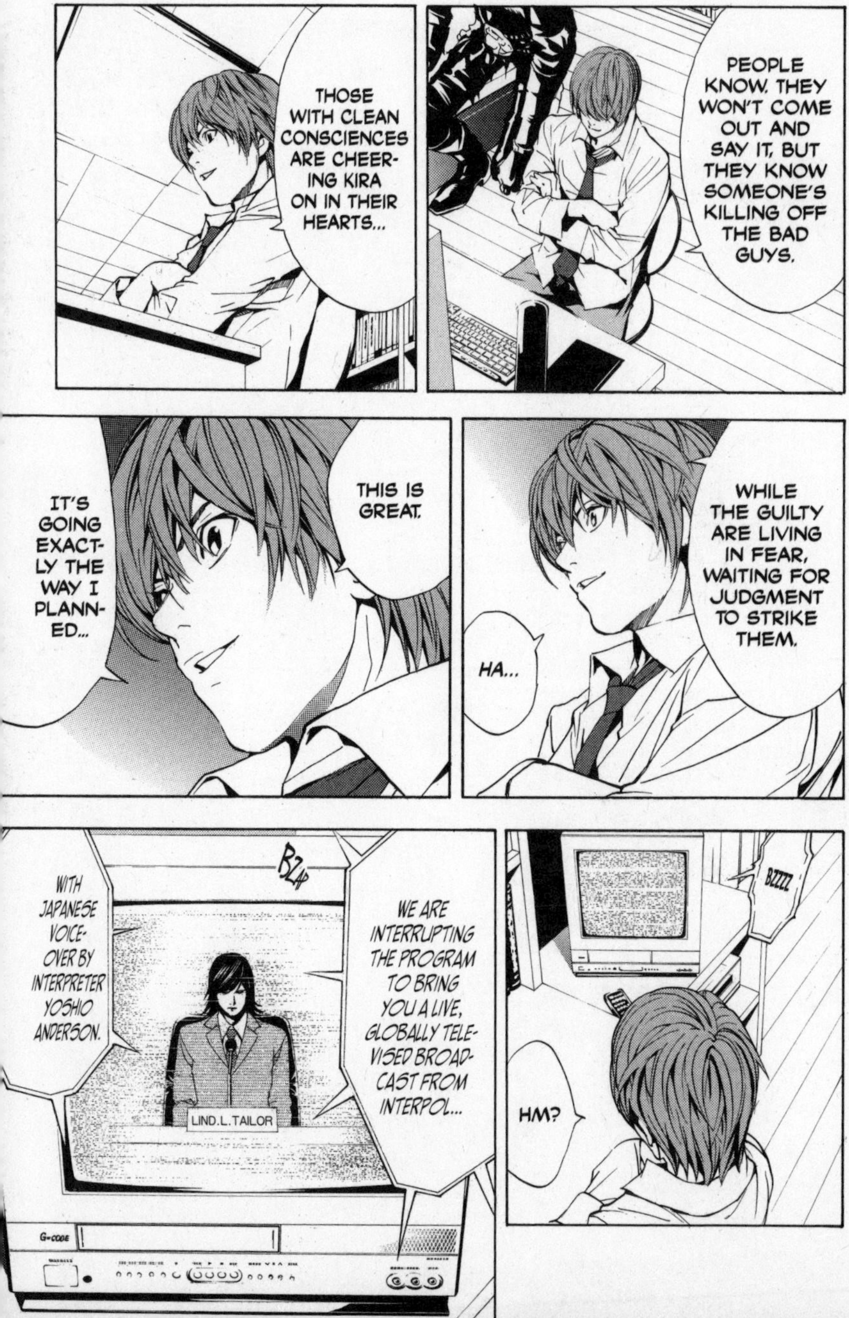
PEOPLE KNOW. THEY WON'T COME OUT AND SAY IT, BUT THEY KNOW SOMEONE'S KILLING OFF THE BAD GUYS.
THOSE WITH CLEAN CONSCIENCES ARE CHEERING KIRA ON IN THEIR HEARTS...
WHILE THE GUILTY ARE LIVING IN FEAR, WAITING FOR JUDGMENT TO STRIKE THEM.
HA...
THIS IS GREAT.
IT'S GOING EXACTLY THE WAY I PLANNED...
BZZZZ
HM?
BZAP
WE ARE INTERRUPTING THE PROGRAM TO BRING YOU A LIVE, GLOBALLY TELEVISED BROADCAST FROM INTERPOL...
WITH JAPANESE VOICE-OVER BY INTERPRETER YOSHIO ANDERSON.
LIND.L.TAILOR
G-CODE

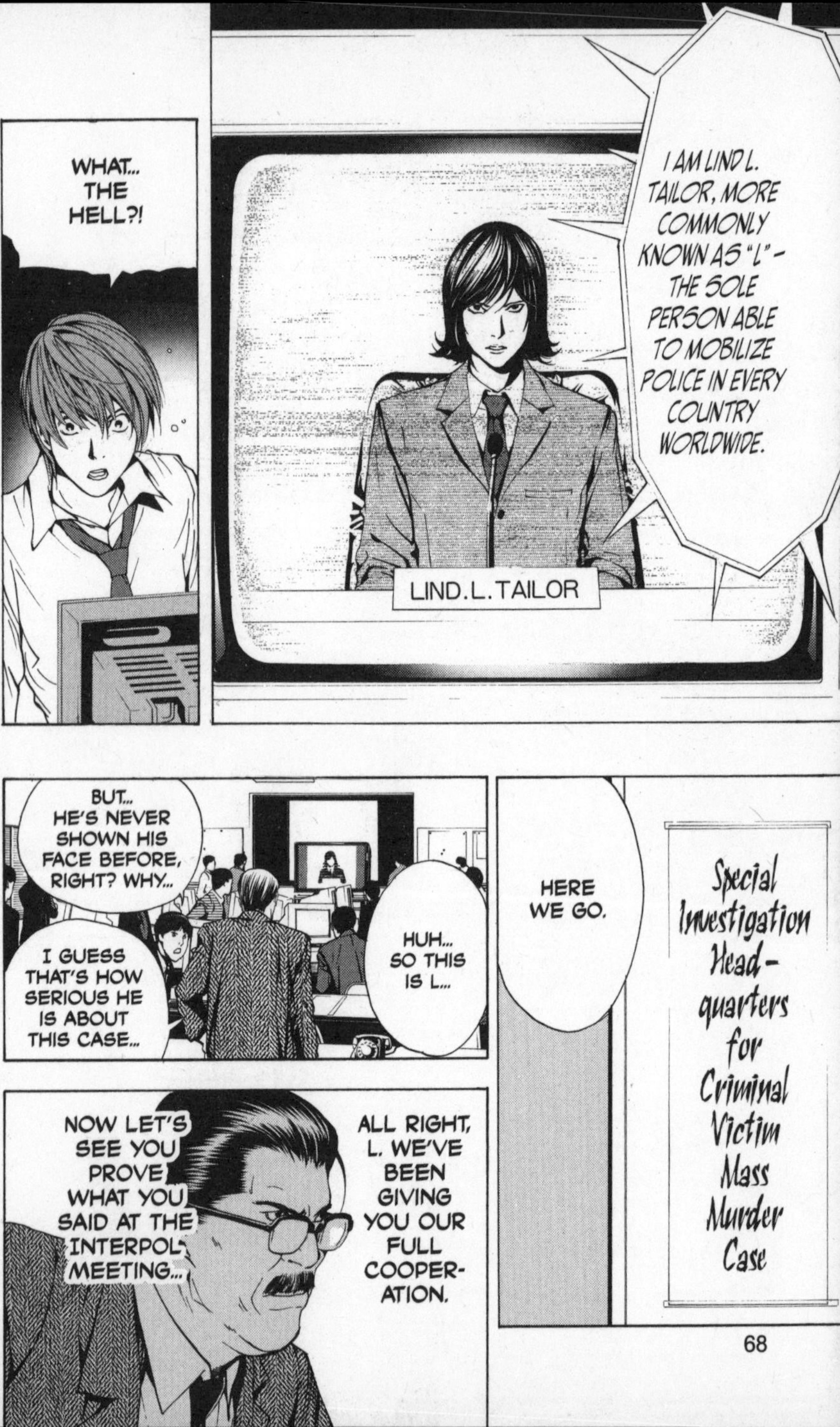
I AM LIND L. TAILOR, MORE COMMONLY KNOWN AS "L" - THE SOLE PERSON ABLE TO MOBILIZE POLICE IN EVERY COUNTRY WORLDWIDE.
LIND.L.TAILOR
WHAT... THE HELL?!
Special Investigation Head-quarters for Criminal Victim Mass Murder Case
HERE WE GO.
HUH... SO THIS IS L...
BUT... HE'S NEVER SHOWN HIS FACE BEFORE, RIGHT? WHY...
I GUESS THAT'S HOW SERIOUS HE IS ABOUT THIS CASE...
ALL RIGHT, L. WE'VE BEEN GIVING YOU OUR FULL COOPER-ATION.
NOW LET'S SEE YOU PROVE WHAT YOU SAID AT THE INTERPOL MEETING...

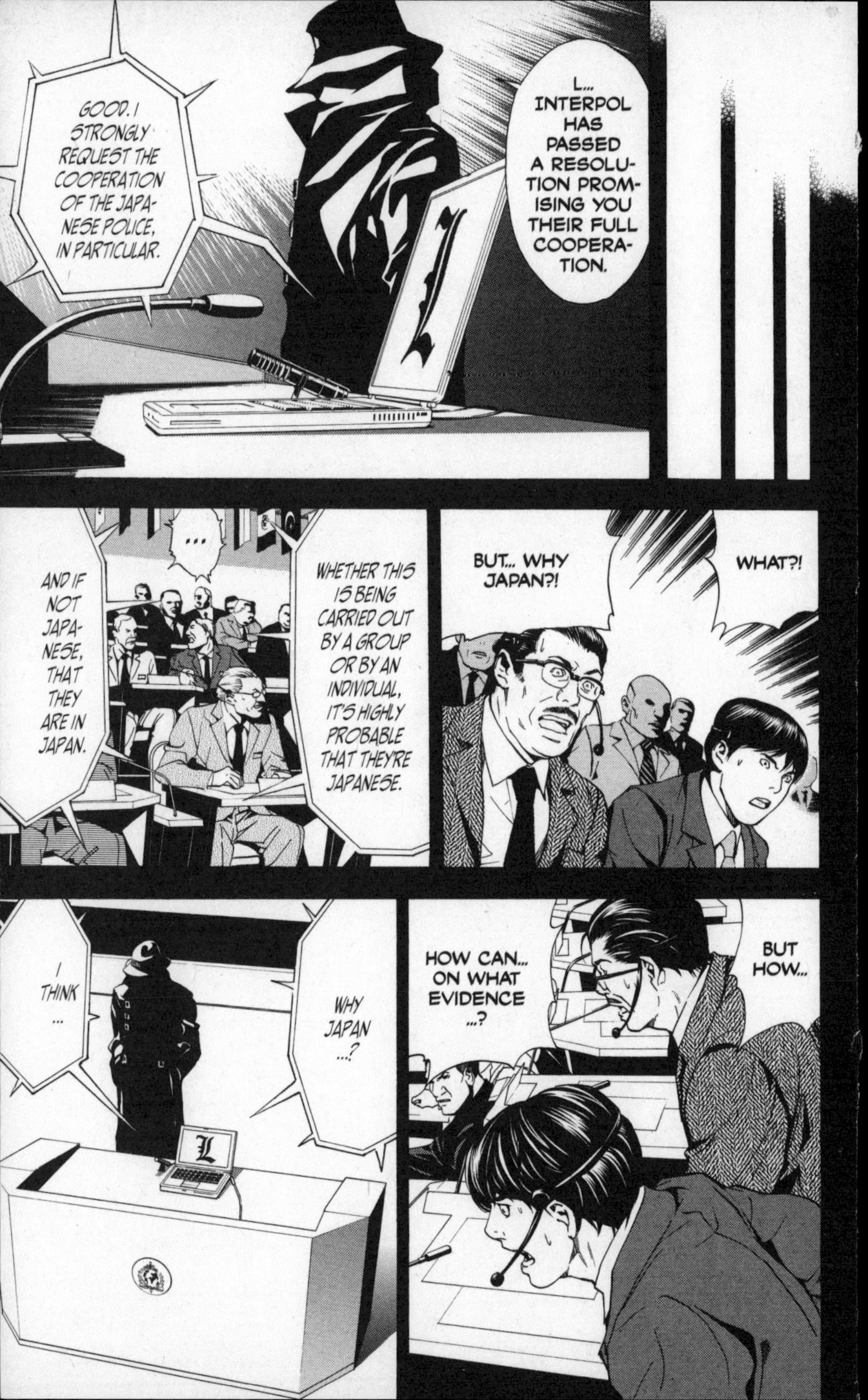
L... INTERPOL HAS PASSED A RESOLUTION PROMISING YOU THEIR FULL COOPERATION.
GOOD. I STRONGLY REQUEST THE COOPERATION OF THE JAPANESE POLICE, IN PARTICULAR.
WHAT?!
BUT... WHY JAPAN?!
WHETHER THIS IS BEING CARRIED OUT BY A GROUP OR BY AN INDIVIDUAL, IT'S HIGHLY PROBABLE THAT THEY'RE JAPANESE.
...
AND IF NOT JAPANESE, THAT THEY ARE IN JAPAN.
BUT HOW...
HOW CAN... ON WHAT EVIDENCE ...?
WHY JAPAN ...?
I THINK ...

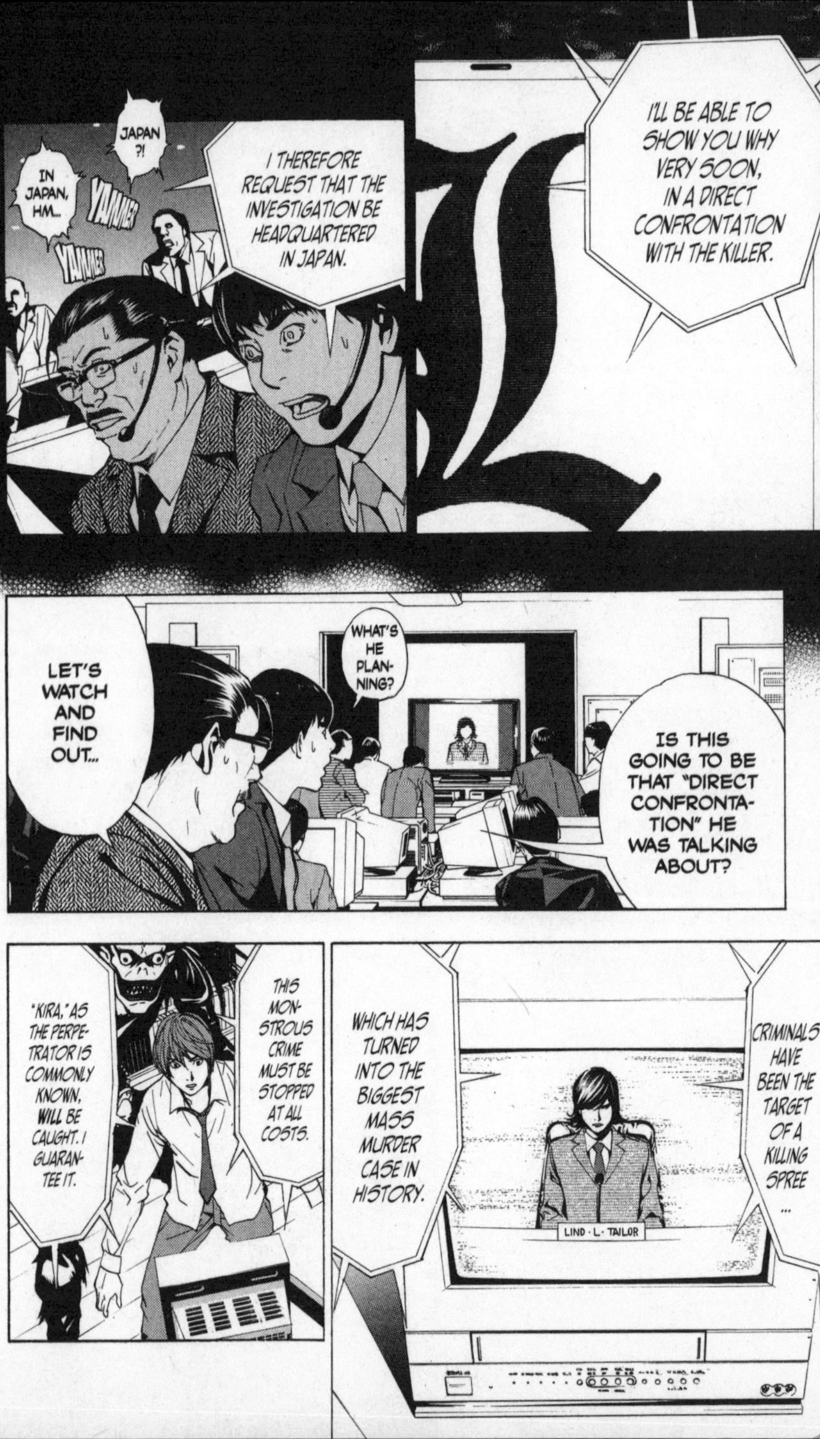
I'LL BE ABLE TO SHOW YOU WHY VERY SOON, IN A DIRECT CONFRONTATION WITH THE KILLER.
I THEREFORE REQUEST THAT THE INVESTIGATION BE HEADQUARTERED IN JAPAN.
JAPAN ?!
YAMMER
IN JAPAN, HM...
YAMMER
IS THIS GOING TO BE THAT "DIRECT CONFRONTATION" HE WAS TALKING ABOUT?
WHAT'S HE PLANNING?
LET'S WATCH AND FIND OUT...
CRIMINALS HAVE BEEN THE TARGET OF A KILLING SPREE ...
WHICH HAS TURNED INTO THE BIGGEST MASS MURDER CASE IN HISTORY.
LIND · L · TAILOR
THIS MONSTROUS CRIME MUST BE STOPPED AT ALL COSTS.
"KIRA," AS THE PERPETRATOR IS COMMONLY KNOWN, **WILL** BE CAUGHT. I GUARANTEE IT.

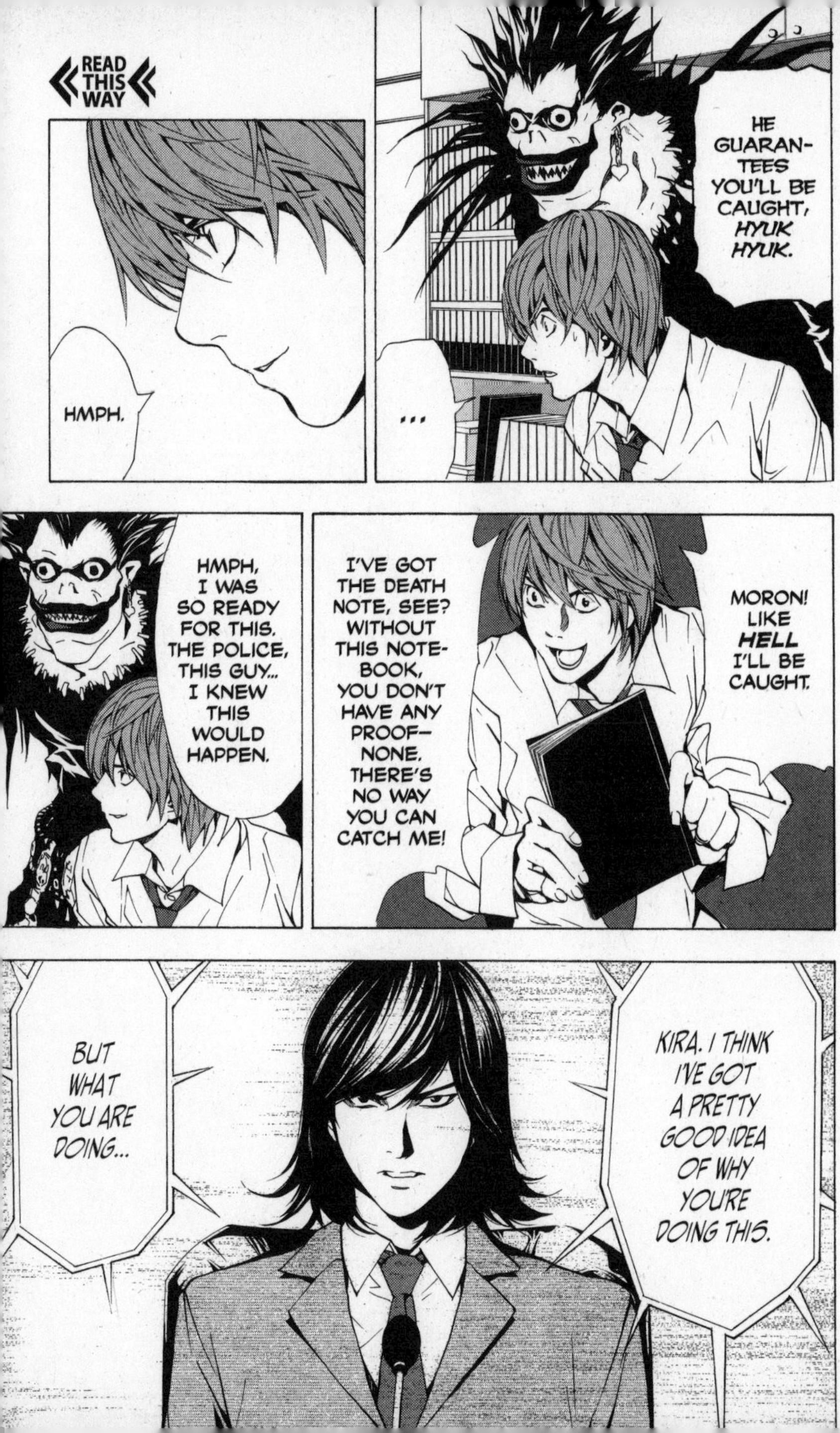
READ THIS WAY
HE GUARANTEES YOU'LL BE CAUGHT, *HYUK HYUK.*
...
HMPH.
MORON! LIKE **HELL** I'LL BE CAUGHT.
I'VE GOT THE DEATH NOTE, SEE? WITHOUT THIS NOTEBOOK, YOU DON'T HAVE ANY PROOF— NONE. THERE'S NO WAY YOU CAN CATCH ME!
HMPH, I WAS SO READY FOR THIS. THE POLICE, THIS GUY... I KNEW THIS WOULD HAPPEN.
KIRA. I THINK I'VE GOT A PRETTY GOOD IDEA OF WHY YOU'RE DOING THIS.
BUT WHAT YOU ARE DOING...

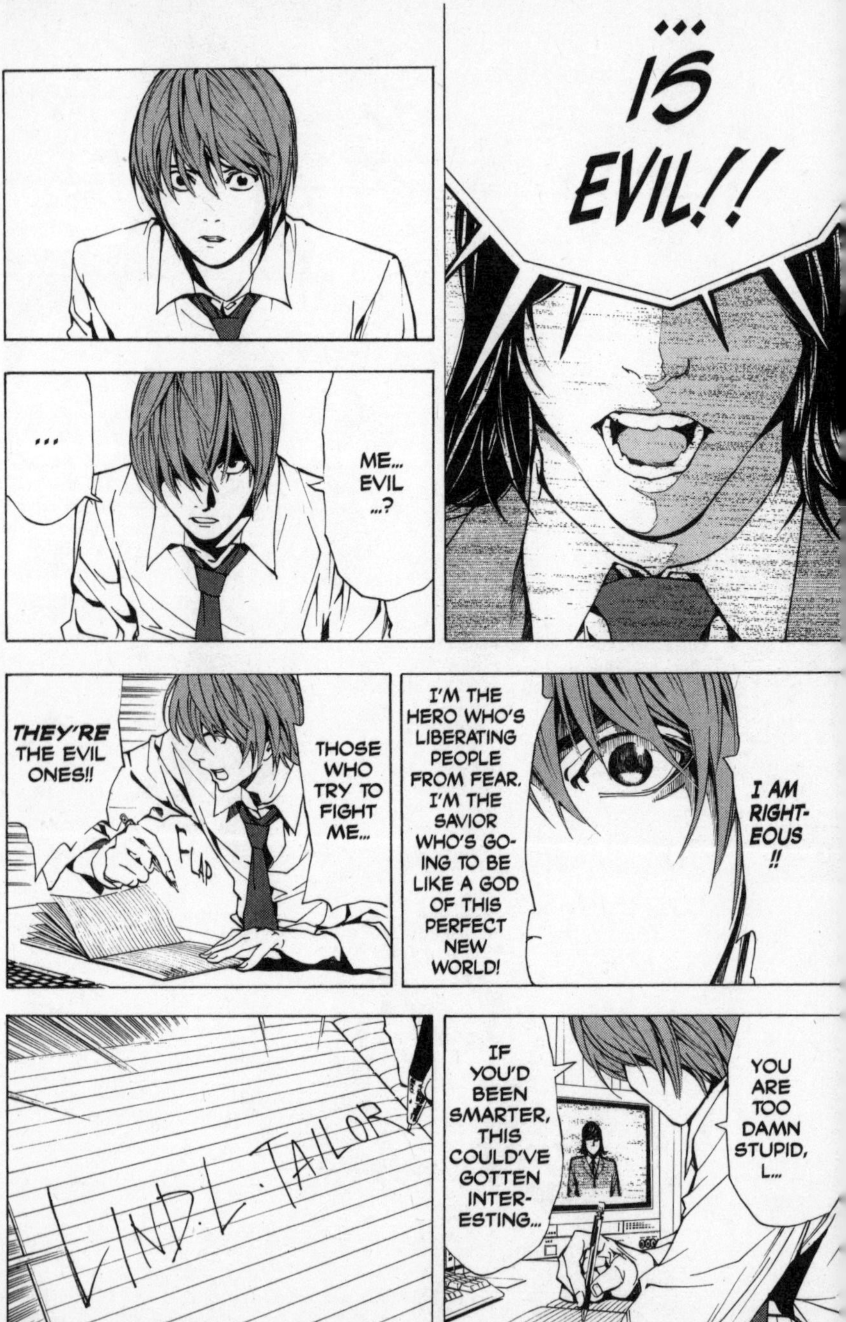
...IS EVIL!!
ME... EVIL ...?
...
I AM RIGHT-EOUS!!
I'M THE HERO WHO'S LIBERATING PEOPLE FROM FEAR. I'M THE SAVIOR WHO'S GO-ING TO BE LIKE A GOD OF THIS PERFECT NEW WORLD!
THOSE WHO TRY TO FIGHT ME...
THEY'RE THE EVIL ONES!!
FLAP
YOU ARE TOO DAMN STUPID, L...
IF YOU'D BEEN SMARTER, THIS COULD'VE GOTTEN INTER-ESTING...
LIND L. TAILOR

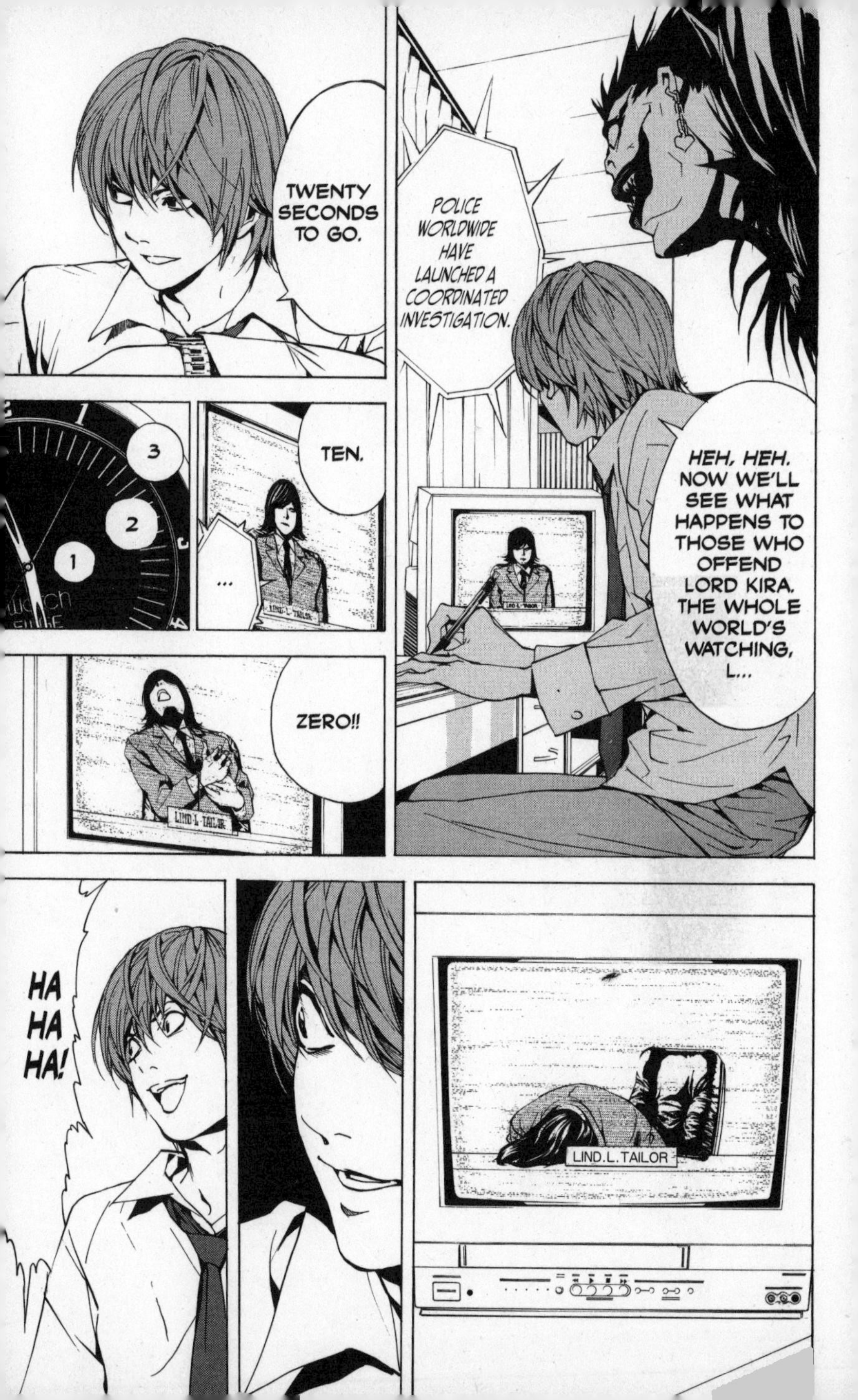
POLICE WORLDWIDE HAVE LAUNCHED A COORDINATED INVESTIGATION.
HEH, HEH. NOW WE'LL SEE WHAT HAPPENS TO THOSE WHO OFFEND LORD KIRA. THE WHOLE WORLD'S WATCHING, L...
TWENTY SECONDS TO GO.
TEN.
...
LIND.L.TAILOR
3
2
1
ZERO!!
LIND.L.TAILOR
LIND.L.TAILOR
HA HA HA!

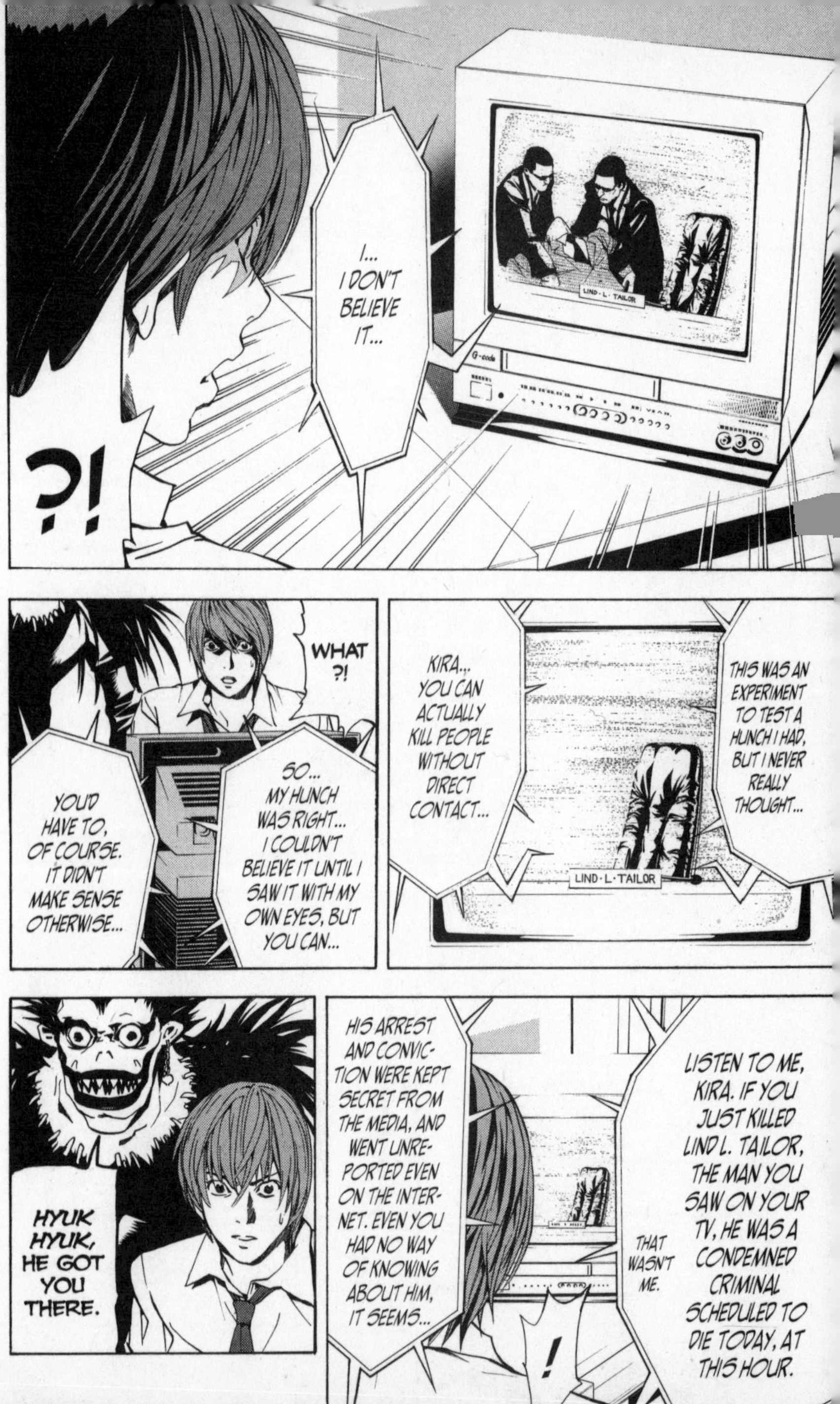

I... I DON'T BELIEVE IT...
?!
THIS WAS AN EXPERIMENT TO TEST A HUNCH I HAD, BUT I NEVER REALLY THOUGHT...
KIRA... YOU CAN ACTUALLY KILL PEOPLE WITHOUT DIRECT CONTACT...
LIND · L · TAILOR
WHAT?!
SO... MY HUNCH WAS RIGHT... I COULDN'T BELIEVE IT UNTIL I SAW IT WITH MY OWN EYES, BUT YOU CAN...
YOU'D HAVE TO, OF COURSE. IT DIDN'T MAKE SENSE OTHERWISE...
LISTEN TO ME, KIRA. IF YOU JUST KILLED LIND L. TAILOR, THE MAN YOU SAW ON YOUR TV, HE WAS A CONDEMNED CRIMINAL SCHEDULED TO DIE TODAY, AT THIS HOUR.
THAT WASN'T ME.
HIS ARREST AND CONVICTION WERE KEPT SECRET FROM THE MEDIA, AND WENT UNREPORTED EVEN ON THE INTERNET. EVEN YOU HAD NO WAY OF KNOWING ABOUT HIM, IT SEEMS...
!
HYUK HYUK, HE GOT YOU THERE.

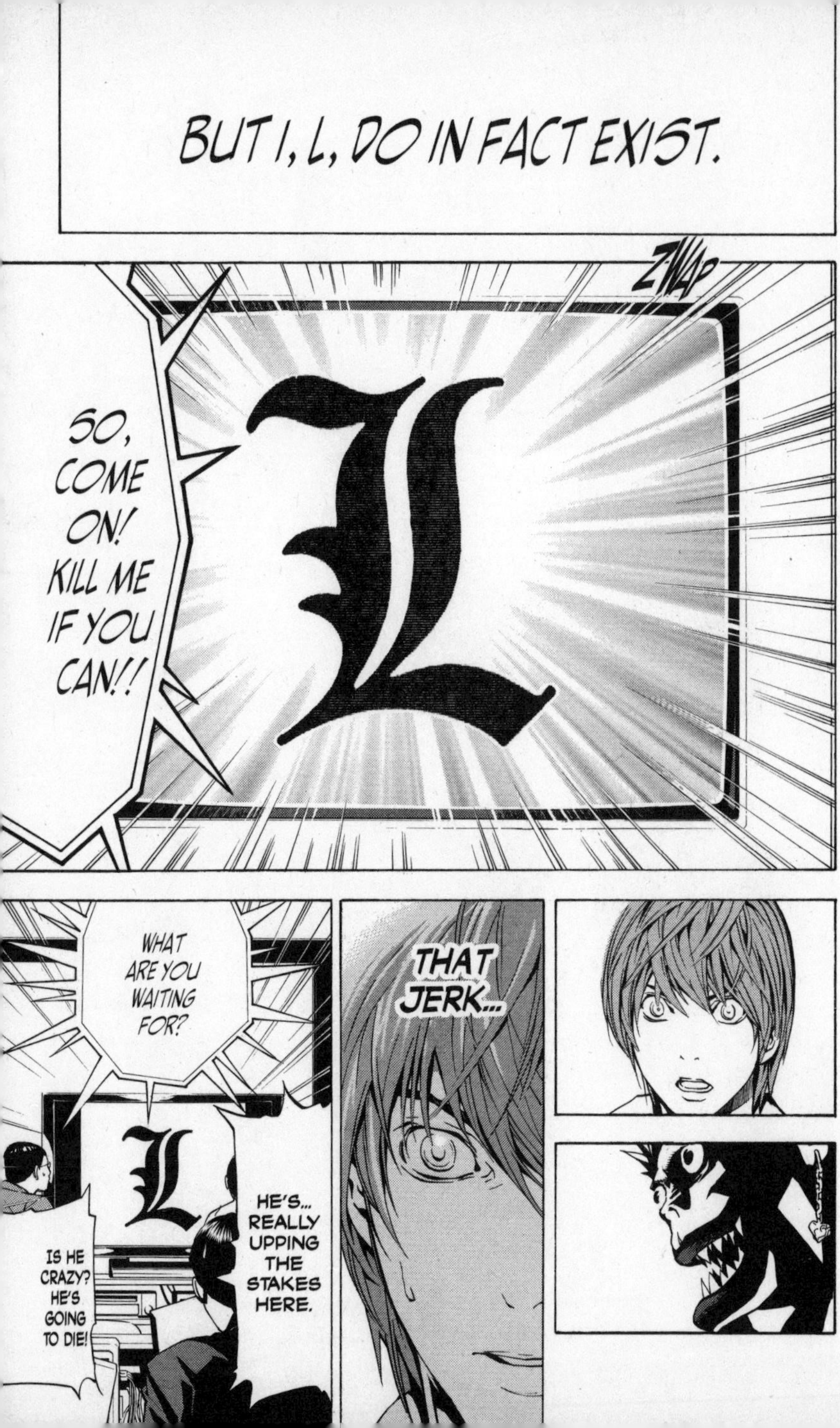
BUT I, L, DO IN FACT EXIST.
Z-WAP
SO, COME ON! KILL ME IF YOU CAN!!
THAT JERK...
WHAT ARE YOU WAITING FOR?
HE'S... REALLY UPPING THE STAKES HERE.
IS HE CRAZY? HE'S GOING TO DIE!

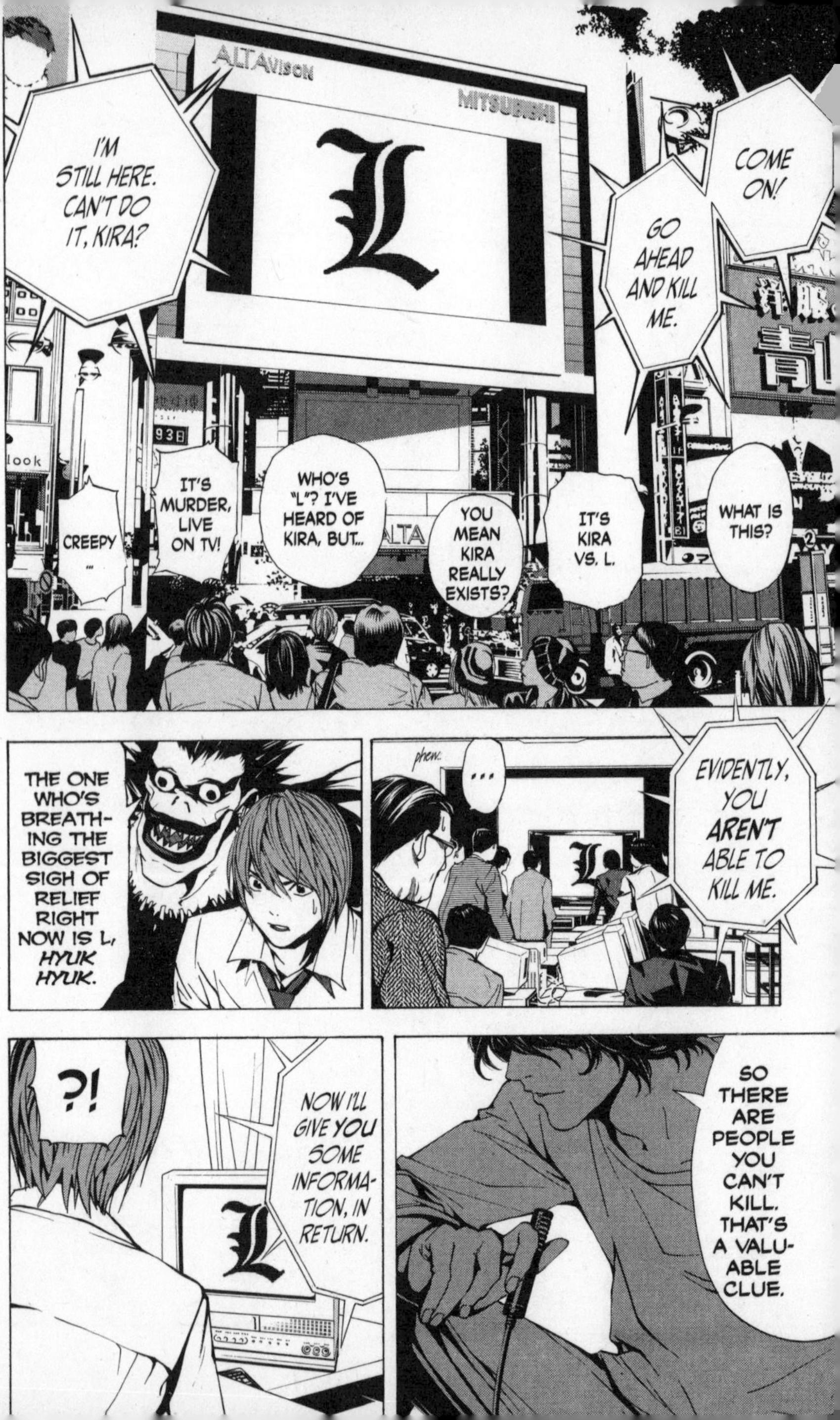
ALTAvison
MITSUBISHI
COME ON!
GO AHEAD AND KILL ME.
I'M STILL HERE. CAN'T DO IT, KIRA?
WHAT IS THIS?
IT'S KIRA VS. L.
YOU MEAN KIRA REALLY EXISTS?
WHO'S "L"? I'VE HEARD OF KIRA, BUT...
ALTA
IT'S MURDER, LIVE ON TV!
CREEPY ...
EVIDENTLY, YOU *AREN'T* ABLE TO KILL ME.
...
phew..
THE ONE WHO'S BREATHING THE BIGGEST SIGH OF RELIEF RIGHT NOW IS L, *HYUK HYUK*.
SO THERE ARE PEOPLE YOU CAN'T KILL. THAT'S A VALUABLE CLUE.
NOW I'LL GIVE *YOU* SOME INFORMATION, IN RETURN.
?!

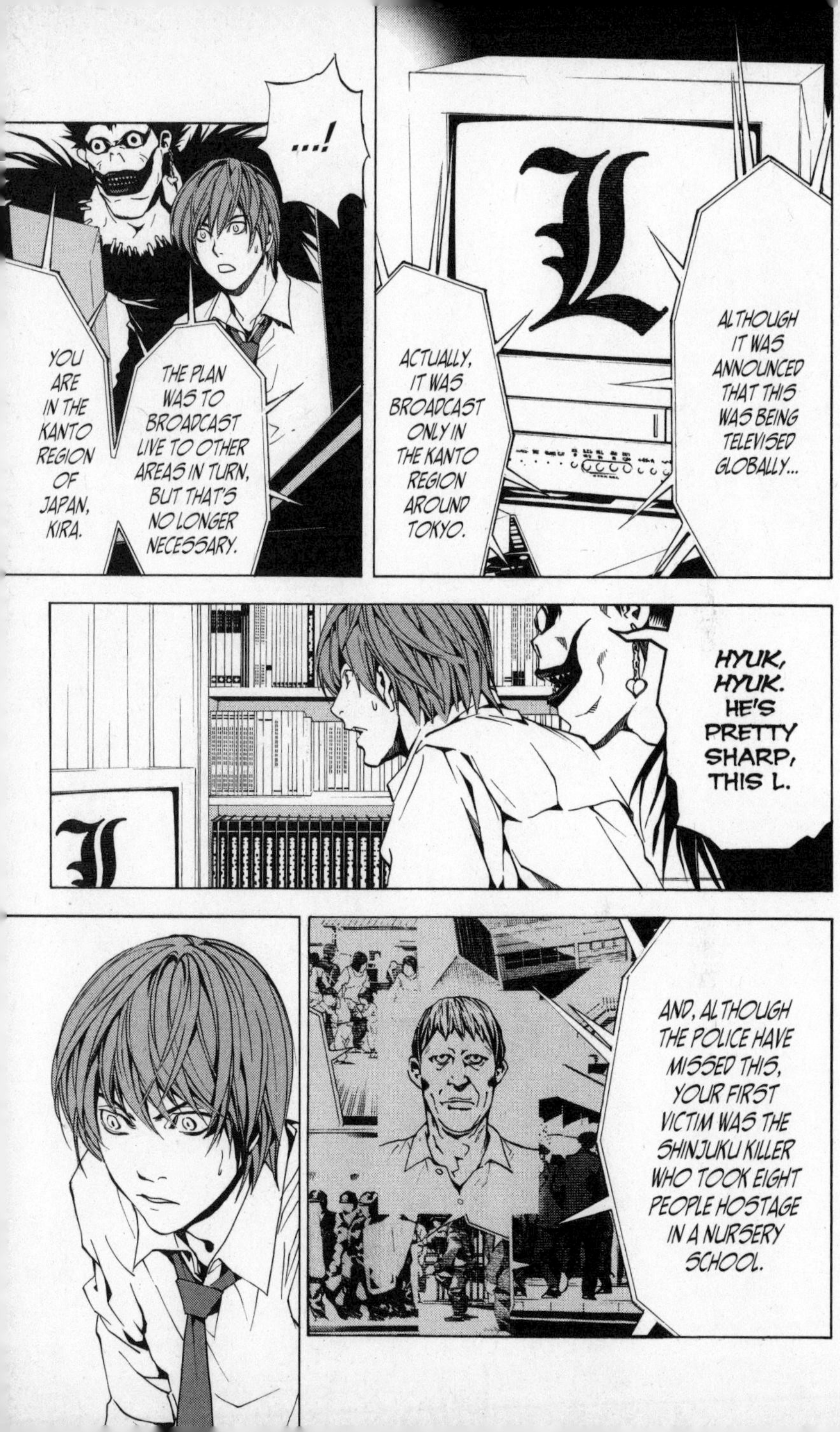
ALTHOUGH IT WAS ANNOUNCED THAT THIS WAS BEING TELEVISED GLOBALLY...
ACTUALLY, IT WAS BROADCAST ONLY IN THE KANTO REGION AROUND TOKYO.
...!
THE PLAN WAS TO BROADCAST LIVE TO OTHER AREAS IN TURN, BUT THAT'S NO LONGER NECESSARY.
YOU ARE IN THE KANTO REGION OF JAPAN, KIRA.
HYUK, HYUK. HE'S PRETTY SHARP, THIS L.
AND, ALTHOUGH THE POLICE HAVE MISSED THIS, YOUR FIRST VICTIM WAS THE SHINJUKU KILLER WHO TOOK EIGHT PEOPLE HOSTAGE IN A NURSERY SCHOOL.

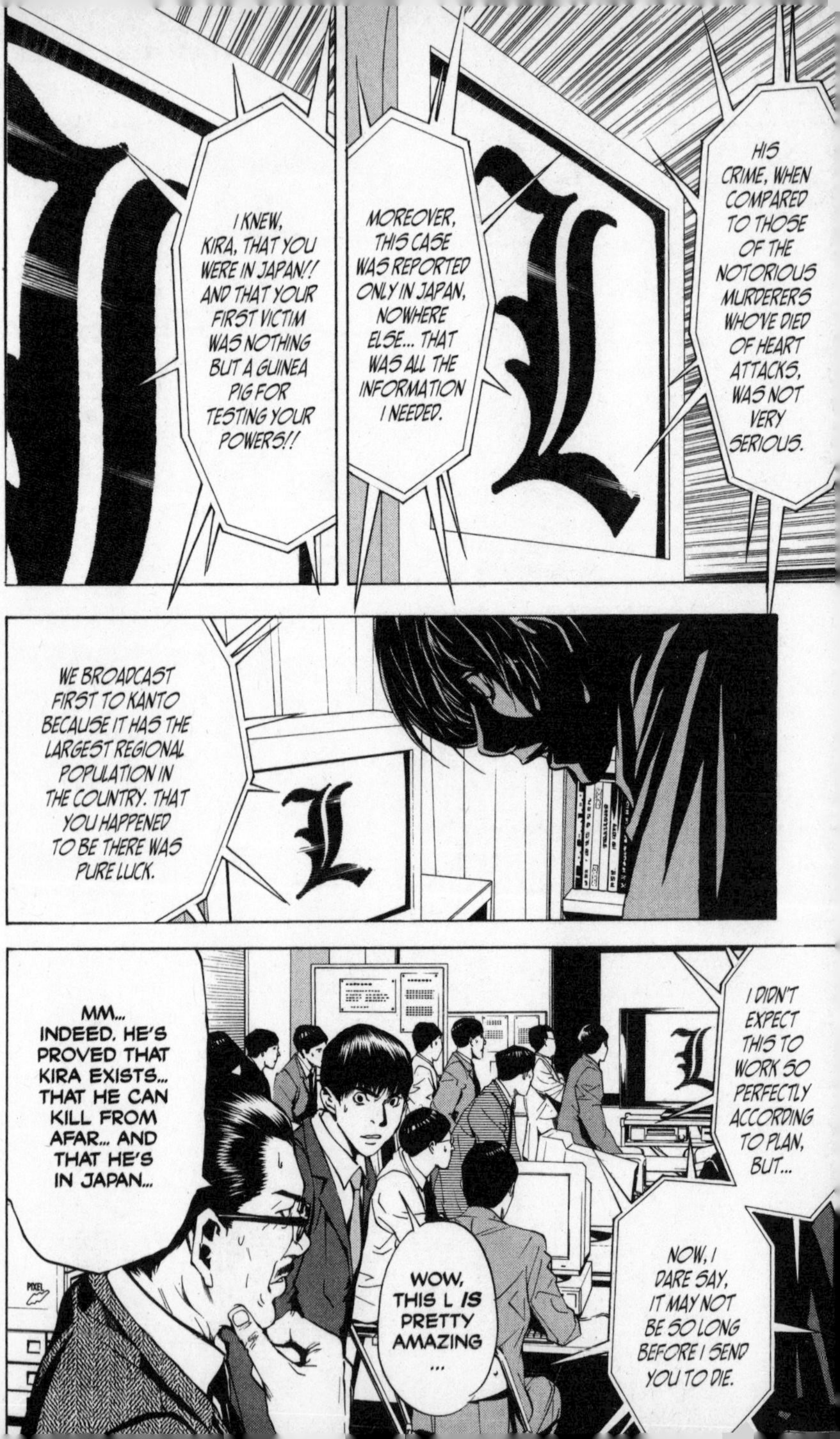
HIS CRIME, WHEN COMPARED TO THOSE OF THE NOTORIOUS MURDERERS WHO'VE DIED OF HEART ATTACKS, WAS NOT VERY SERIOUS.
MOREOVER, THIS CASE WAS REPORTED ONLY IN JAPAN, NOWHERE ELSE... THAT WAS ALL THE INFORMATION I NEEDED.
I KNEW, KIRA, THAT YOU WERE IN JAPAN!! AND THAT YOUR FIRST VICTIM WAS NOTHING BUT A GUINEA PIG FOR TESTING YOUR POWERS!!
WE BROADCAST FIRST TO KANTO BECAUSE IT HAS THE LARGEST REGIONAL POPULATION IN THE COUNTRY. THAT YOU HAPPENED TO BE THERE WAS PURE LUCK.
I DIDN'T EXPECT THIS TO WORK SO PERFECTLY ACCORDING TO PLAN, BUT...
NOW, I DARE SAY, IT MAY NOT BE SO LONG BEFORE I SEND YOU TO DIE.
WOW, THIS L *IS* PRETTY AMAZING ...
MM... INDEED. HE'S PROVED THAT KIRA EXISTS... THAT HE CAN KILL FROM AFAR... AND THAT HE'S IN JAPAN...

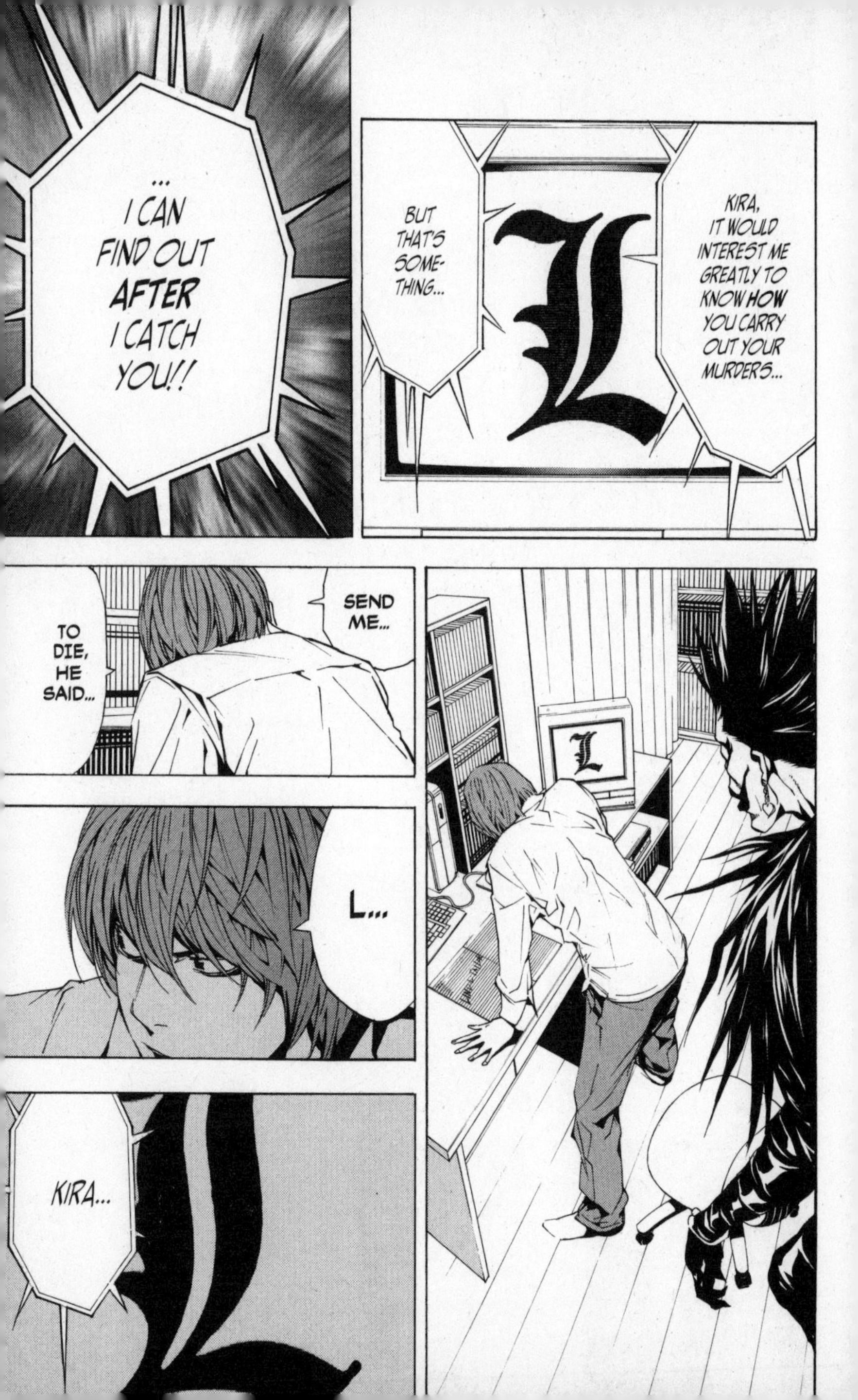
KIRA, IT WOULD INTEREST ME GREATLY TO KNOW HOW YOU CARRY OUT YOUR MURDERS...
BUT THAT'S SOME-THING...
... I CAN FIND OUT AFTER I CATCH YOU!!
SEND ME...
TO DIE, HE SAID...
L...
KIRA...

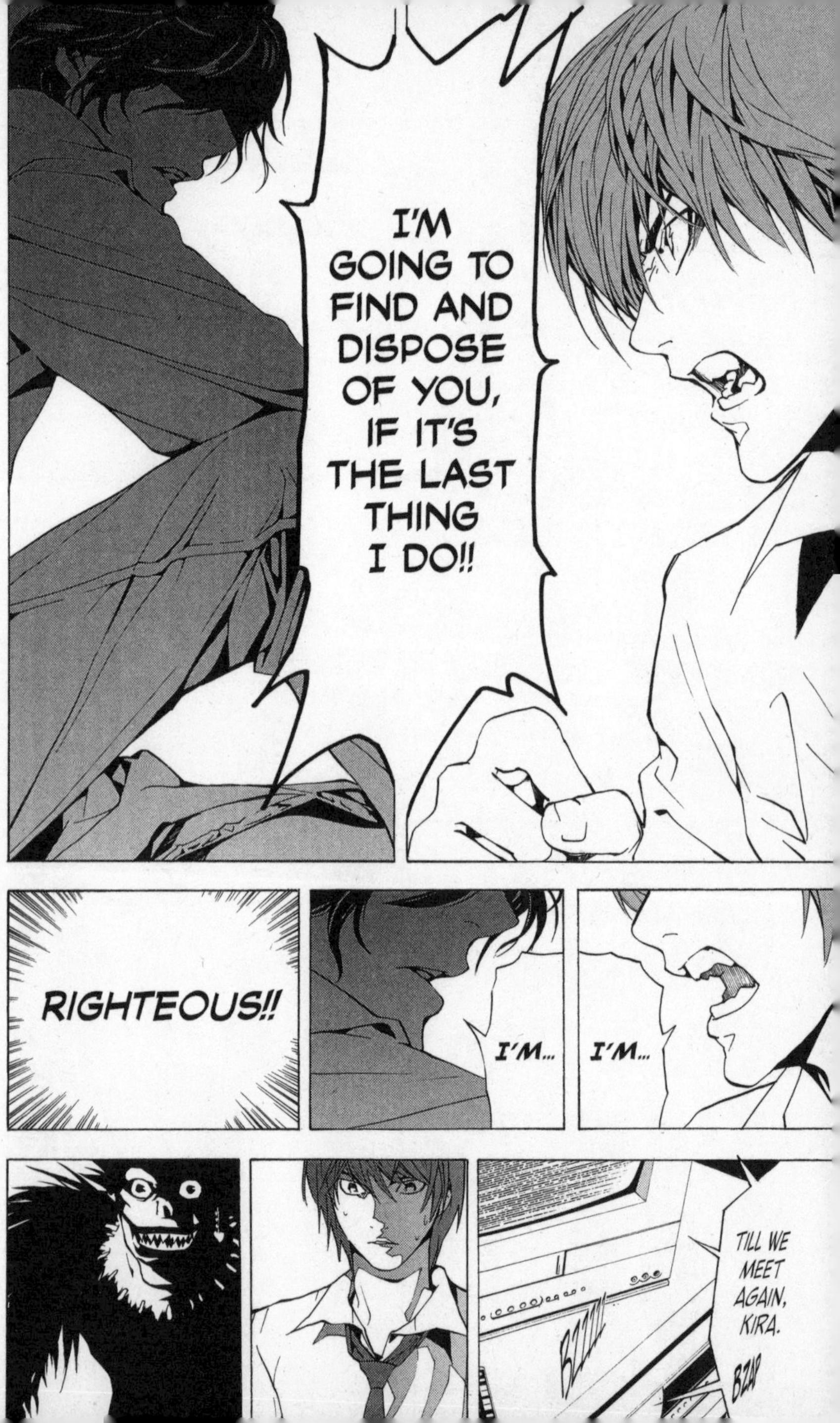
I'M GOING TO FIND AND DISPOSE OF YOU, IF IT'S THE LAST THING I DO!!
I'M...
I'M...
RIGHTEOUS!!
TILL WE MEET AGAIN, KIRA.
BZAP
BZZZZ

READ THIS WAY

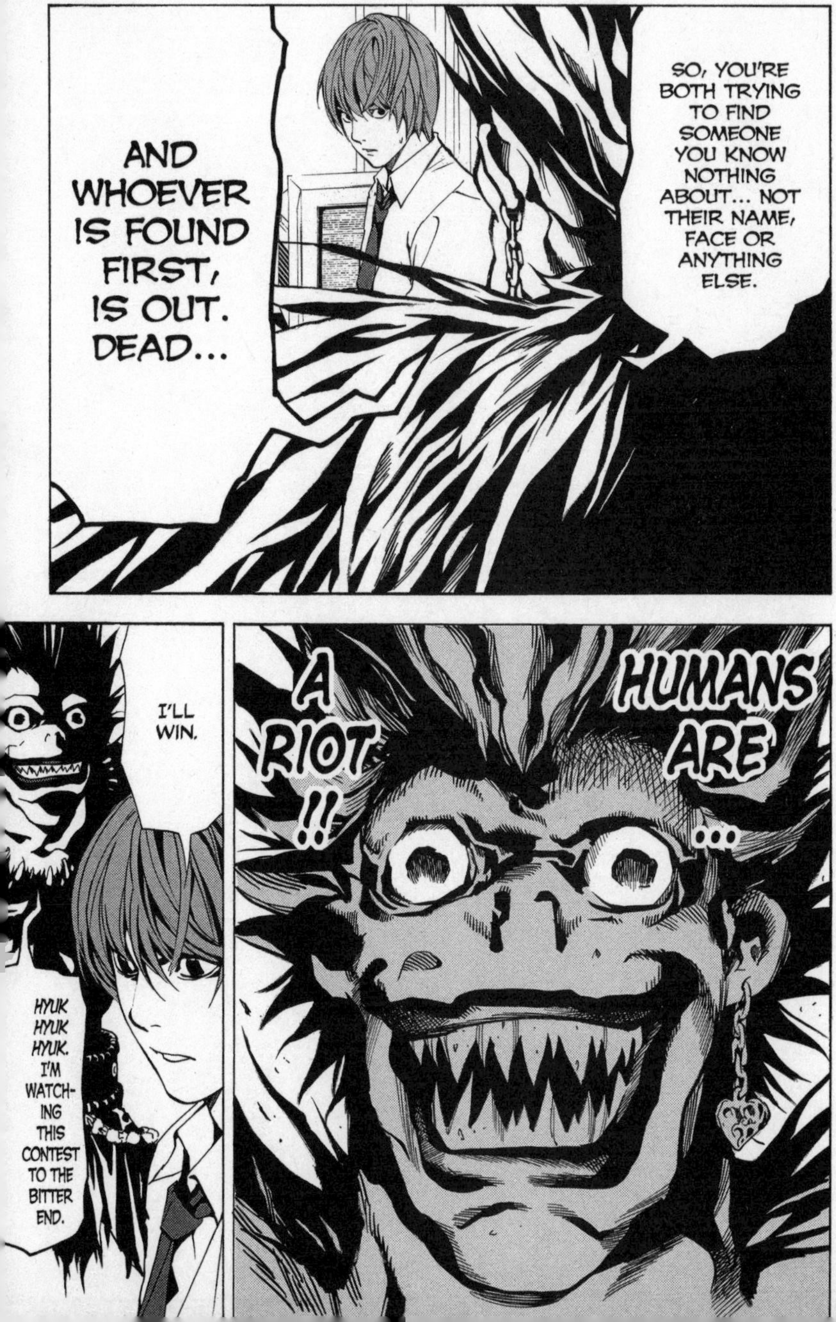
SO, YOU'RE BOTH TRYING TO FIND SOMEONE YOU KNOW NOTHING ABOUT... NOT THEIR NAME, FACE OR ANYTHING ELSE.
AND WHOEVER IS FOUND FIRST, IS OUT. DEAD...
HUMANS ARE...
A RIOT!!
I'LL WIN.
HYUK HYUK HYUK. I'M WATCHING THIS CONTEST TO THE BITTER END.

DEATH NOTE
How to Use It
II

○ This note shall become the property of the human world, once it touches the ground of (arrives in) the human world.

このノートは人間界の地に着いた時点から人間界の物となる。

○ The owner of the note can recognize the image and voice of its original owner, i.e. a god of death.

所有者はノートの元の持ち主である死神の姿や声を認知する事ができる。

○ The human who uses this note can neither go to Heaven nor Hell.

このノートを使った人間は天国にも地獄にも行けない。

chapter 3 Family

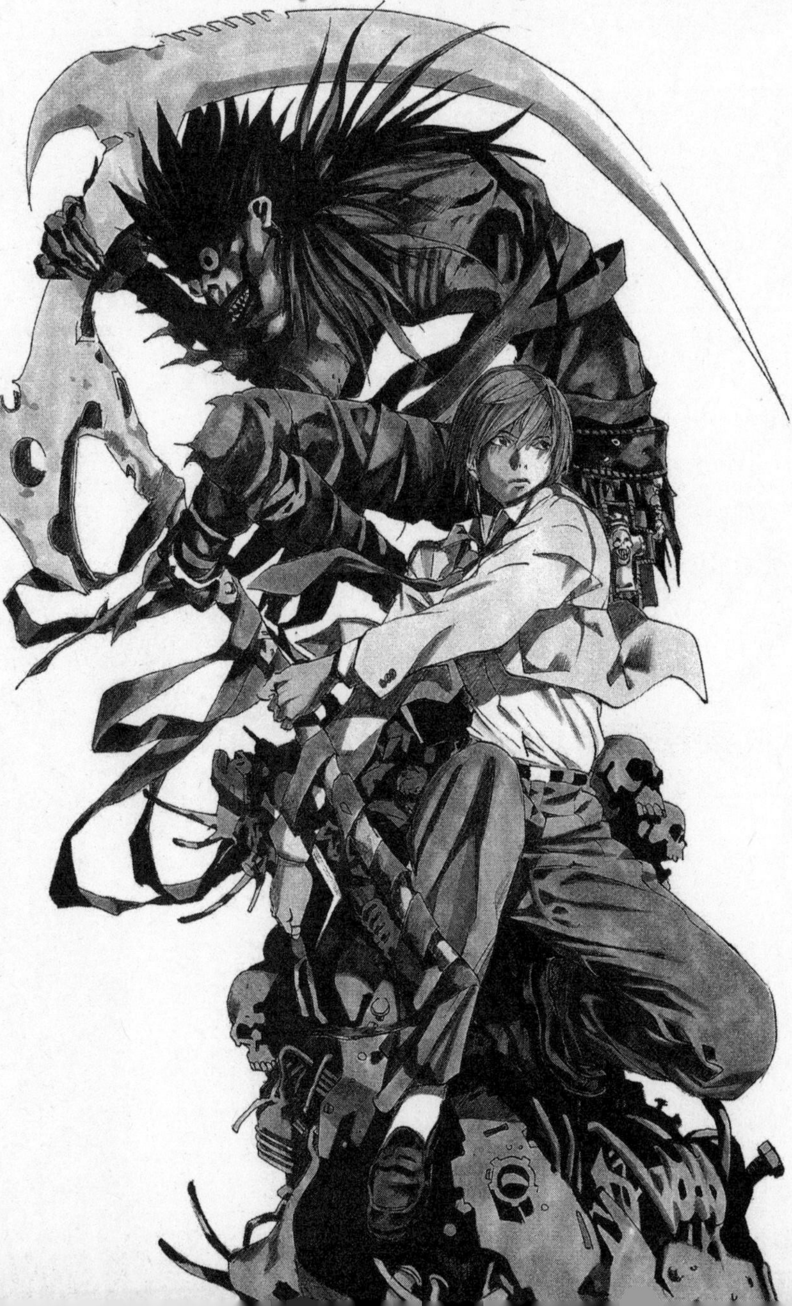

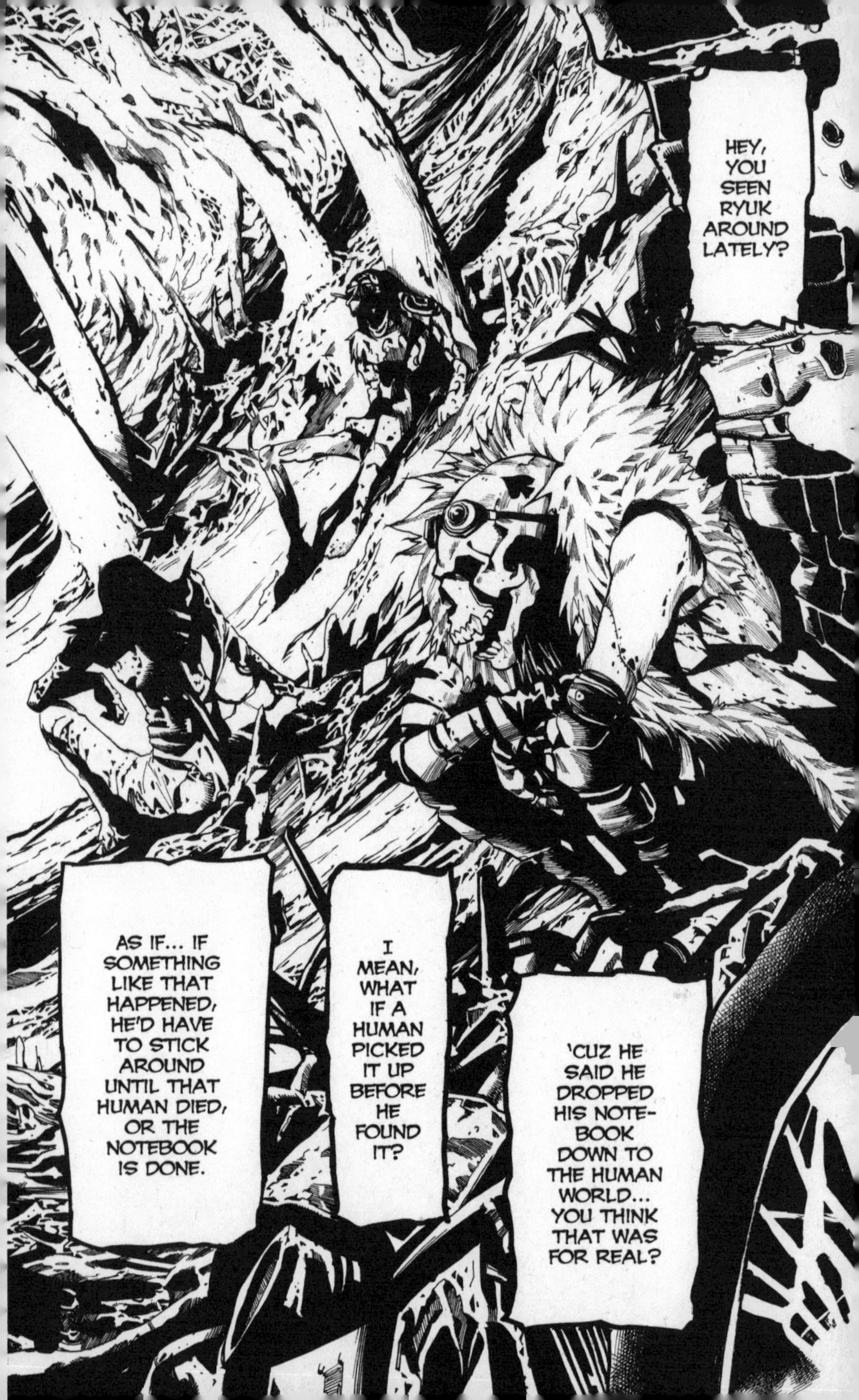
HEY, YOU SEEN RYUK AROUND LATELY?
'CUZ HE SAID HE DROPPED HIS NOTE-BOOK DOWN TO THE HUMAN WORLD... YOU THINK THAT WAS FOR REAL?
I MEAN, WHAT IF A HUMAN PICKED IT UP BEFORE HE FOUND IT?
AS IF... IF SOMETHING LIKE THAT HAPPENED, HE'D HAVE TO STICK AROUND UNTIL THAT HUMAN DIED, OR THE NOTEBOOK IS DONE.

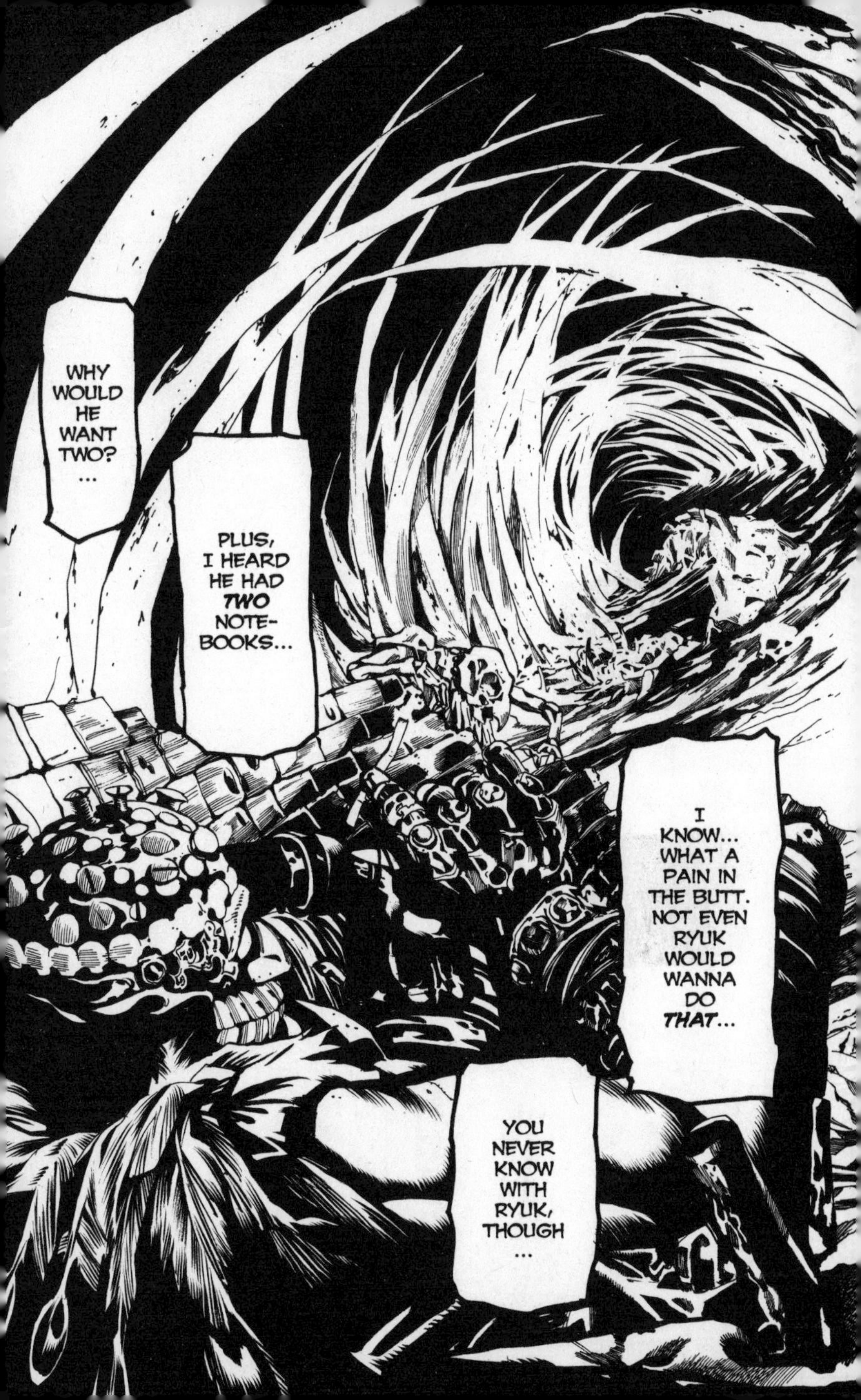
PLUS, I HEARD HE HAD *TWO* NOTE-BOOKS...
WHY WOULD HE WANT TWO? ...
I KNOW... WHAT A PAIN IN THE BUTT. NOT EVEN RYUK WOULD WANNA DO *THAT*...
YOU NEVER KNOW WITH RYUK, THOUGH ...

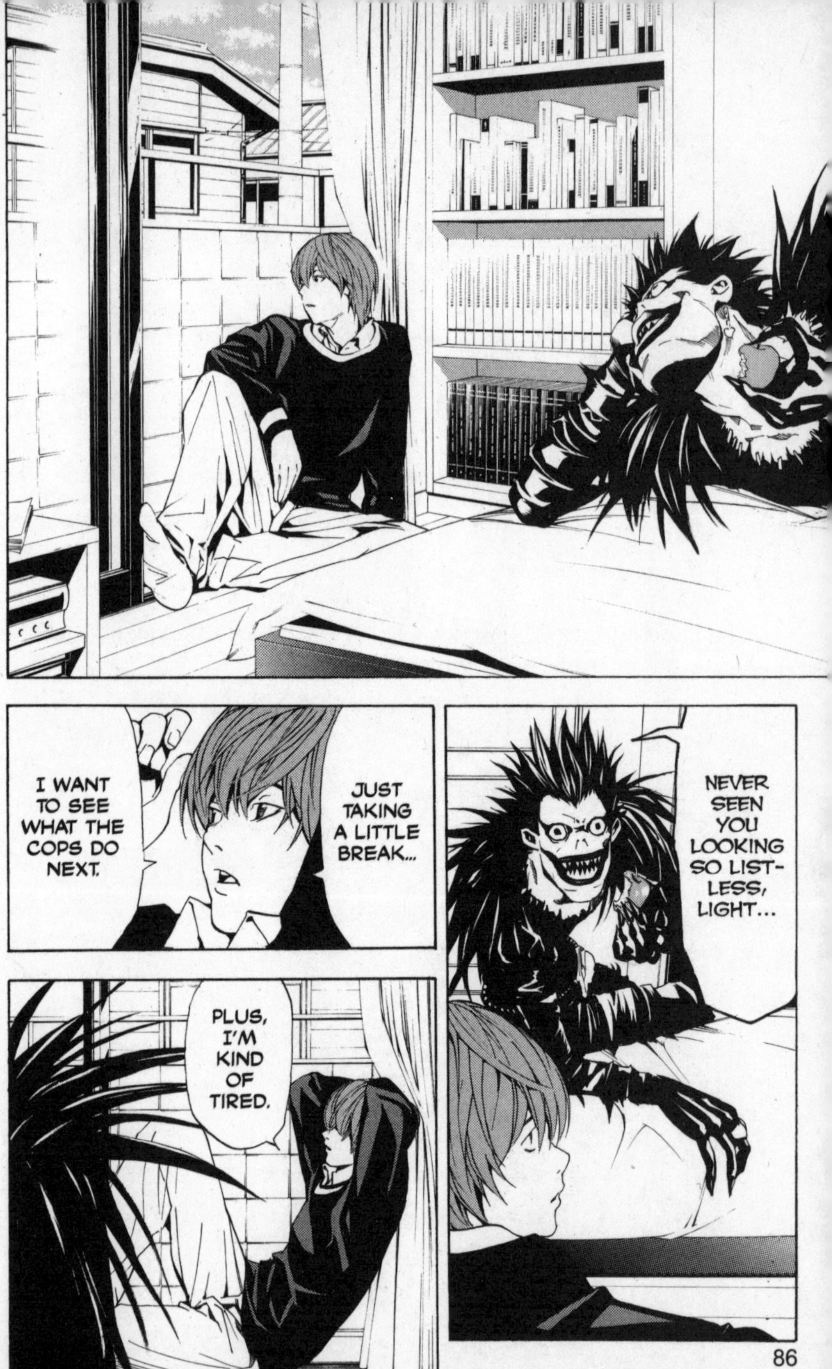
NEVER SEEN YOU LOOKING SO LIST-LESS, LIGHT...
JUST TAKING A LITTLE BREAK...
I WANT TO SEE WHAT THE COPS DO NEXT.
PLUS, I'M KIND OF TIRED.

READ THIS WAY

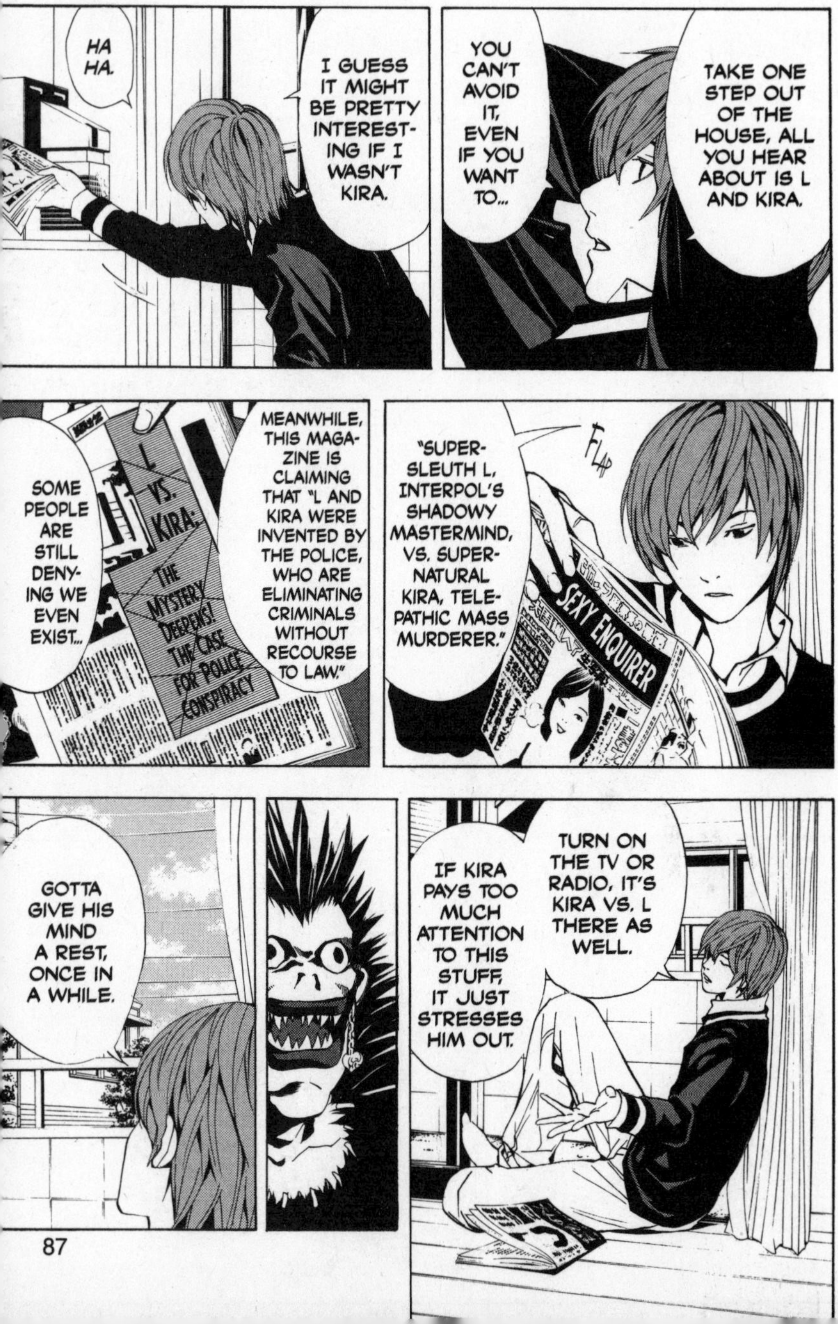
TAKE ONE STEP OUT OF THE HOUSE, ALL YOU HEAR ABOUT IS L AND KIRA.
YOU CAN'T AVOID IT, EVEN IF YOU WANT TO...
I GUESS IT MIGHT BE PRETTY INTEREST-ING IF I WASN'T KIRA.
HA HA.
FLAP
"SUPER-SLEUTH L, INTERPOL'S SHADOWY MASTERMIND, VS. SUPER-NATURAL KIRA, TELE-PATHIC MASS MURDERER."
SEXY ENQUIRER
MEANWHILE, THIS MAGA-ZINE IS CLAIMING THAT "L AND KIRA WERE INVENTED BY THE POLICE, WHO ARE ELIMINATING CRIMINALS WITHOUT RECOURSE TO LAW."
L VS. KIRA:
THE MYSTERY DEEPENS! THE CASE FOR POLICE CONSPIRACY
SOME PEOPLE ARE STILL DENY-ING WE EVEN EXIST...
TURN ON THE TV OR RADIO, IT'S KIRA VS. L THERE AS WELL.
IF KIRA PAYS TOO MUCH ATTENTION TO THIS STUFF, IT JUST STRESSES HIM OUT.
GOTTA GIVE HIS MIND A REST, ONCE IN A WHILE.

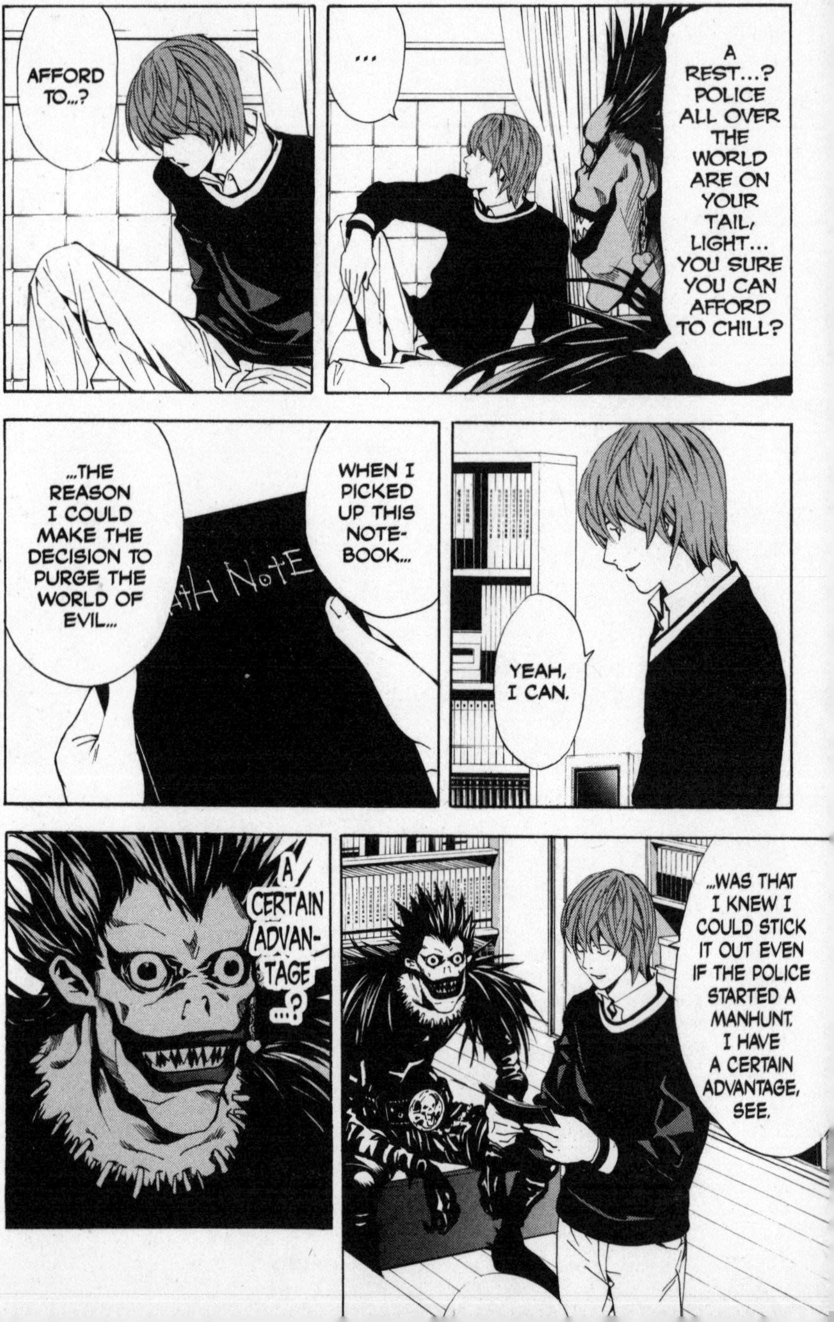
A REST...? POLICE ALL OVER THE WORLD ARE ON YOUR TAIL, LIGHT... YOU SURE YOU CAN AFFORD TO CHILL?
...
AFFORD TO...?
YEAH, I CAN.
WHEN I PICKED UP THIS NOTE-BOOK...
...THE REASON I COULD MAKE THE DECISION TO PURGE THE WORLD OF EVIL...
...WAS THAT I KNEW I COULD STICK IT OUT EVEN IF THE POLICE STARTED A MANHUNT. I HAVE A CERTAIN ADVANTAGE, SEE.
A CERTAIN ADVAN-TAGE...?

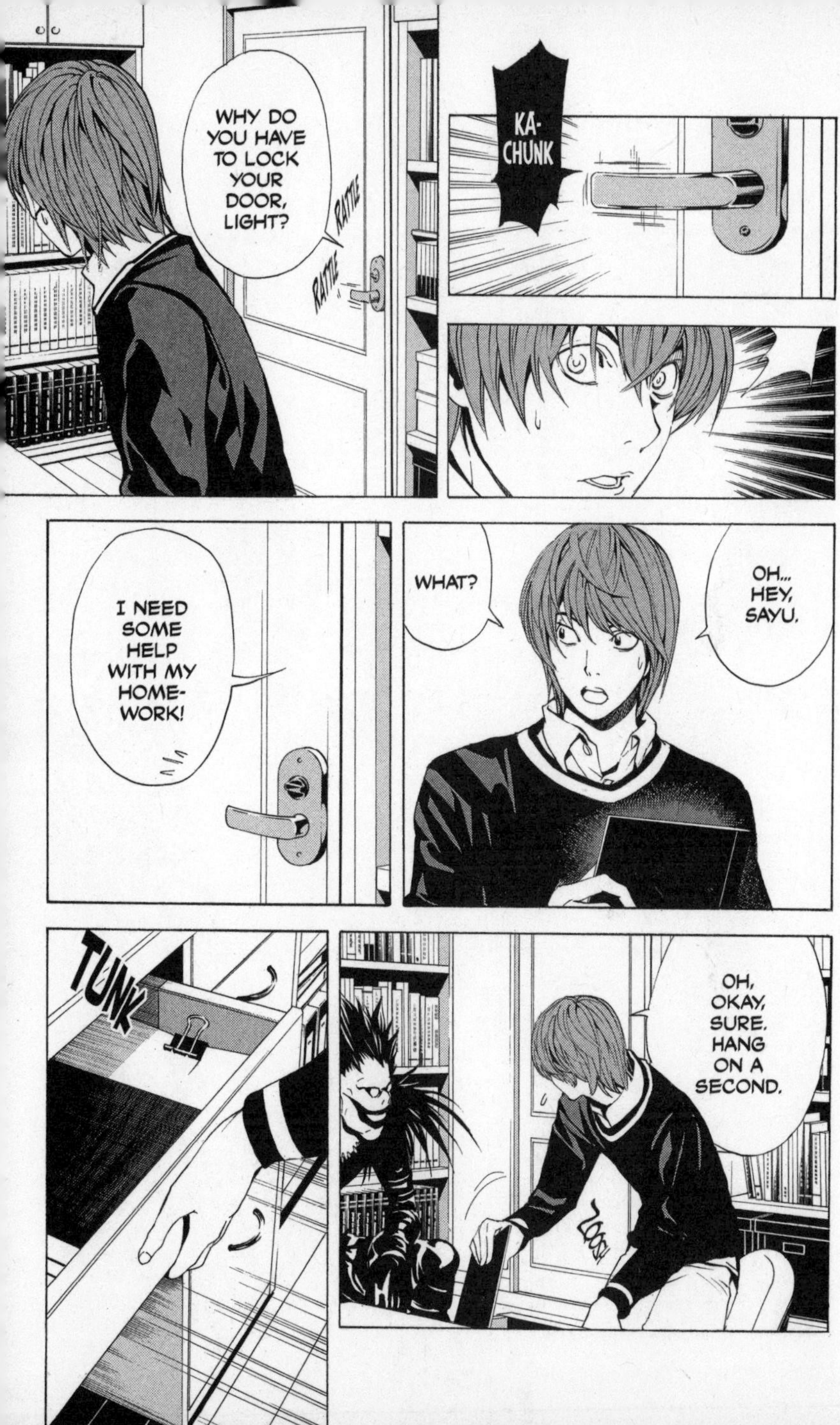
KA-CHUNK
WHY DO YOU HAVE TO LOCK YOUR DOOR, LIGHT?
RATTLE RATTLE
OH... HEY, SAYU.
WHAT?
I NEED SOME HELP WITH MY HOMEWORK!
OH, OKAY, SURE. HANG ON A SECOND.
ZOOSH
TUNK

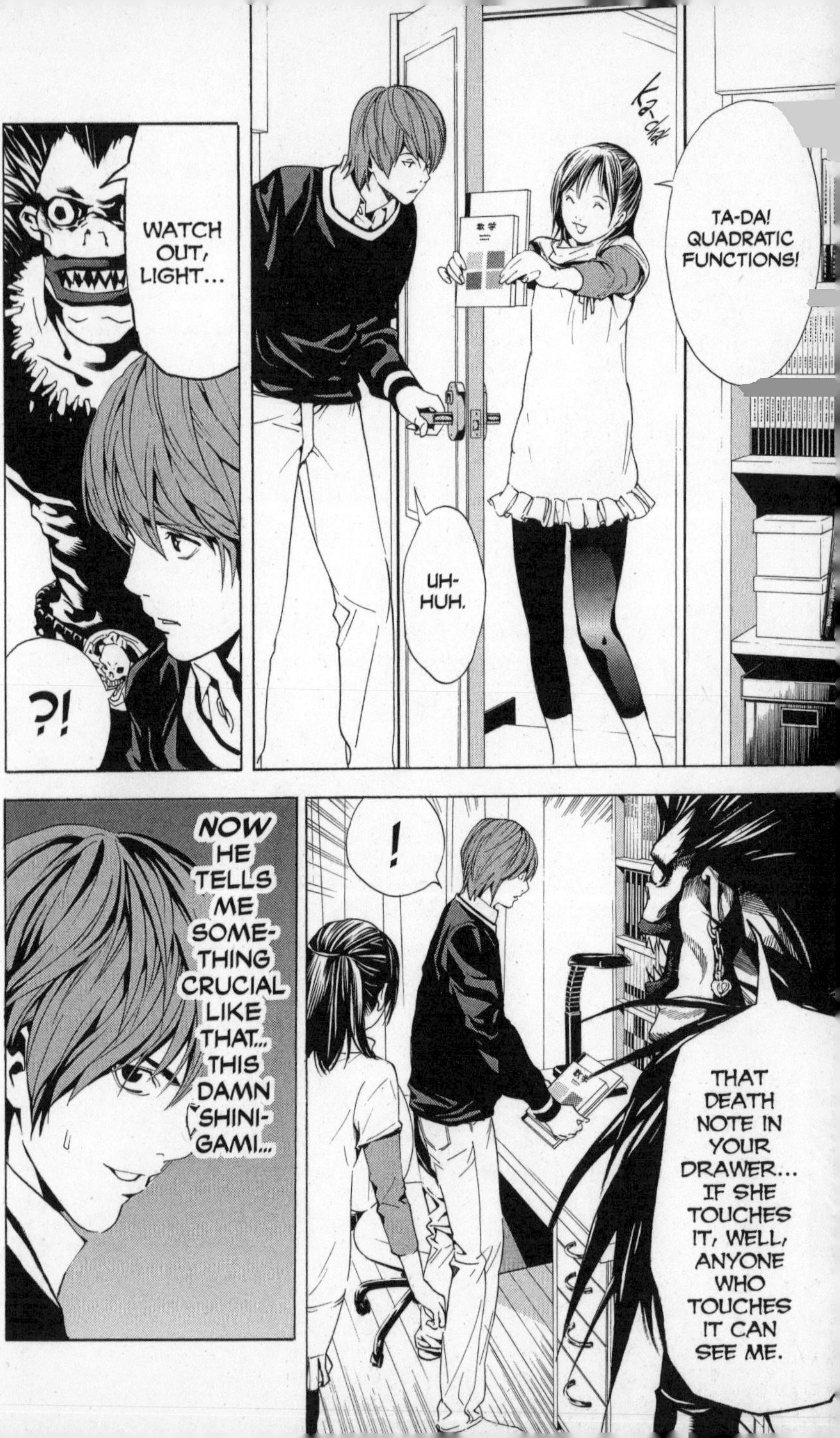
TA-DA! QUADRATIC FUNCTIONS!
CLICK
UH-HUH.
WATCH OUT, LIGHT...
?!
THAT DEATH NOTE IN YOUR DRAWER... IF SHE TOUCHES IT, WELL, ANYONE WHO TOUCHES IT CAN SEE ME.
!
NOW HE TELLS ME SOMETHING CRUCIAL LIKE THAT... THIS DAMN SHINIGAMI...

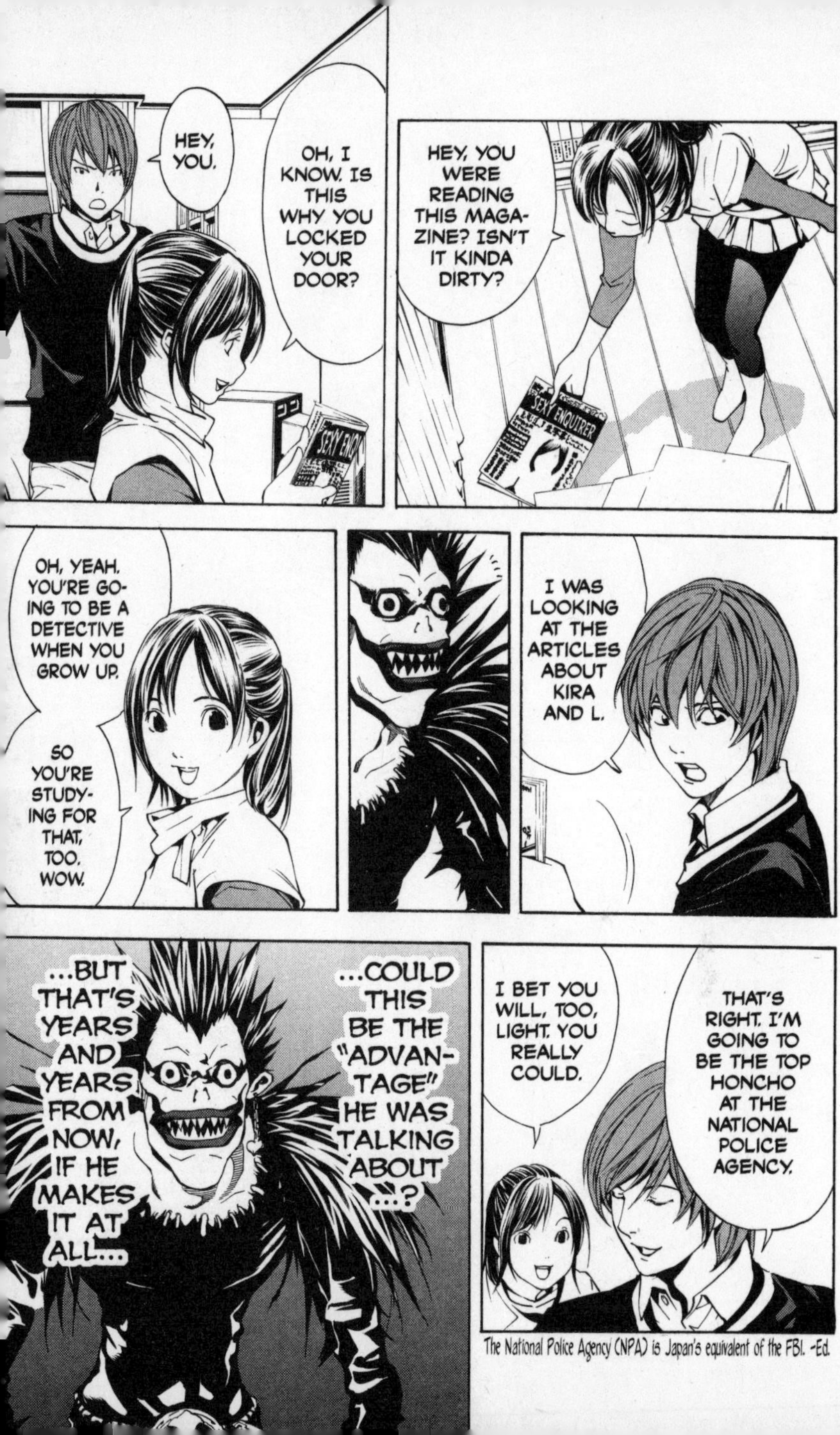
HEY, YOU WERE READING THIS MAGAZINE? ISN'T IT KINDA DIRTY?
SEXY ENQUIRER
OH, I KNOW. IS THIS WHY YOU LOCKED YOUR DOOR?
HEY, YOU.
I WAS LOOKING AT THE ARTICLES ABOUT KIRA AND L.
OH, YEAH. YOU'RE GOING TO BE A DETECTIVE WHEN YOU GROW UP.
SO YOU'RE STUDYING FOR THAT, TOO. WOW.
THAT'S RIGHT. I'M GOING TO BE THE TOP HONCHO AT THE NATIONAL POLICE AGENCY.
I BET YOU WILL, TOO, LIGHT. YOU REALLY COULD.
...COULD THIS BE THE "ADVANTAGE" HE WAS TALKING ABOUT...?
...BUT THAT'S YEARS AND YEARS FROM NOW, IF HE MAKES IT AT ALL...

The National Police Agency (NPA) is Japan's equivalent of the FBI. -Ed.

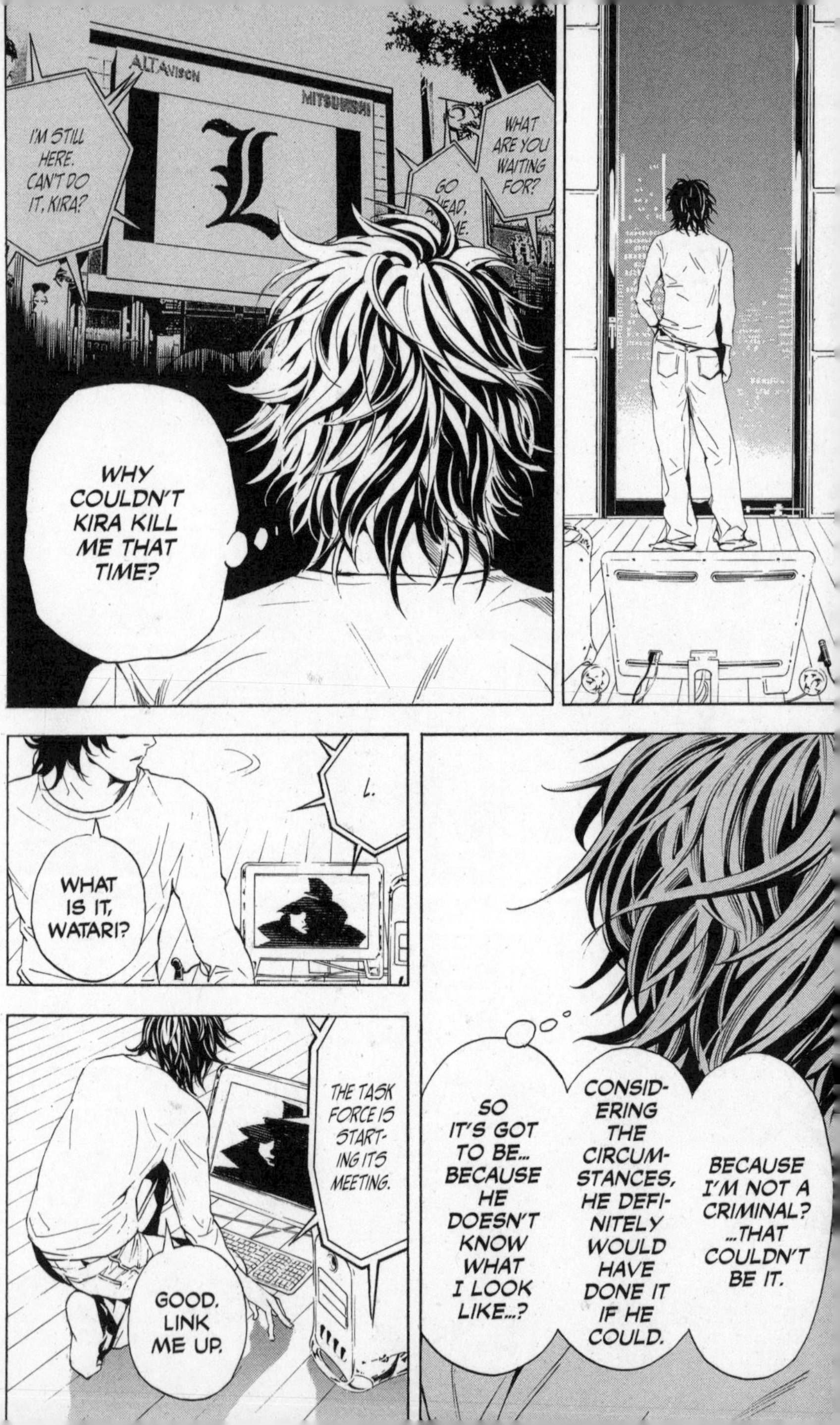
WHAT ARE YOU WAITING FOR?
GO AHEAD,
I'M STILL HERE. CAN'T DO IT, KIRA?
WHY COULDN'T KIRA KILL ME THAT TIME?
BECAUSE I'M NOT A CRIMINAL? ...THAT COULDN'T BE IT.
CONSIDERING THE CIRCUMSTANCES, HE DEFINITELY WOULD HAVE DONE IT IF HE COULD.
SO IT'S GOT TO BE... BECAUSE HE DOESN'T KNOW WHAT I LOOK LIKE...?
L.
WHAT IS IT, WATARI?
THE TASK FORCE IS STARTING ITS MEETING.
GOOD. LINK ME UP.

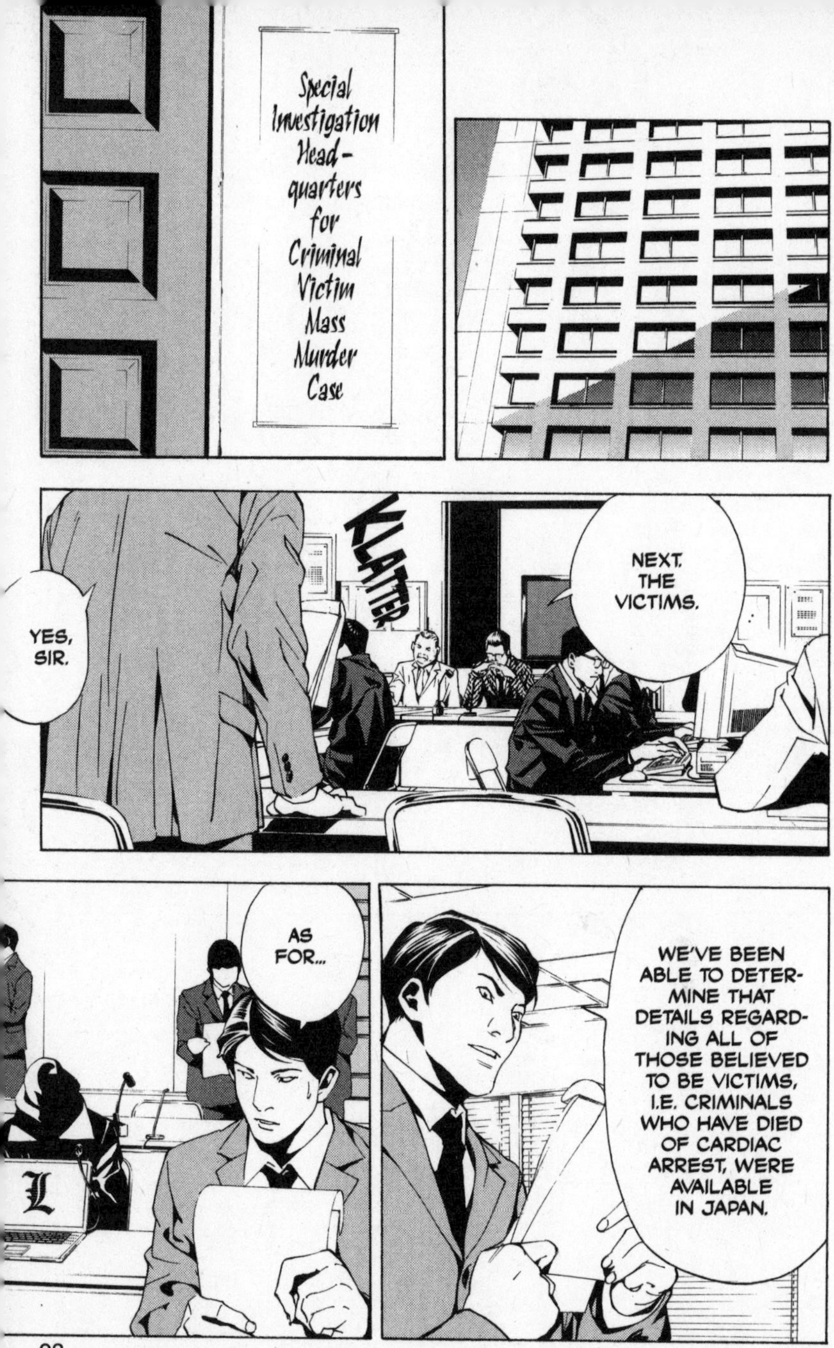
Special Investigation Head-quarters for Criminal Victim Mass Murder Case
NEXT, THE VICTIMS.
KLATTER
YES, SIR.
WE'VE BEEN ABLE TO DETER-MINE THAT DETAILS REGARD-ING ALL OF THOSE BELIEVED TO BE VICTIMS, I.E. CRIMINALS WHO HAVE DIED OF CARDIAC ARREST, WERE AVAILABLE IN JAPAN.
AS FOR...

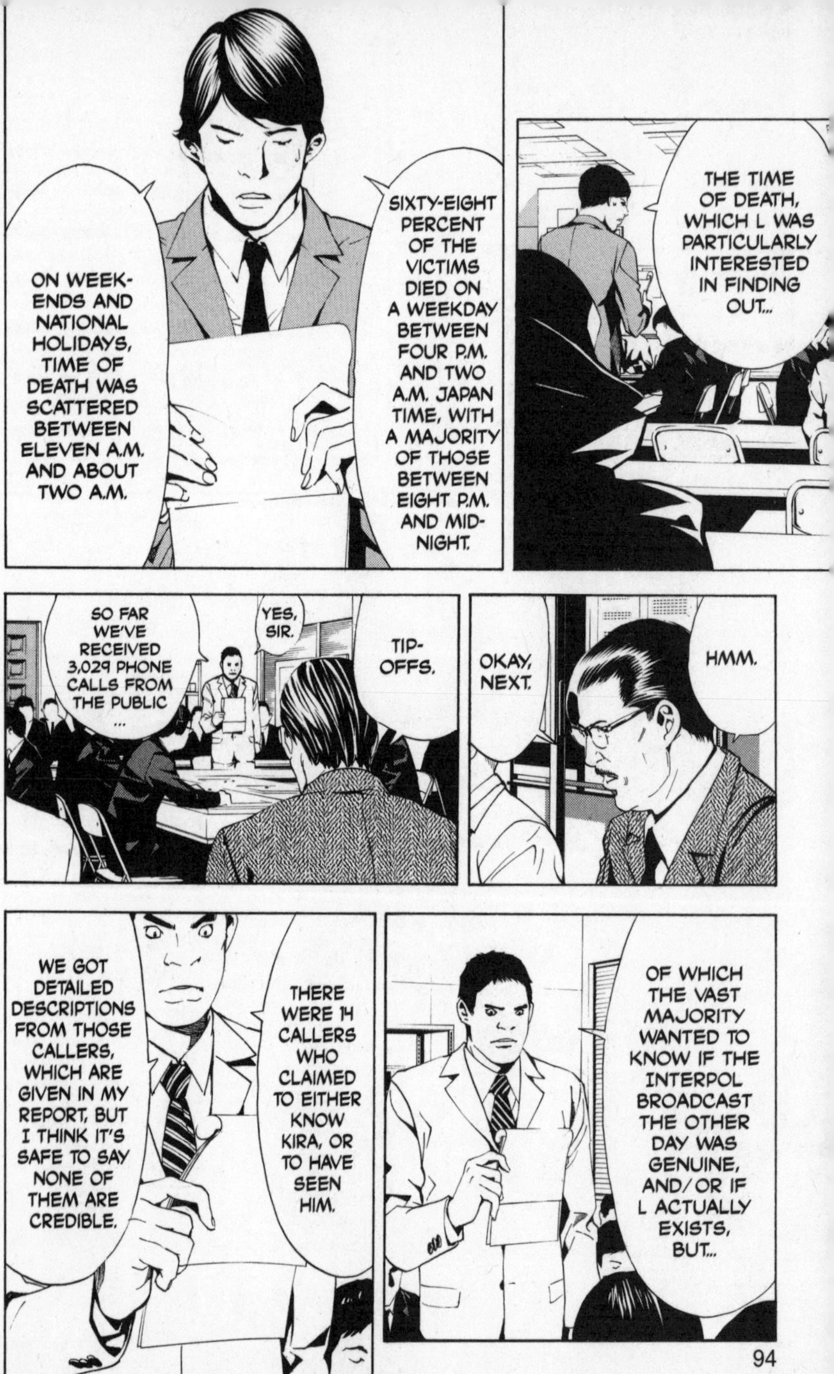
THE TIME OF DEATH, WHICH L WAS PARTICULARLY INTERESTED IN FINDING OUT...
SIXTY-EIGHT PERCENT OF THE VICTIMS DIED ON A WEEKDAY BETWEEN FOUR P.M. AND TWO A.M. JAPAN TIME, WITH A MAJORITY OF THOSE BETWEEN EIGHT P.M. AND MID-NIGHT.
ON WEEK-ENDS AND NATIONAL HOLIDAYS, TIME OF DEATH WAS SCATTERED BETWEEN ELEVEN A.M. AND ABOUT TWO A.M.
HMM.
OKAY, NEXT.
TIP-OFFS.
YES, SIR.
SO FAR WE'VE RECEIVED 3,029 PHONE CALLS FROM THE PUBLIC ...
OF WHICH THE VAST MAJORITY WANTED TO KNOW IF THE INTERPOL BROADCAST THE OTHER DAY WAS GENUINE, AND/OR IF L ACTUALLY EXISTS, BUT...
THERE WERE 14 CALLERS WHO CLAIMED TO EITHER KNOW KIRA, OR TO HAVE SEEN HIM.
WE GOT DETAILED DESCRIPTIONS FROM THOSE CALLERS, WHICH ARE GIVEN IN MY REPORT, BUT I THINK IT'S SAFE TO SAY NONE OF THEM ARE CREDIBLE.

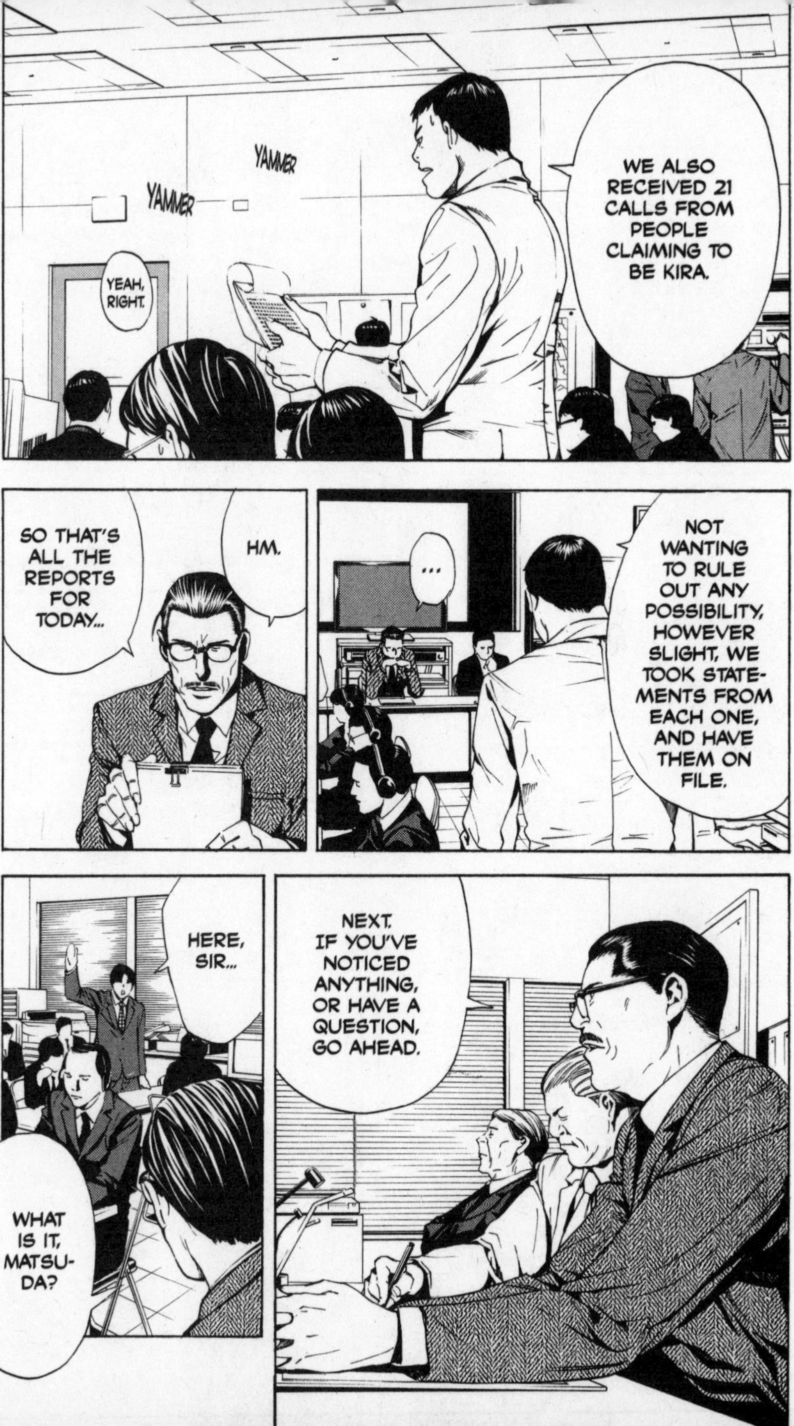
WE ALSO RECEIVED 21 CALLS FROM PEOPLE CLAIMING TO BE KIRA.
YAMMER
YAMMER
YEAH, RIGHT.
NOT WANTING TO RULE OUT ANY POSSIBILITY, HOWEVER SLIGHT, WE TOOK STATE-MENTS FROM EACH ONE, AND HAVE THEM ON FILE.
...
HM.
SO THAT'S ALL THE REPORTS FOR TODAY...
NEXT. IF YOU'VE NOTICED ANYTHING, OR HAVE A QUESTION, GO AHEAD.
HERE, SIR...
WHAT IS IT, MATSU-DA?

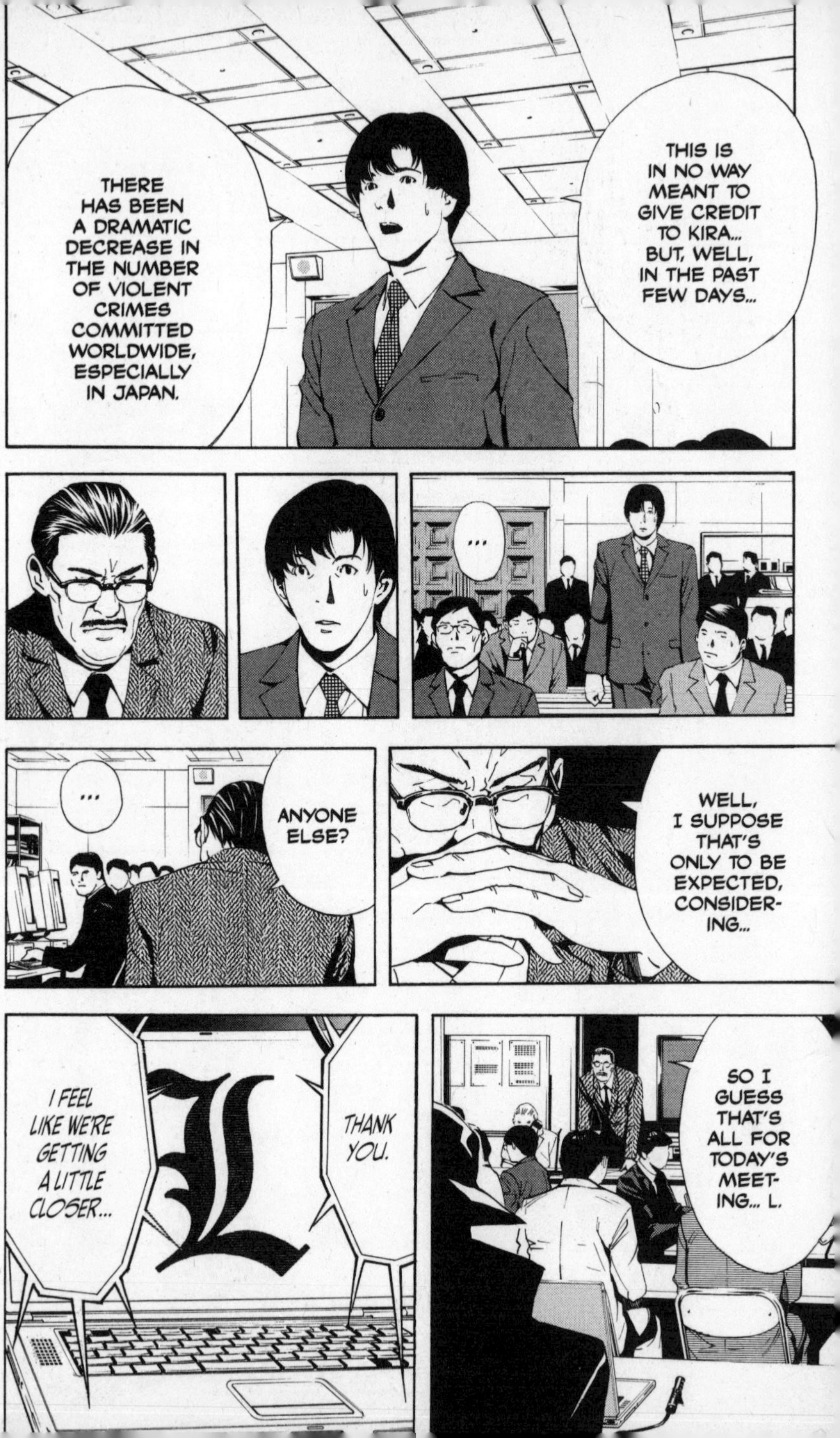
THIS IS IN NO WAY MEANT TO GIVE CREDIT TO KIRA... BUT, WELL, IN THE PAST FEW DAYS...
THERE HAS BEEN A DRAMATIC DECREASE IN THE NUMBER OF VIOLENT CRIMES COMMITTED WORLDWIDE, ESPECIALLY IN JAPAN.
...
WELL, I SUPPOSE THAT'S ONLY TO BE EXPECTED, CONSIDER-ING...
ANYONE ELSE?
...
SO I GUESS THAT'S ALL FOR TODAY'S MEET-ING... L.
THANK YOU.
I FEEL LIKE WE'RE GETTING A LITTLE CLOSER...

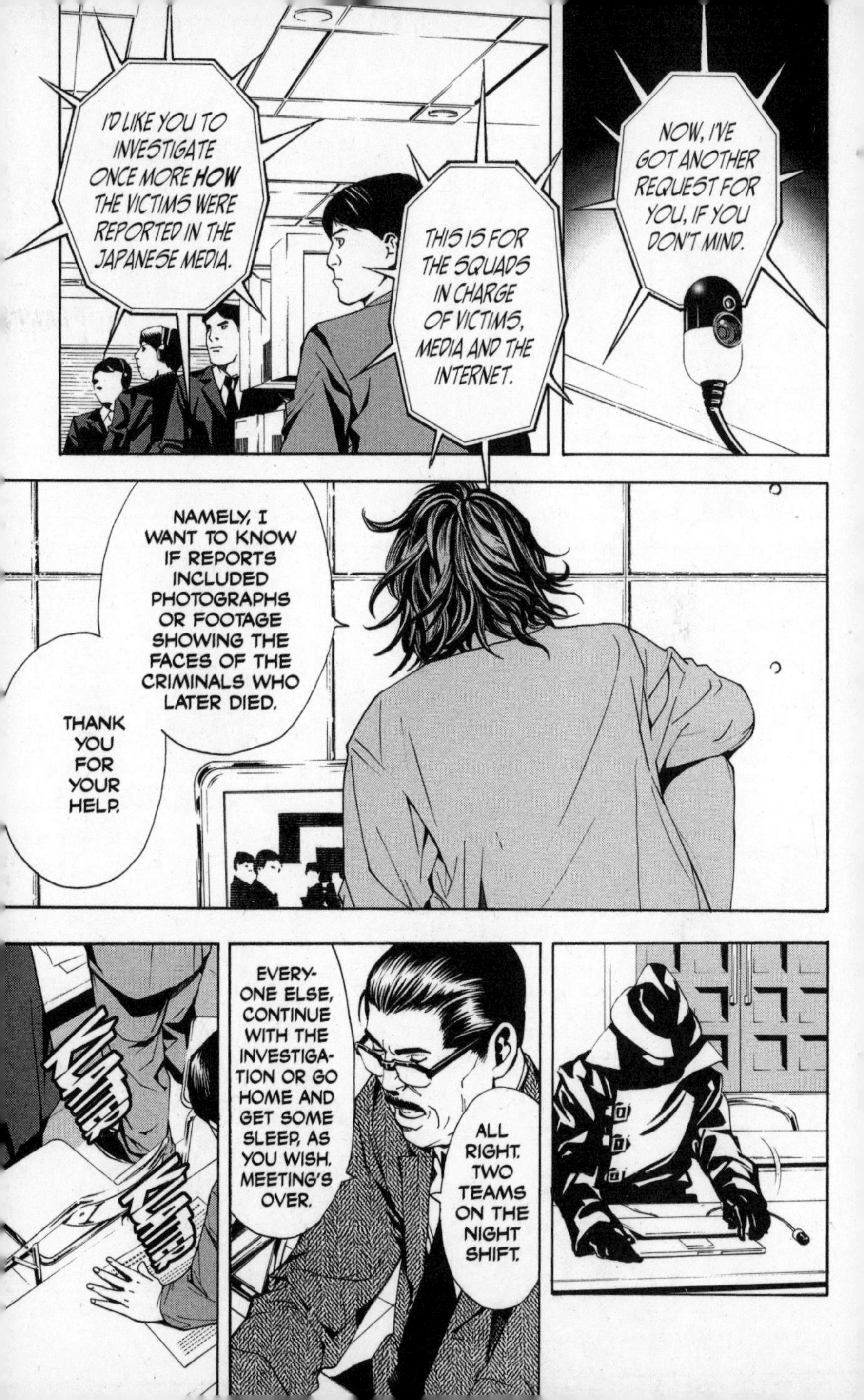
NOW, I'VE GOT ANOTHER REQUEST FOR YOU, IF YOU DON'T MIND.
THIS IS FOR THE SQUADS IN CHARGE OF VICTIMS, MEDIA AND THE INTERNET.
I'D LIKE YOU TO INVESTIGATE ONCE MORE **HOW** THE VICTIMS WERE REPORTED IN THE JAPANESE MEDIA.
NAMELY, I WANT TO KNOW IF REPORTS INCLUDED PHOTOGRAPHS OR FOOTAGE SHOWING THE FACES OF THE CRIMINALS WHO LATER DIED.
THANK YOU FOR YOUR HELP.
ALL RIGHT. TWO TEAMS ON THE NIGHT SHIFT.
EVERYONE ELSE, CONTINUE WITH THE INVESTIGATION OR GO HOME AND GET SOME SLEEP, AS YOU WISH. MEETING'S OVER.

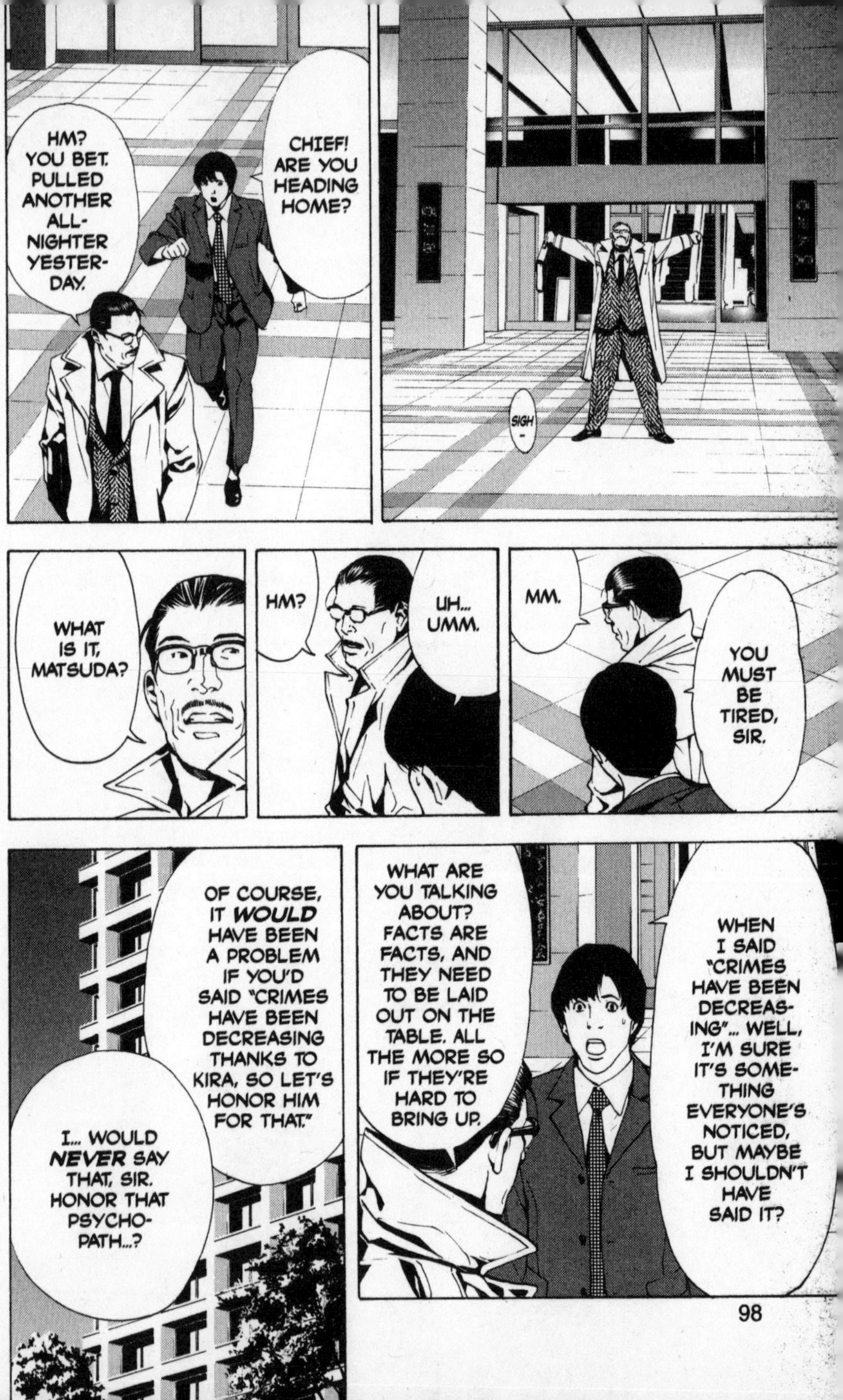
SIGH
CHIEF! ARE YOU HEADING HOME?
HM? YOU BET. PULLED ANOTHER ALL-NIGHTER YESTER-DAY.
YOU MUST BE TIRED, SIR.
MM.
UH... UMM.
HM?
WHAT IS IT, MATSUDA?
WHEN I SAID "CRIMES HAVE BEEN DECREAS-ING"... WELL, I'M SURE IT'S SOME-THING EVERYONE'S NOTICED, BUT MAYBE I SHOULDN'T HAVE SAID IT?
WHAT ARE YOU TALKING ABOUT? FACTS ARE FACTS, AND THEY NEED TO BE LAID OUT ON THE TABLE. ALL THE MORE SO IF THEY'RE HARD TO BRING UP.
OF COURSE, IT *WOULD* HAVE BEEN A PROBLEM IF YOU'D SAID "CRIMES HAVE BEEN DECREASING THANKS TO KIRA, SO LET'S HONOR HIM FOR THAT."
I... WOULD ***NEVER*** SAY THAT, SIR. HONOR THAT PSYCHO-PATH...?

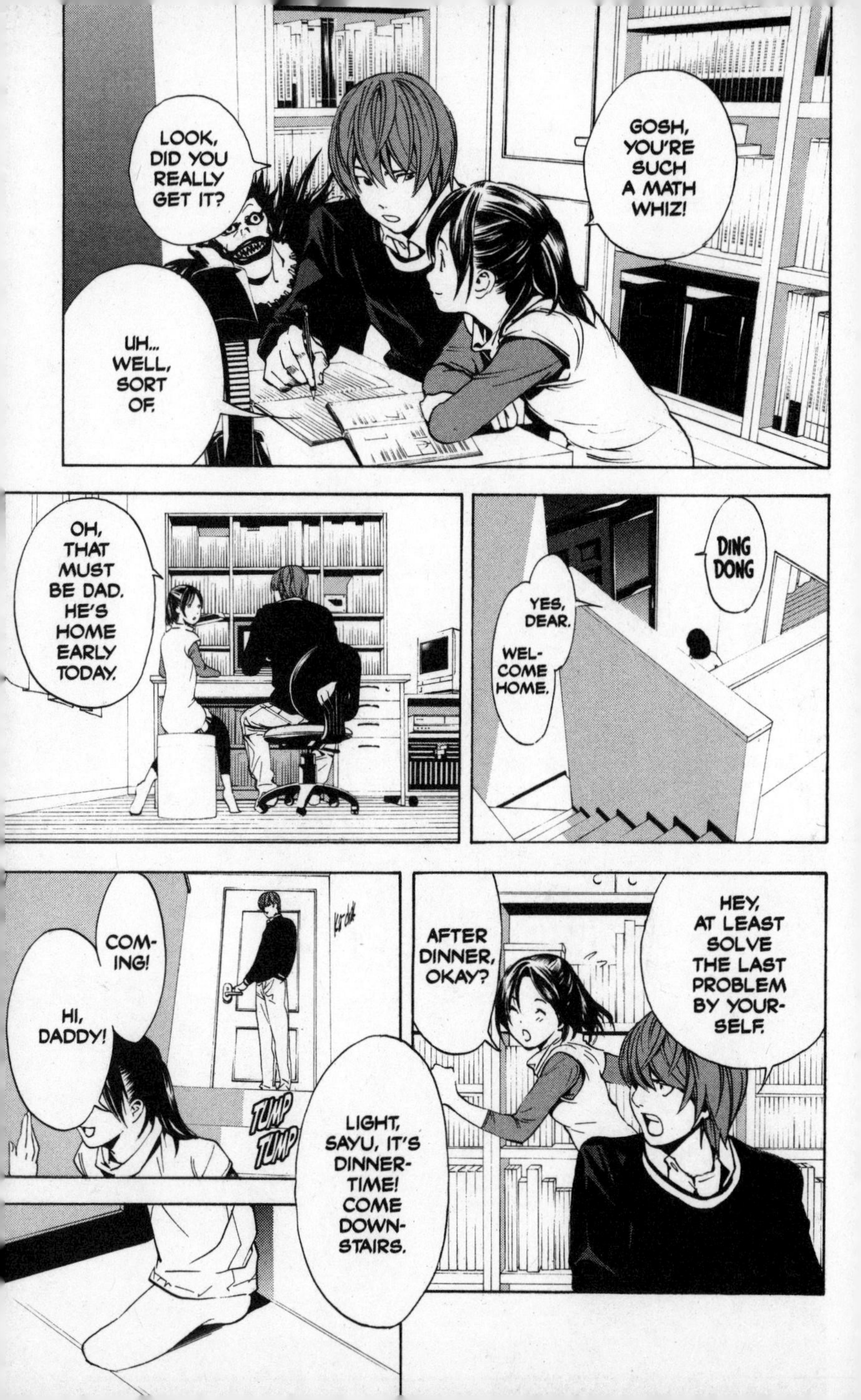
GOSH, YOU'RE SUCH A MATH WHIZ!
LOOK, DID YOU REALLY GET IT?
UH... WELL, SORT OF.
DING DONG
YES, DEAR.
WEL-COME HOME.
OH, THAT MUST BE DAD. HE'S HOME EARLY TODAY.
HEY, AT LEAST SOLVE THE LAST PROBLEM BY YOUR-SELF.
AFTER DINNER, OKAY?
LIGHT, SAYU, IT'S DINNER-TIME! COME DOWN-STAIRS.
TUMP TUMP
COM-ING!
HI, DADDY!

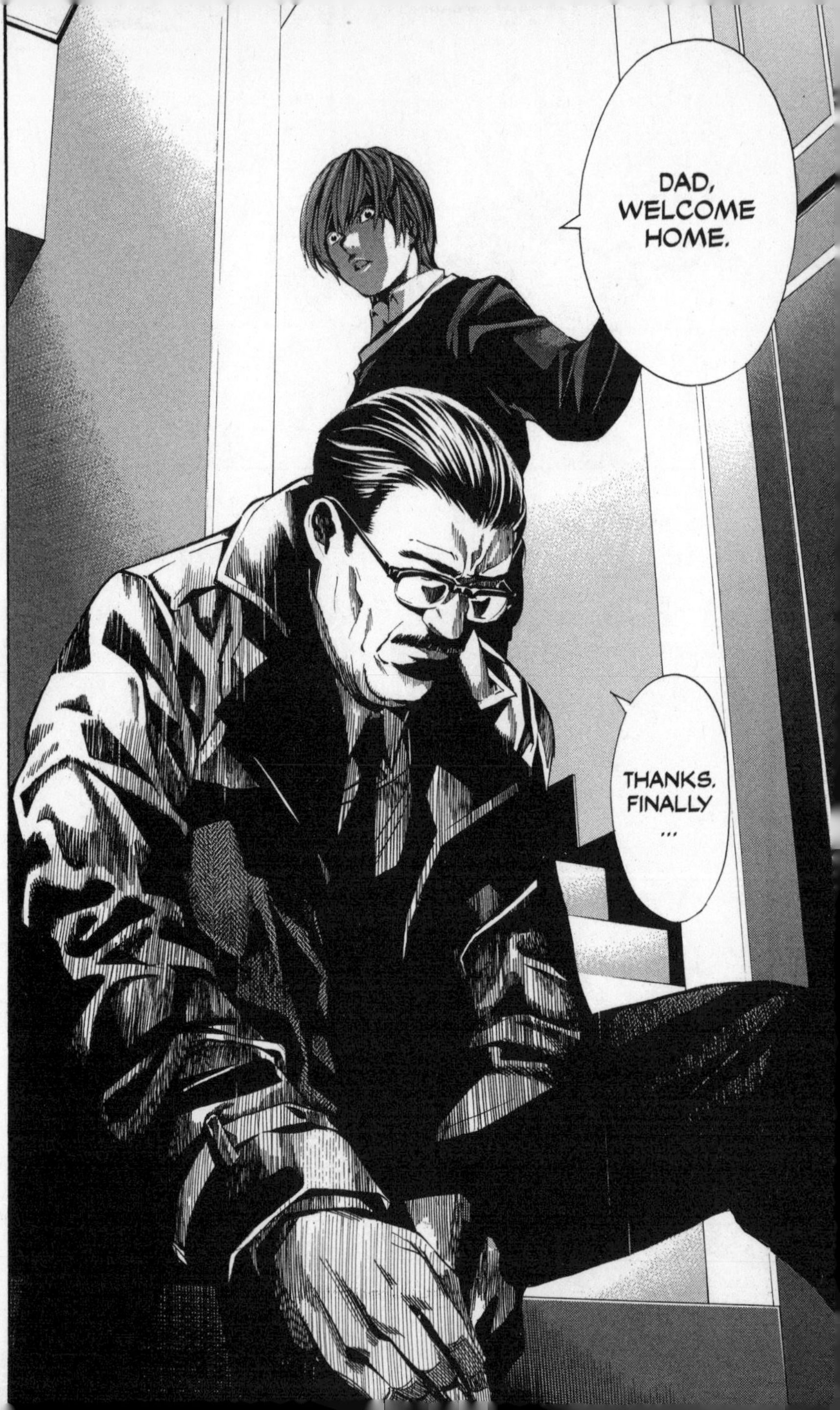
DAD, WELCOME HOME.
THANKS. FINALLY ...

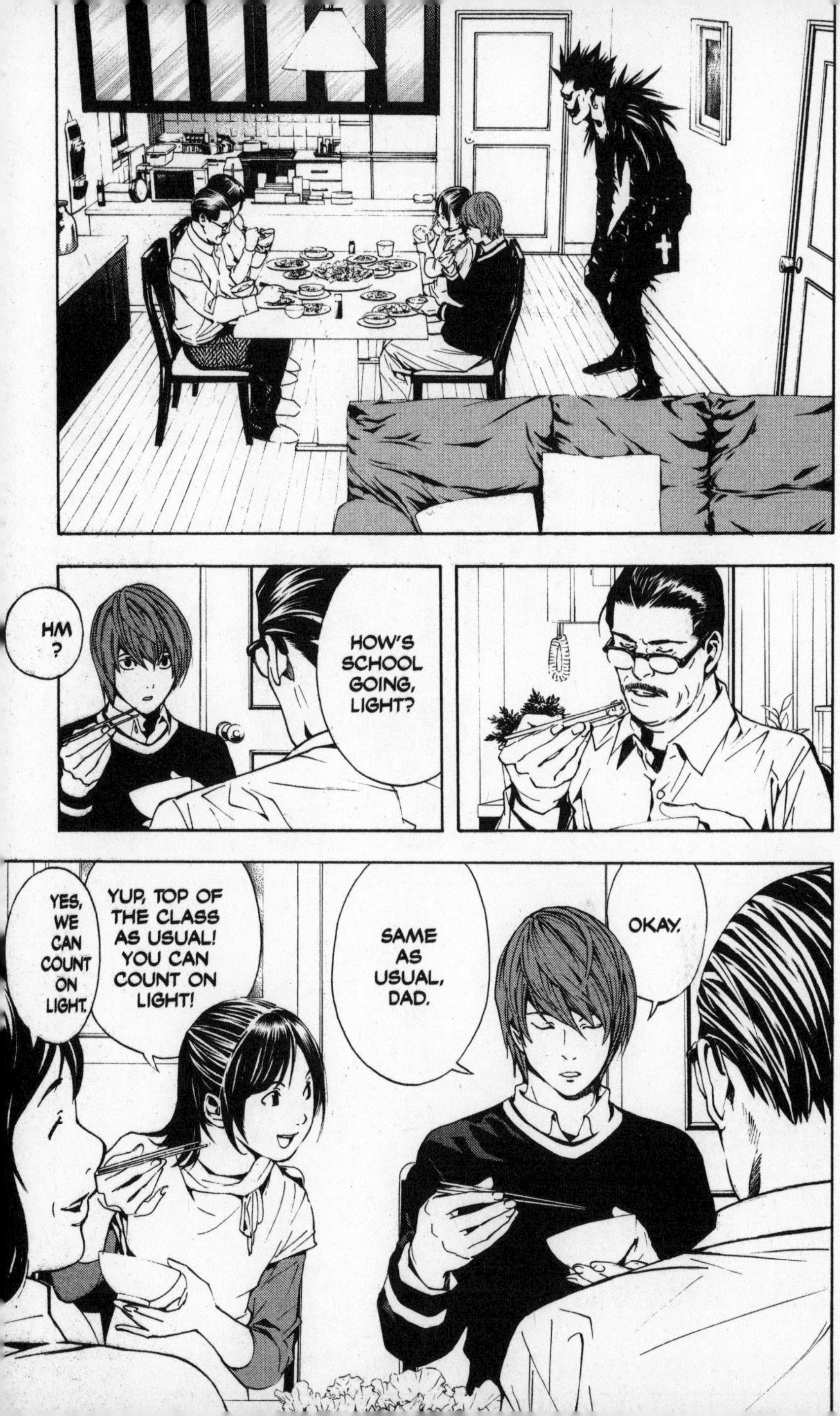
HOW'S SCHOOL GOING, LIGHT?
HM ?
OKAY.
SAME AS USUAL, DAD.
YUP, TOP OF THE CLASS AS USUAL! YOU CAN COUNT ON LIGHT!
YES, WE CAN COUNT ON LIGHT.

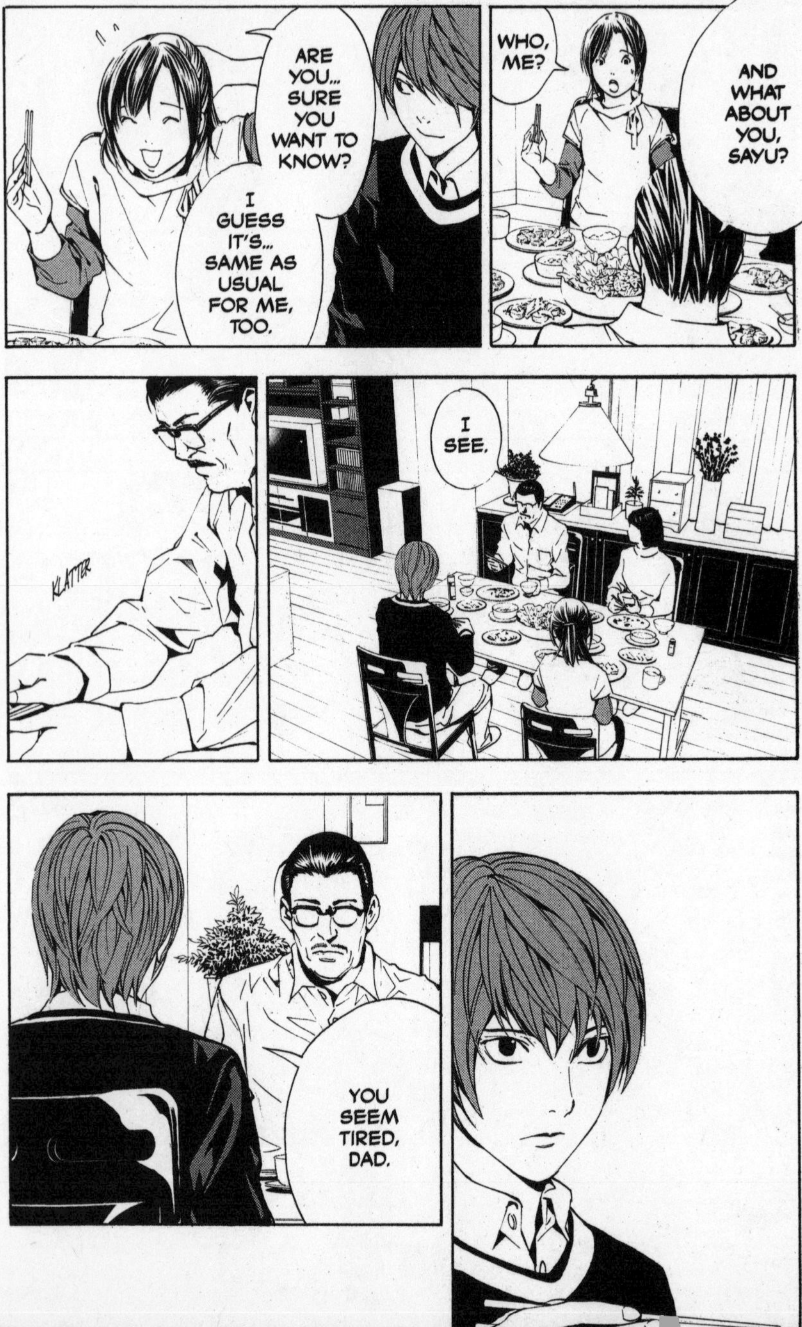
AND WHAT ABOUT YOU, SAYU?
WHO, ME?
ARE YOU... SURE YOU WANT TO KNOW?
I GUESS IT'S... SAME AS USUAL FOR ME, TOO.
I SEE.
KLATTER
YOU SEEM TIRED, DAD.

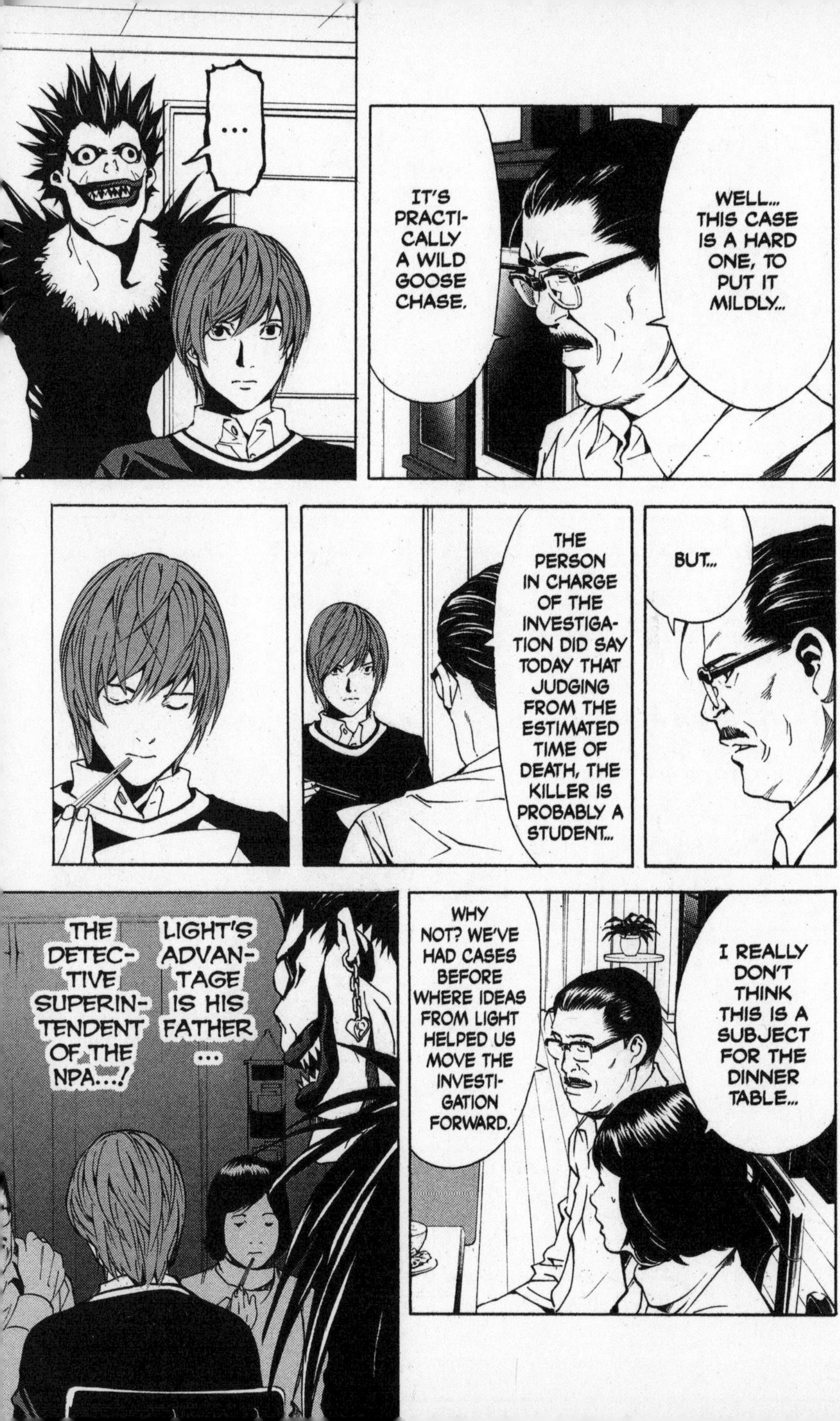
WELL... THIS CASE IS A HARD ONE, TO PUT IT MILDLY...
IT'S PRACTICALLY A WILD GOOSE CHASE.
...
BUT...
THE PERSON IN CHARGE OF THE INVESTIGATION DID SAY TODAY THAT JUDGING FROM THE ESTIMATED TIME OF DEATH, THE KILLER IS PROBABLY A STUDENT...
I REALLY DON'T THINK THIS IS A SUBJECT FOR THE DINNER TABLE...
WHY NOT? WE'VE HAD CASES BEFORE WHERE IDEAS FROM LIGHT HELPED US MOVE THE INVESTIGATION FORWARD.
LIGHT'S ADVANTAGE IS HIS FATHER...
THE DETECTIVE SUPERINTENDENT OF THE NPA...!

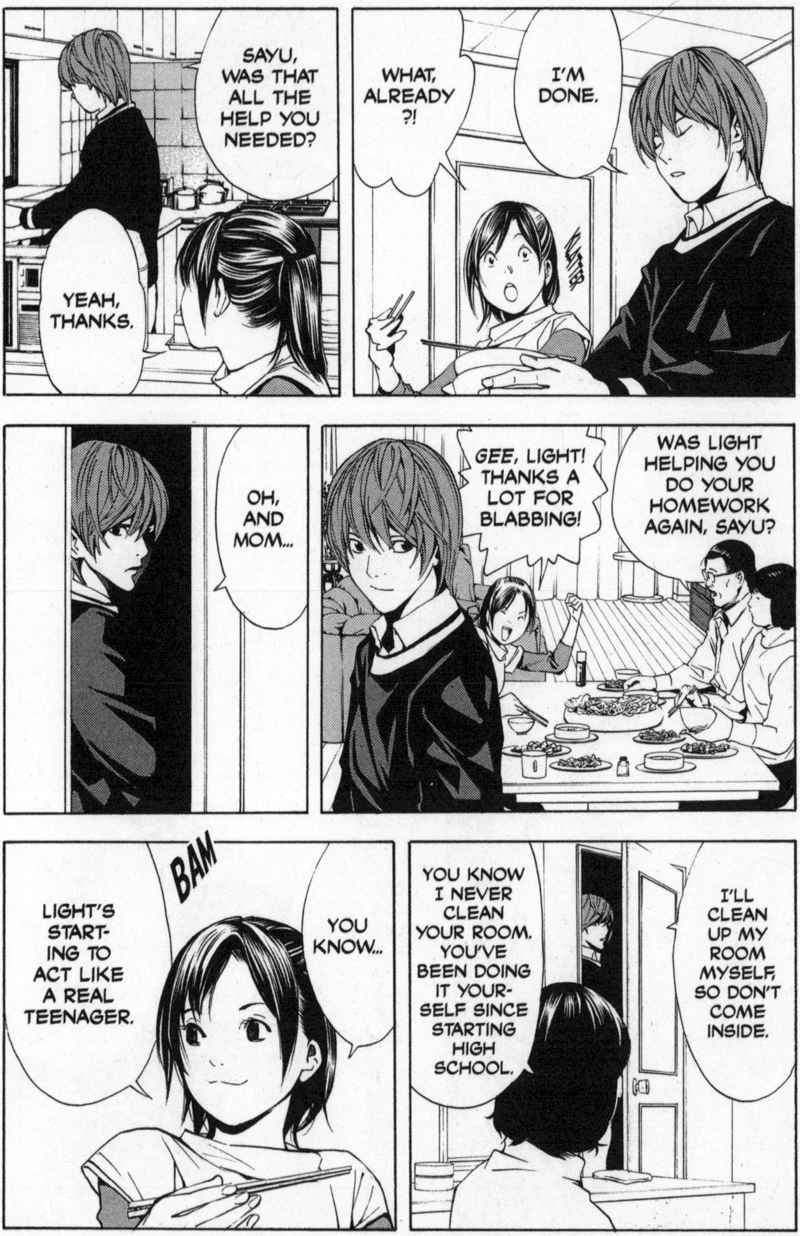
I'M DONE.
WHAT, ALREADY?!
SAYU, WAS THAT ALL THE HELP YOU NEEDED?
YEAH, THANKS.
WAS LIGHT HELPING YOU DO YOUR HOMEWORK AGAIN, SAYU?
GEE, LIGHT! THANKS A LOT FOR BLABBING!
OH, AND MOM...
I'LL CLEAN UP MY ROOM MYSELF, SO DON'T COME INSIDE.
YOU KNOW I NEVER CLEAN YOUR ROOM. YOU'VE BEEN DOING IT YOUR-SELF SINCE STARTING HIGH SCHOOL.
BAM
YOU KNOW...
LIGHT'S START-ING TO ACT LIKE A REAL TEENAGER.

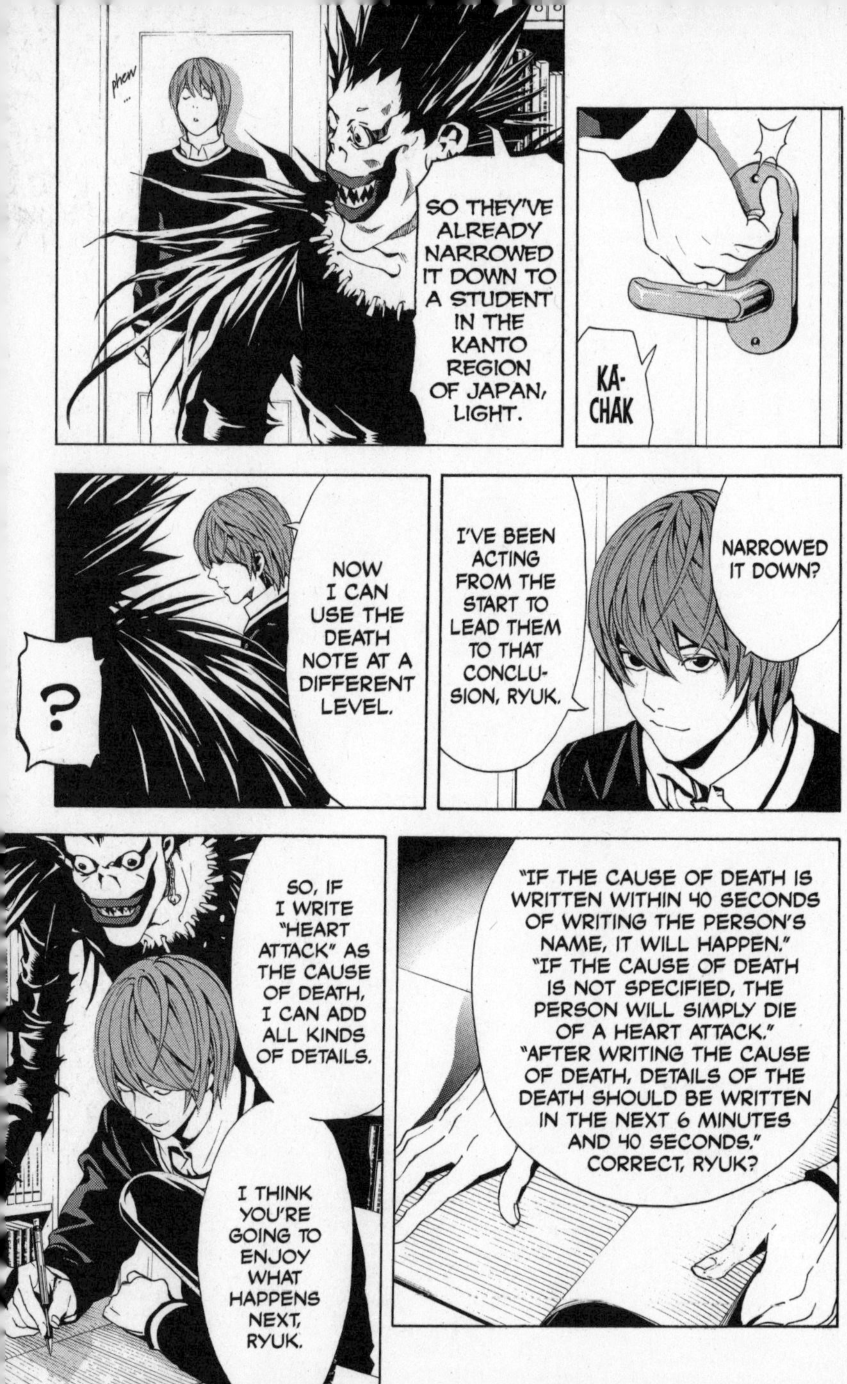
KA-CHAK
phew ...
SO THEY'VE ALREADY NARROWED IT DOWN TO A STUDENT IN THE KANTO REGION OF JAPAN, LIGHT.
NARROWED IT DOWN?
I'VE BEEN ACTING FROM THE START TO LEAD THEM TO THAT CONCLUSION, RYUK.
NOW I CAN USE THE DEATH NOTE AT A DIFFERENT LEVEL.
?
"IF THE CAUSE OF DEATH IS WRITTEN WITHIN 40 SECONDS OF WRITING THE PERSON'S NAME, IT WILL HAPPEN." "IF THE CAUSE OF DEATH IS NOT SPECIFIED, THE PERSON WILL SIMPLY DIE OF A HEART ATTACK." "AFTER WRITING THE CAUSE OF DEATH, DETAILS OF THE DEATH SHOULD BE WRITTEN IN THE NEXT 6 MINUTES AND 40 SECONDS." CORRECT, RYUK?
SO, IF I WRITE "HEART ATTACK" AS THE CAUSE OF DEATH, I CAN ADD ALL KINDS OF DETAILS.
I THINK YOU'RE GOING TO ENJOY WHAT HAPPENS NEXT, RYUK.

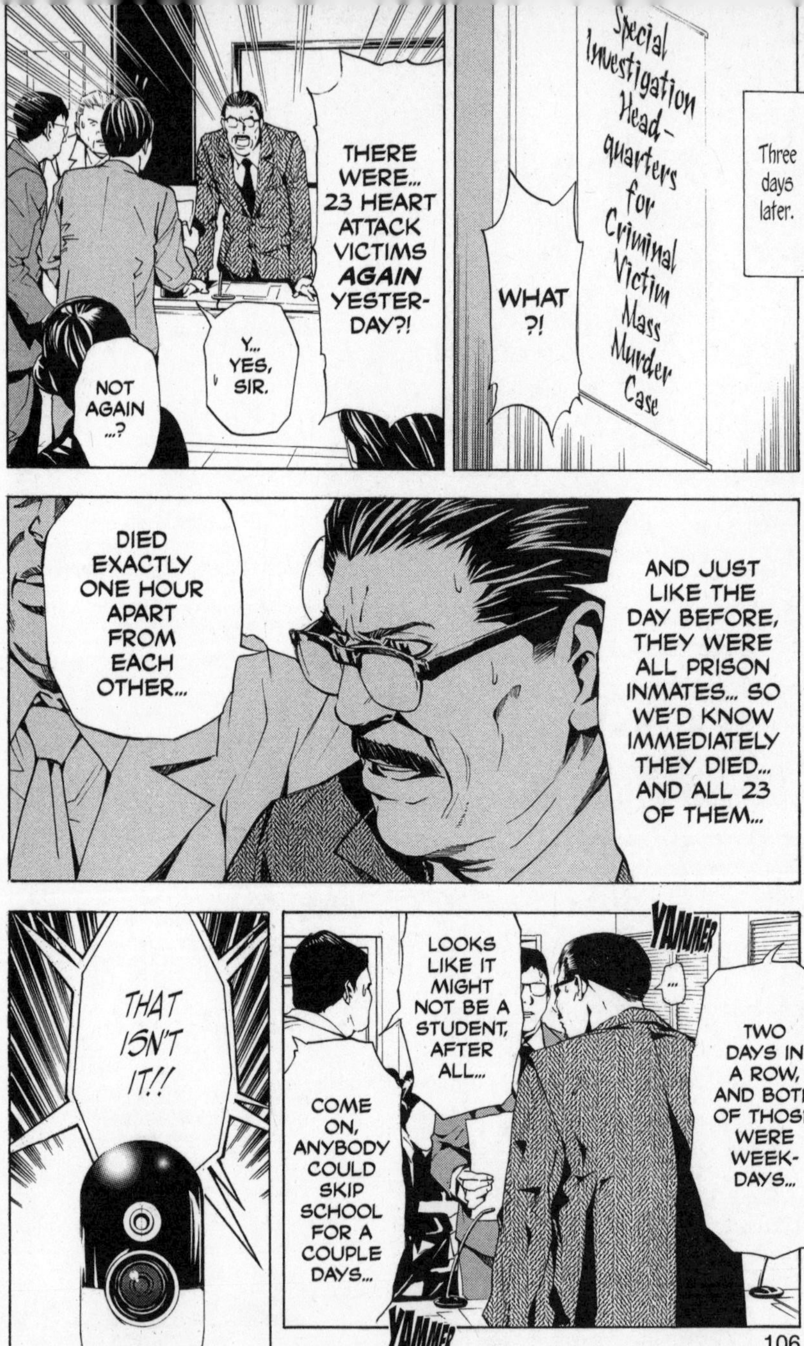
Three days later.
Special Investigation Headquarters for Criminal Victim Mass Murder Case
WHAT?!
THERE WERE... 23 HEART ATTACK VICTIMS **AGAIN** YESTERDAY?!
Y... YES, SIR.
NOT AGAIN ...?
AND JUST LIKE THE DAY BEFORE, THEY WERE ALL PRISON INMATES... SO WE'D KNOW IMMEDIATELY THEY DIED... AND ALL 23 OF THEM...
DIED EXACTLY ONE HOUR APART FROM EACH OTHER...
YAMMER
TWO DAYS IN A ROW, AND BOTH OF THOSE WERE WEEKDAYS...
...
LOOKS LIKE IT MIGHT NOT BE A STUDENT, AFTER ALL...
COME ON, ANYBODY COULD SKIP SCHOOL FOR A COUPLE DAYS...
YAMMER
THAT ISN'T IT!!

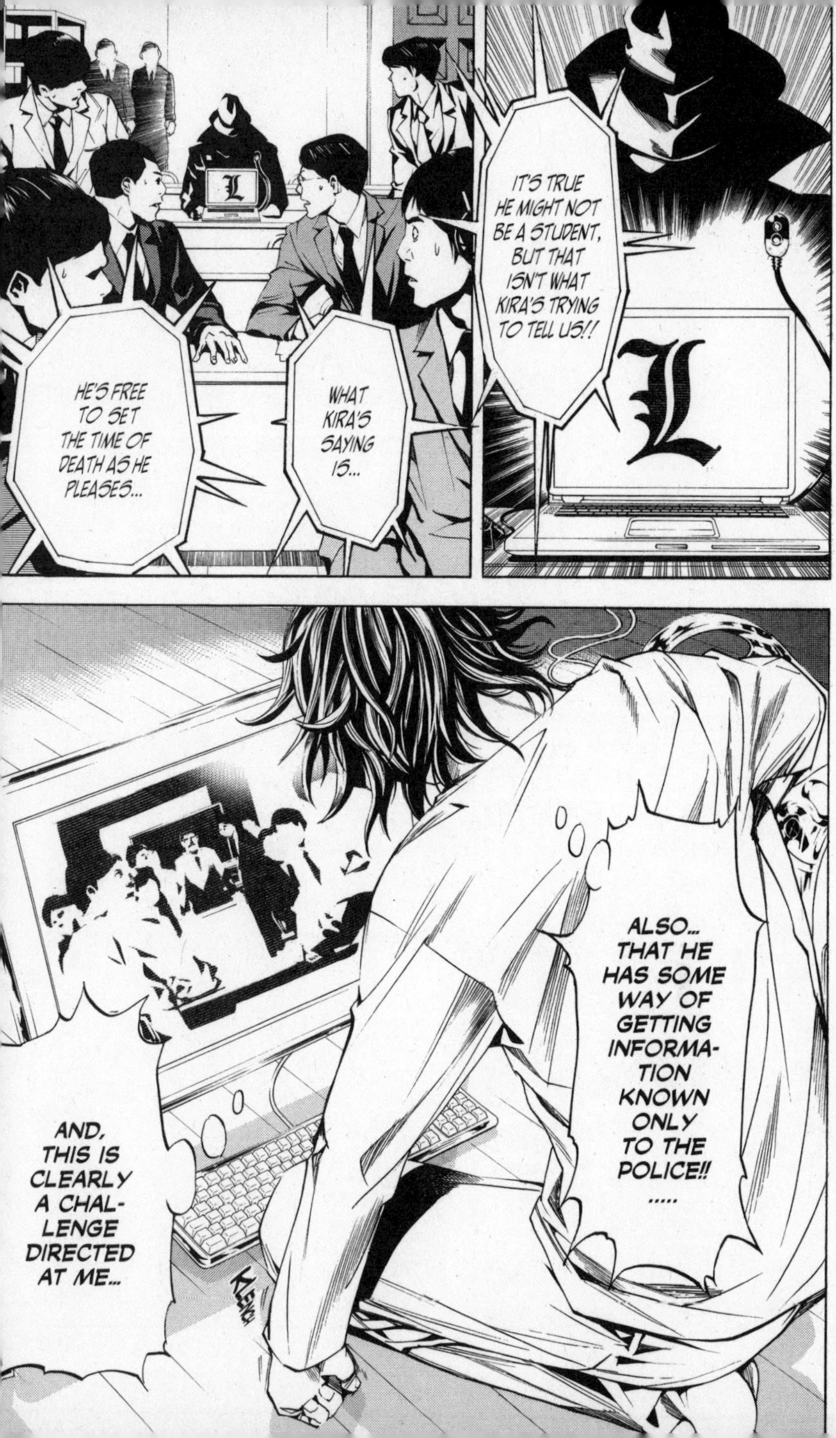
IT'S TRUE HE MIGHT NOT BE A STUDENT, BUT THAT ISN'T WHAT KIRA'S TRYING TO TELL US!!
WHAT KIRA'S SAYING IS...
HE'S FREE TO SET THE TIME OF DEATH AS HE PLEASES...
ALSO... THAT HE HAS SOME WAY OF GETTING INFORMATION KNOWN ONLY TO THE POLICE!! .....
AND, THIS IS CLEARLY A CHALLENGE DIRECTED AT ME...
KLENCH

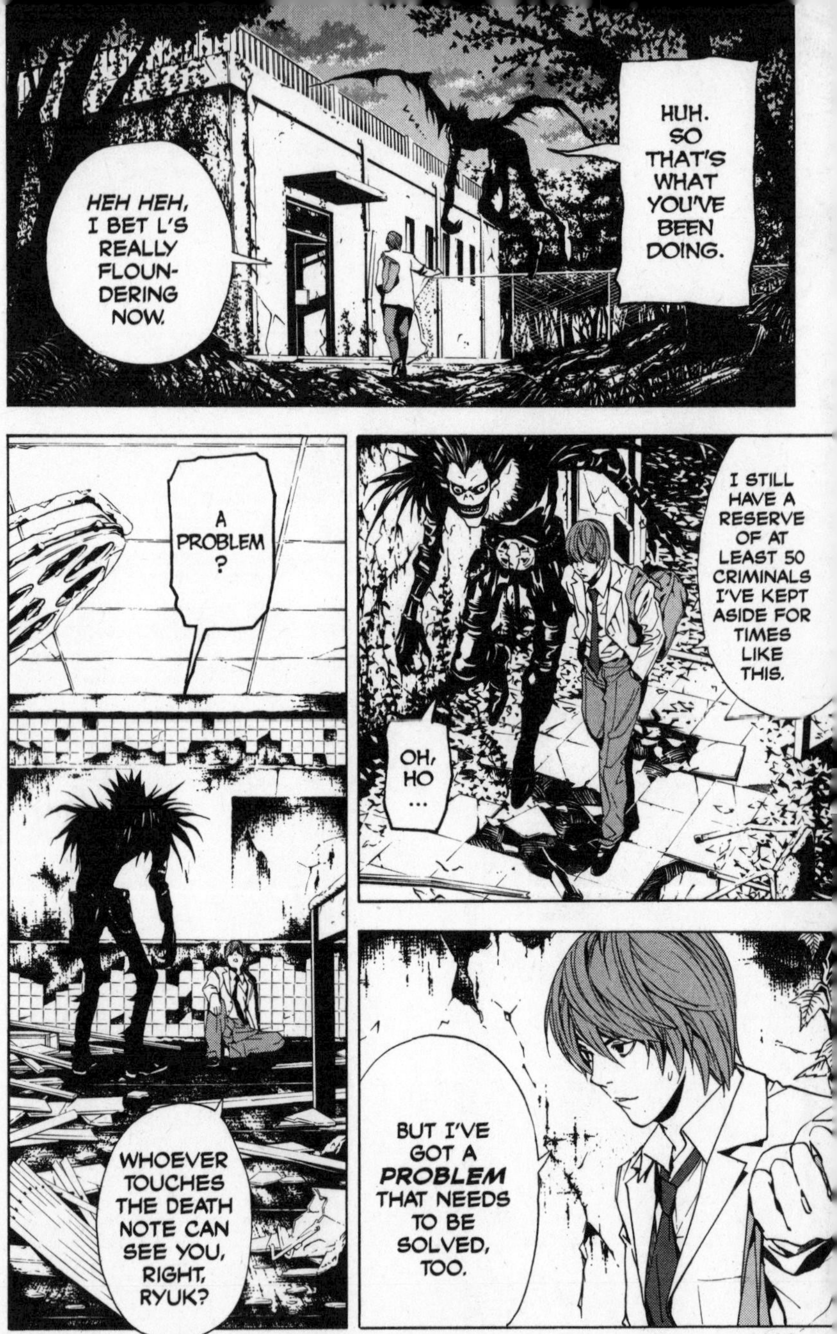
HUH. SO THAT'S WHAT YOU'VE BEEN DOING.
HEH HEH, I BET L'S REALLY FLOUN-DERING NOW.
I STILL HAVE A RESERVE OF AT LEAST 50 CRIMINALS I'VE KEPT ASIDE FOR TIMES LIKE THIS.
OH, HO ...
BUT I'VE GOT A ***PROBLEM*** THAT NEEDS TO BE SOLVED, TOO.
A PROBLEM ?
WHOEVER TOUCHES THE DEATH NOTE CAN SEE YOU, RIGHT, RYUK?

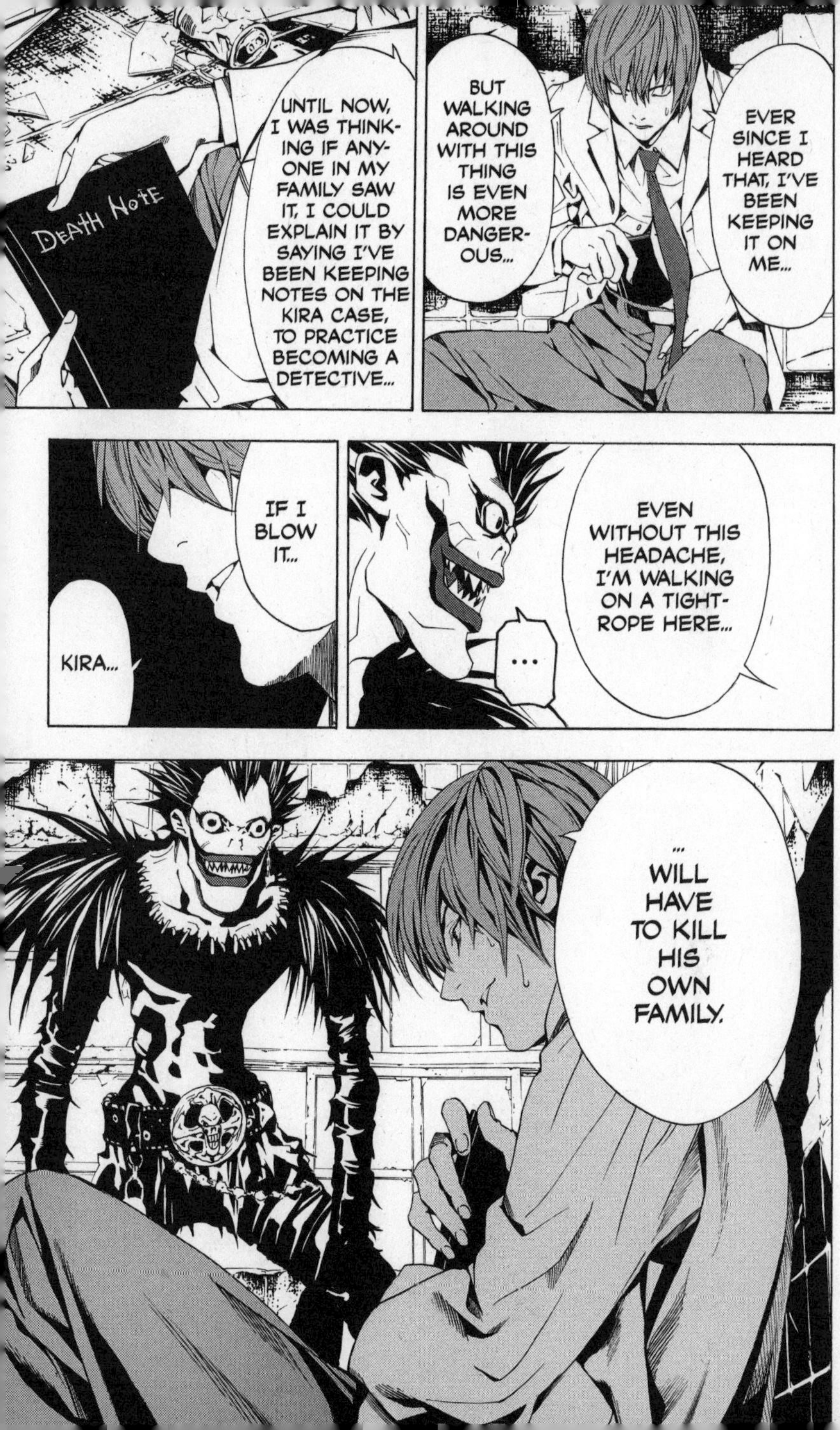
EVER SINCE I HEARD THAT, I'VE BEEN KEEPING IT ON ME...
BUT WALKING AROUND WITH THIS THING IS EVEN MORE DANGEROUS...
UNTIL NOW, I WAS THINKING IF ANYONE IN MY FAMILY SAW IT, I COULD EXPLAIN IT BY SAYING I'VE BEEN KEEPING NOTES ON THE KIRA CASE, TO PRACTICE BECOMING A DETECTIVE...
DEATH NOTE
EVEN WITHOUT THIS HEADACHE, I'M WALKING ON A TIGHTROPE HERE...
...
IF I BLOW IT...
KIRA...
... WILL HAVE TO KILL HIS OWN FAMILY.

DEATH NOTE
HOW to USE It
III

- If the time of death is written within 40 seconds after writing the cause of death as a heart attack, the time of death can be manipulated, and the time can go into effect within 40 seconds after writing the name.

死因に心臓麻痺と書いた後、40秒以内に死亡時刻を書けば、
心臓麻痺であっても死の時間を操れ、その時刻は名前を書いてからの
40秒以内でも可能である。

- The human who touches the DEATH NOTE can recognize the image and voice of its original owner, a god of death, even if the human is not the owner of the note.

デスノートに触った人間には、そのノートの所有者でなくとも、
元持ち主の死神の姿や声が認知できる。

chapter 4 Current

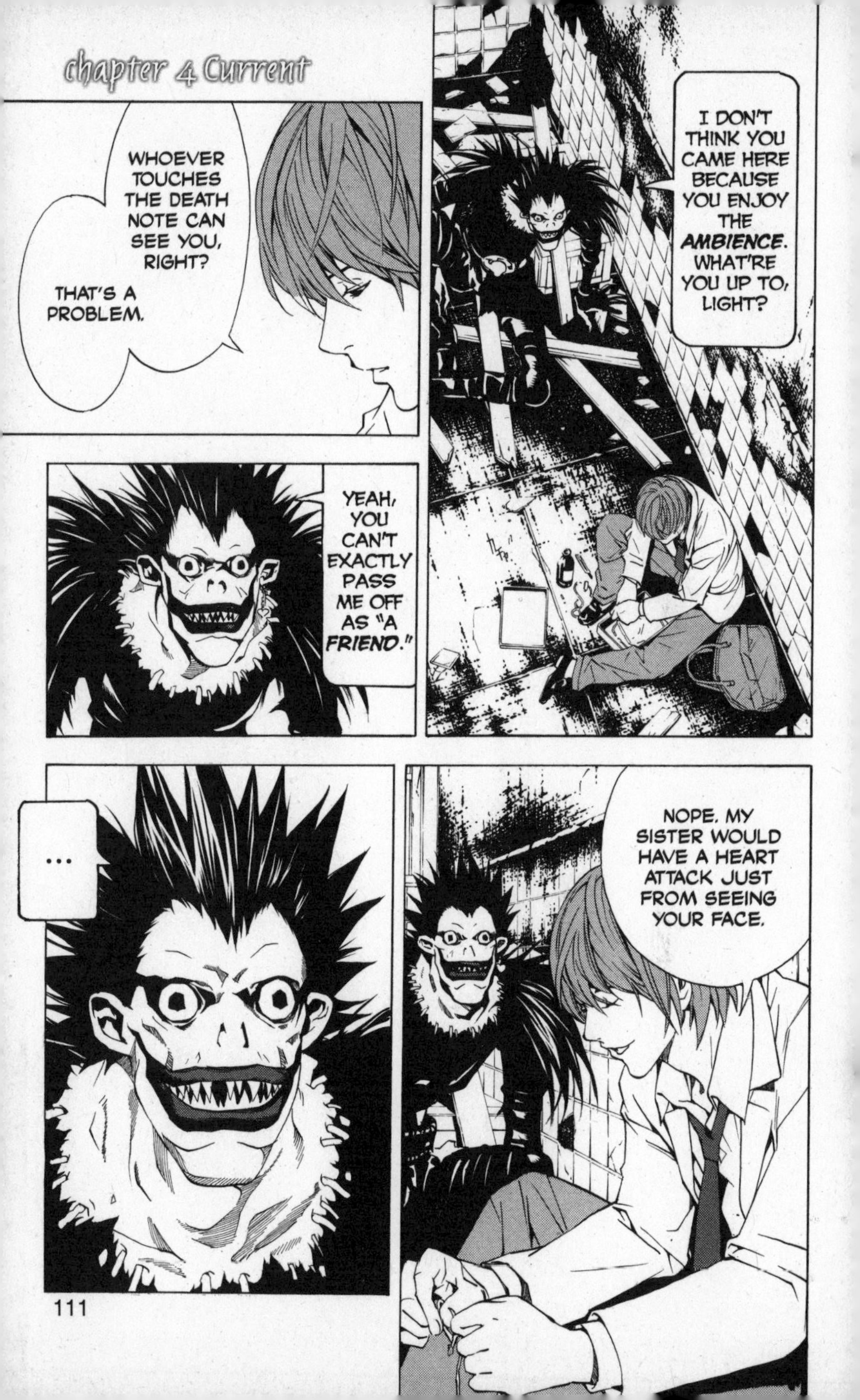
I DON'T THINK YOU CAME HERE BECAUSE YOU ENJOY THE *AMBIENCE*. WHAT'RE YOU UP TO, LIGHT?
WHOEVER TOUCHES THE DEATH NOTE CAN SEE YOU, RIGHT?
THAT'S A PROBLEM.
YEAH, YOU CAN'T EXACTLY PASS ME OFF AS "A *FRIEND*."
NOPE. MY SISTER WOULD HAVE A HEART ATTACK JUST FROM SEEING YOUR FACE.
...

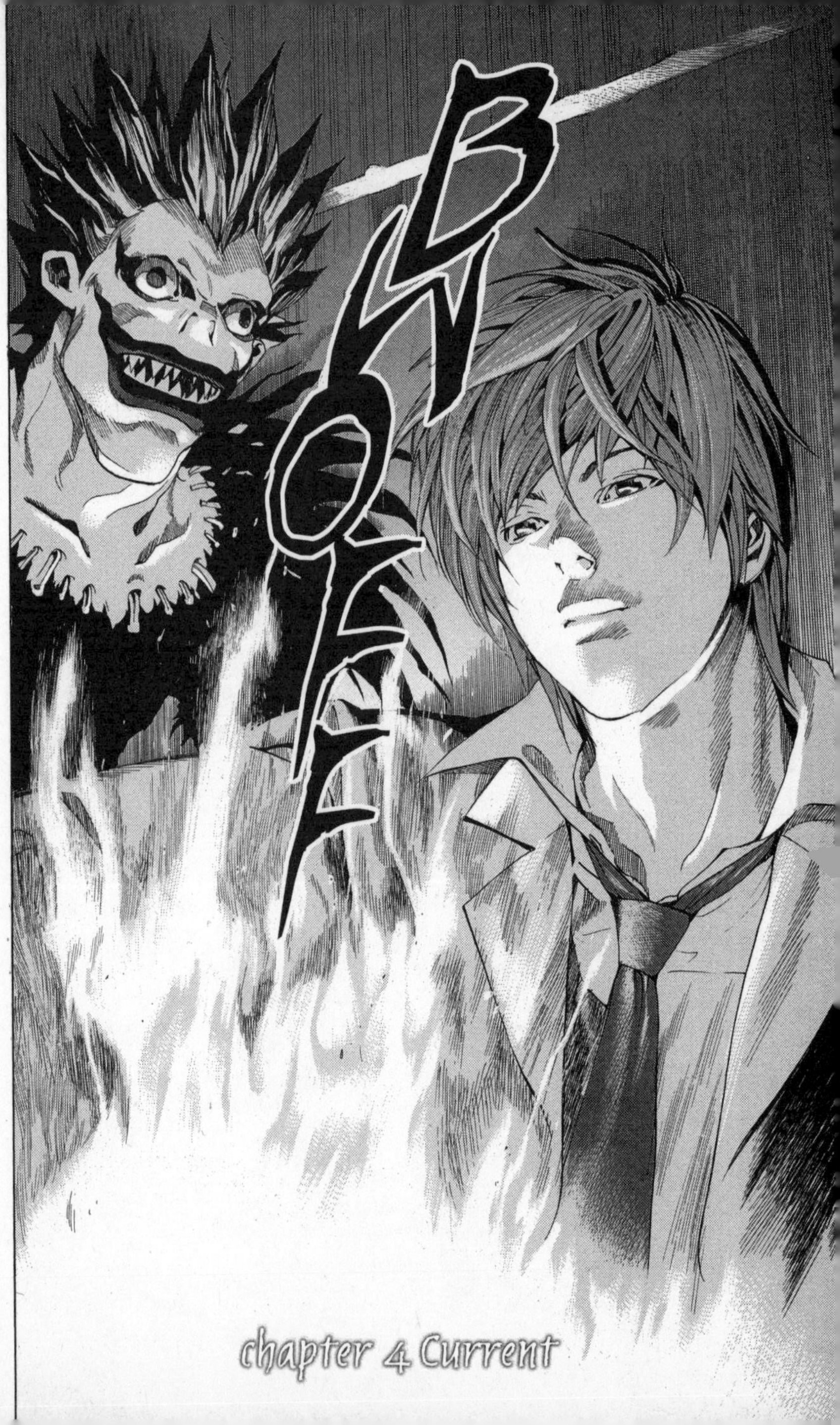
BWOOFF

chapter 4 Current

READ THIS WAY

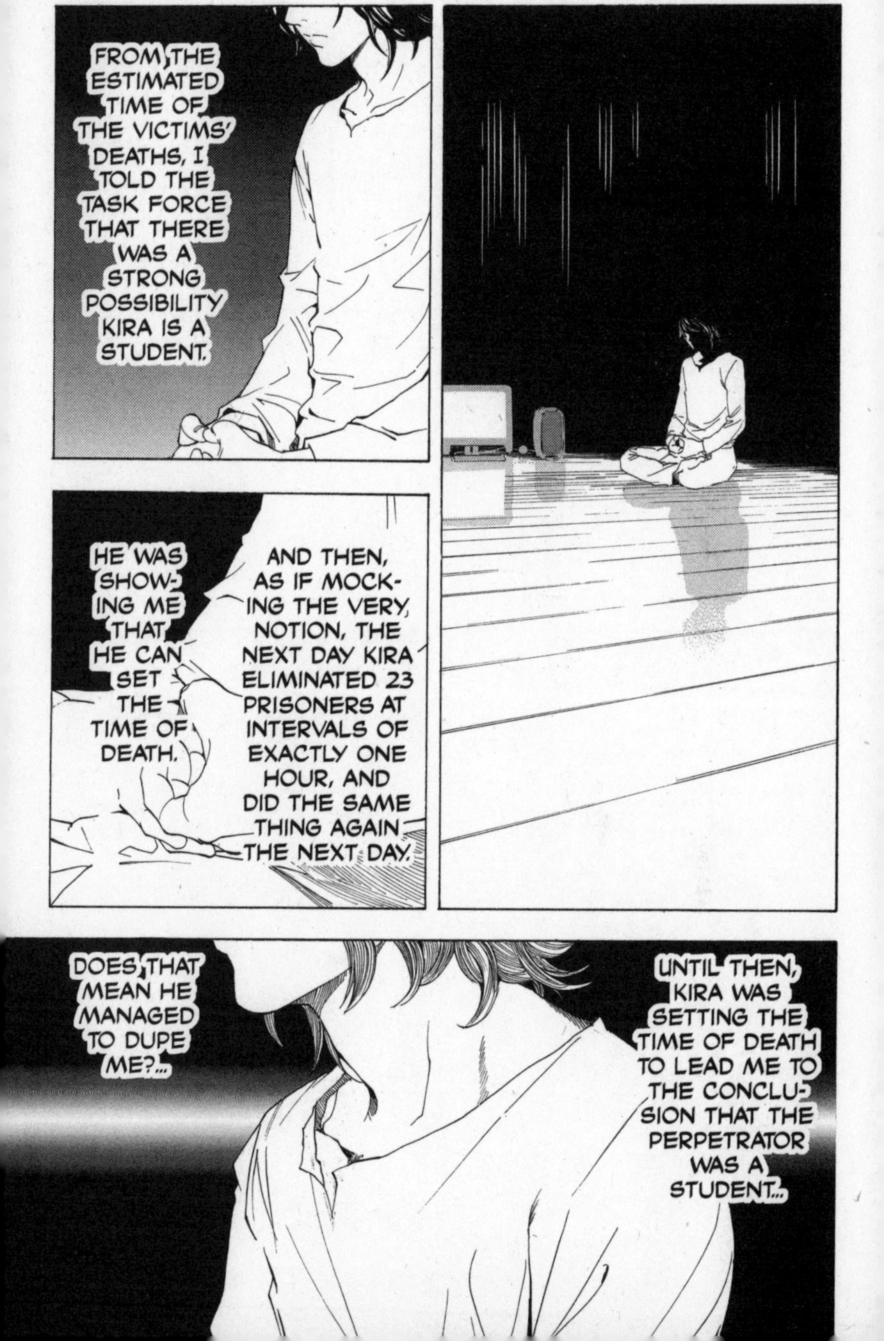
FROM THE ESTIMATED TIME OF THE VICTIMS' DEATHS, I TOLD THE TASK FORCE THAT THERE WAS A STRONG POSSIBILITY KIRA IS A STUDENT.
AND THEN, AS IF MOCKING THE VERY NOTION, THE NEXT DAY KIRA ELIMINATED 23 PRISONERS AT INTERVALS OF EXACTLY ONE HOUR, AND DID THE SAME THING AGAIN THE NEXT DAY.
HE WAS SHOWING ME THAT HE CAN SET THE TIME OF DEATH.
UNTIL THEN, KIRA WAS SETTING THE TIME OF DEATH TO LEAD ME TO THE CONCLUSION THAT THE PERPETRATOR WAS A STUDENT...
DOES THAT MEAN HE MANAGED TO DUPE ME?...

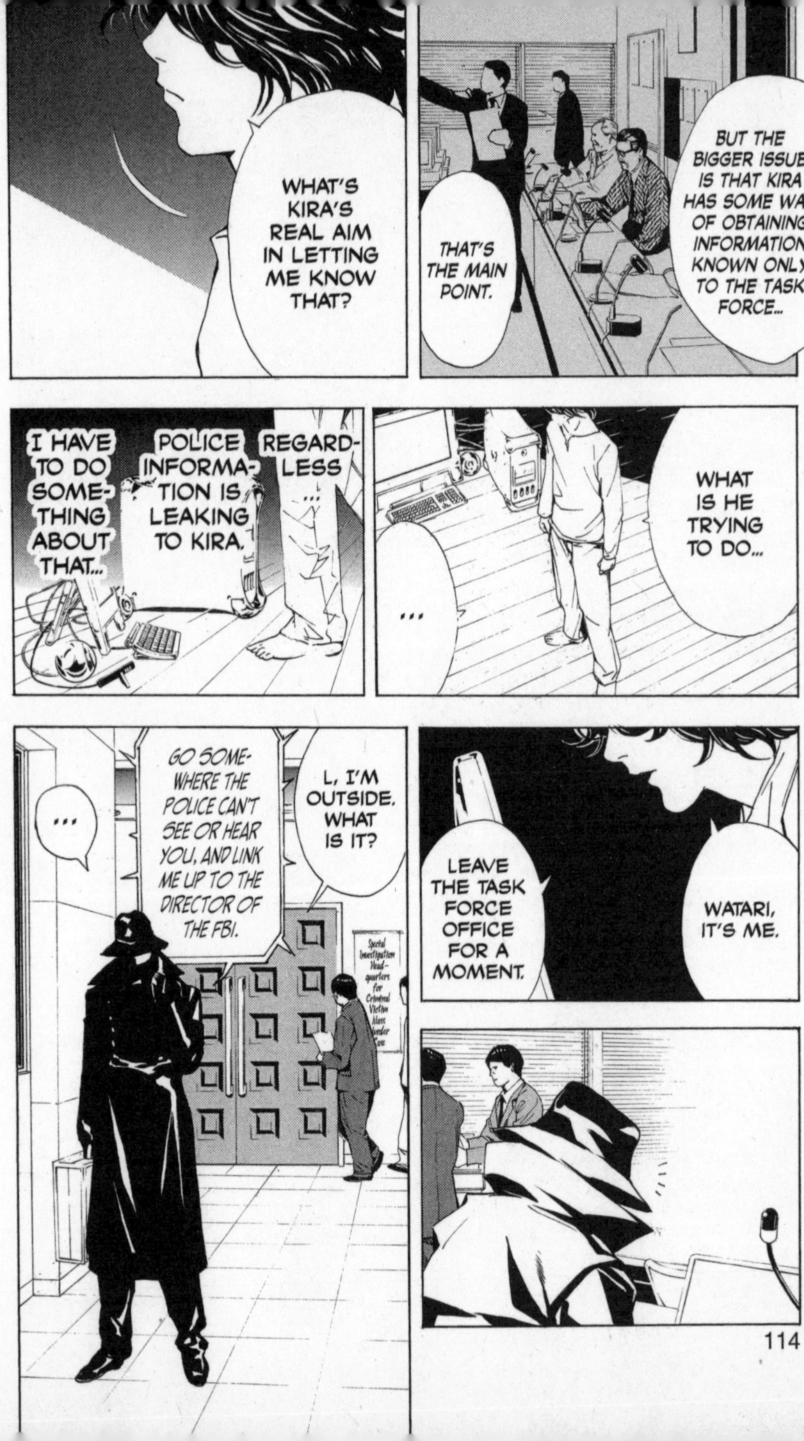
BUT THE BIGGER ISSUE IS THAT KIRA HAS SOME WAY OF OBTAINING INFORMATION KNOWN ONLY TO THE TASK FORCE...
THAT'S THE MAIN POINT.
WHAT'S KIRA'S REAL AIM IN LETTING ME KNOW THAT?
WHAT IS HE TRYING TO DO...
...
REGARDLESS...
POLICE INFORMATION IS LEAKING TO KIRA.
I HAVE TO DO SOMETHING ABOUT THAT...
WATARI, IT'S ME.
LEAVE THE TASK FORCE OFFICE FOR A MOMENT.
L, I'M OUTSIDE. WHAT IS IT?
GO SOMEWHERE THE POLICE CAN'T SEE OR HEAR YOU, AND LINK ME UP TO THE DIRECTOR OF THE FBI.
...

READ THIS WAY

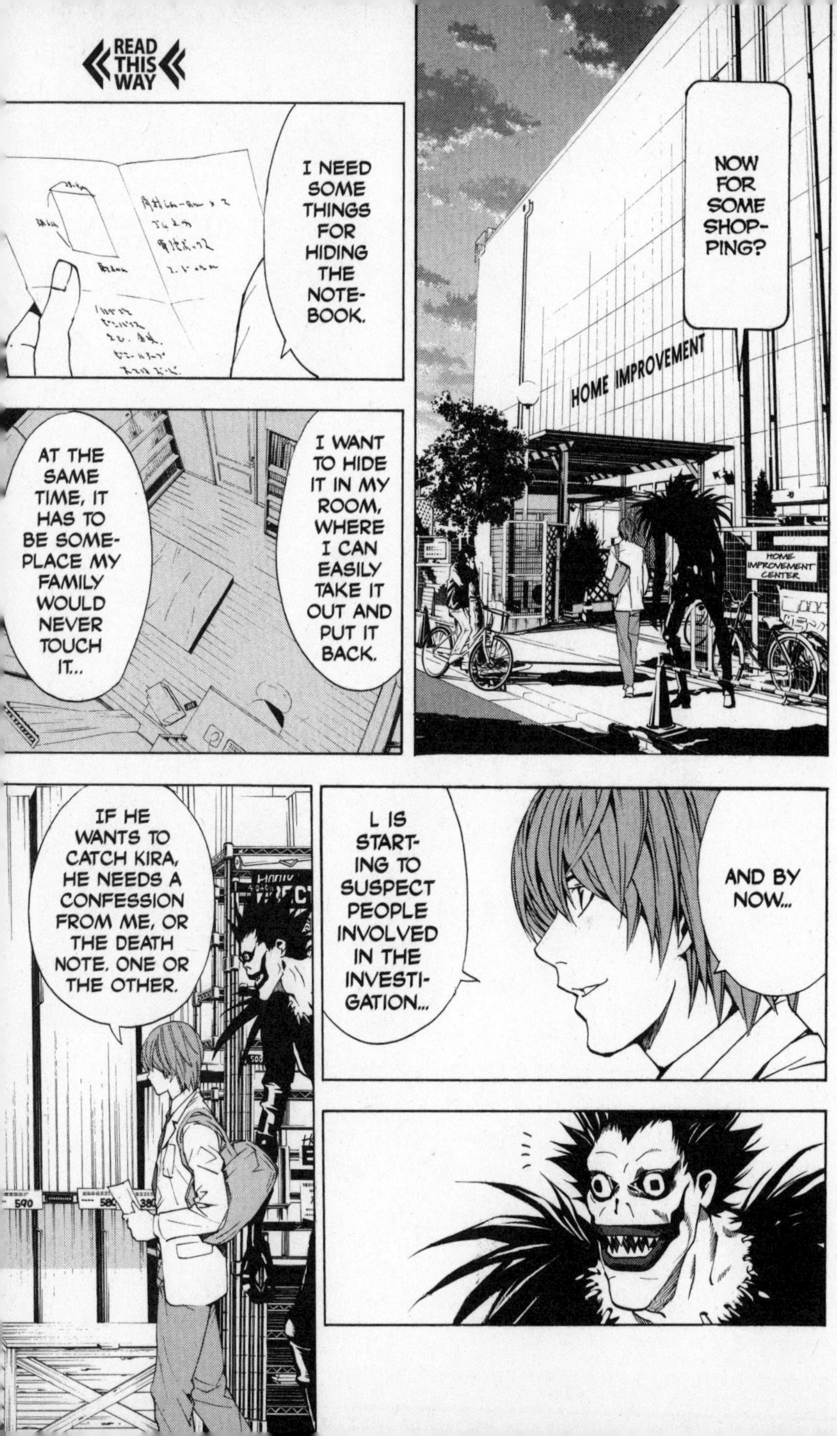

NOW FOR SOME SHOP-PING?
HOME IMPROVEMENT
HOME IMPROVEMENT CENTER
I NEED SOME THINGS FOR HIDING THE NOTE-BOOK.
I WANT TO HIDE IT IN MY ROOM, WHERE I CAN EASILY TAKE IT OUT AND PUT IT BACK.
AT THE SAME TIME, IT HAS TO BE SOME-PLACE MY FAMILY WOULD NEVER TOUCH IT...
AND BY NOW...
L IS START-ING TO SUSPECT PEOPLE INVOLVED IN THE INVESTI-GATION...
IF HE WANTS TO CATCH KIRA, HE NEEDS A CONFESSION FROM ME, OR THE DEATH NOTE. ONE OR THE OTHER.
590
580
380

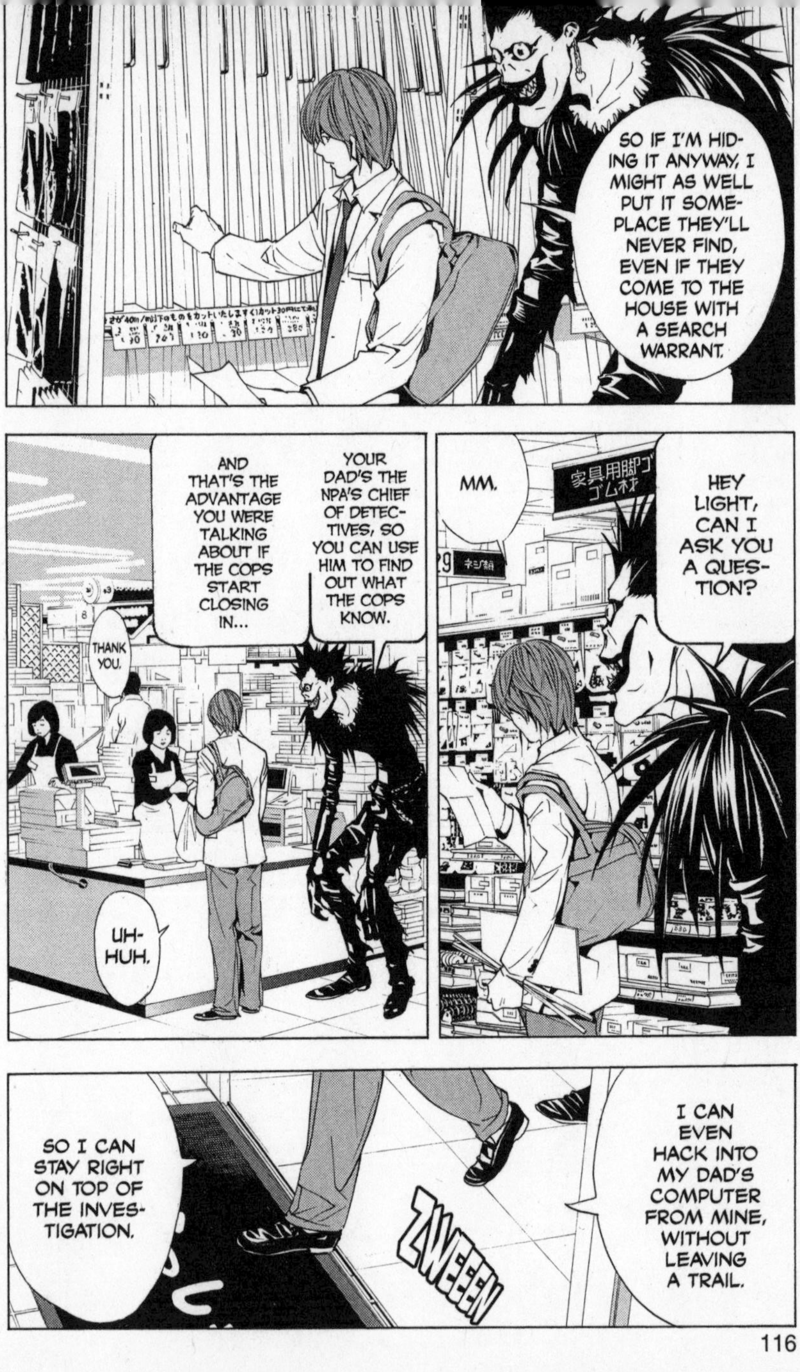
SO IF I'M HIDING IT ANYWAY, I MIGHT AS WELL PUT IT SOMEPLACE THEY'LL NEVER FIND, EVEN IF THEY COME TO THE HOUSE WITH A SEARCH WARRANT.
HEY LIGHT, CAN I ASK YOU A QUESTION?
家具用脚ゴ
ゴム材
MM.
YOUR DAD'S THE NPA'S CHIEF OF DETECTIVES, SO YOU CAN USE HIM TO FIND OUT WHAT THE COPS KNOW.
AND THAT'S THE ADVANTAGE YOU WERE TALKING ABOUT IF THE COPS START CLOSING IN...
THANK YOU.
UH-HUH.
I CAN EVEN HACK INTO MY DAD'S COMPUTER FROM MINE, WITHOUT LEAVING A TRAIL.
ZWEEEN
SO I CAN STAY RIGHT ON TOP OF THE INVESTIGATION.

READ THIS WAY

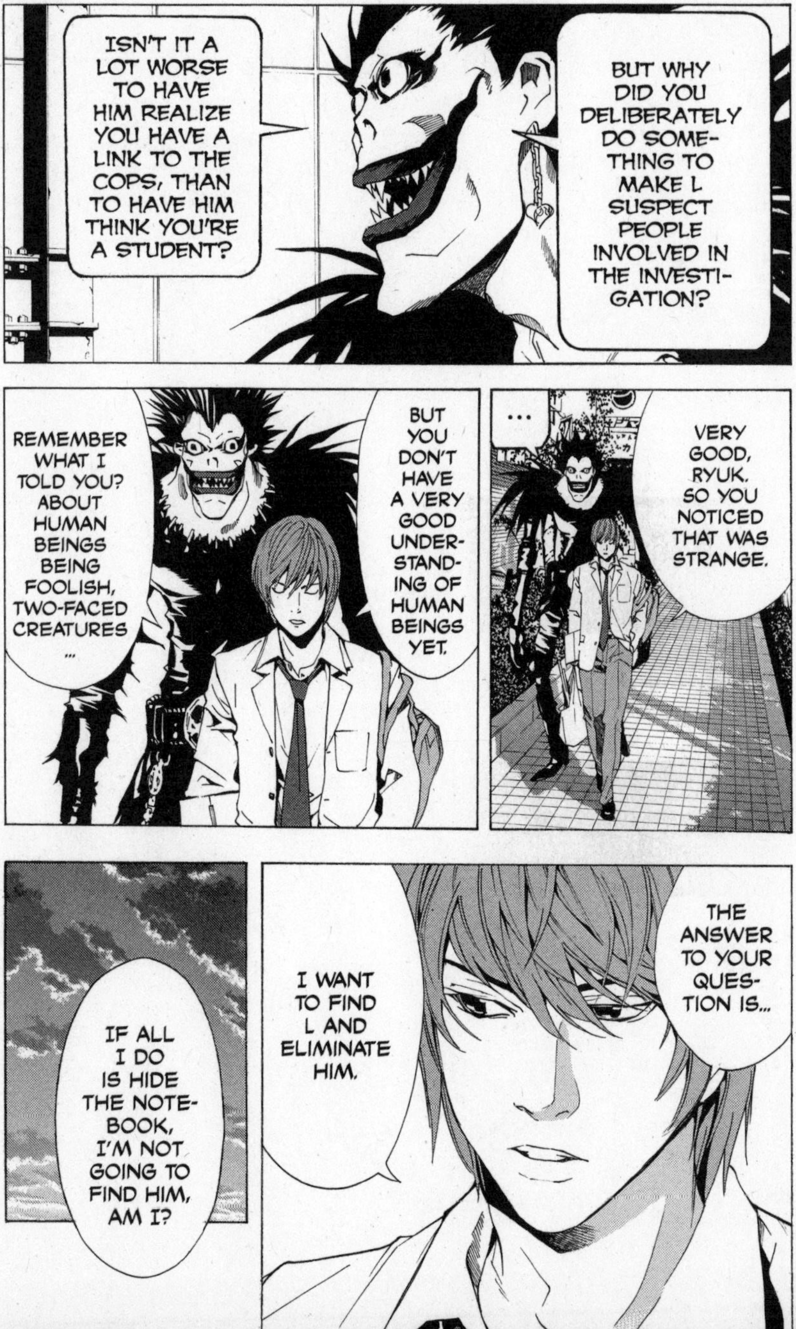
BUT WHY DID YOU DELIBERATELY DO SOMETHING TO MAKE L SUSPECT PEOPLE INVOLVED IN THE INVESTIGATION?
ISN'T IT A LOT WORSE TO HAVE HIM REALIZE YOU HAVE A LINK TO THE COPS, THAN TO HAVE HIM THINK YOU'RE A STUDENT?
VERY GOOD, RYUK. SO YOU NOTICED THAT WAS STRANGE.
...
BUT YOU DON'T HAVE A VERY GOOD UNDERSTANDING OF HUMAN BEINGS YET.
REMEMBER WHAT I TOLD YOU? ABOUT HUMAN BEINGS BEING FOOLISH, TWO-FACED CREATURES ...
THE ANSWER TO YOUR QUESTION IS...
I WANT TO FIND L AND ELIMINATE HIM.
IF ALL I DO IS HIDE THE NOTEBOOK, I'M NOT GOING TO FIND HIM, AM I?

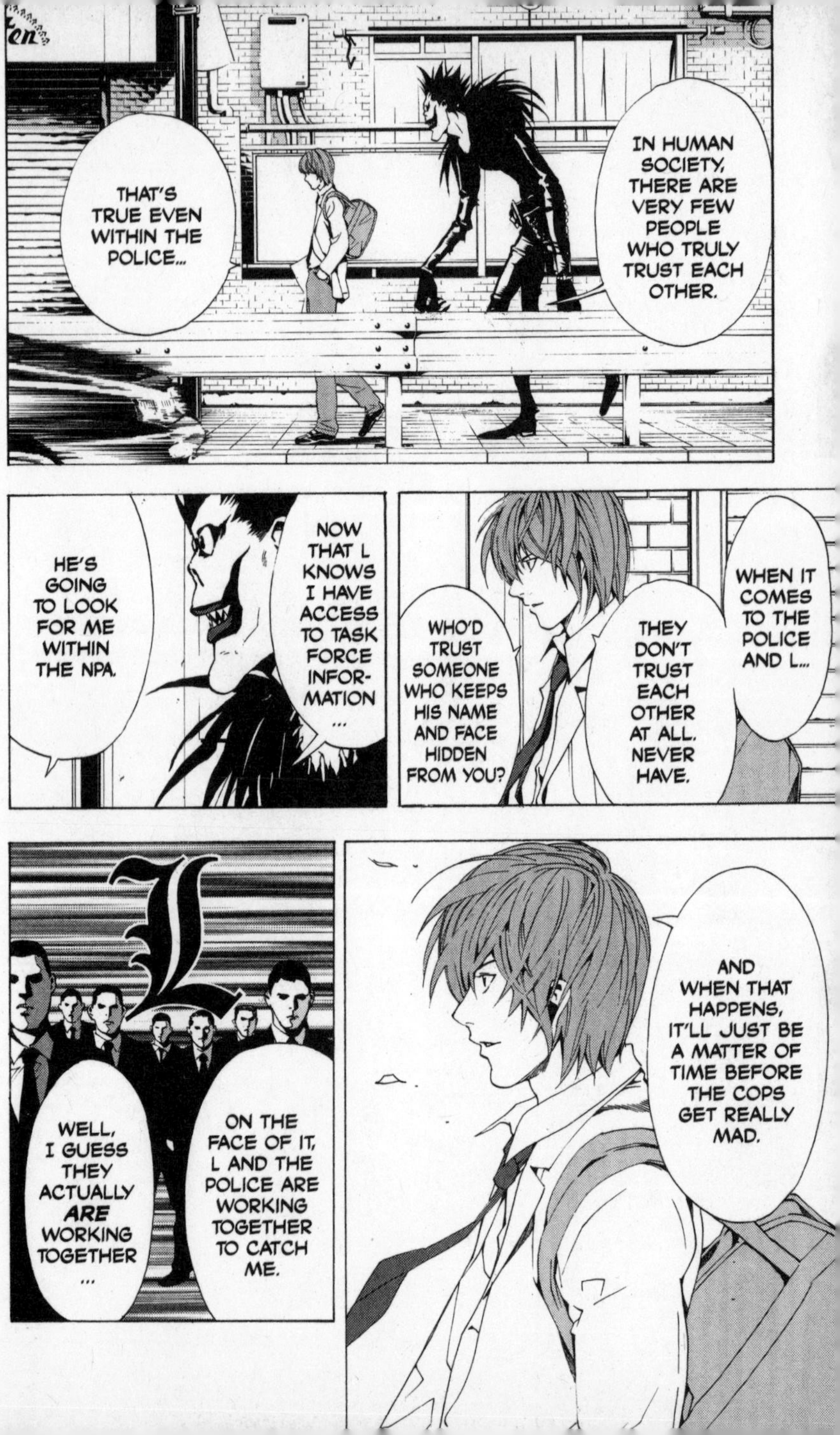
IN HUMAN SOCIETY, THERE ARE VERY FEW PEOPLE WHO TRULY TRUST EACH OTHER.
THAT'S TRUE EVEN WITHIN THE POLICE...
WHEN IT COMES TO THE POLICE AND L...
THEY DON'T TRUST EACH OTHER AT ALL. NEVER HAVE.
WHO'D TRUST SOMEONE WHO KEEPS HIS NAME AND FACE HIDDEN FROM YOU?
NOW THAT L KNOWS I HAVE ACCESS TO TASK FORCE INFOR-MATION...
HE'S GOING TO LOOK FOR ME WITHIN THE NPA.
AND WHEN THAT HAPPENS, IT'LL JUST BE A MATTER OF TIME BEFORE THE COPS GET REALLY MAD.
ON THE FACE OF IT, L AND THE POLICE ARE WORKING TOGETHER TO CATCH ME.
WELL, I GUESS THEY ACTUALLY *ARE* WORKING TOGETHER...

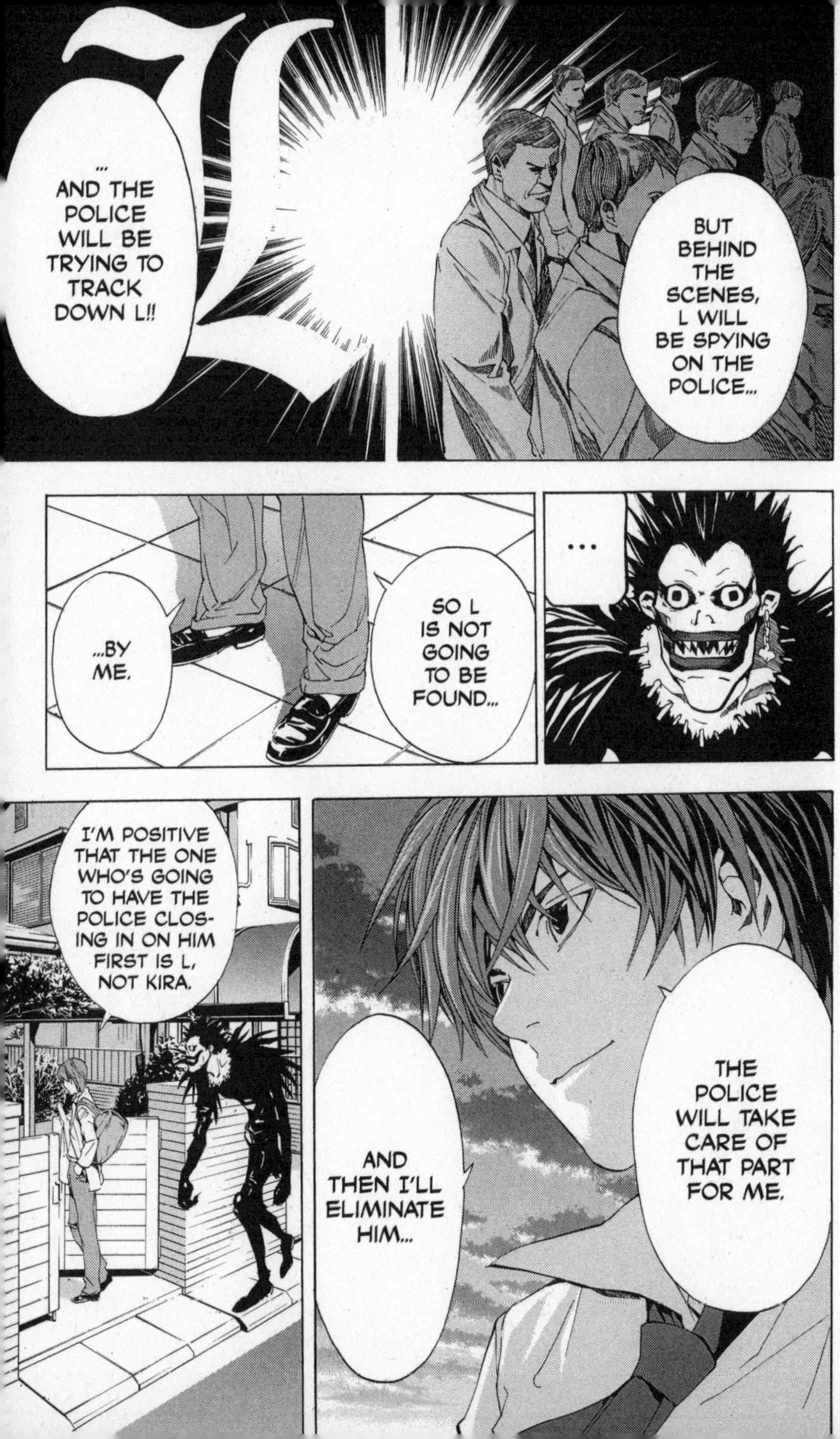
BUT BEHIND THE SCENES, L WILL BE SPYING ON THE POLICE...
... AND THE POLICE WILL BE TRYING TO TRACK DOWN L!!
...
SO L IS NOT GOING TO BE FOUND...
...BY ME.
THE POLICE WILL TAKE CARE OF THAT PART FOR ME.
AND THEN I'LL ELIMINATE HIM...
I'M POSITIVE THAT THE ONE WHO'S GOING TO HAVE THE POLICE CLOSING IN ON HIM FIRST IS L, NOT KIRA.

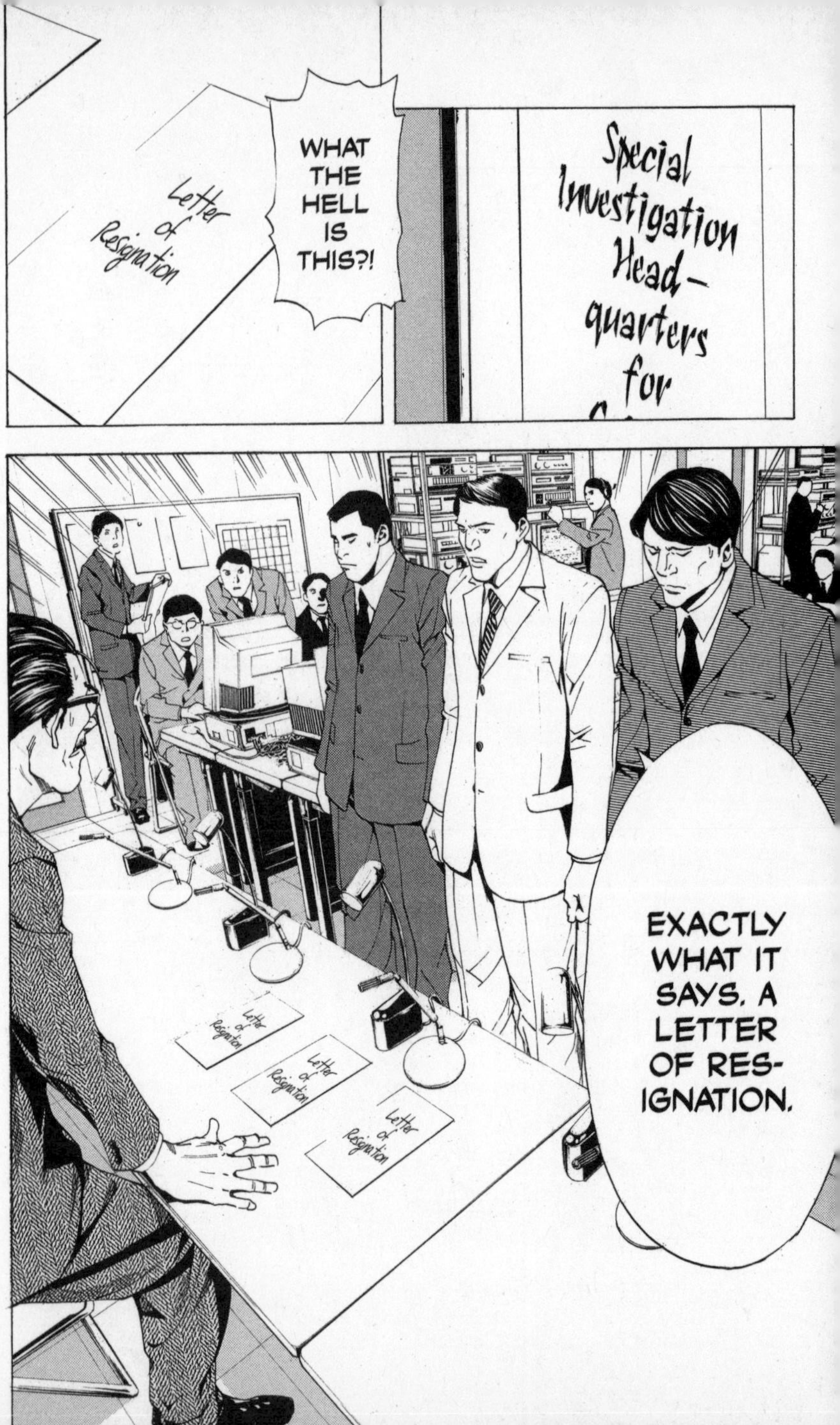
Special Investigation Head-quarters for
WHAT THE HELL IS THIS?!
Letter of Resignation
Letter of Resignation
Letter of Resignation
Letter of Resignation
EXACTLY WHAT IT SAYS. A LETTER OF RES-IGNATION.

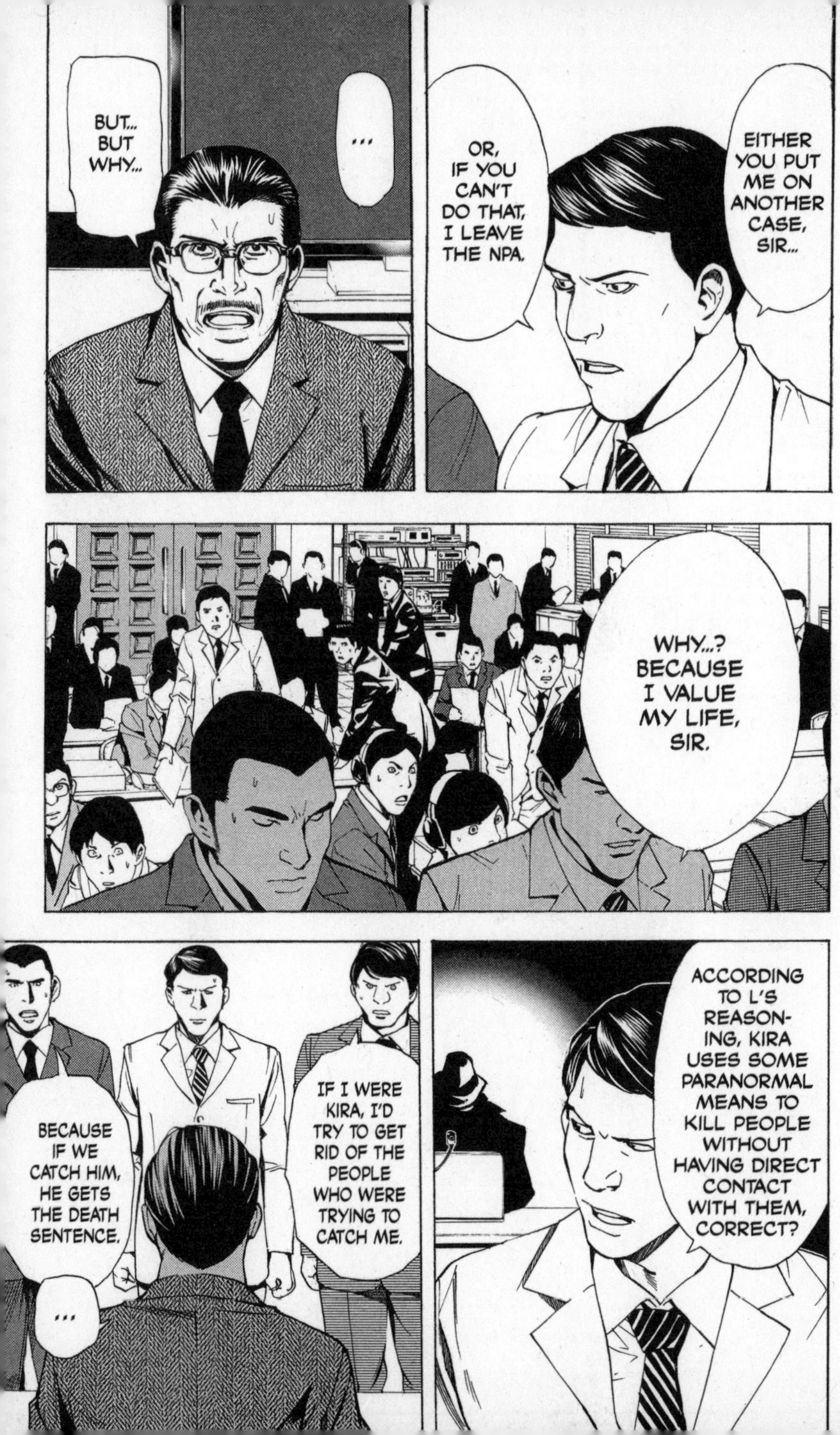
EITHER YOU PUT ME ON ANOTHER CASE, SIR...
OR, IF YOU CAN'T DO THAT, I LEAVE THE NPA.
...
BUT... BUT WHY...
WHY...? BECAUSE I VALUE MY LIFE, SIR.
ACCORDING TO L'S REASON-ING, KIRA USES SOME PARANORMAL MEANS TO KILL PEOPLE WITHOUT HAVING DIRECT CONTACT WITH THEM, CORRECT?
IF I WERE KIRA, I'D TRY TO GET RID OF THE PEOPLE WHO WERE TRYING TO CATCH ME.
BECAUSE IF WE CATCH HIM, HE GETS THE DEATH SENTENCE.
...

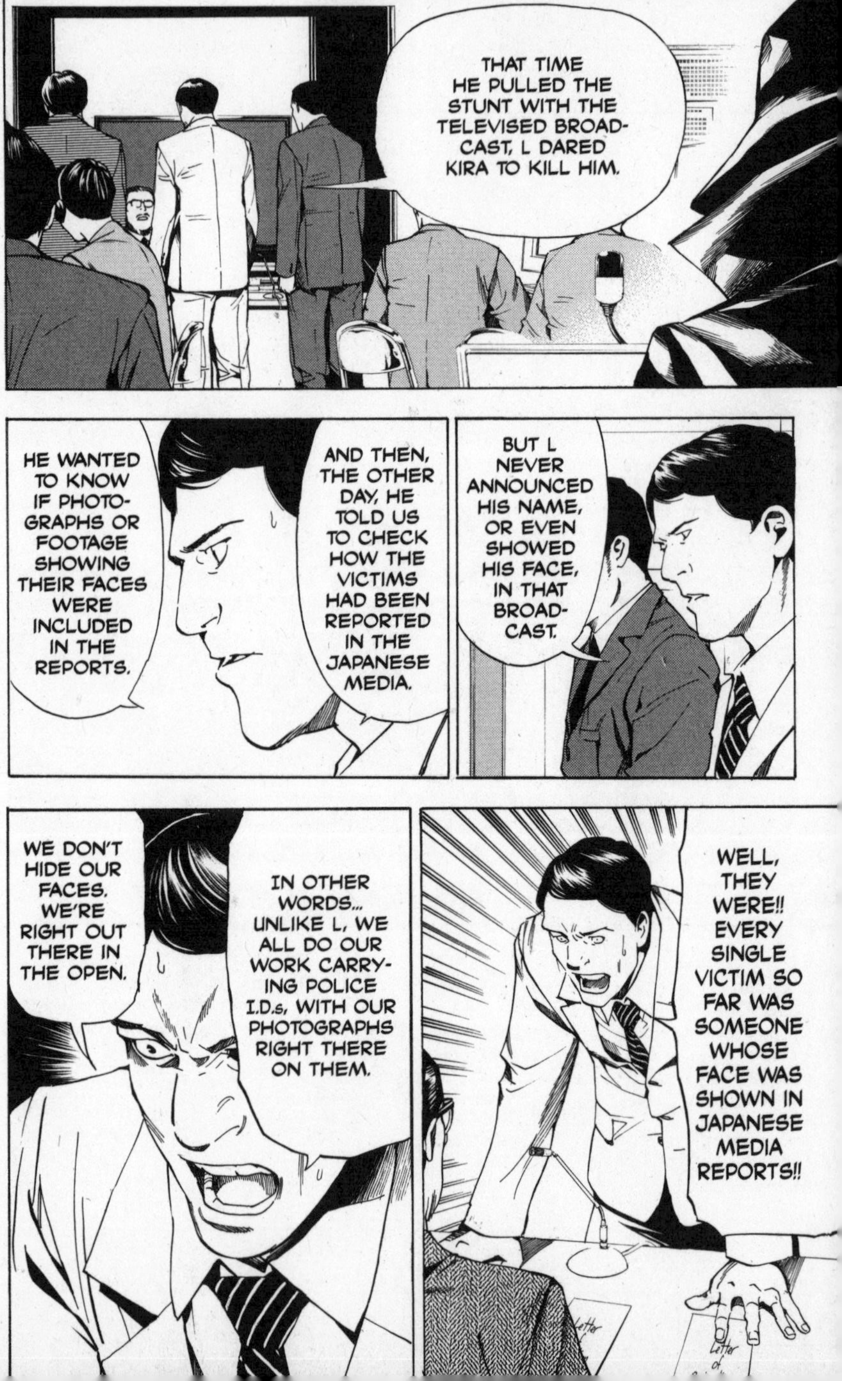
THAT TIME HE PULLED THE STUNT WITH THE TELEVISED BROAD-CAST, L DARED KIRA TO KILL HIM.
BUT L NEVER ANNOUNCED HIS NAME, OR EVEN SHOWED HIS FACE, IN THAT BROAD-CAST.
AND THEN, THE OTHER DAY, HE TOLD US TO CHECK HOW THE VICTIMS HAD BEEN REPORTED IN THE JAPANESE MEDIA.
HE WANTED TO KNOW IF PHOTO-GRAPHS OR FOOTAGE SHOWING THEIR FACES WERE INCLUDED IN THE REPORTS.
WELL, THEY WERE!! EVERY SINGLE VICTIM SO FAR WAS SOMEONE WHOSE FACE WAS SHOWN IN JAPANESE MEDIA REPORTS!!
IN OTHER WORDS... UNLIKE L, WE ALL DO OUR WORK CARRY-ING POLICE I.D.s, WITH OUR PHOTOGRAPHS RIGHT THERE ON THEM.
WE DON'T HIDE OUR FACES. WE'RE RIGHT OUT THERE IN THE OPEN.

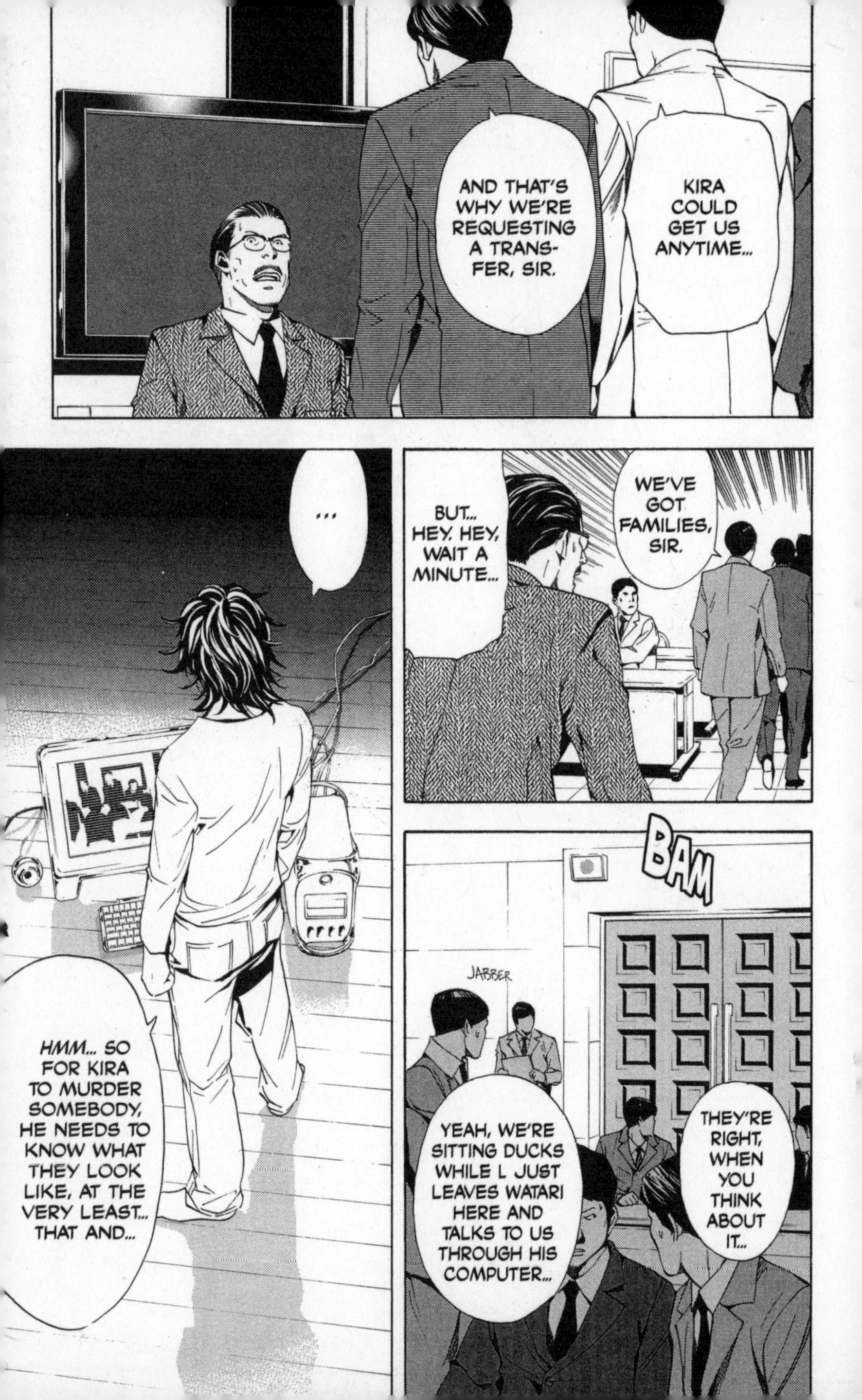
KIRA COULD GET US ANYTIME...
AND THAT'S WHY WE'RE REQUESTING A TRANSFER, SIR.
WE'VE GOT FAMILIES, SIR.
BUT... HEY. HEY, WAIT A MINUTE...
BAM
JABBER
THEY'RE RIGHT, WHEN YOU THINK ABOUT IT...
YEAH, WE'RE SITTING DUCKS WHILE L JUST LEAVES WATARI HERE AND TALKS TO US THROUGH HIS COMPUTER...
...
HMM... SO FOR KIRA TO MURDER SOMEBODY, HE NEEDS TO KNOW WHAT THEY LOOK LIKE, AT THE VERY LEAST... THAT AND...

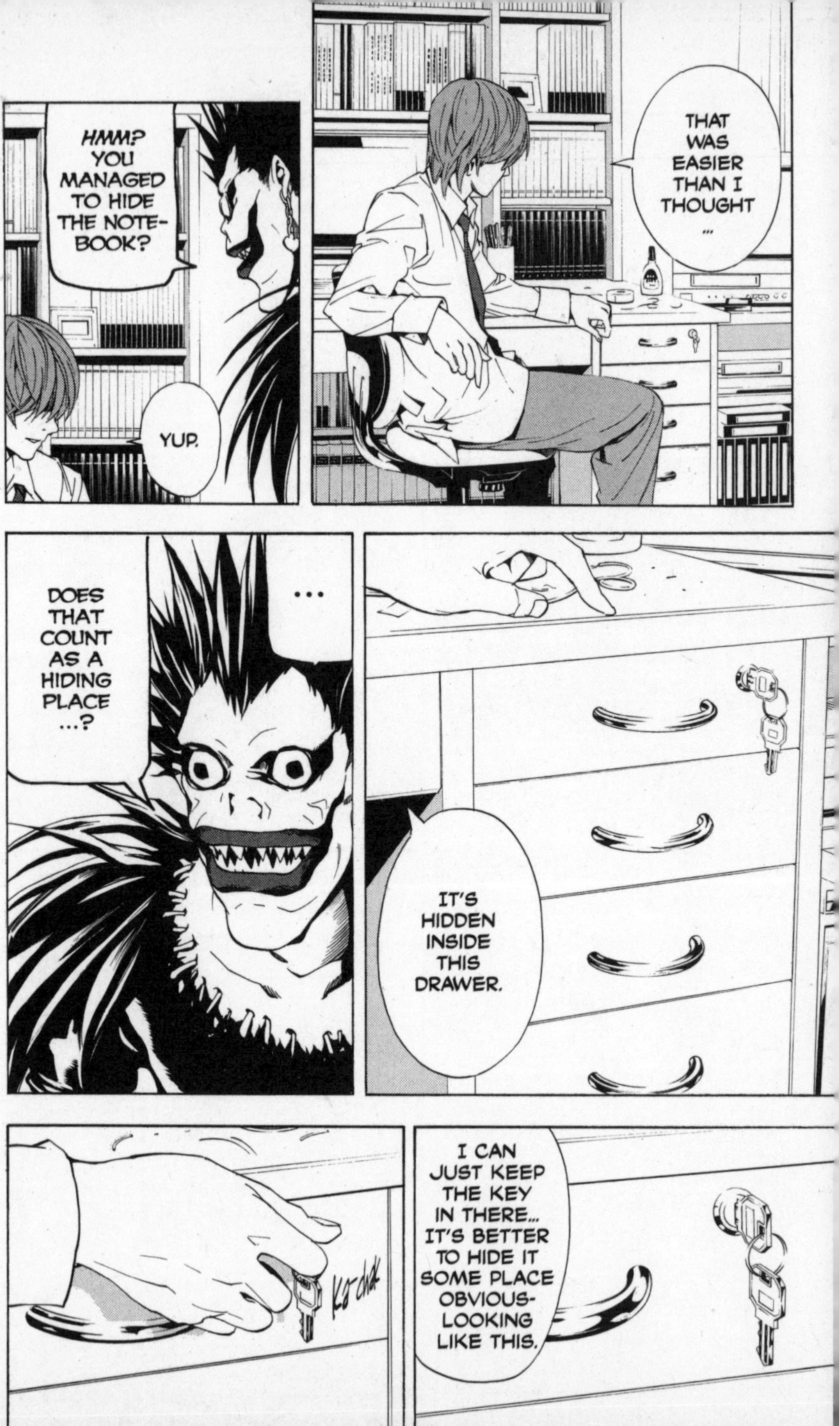
THAT WAS EASIER THAN I THOUGHT ...
HMM? YOU MANAGED TO HIDE THE NOTE-BOOK?
YUP.
IT'S HIDDEN INSIDE THIS DRAWER.
...
DOES THAT COUNT AS A HIDING PLACE ...?
I CAN JUST KEEP THE KEY IN THERE... IT'S BETTER TO HIDE IT SOME PLACE OBVIOUS-LOOKING LIKE THIS.
Ka-chak

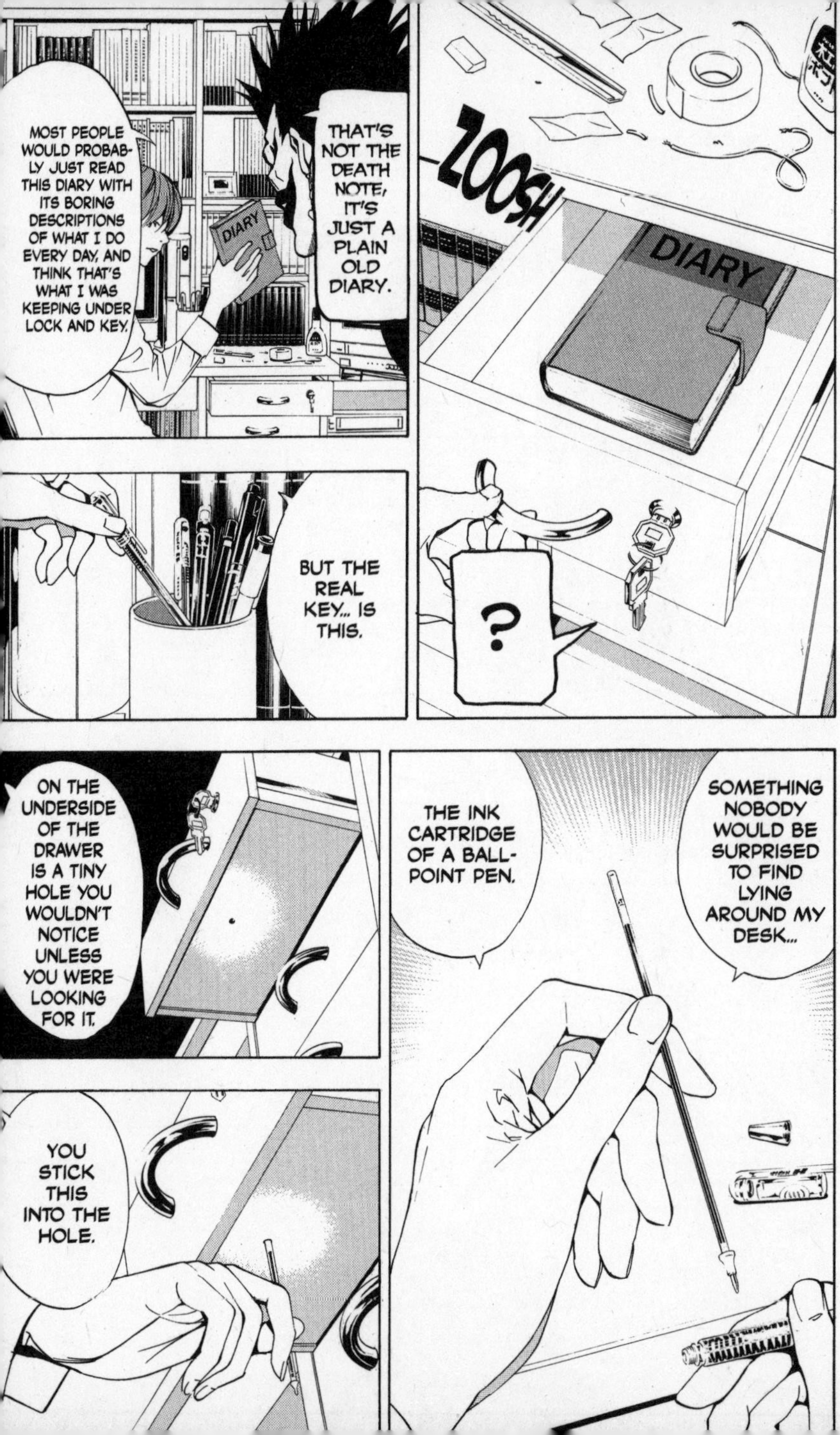
ZOOSH
DIARY
DIARY
THAT'S NOT THE DEATH NOTE, IT'S JUST A PLAIN OLD DIARY.
MOST PEOPLE WOULD PROBABLY JUST READ THIS DIARY WITH ITS BORING DESCRIPTIONS OF WHAT I DO EVERY DAY, AND THINK THAT'S WHAT I WAS KEEPING UNDER LOCK AND KEY.
?
BUT THE REAL KEY... IS THIS.
SOMETHING NOBODY WOULD BE SURPRISED TO FIND LYING AROUND MY DESK...
THE INK CARTRIDGE OF A BALL-POINT PEN.
ON THE UNDERSIDE OF THE DRAWER IS A TINY HOLE YOU WOULDN'T NOTICE UNLESS YOU WERE LOOKING FOR IT.
YOU STICK THIS INTO THE HOLE.

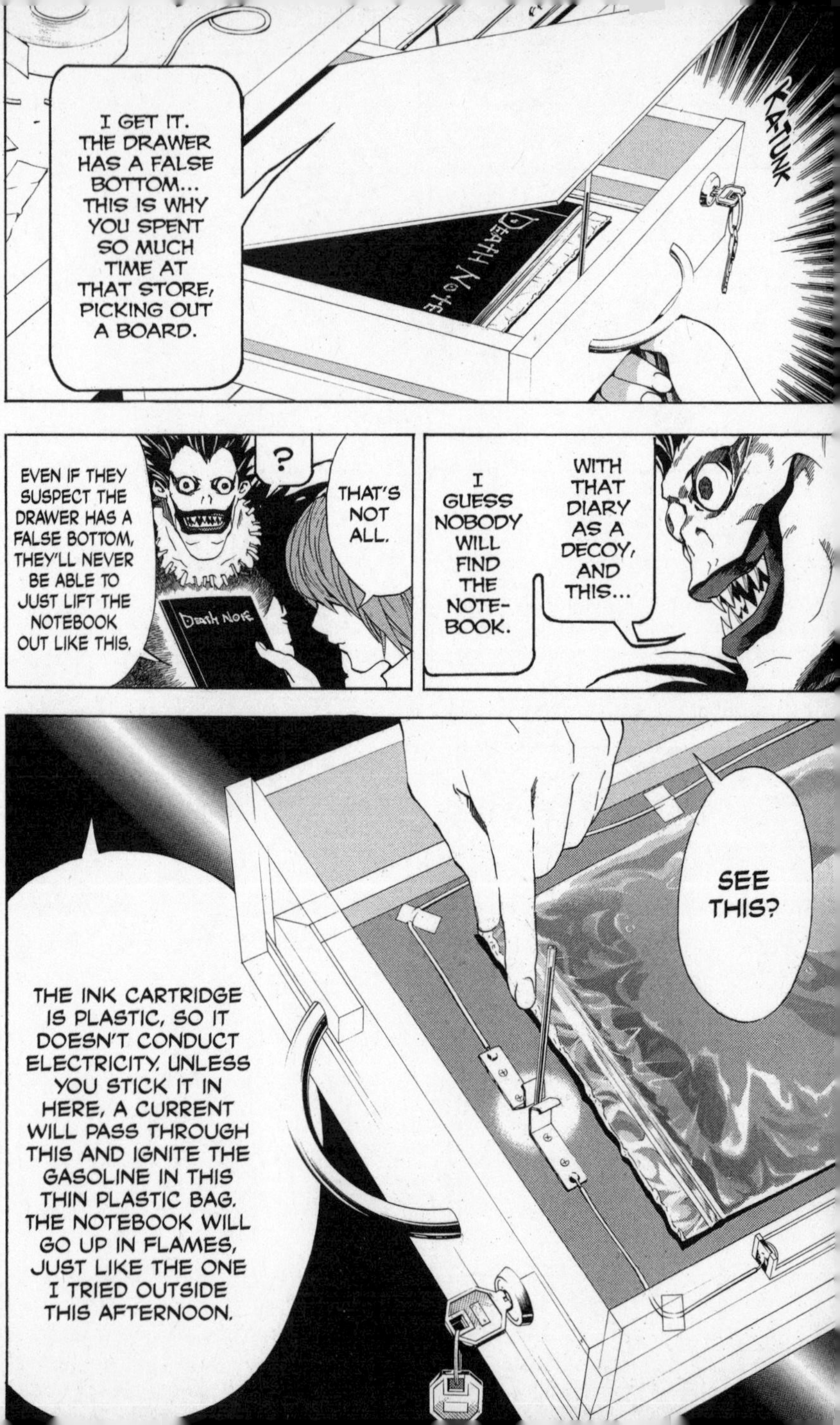
KATUNK
I GET IT. THE DRAWER HAS A FALSE BOTTOM... THIS IS WHY YOU SPENT SO MUCH TIME AT THAT STORE, PICKING OUT A BOARD.
DEATH NOTE
WITH THAT DIARY AS A DECOY, AND THIS...
I GUESS NOBODY WILL FIND THE NOTE-BOOK.
?
THAT'S NOT ALL.
EVEN IF THEY SUSPECT THE DRAWER HAS A FALSE BOTTOM, THEY'LL NEVER BE ABLE TO JUST LIFT THE NOTEBOOK OUT LIKE THIS.
DEATH NOTE
SEE THIS?
THE INK CARTRIDGE IS PLASTIC, SO IT DOESN'T CONDUCT ELECTRICITY. UNLESS YOU STICK IT IN HERE, A CURRENT WILL PASS THROUGH THIS AND IGNITE THE GASOLINE IN THIS THIN PLASTIC BAG. THE NOTEBOOK WILL GO UP IN FLAMES, JUST LIKE THE ONE I TRIED OUTSIDE THIS AFTERNOON.

READ THIS WAY

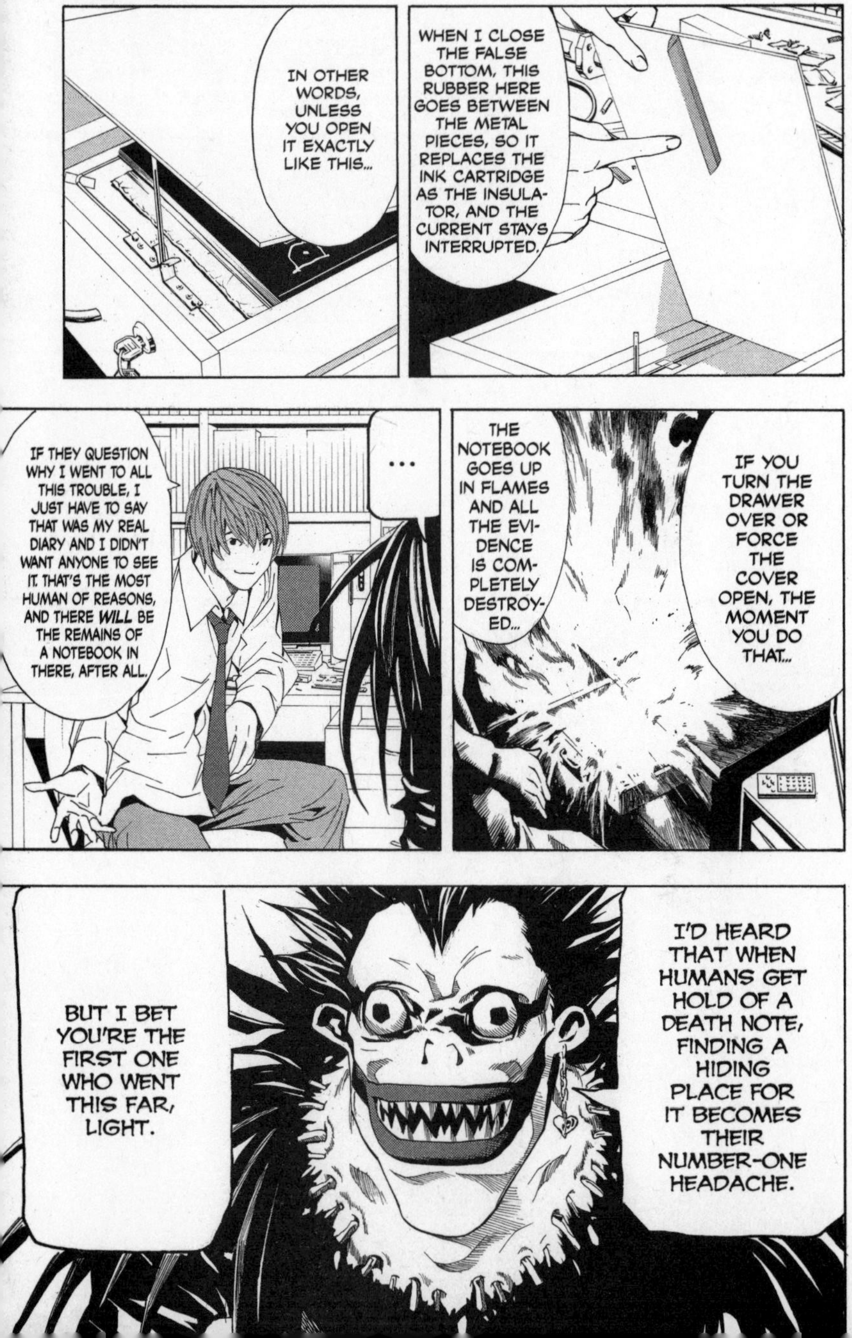
WHEN I CLOSE THE FALSE BOTTOM, THIS RUBBER HERE GOES BETWEEN THE METAL PIECES, SO IT REPLACES THE INK CARTRIDGE AS THE INSULATOR, AND THE CURRENT STAYS INTERRUPTED.
IN OTHER WORDS, UNLESS YOU OPEN IT EXACTLY LIKE THIS...
IF YOU TURN THE DRAWER OVER OR FORCE THE COVER OPEN, THE MOMENT YOU DO THAT...
THE NOTEBOOK GOES UP IN FLAMES AND ALL THE EVIDENCE IS COMPLETELY DESTROYED...
...
IF THEY QUESTION WHY I WENT TO ALL THIS TROUBLE, I JUST HAVE TO SAY THAT WAS MY REAL DIARY AND I DIDN'T WANT ANYONE TO SEE IT. THAT'S THE MOST HUMAN OF REASONS, AND THERE *WILL* BE THE REMAINS OF A NOTEBOOK IN THERE, AFTER ALL.
I'D HEARD THAT WHEN HUMANS GET HOLD OF A DEATH NOTE, FINDING A HIDING PLACE FOR IT BECOMES THEIR NUMBER-ONE HEADACHE.
BUT I BET YOU'RE THE FIRST ONE WHO WENT THIS FAR, LIGHT.

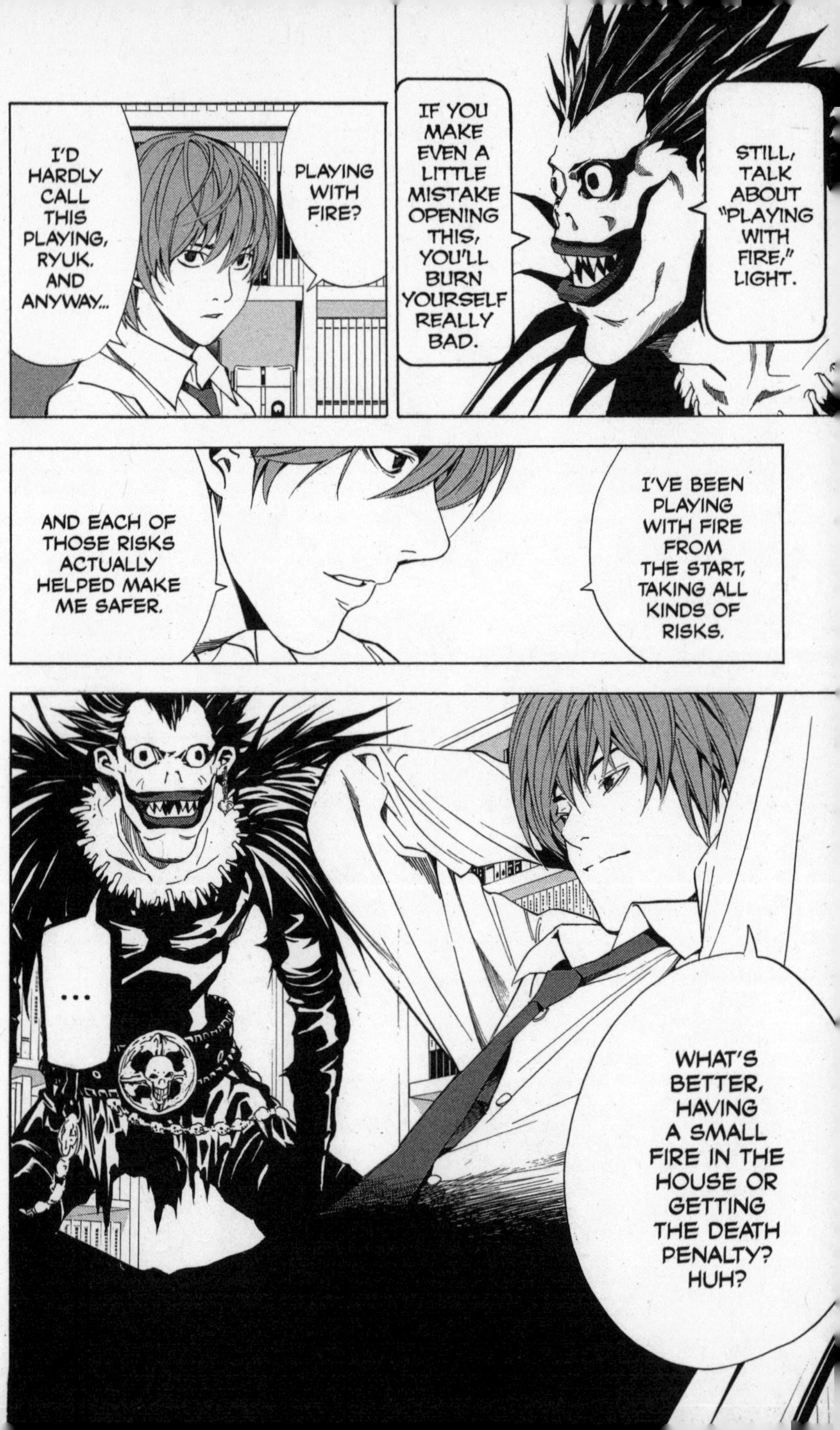
STILL, TALK ABOUT "PLAYING WITH FIRE," LIGHT.
IF YOU MAKE EVEN A LITTLE MISTAKE OPENING THIS, YOU'LL BURN YOURSELF REALLY BAD.
PLAYING WITH FIRE?
I'D HARDLY CALL THIS PLAYING, RYUK. AND ANYWAY...
I'VE BEEN PLAYING WITH FIRE FROM THE START, TAKING ALL KINDS OF RISKS.
AND EACH OF THOSE RISKS ACTUALLY HELPED MAKE ME SAFER.
WHAT'S BETTER, HAVING A SMALL FIRE IN THE HOUSE OR GETTING THE DEATH PENALTY? HUH?
...

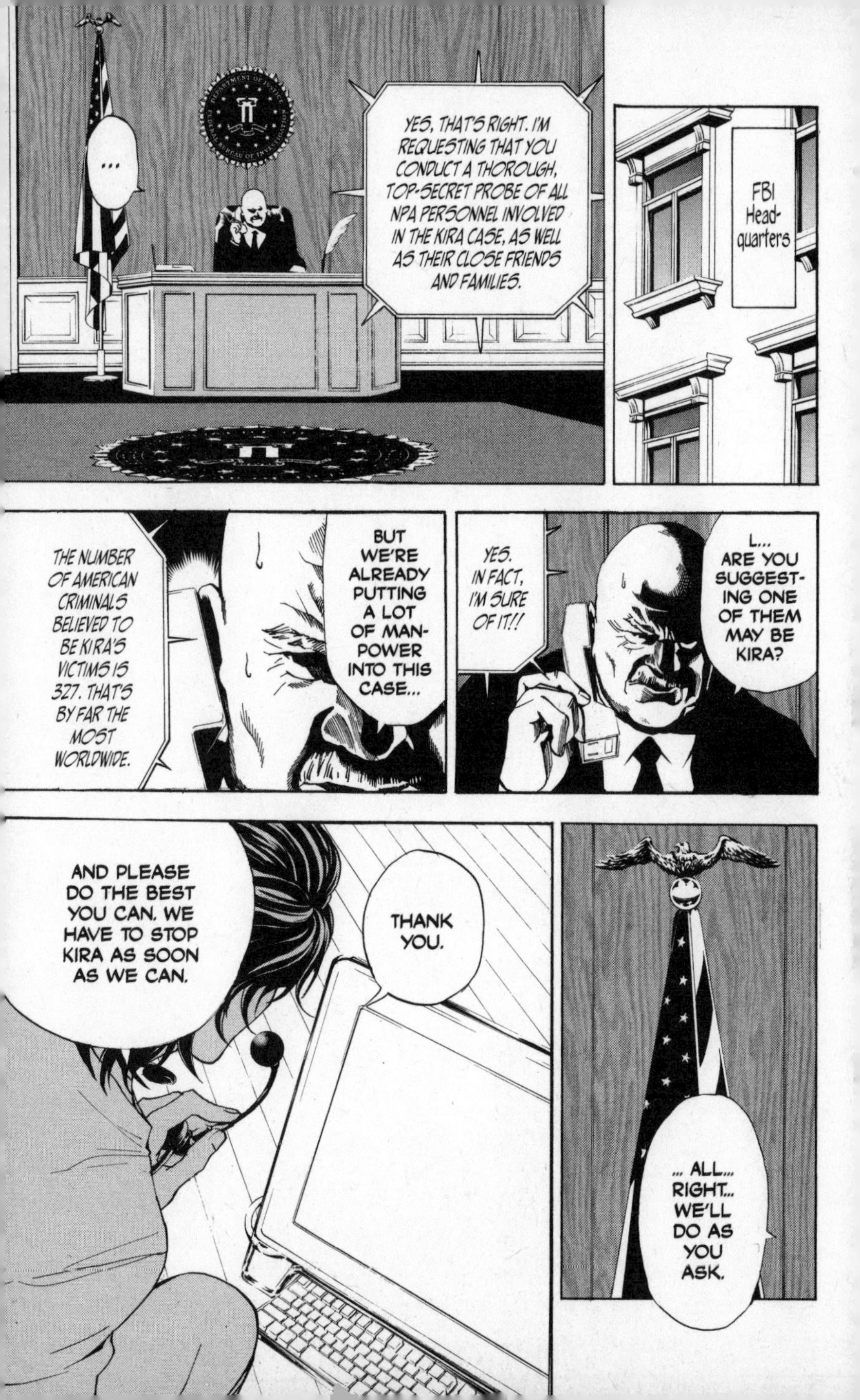
FBI Headquarters
YES, THAT'S RIGHT. I'M REQUESTING THAT YOU CONDUCT A THOROUGH, TOP-SECRET PROBE OF ALL NPA PERSONNEL INVOLVED IN THE KIRA CASE, AS WELL AS THEIR CLOSE FRIENDS AND FAMILIES.
...
L... ARE YOU SUGGESTING ONE OF THEM MAY BE KIRA?
YES. IN FACT, I'M SURE OF IT!!
BUT WE'RE ALREADY PUTTING A LOT OF MANPOWER INTO THIS CASE...
THE NUMBER OF AMERICAN CRIMINALS BELIEVED TO BE KIRA'S VICTIMS IS 327. THAT'S BY FAR THE MOST WORLDWIDE.
... ALL... RIGHT... WE'LL DO AS YOU ASK.
THANK YOU.
AND PLEASE DO THE BEST YOU CAN. WE HAVE TO STOP KIRA AS SOON AS WE CAN.

DEATH NOTE
How to use it
IV

- The person in possession of the DEATH NOTE is possessed by a god of death, its original owner, until they die.

  デスノートを持っている限り、自分が死ぬまで元持ち主である死神が憑いてまわる。

- If a human uses the note, a god of death usually appears in front of him/her within 39 days after he/she uses the note.

  死神は通常、人間がノートを使った39日以内に使った者の前に姿を現す。

- Gods of death, the original owners of the DEATH NOTE, do not do, in principle, anything which will help or prevent the deaths in the note.

  デスノートの元持ち主である死神は、そのノートでの死の手伝いや妨げになる行為は基本的にはしない。

- A god of death has no obligation to completely explain how to use the note or rules which will apply to the human who owns it.

  デスノートの使い方や、それを持つ人間に発生する掟を死神が全て説明する義務はない。

chapter 5 Eyeballs

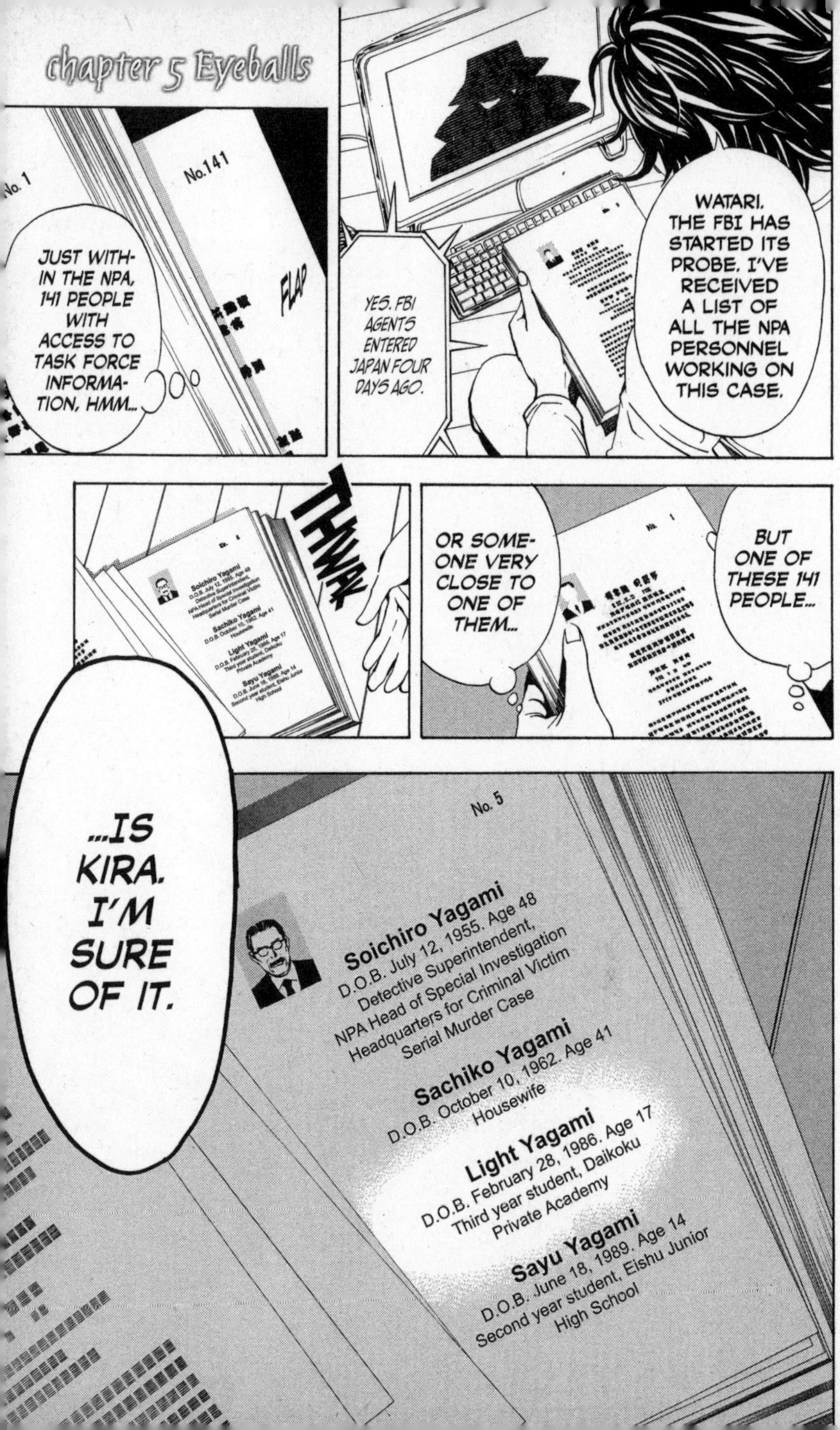
WATARI. THE FBI HAS STARTED ITS PROBE. I'VE RECEIVED A LIST OF ALL THE NPA PERSONNEL WORKING ON THIS CASE.
YES. FBI AGENTS ENTERED JAPAN FOUR DAYS AGO.
No.141
No. 1
FLAP
JUST WITHIN THE NPA, 141 PEOPLE WITH ACCESS TO TASK FORCE INFORMATION, HMM...
BUT ONE OF THESE 141 PEOPLE...
OR SOMEONE VERY CLOSE TO ONE OF THEM...
THWAK
...IS KIRA. I'M SURE OF IT.
No. 5
Soichiro Yagami
D.O.B. July 12, 1955. Age 48
Detective Superintendent,
NPA Head of Special Investigation
Headquarters for Criminal Victim
Serial Murder Case
Sachiko Yagami
D.O.B. October 10, 1962. Age 41
Housewife
Light Yagami
D.O.B. February 28, 1986. Age 17
Third year student, Daikoku
Private Academy
Sayu Yagami
D.O.B. June 18, 1989. Age 14
Second year student, Eishu Junior
High School

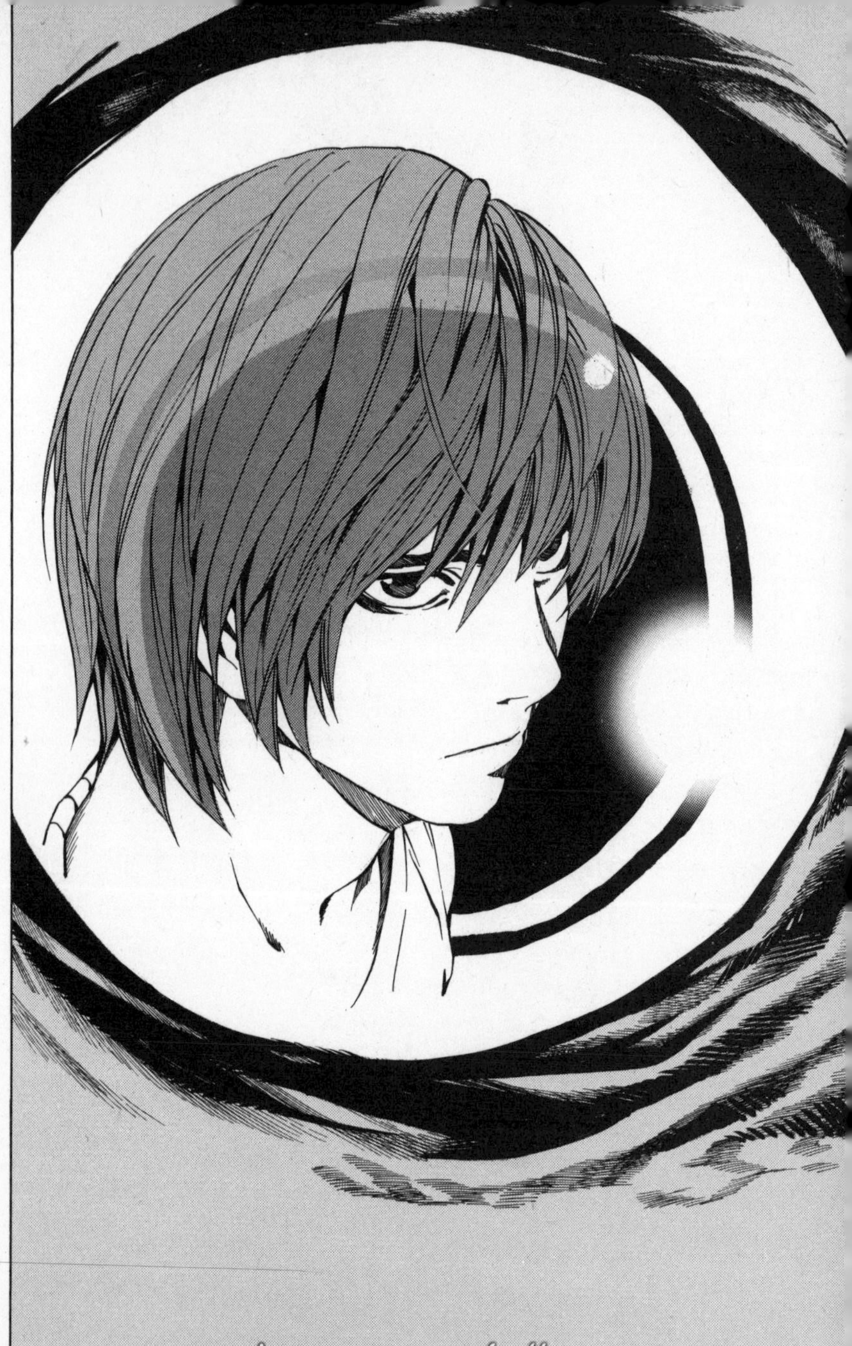

chapter 5 Eyeballs

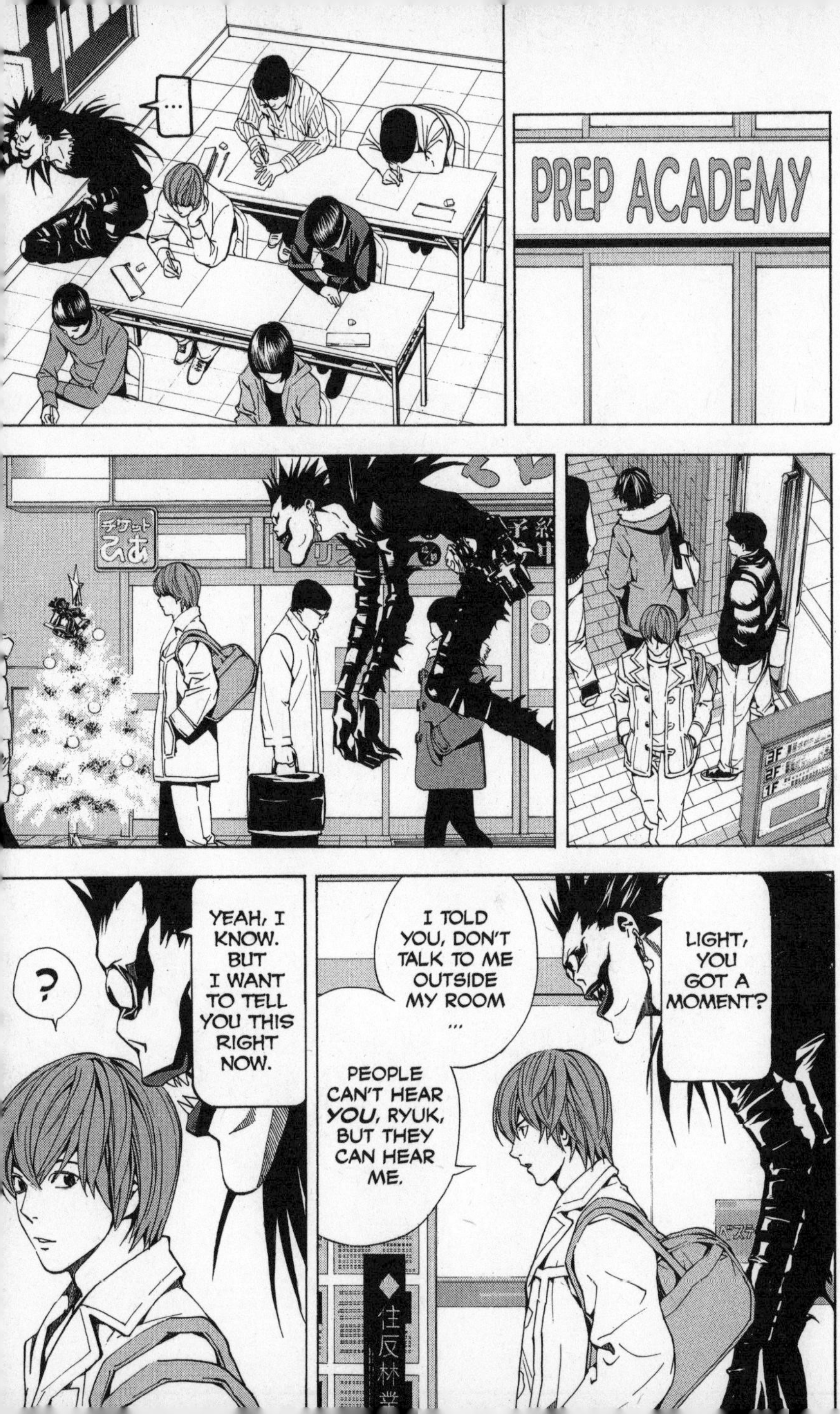
PREP ACADEMY
…
LIGHT, YOU GOT A MOMENT?
I TOLD YOU, DON'T TALK TO ME OUTSIDE MY ROOM …
PEOPLE CAN'T HEAR *YOU*, RYUK, BUT THEY CAN HEAR ME.
YEAH, I KNOW. BUT I WANT TO TELL YOU THIS RIGHT NOW.
?

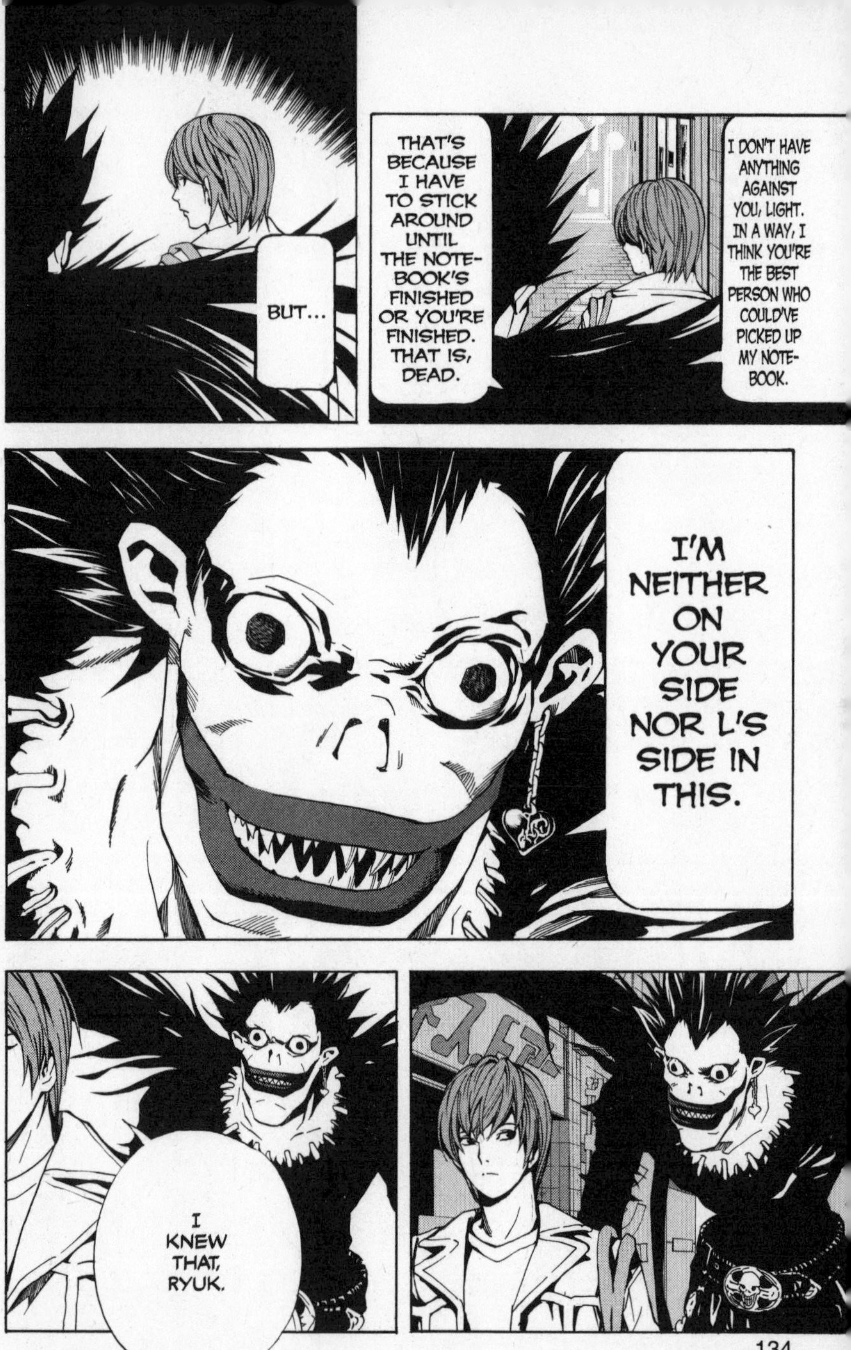
I DON'T HAVE ANYTHING AGAINST YOU, LIGHT. IN A WAY, I THINK YOU'RE THE BEST PERSON WHO COULD'VE PICKED UP MY NOTE-BOOK.
THAT'S BECAUSE I HAVE TO STICK AROUND UNTIL THE NOTE-BOOK'S FINISHED OR YOU'RE FINISHED. THAT IS, DEAD.
BUT...
I'M NEITHER ON YOUR SIDE NOR L'S SIDE IN THIS.
I KNEW THAT, RYUK.

READ THIS WAY

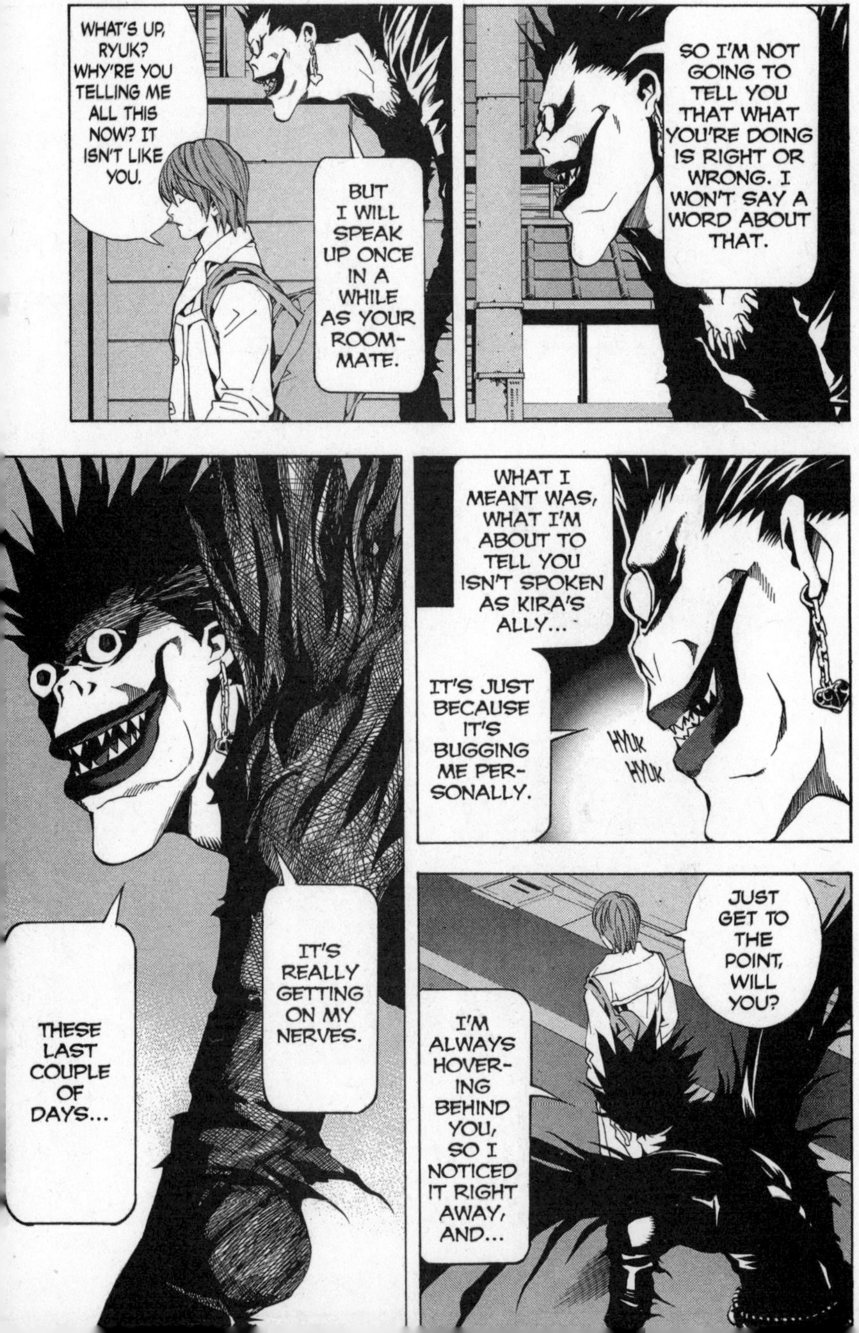
SO I'M NOT GOING TO TELL YOU THAT WHAT YOU'RE DOING IS RIGHT OR WRONG. I WON'T SAY A WORD ABOUT THAT.
BUT I WILL SPEAK UP ONCE IN A WHILE AS YOUR ROOM-MATE.
WHAT'S UP, RYUK? WHY'RE YOU TELLING ME ALL THIS NOW? IT ISN'T LIKE YOU.
WHAT I MEANT WAS, WHAT I'M ABOUT TO TELL YOU ISN'T SPOKEN AS KIRA'S ALLY...
HYUK HYUK
IT'S JUST BECAUSE IT'S BUGGING ME PER-SONALLY.
JUST GET TO THE POINT, WILL YOU?
I'M ALWAYS HOVER-ING BEHIND YOU, SO I NOTICED IT RIGHT AWAY, AND...
IT'S REALLY GETTING ON MY NERVES.
THESE LAST COUPLE OF DAYS...

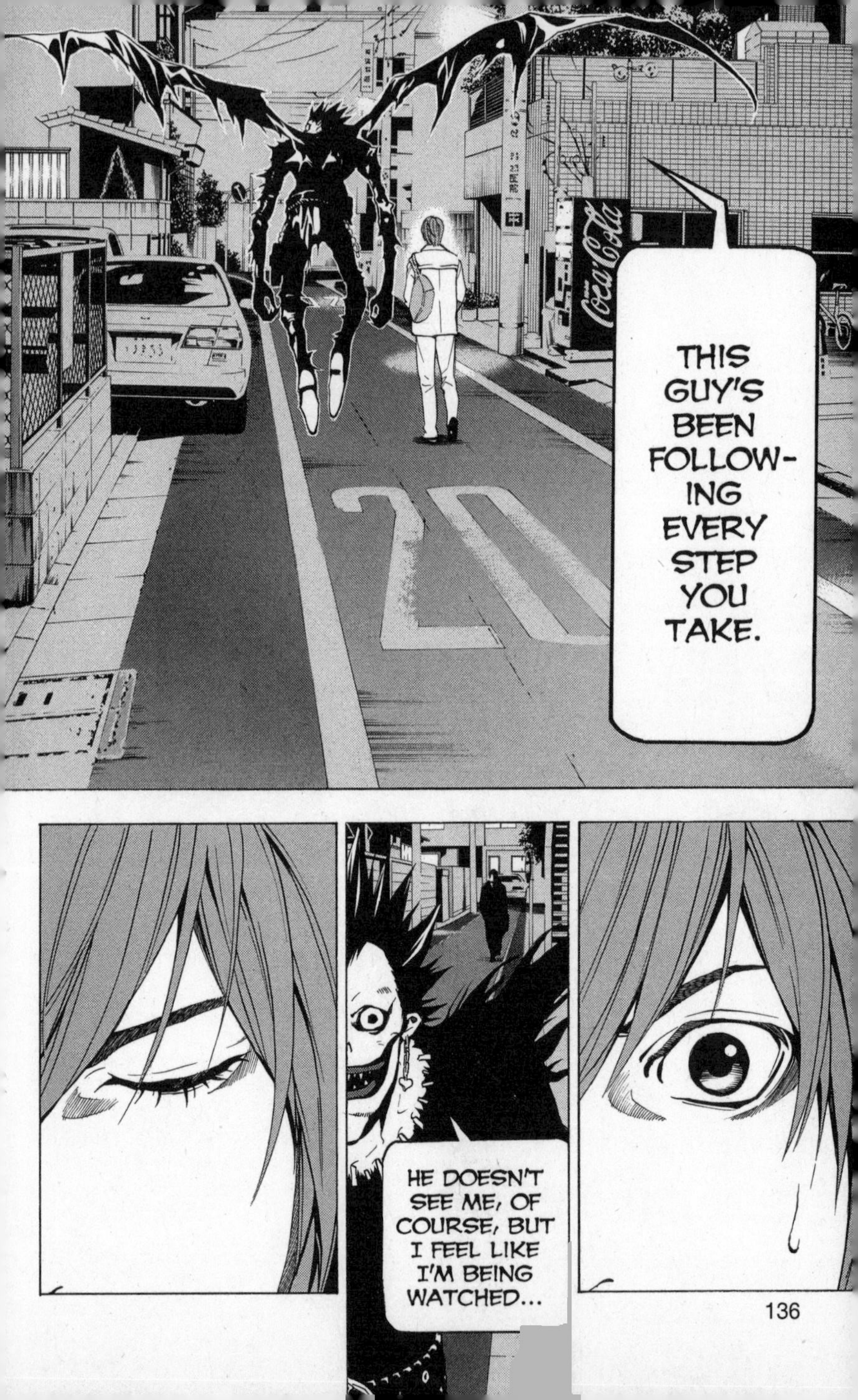
Coca-Cola
THIS GUY'S BEEN FOLLOWING EVERY STEP YOU TAKE.
HE DOESN'T SEE ME, OF COURSE, BUT I FEEL LIKE I'M BEING WATCHED...

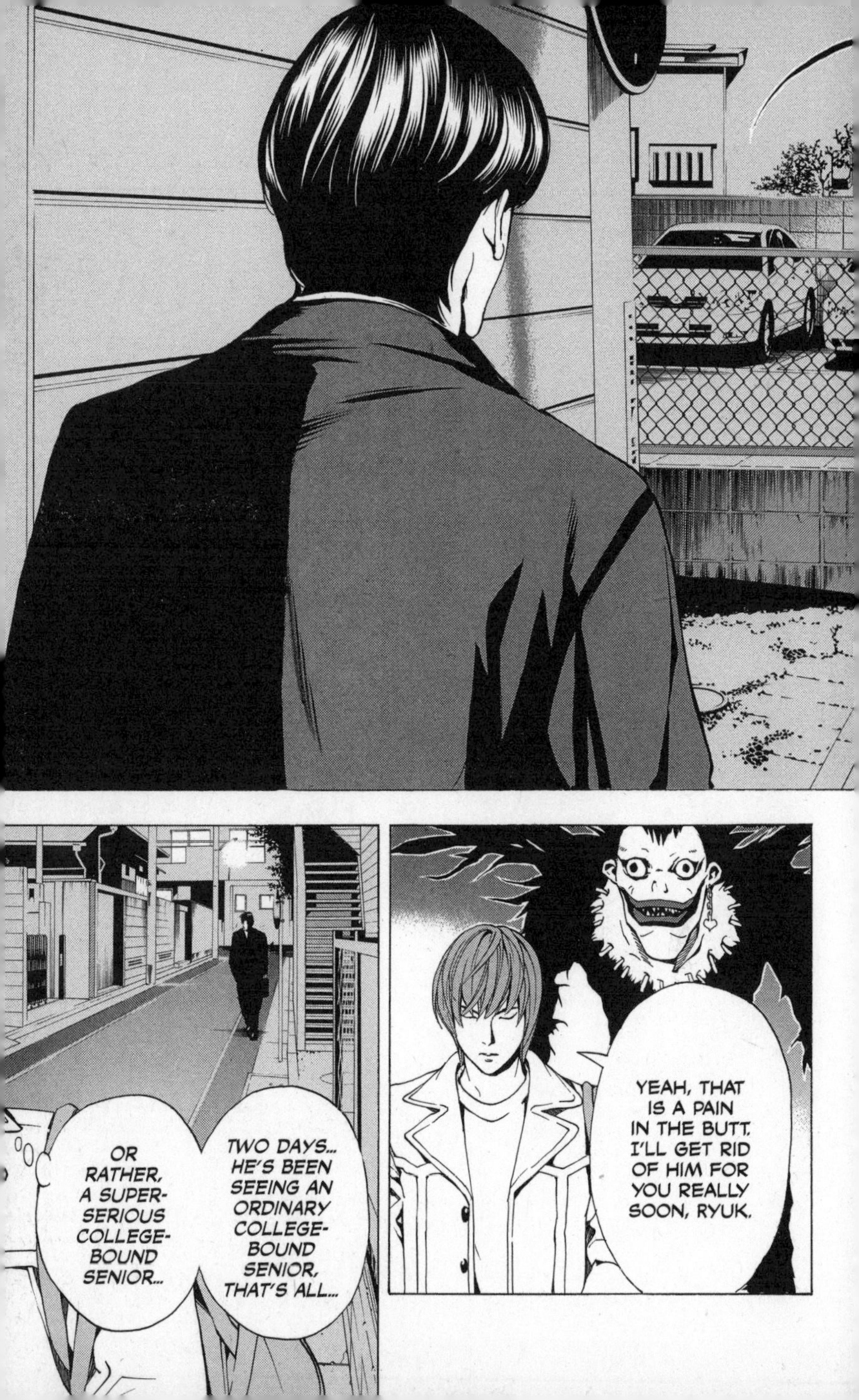
YEAH, THAT IS A PAIN IN THE BUTT. I'LL GET RID OF HIM FOR YOU REALLY SOON, RYUK.
TWO DAYS... HE'S BEEN SEEING AN ORDINARY COLLEGE-BOUND SENIOR, THAT'S ALL...
OR RATHER, A SUPER-SERIOUS COLLEGE-BOUND SENIOR...

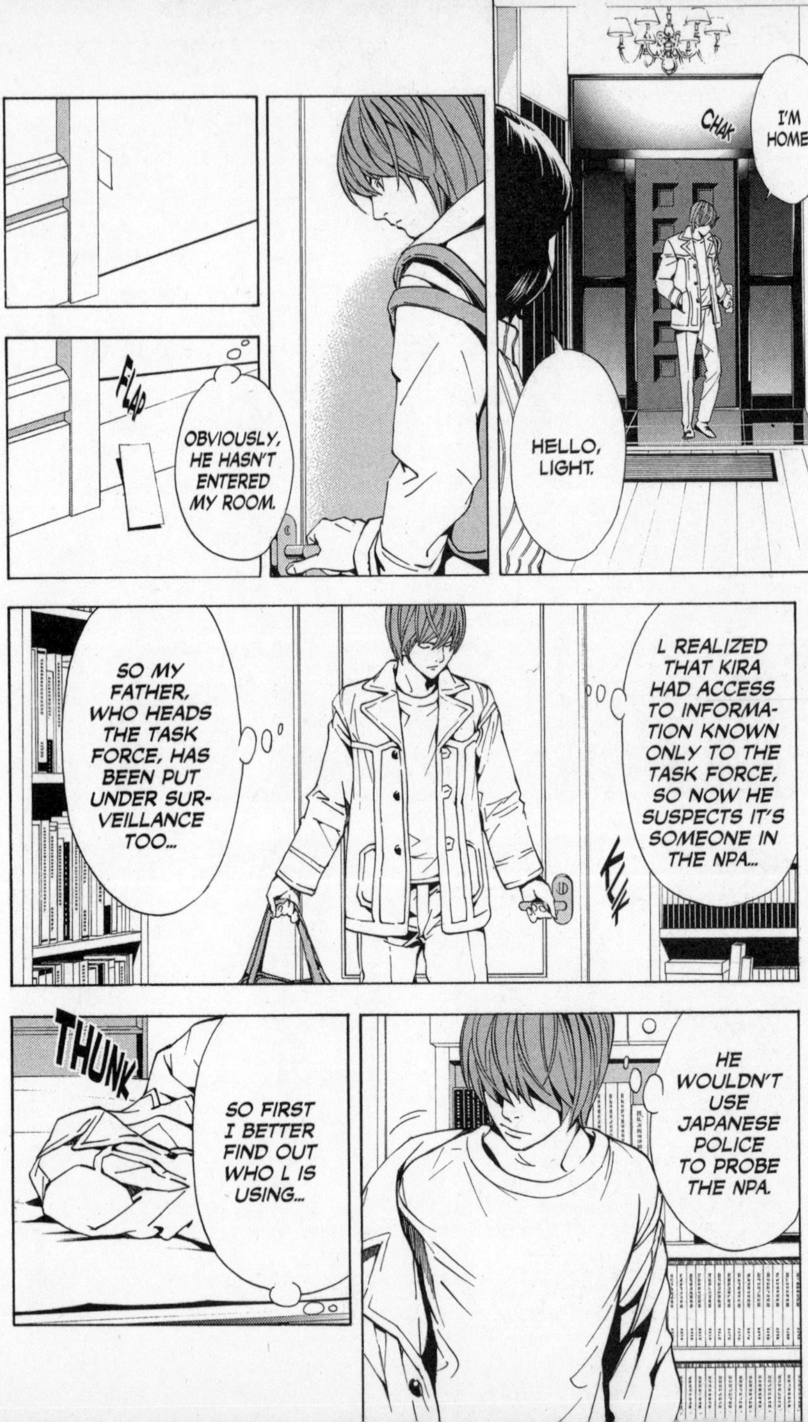
CHAK
I'M HOME.
HELLO, LIGHT.
FLAP
OBVIOUSLY, HE HASN'T ENTERED MY ROOM.
L REALIZED THAT KIRA HAD ACCESS TO INFORMATION KNOWN ONLY TO THE TASK FORCE, SO NOW HE SUSPECTS IT'S SOMEONE IN THE NPA...
KLIK
SO MY FATHER, WHO HEADS THE TASK FORCE, HAS BEEN PUT UNDER SURVEILLANCE TOO...
HE WOULDN'T USE JAPANESE POLICE TO PROBE THE NPA.
THUNK
SO FIRST I BETTER FIND OUT WHO L IS USING...

READ THIS WAY

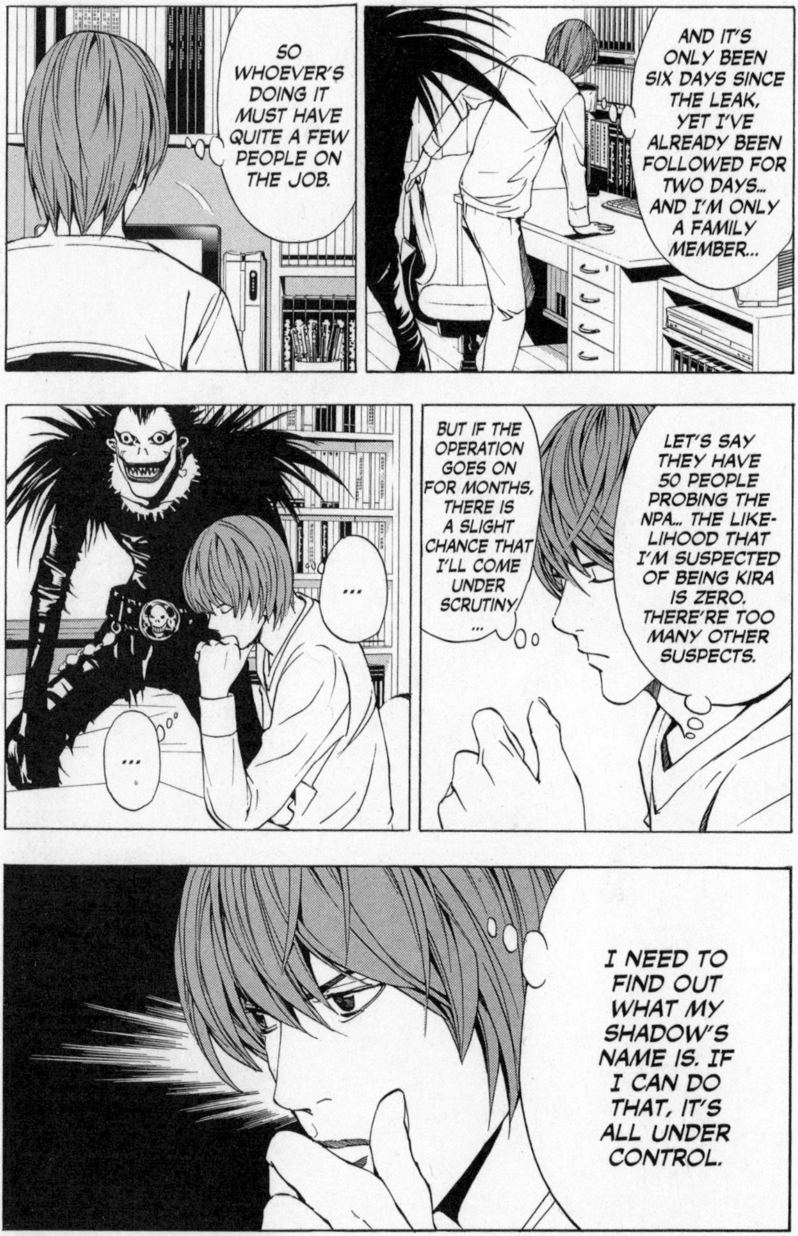
AND IT'S ONLY BEEN SIX DAYS SINCE THE LEAK, YET I'VE ALREADY BEEN FOLLOWED FOR TWO DAYS... AND I'M ONLY A FAMILY MEMBER...
SO WHOEVER'S DOING IT MUST HAVE QUITE A FEW PEOPLE ON THE JOB.
LET'S SAY THEY HAVE 50 PEOPLE PROBING THE NPA... THE LIKE-LIHOOD THAT I'M SUSPECTED OF BEING KIRA IS ZERO. THERE'RE TOO MANY OTHER SUSPECTS.
BUT IF THE OPERATION GOES ON FOR MONTHS, THERE IS A SLIGHT CHANCE THAT I'LL COME UNDER SCRUTINY ...
...
...
I NEED TO FIND OUT WHAT MY SHADOW'S NAME IS. IF I CAN DO THAT, IT'S ALL UNDER CONTROL.

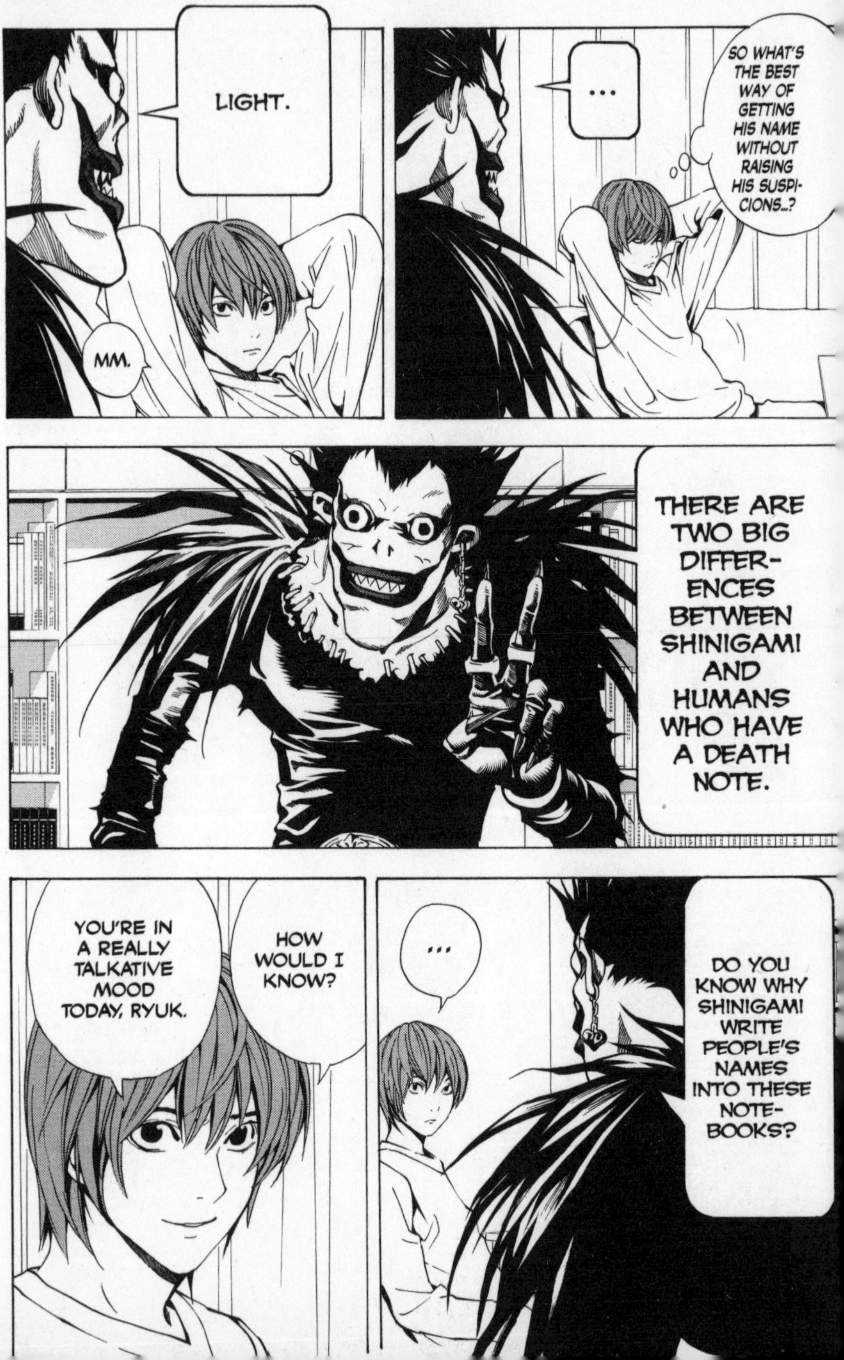
SO WHAT'S THE BEST WAY OF GETTING HIS NAME WITHOUT RAISING HIS SUSPICIONS...?
...
LIGHT.
MM.
THERE ARE TWO BIG DIFFERENCES BETWEEN SHINIGAMI AND HUMANS WHO HAVE A DEATH NOTE.
DO YOU KNOW WHY SHINIGAMI WRITE PEOPLE'S NAMES INTO THESE NOTEBOOKS?
...
HOW WOULD I KNOW?
YOU'RE IN A REALLY TALKATIVE MOOD TODAY, RYUK.

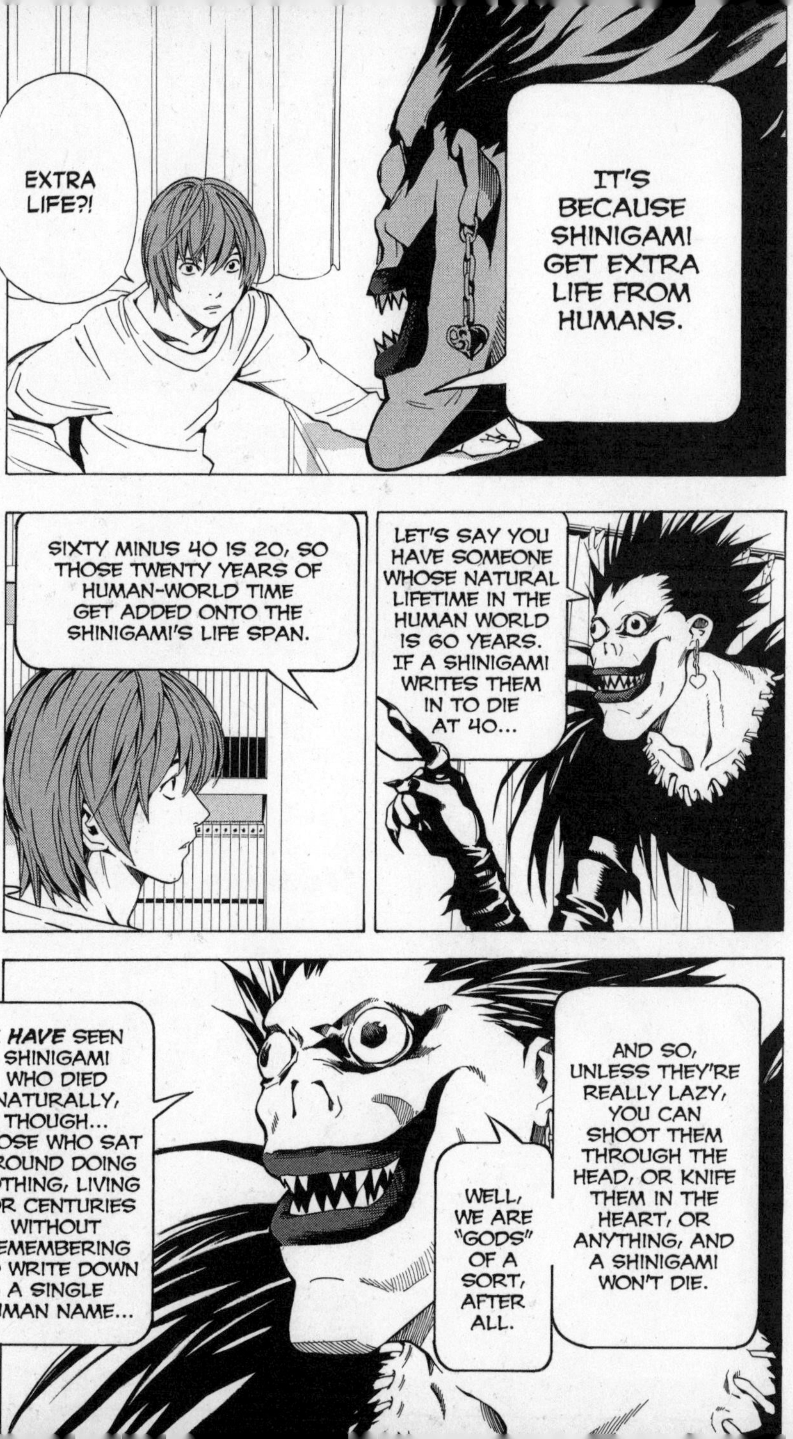

IT'S BECAUSE SHINIGAMI GET EXTRA LIFE FROM HUMANS.
EXTRA LIFE?!
LET'S SAY YOU HAVE SOMEONE WHOSE NATURAL LIFETIME IN THE HUMAN WORLD IS 60 YEARS. IF A SHINIGAMI WRITES THEM IN TO DIE AT 40...
SIXTY MINUS 40 IS 20, SO THOSE TWENTY YEARS OF HUMAN-WORLD TIME GET ADDED ONTO THE SHINIGAMI'S LIFE SPAN.
AND SO, UNLESS THEY'RE REALLY LAZY, YOU CAN SHOOT THEM THROUGH THE HEAD, OR KNIFE THEM IN THE HEART, OR ANYTHING, AND A SHINIGAMI WON'T DIE.
WELL, WE ARE "GODS" OF A SORT, AFTER ALL.
I *HAVE* SEEN SHINIGAMI WHO DIED NATURALLY, THOUGH... THOSE WHO SAT AROUND DOING NOTHING, LIVING FOR CENTURIES WITHOUT REMEMBERING TO WRITE DOWN A SINGLE HUMAN NAME...

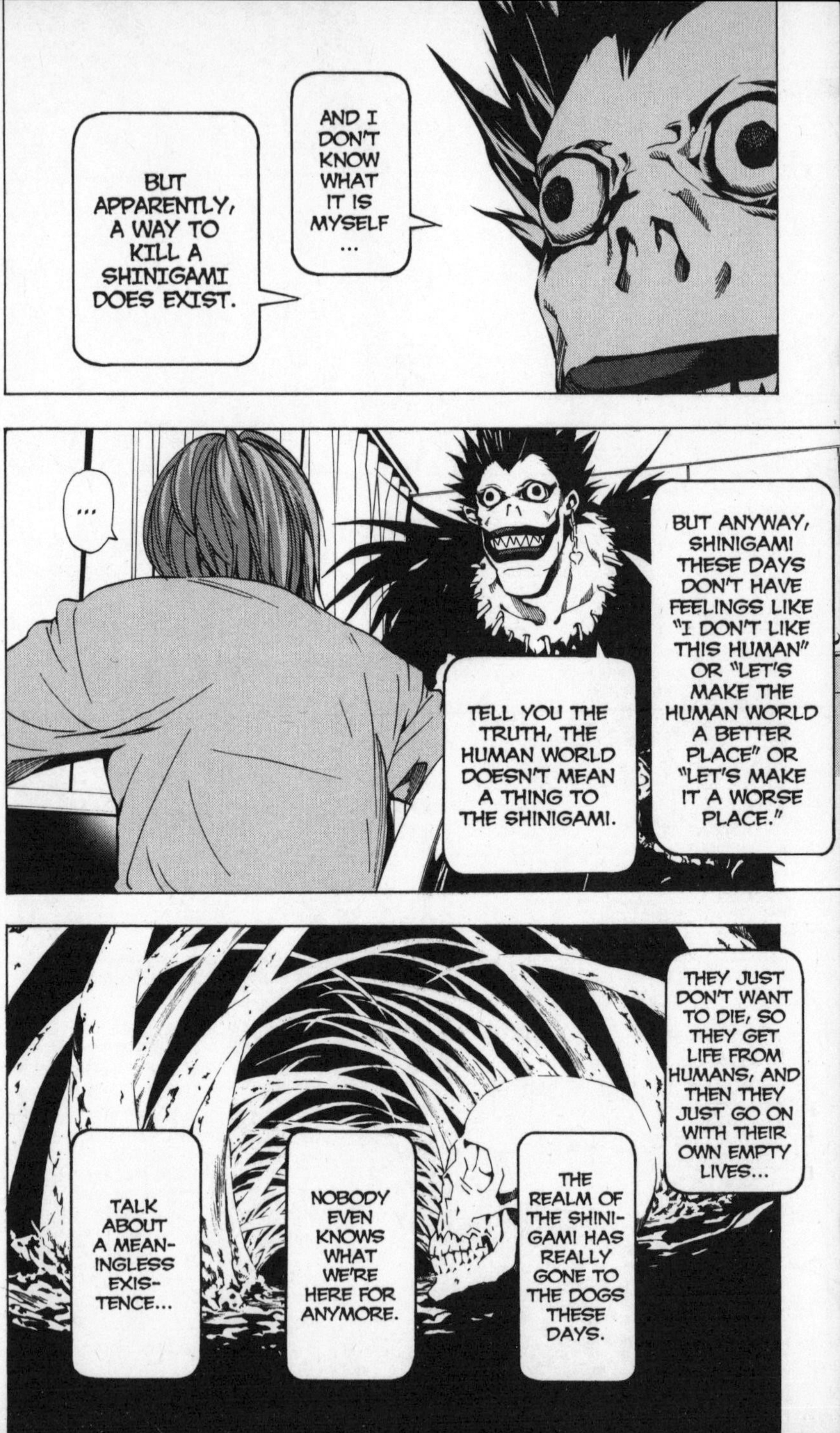
AND I DON'T KNOW WHAT IT IS MYSELF ...
BUT APPARENTLY, A WAY TO KILL A SHINIGAMI DOES EXIST.
BUT ANYWAY, SHINIGAMI THESE DAYS DON'T HAVE FEELINGS LIKE "I DON'T LIKE THIS HUMAN" OR "LET'S MAKE THE HUMAN WORLD A BETTER PLACE" OR "LET'S MAKE IT A WORSE PLACE."
TELL YOU THE TRUTH, THE HUMAN WORLD DOESN'T MEAN A THING TO THE SHINIGAMI.
...
THEY JUST DON'T WANT TO DIE, SO THEY GET LIFE FROM HUMANS, AND THEN THEY JUST GO ON WITH THEIR OWN EMPTY LIVES...
THE REALM OF THE SHINI-GAMI HAS REALLY GONE TO THE DOGS THESE DAYS.
NOBODY EVEN KNOWS WHAT WE'RE HERE FOR ANYMORE.
TALK ABOUT A MEAN-INGLESS EXIS-TENCE...

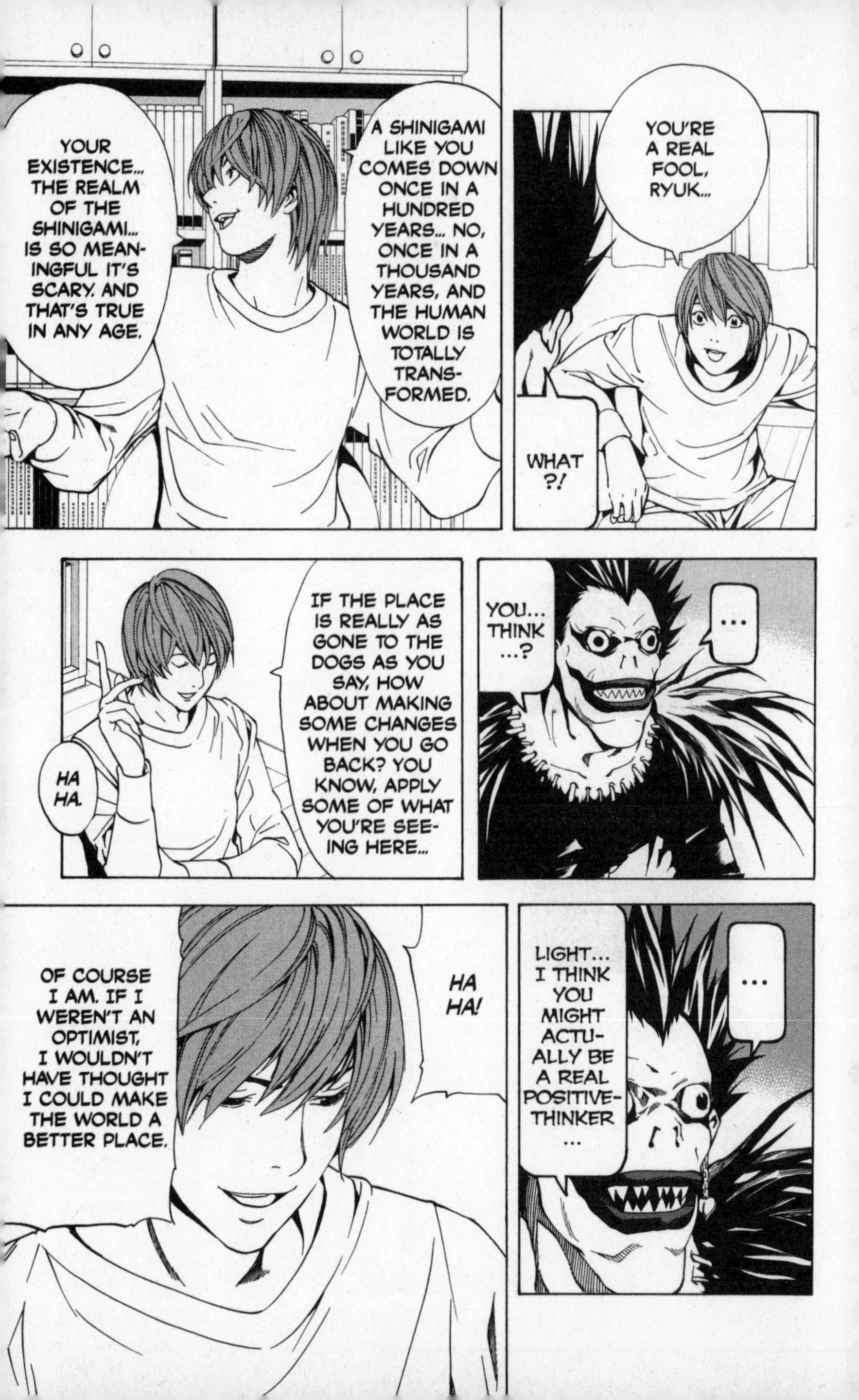
YOU'RE A REAL FOOL, RYUK...
WHAT?!
A SHINIGAMI LIKE YOU COMES DOWN ONCE IN A HUNDRED YEARS... NO, ONCE IN A THOUSAND YEARS, AND THE HUMAN WORLD IS TOTALLY TRANSFORMED.
YOUR EXISTENCE... THE REALM OF THE SHINIGAMI... IS SO MEANINGFUL IT'S SCARY. AND THAT'S TRUE IN ANY AGE.
...
YOU... THINK ...?
IF THE PLACE IS REALLY AS GONE TO THE DOGS AS YOU SAY, HOW ABOUT MAKING SOME CHANGES WHEN YOU GO BACK? YOU KNOW, APPLY SOME OF WHAT YOU'RE SEEING HERE...
HA HA.
...
LIGHT... I THINK YOU MIGHT ACTUALLY BE A REAL POSITIVE-THINKER ...
HA HA!
OF COURSE I AM. IF I WEREN'T AN OPTIMIST, I WOULDN'T HAVE THOUGHT I COULD MAKE THE WORLD A BETTER PLACE.

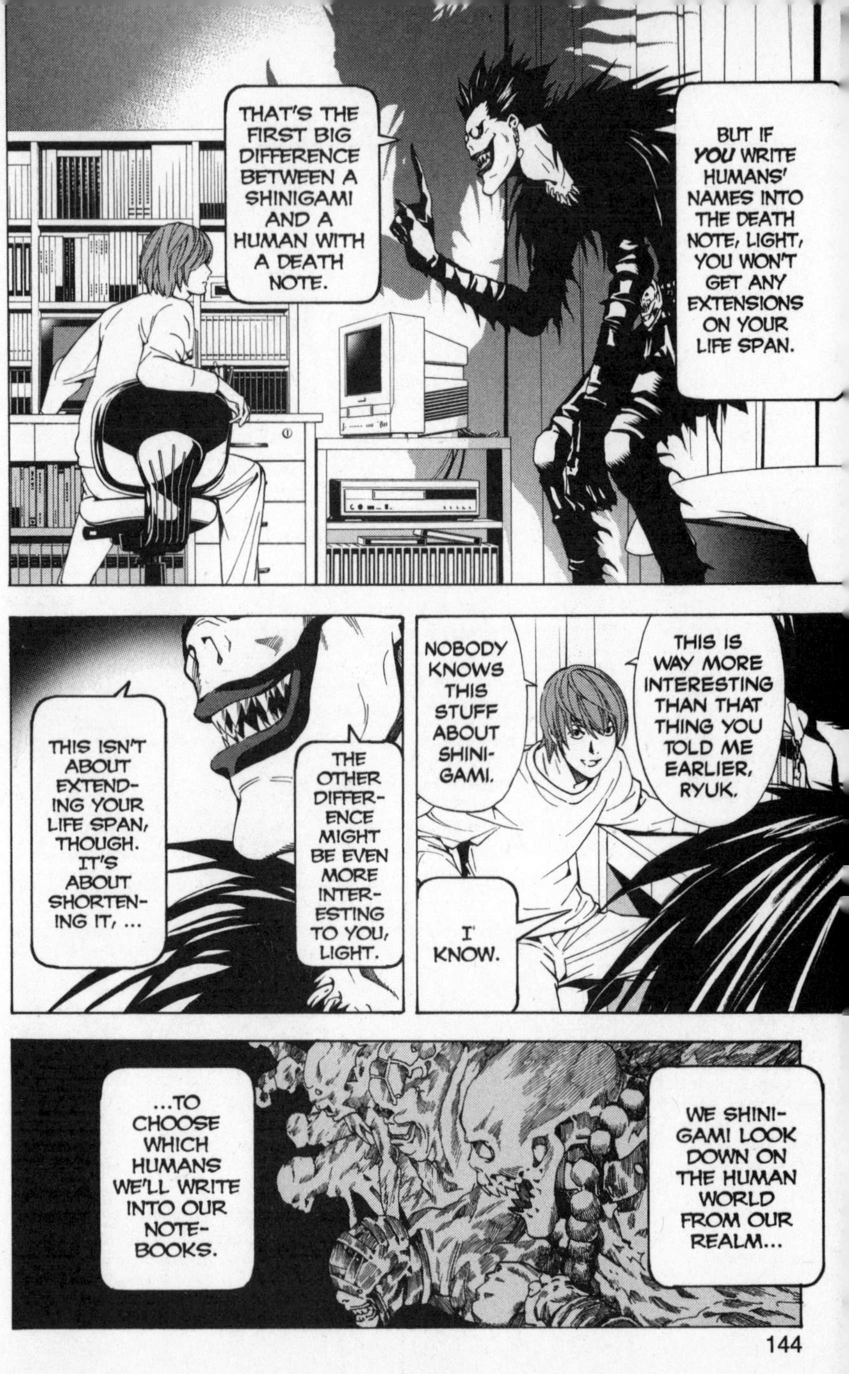
BUT IF YOU WRITE HUMANS' NAMES INTO THE DEATH NOTE, LIGHT, YOU WON'T GET ANY EXTENSIONS ON YOUR LIFE SPAN.
THAT'S THE FIRST BIG DIFFERENCE BETWEEN A SHINIGAMI AND A HUMAN WITH A DEATH NOTE.
THIS IS WAY MORE INTERESTING THAN THAT THING YOU TOLD ME EARLIER, RYUK.
NOBODY KNOWS THIS STUFF ABOUT SHINI-GAMI.
I KNOW.
THE OTHER DIFFER-ENCE MIGHT BE EVEN MORE INTER-ESTING TO YOU, LIGHT.
THIS ISN'T ABOUT EXTEND-ING YOUR LIFE SPAN, THOUGH. IT'S ABOUT SHORTEN-ING IT, ...
WE SHINI-GAMI LOOK DOWN ON THE HUMAN WORLD FROM OUR REALM...
...TO CHOOSE WHICH HUMANS WE'LL WRITE INTO OUR NOTE-BOOKS.

READ THIS WAY

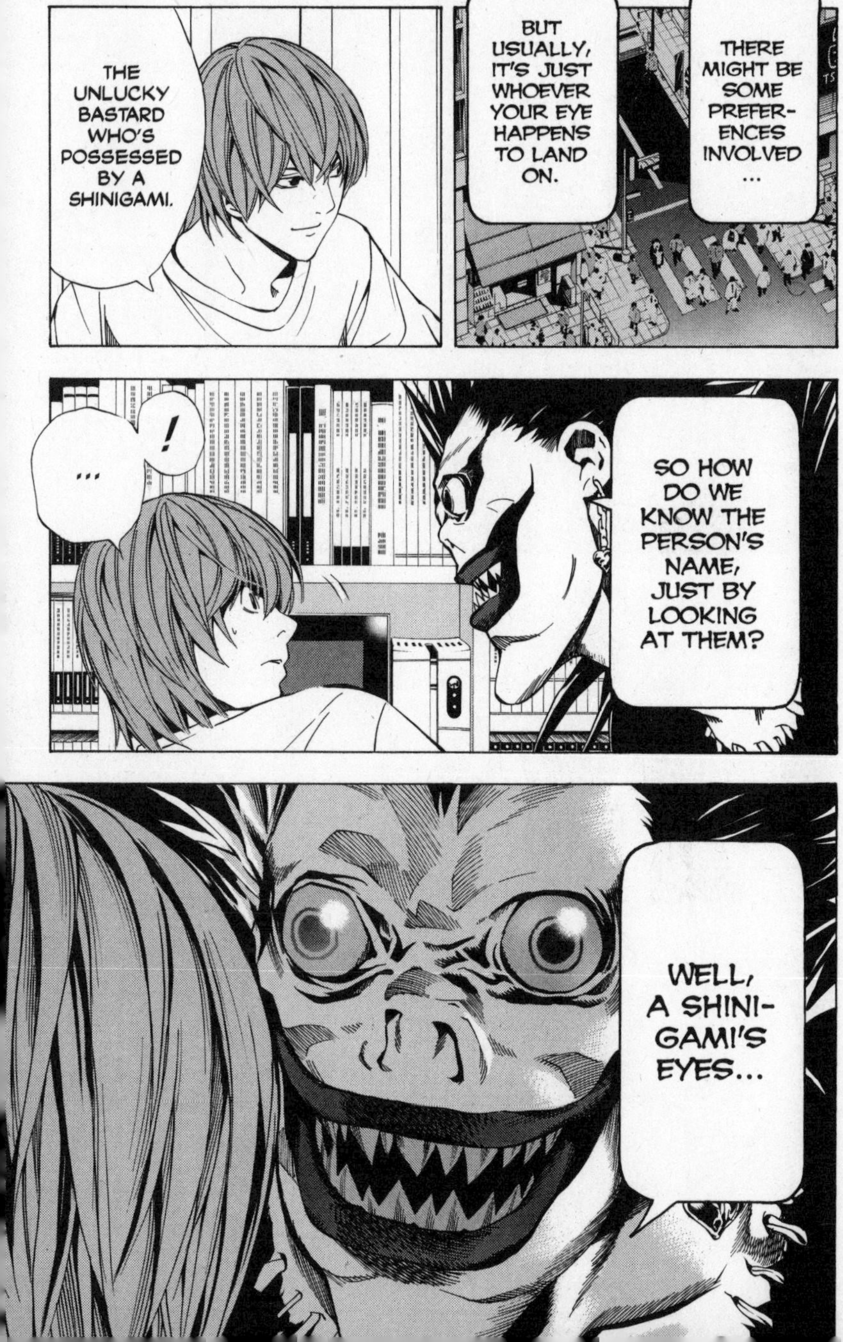
THERE MIGHT BE SOME PREFER-ENCES INVOLVED ...
BUT USUALLY, IT'S JUST WHOEVER YOUR EYE HAPPENS TO LAND ON.
THE UNLUCKY BASTARD WHO'S POSSESSED BY A SHINIGAMI.
SO HOW DO WE KNOW THE PERSON'S NAME, JUST BY LOOKING AT THEM?
!
...
WELL, A SHINI-GAMI'S EYES...

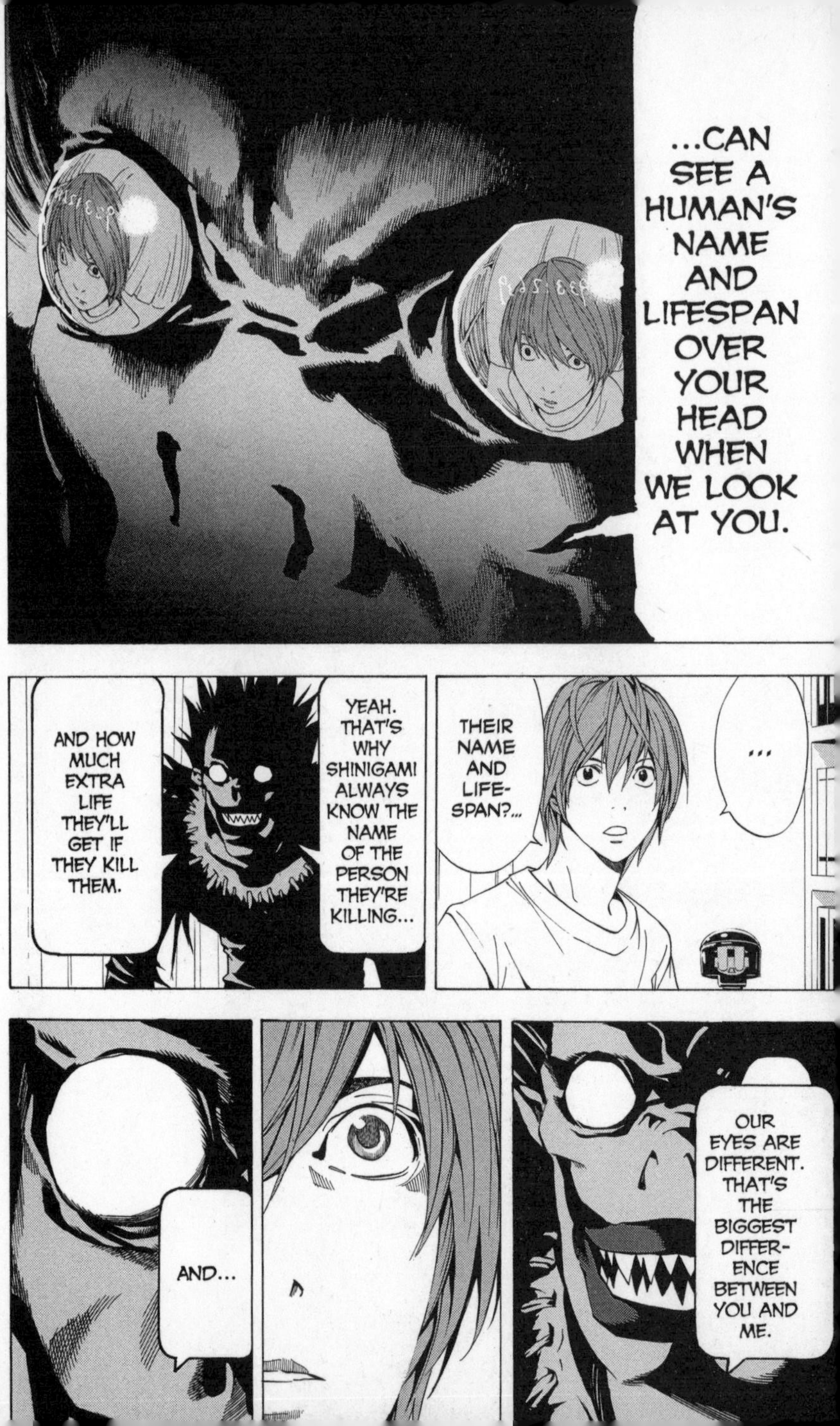
...CAN SEE A HUMAN'S NAME AND LIFESPAN OVER YOUR HEAD WHEN WE LOOK AT YOU.
...
THEIR NAME AND LIFE-SPAN?...
YEAH. THAT'S WHY SHINIGAMI ALWAYS KNOW THE NAME OF THE PERSON THEY'RE KILLING...
AND HOW MUCH EXTRA LIFE THEY'LL GET IF THEY KILL THEM.
OUR EYES ARE DIFFERENT. THAT'S THE BIGGEST DIFFER-ENCE BETWEEN YOU AND ME.
AND...

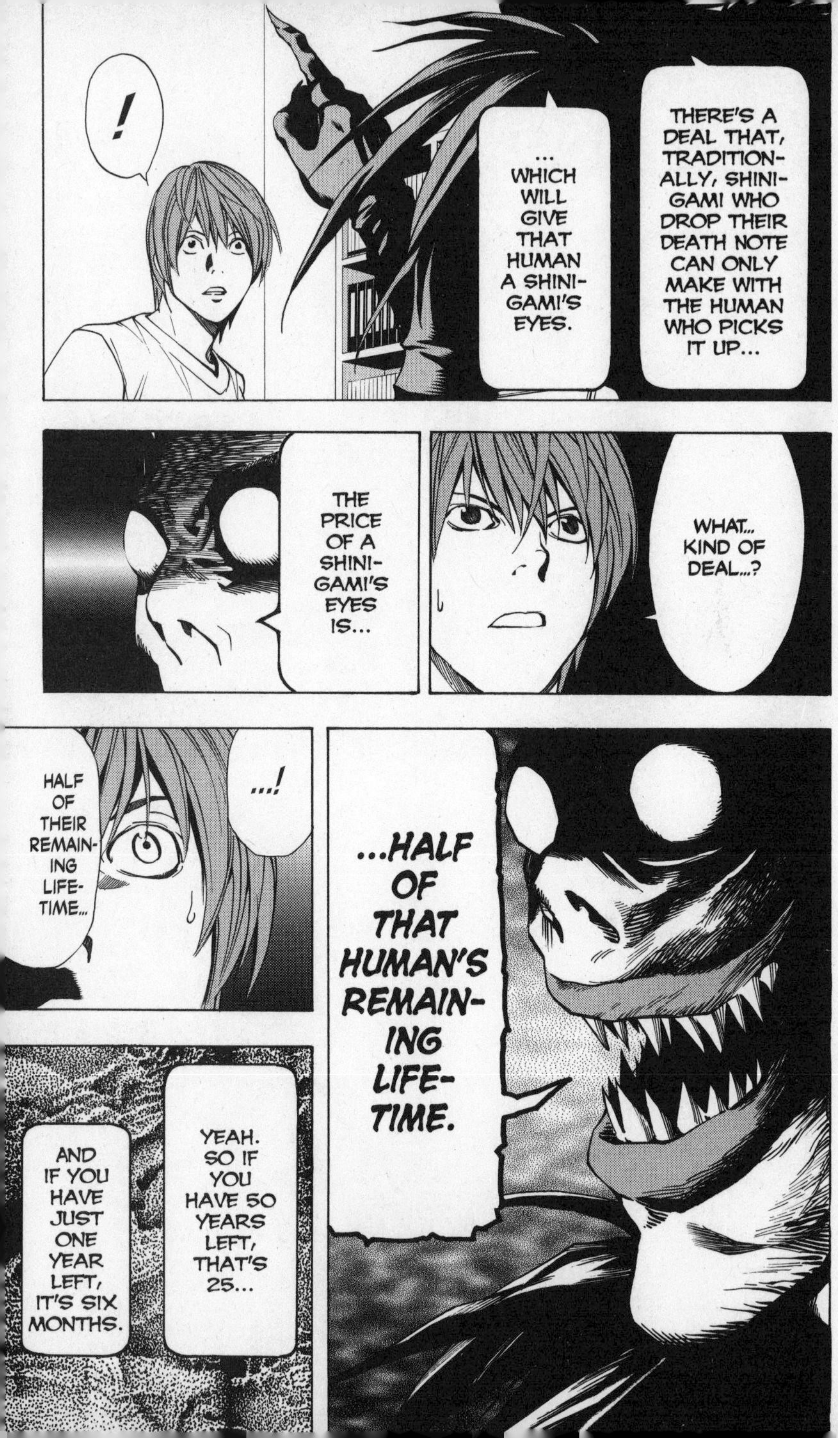
THERE'S A DEAL THAT, TRADITIONALLY, SHINIGAMI WHO DROP THEIR DEATH NOTE CAN ONLY MAKE WITH THE HUMAN WHO PICKS IT UP...
...WHICH WILL GIVE THAT HUMAN A SHINIGAMI'S EYES.
!
WHAT... KIND OF DEAL...?
THE PRICE OF A SHINIGAMI'S EYES IS...
...HALF OF THAT HUMAN'S REMAINING LIFETIME.
...!
HALF OF THEIR REMAINING LIFETIME...
YEAH. SO IF YOU HAVE 50 YEARS LEFT, THAT'S 25...
AND IF YOU HAVE JUST ONE YEAR LEFT, IT'S SIX MONTHS.

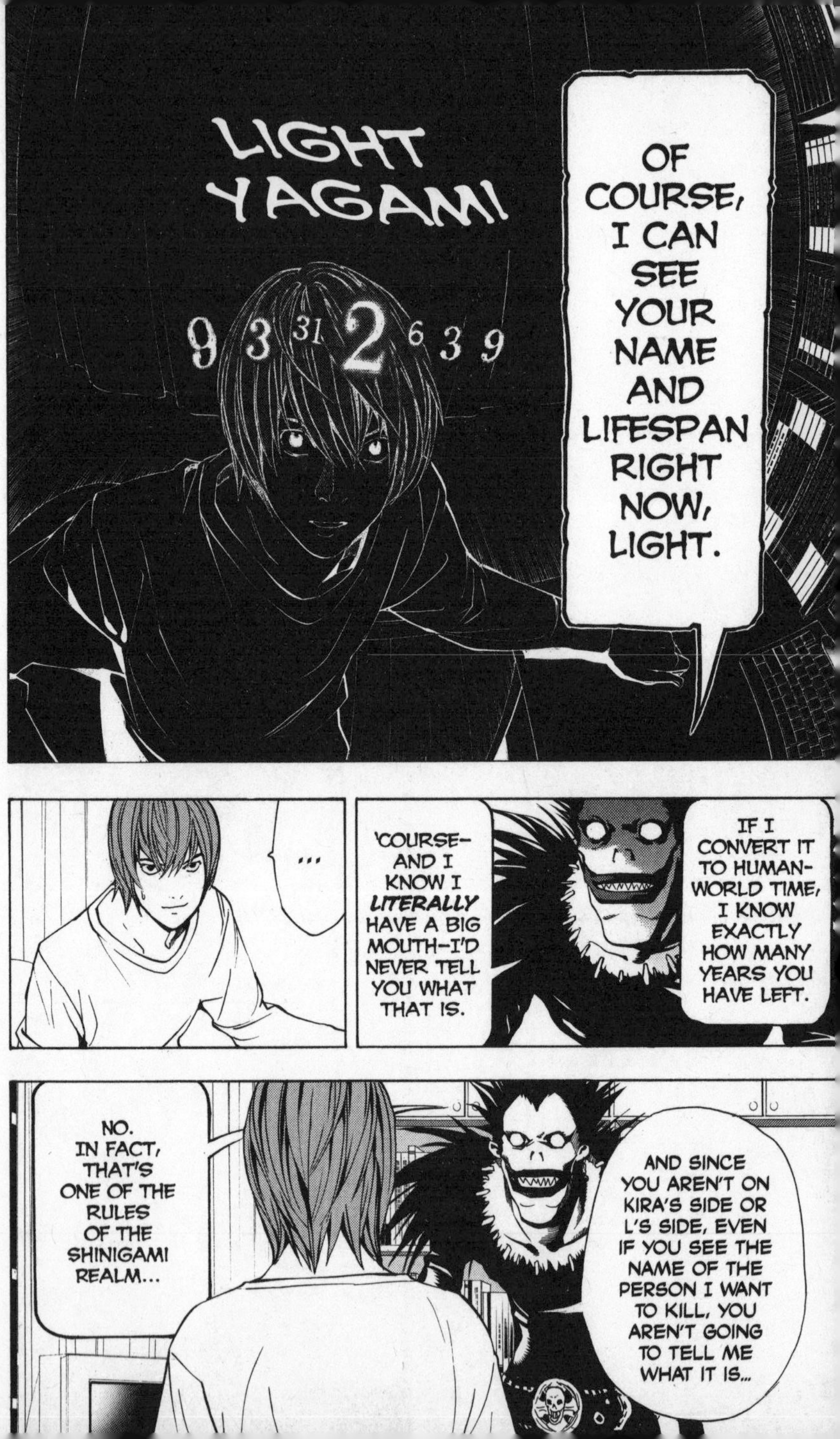
OF COURSE, I CAN SEE YOUR NAME AND LIFESPAN RIGHT NOW, LIGHT.
LIGHT YAGAMI
9 3 31 2 6 3 9
IF I CONVERT IT TO HUMAN-WORLD TIME, I KNOW EXACTLY HOW MANY YEARS YOU HAVE LEFT.
'COURSE-AND I KNOW I *LITERALLY* HAVE A BIG MOUTH-I'D NEVER TELL YOU WHAT THAT IS.
...
AND SINCE YOU AREN'T ON KIRA'S SIDE OR L'S SIDE, EVEN IF YOU SEE THE NAME OF THE PERSON I WANT TO KILL, YOU AREN'T GOING TO TELL ME WHAT IT IS...
NO. IN FACT, THAT'S ONE OF THE RULES OF THE SHINIGAMI REALM...

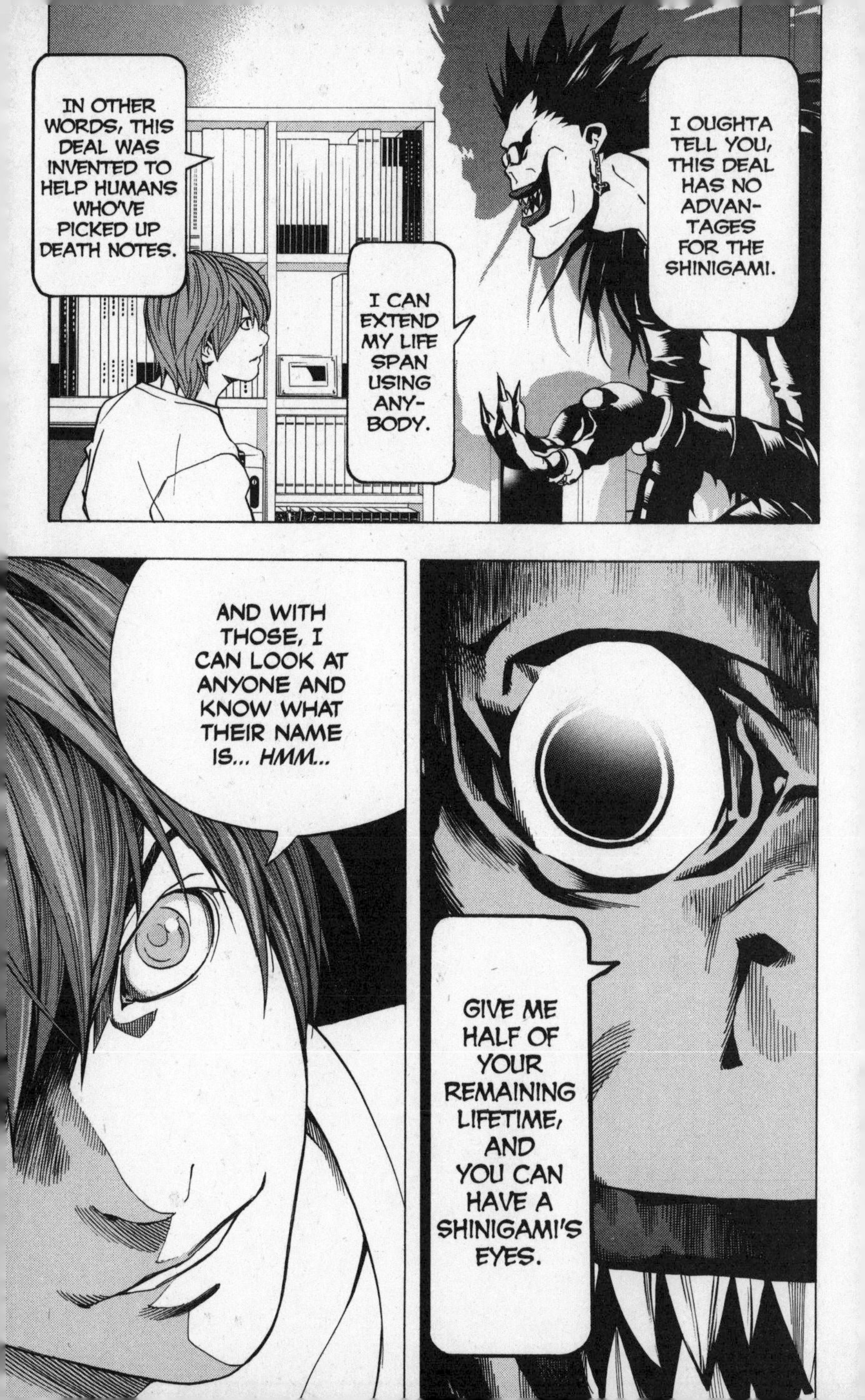
I OUGHTA TELL YOU, THIS DEAL HAS NO ADVAN-TAGES FOR THE SHINIGAMI.
I CAN EXTEND MY LIFE SPAN USING ANY-BODY.
IN OTHER WORDS, THIS DEAL WAS INVENTED TO HELP HUMANS WHO'VE PICKED UP DEATH NOTES.
GIVE ME HALF OF YOUR REMAINING LIFETIME, AND YOU CAN HAVE A SHINIGAMI'S EYES.
AND WITH THOSE, I CAN LOOK AT ANYONE AND KNOW WHAT THEIR NAME IS... *HMM...*

DEATH NOTE
How to use it

- A god of death can extend his life by putting human names on the note, but humans cannot.

  死神はデスノートに人間の名前を書く事で自分の寿命を延ばせるが、人間は延ばせない。

- A person can shorten his or her own life by using the note.

  自分で自分の寿命をデスノートによって縮める事はできる。

- The human who becomes the owner of the DEATH NOTE can, in exchange of half of his/her remaining life, get the eyeballs of the god of death which will enable him/her to see a human's name and remaining lifetime when looking through them.

  デスノートの所有者となった人間は、自分の残された寿命の半分と交換に、人間の顔を見るとその人間の名前と寿命の見える死神の眼球をもらう事ができる。

- A god of death cannot be killed even if stabbed in his heart with a knife or shot in the head with a gun. However, there are ways to kill a god of death, which are not generally known to the gods of death.

  死神は心臓をナイフで刺しても頭を銃で撃ち抜いても殺す事はできない。しかし、一介の死神は知らない死神の殺し方は存在する。

chapter 6 Manipulation

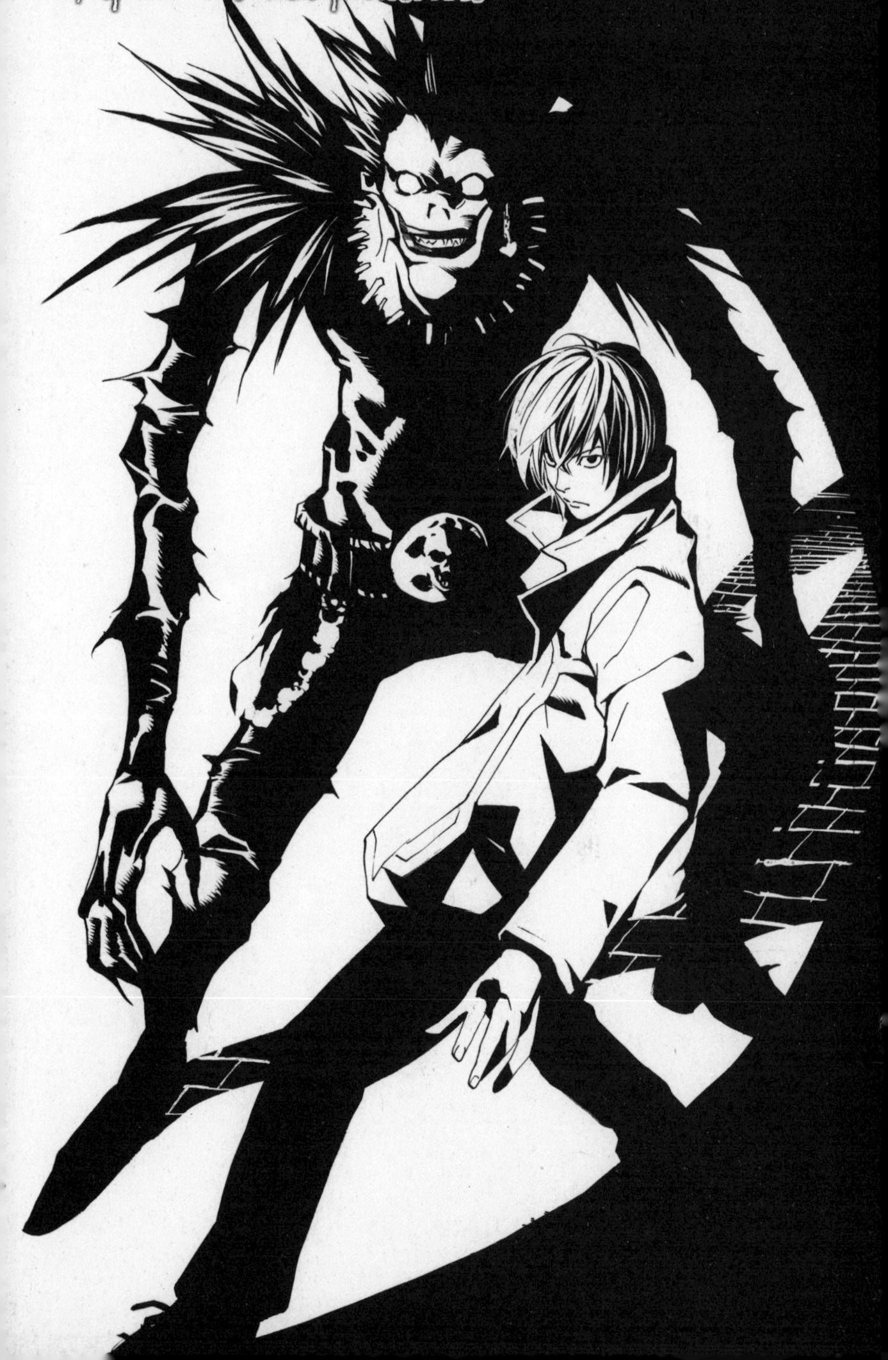

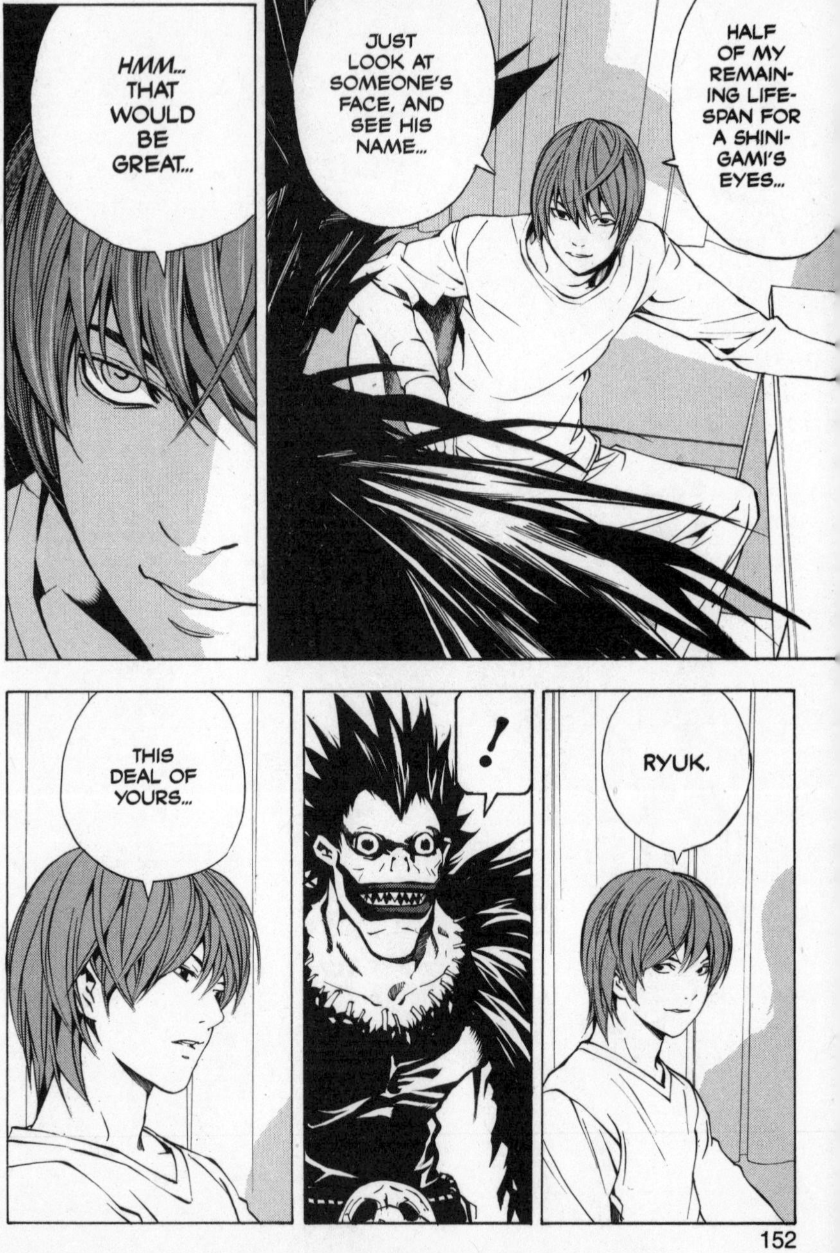
HALF OF MY REMAINING LIFESPAN FOR A SHINIGAMI'S EYES...
JUST LOOK AT SOMEONE'S FACE, AND SEE HIS NAME...
HMM... THAT WOULD BE GREAT...
RYUK.
!
THIS DEAL OF YOURS...

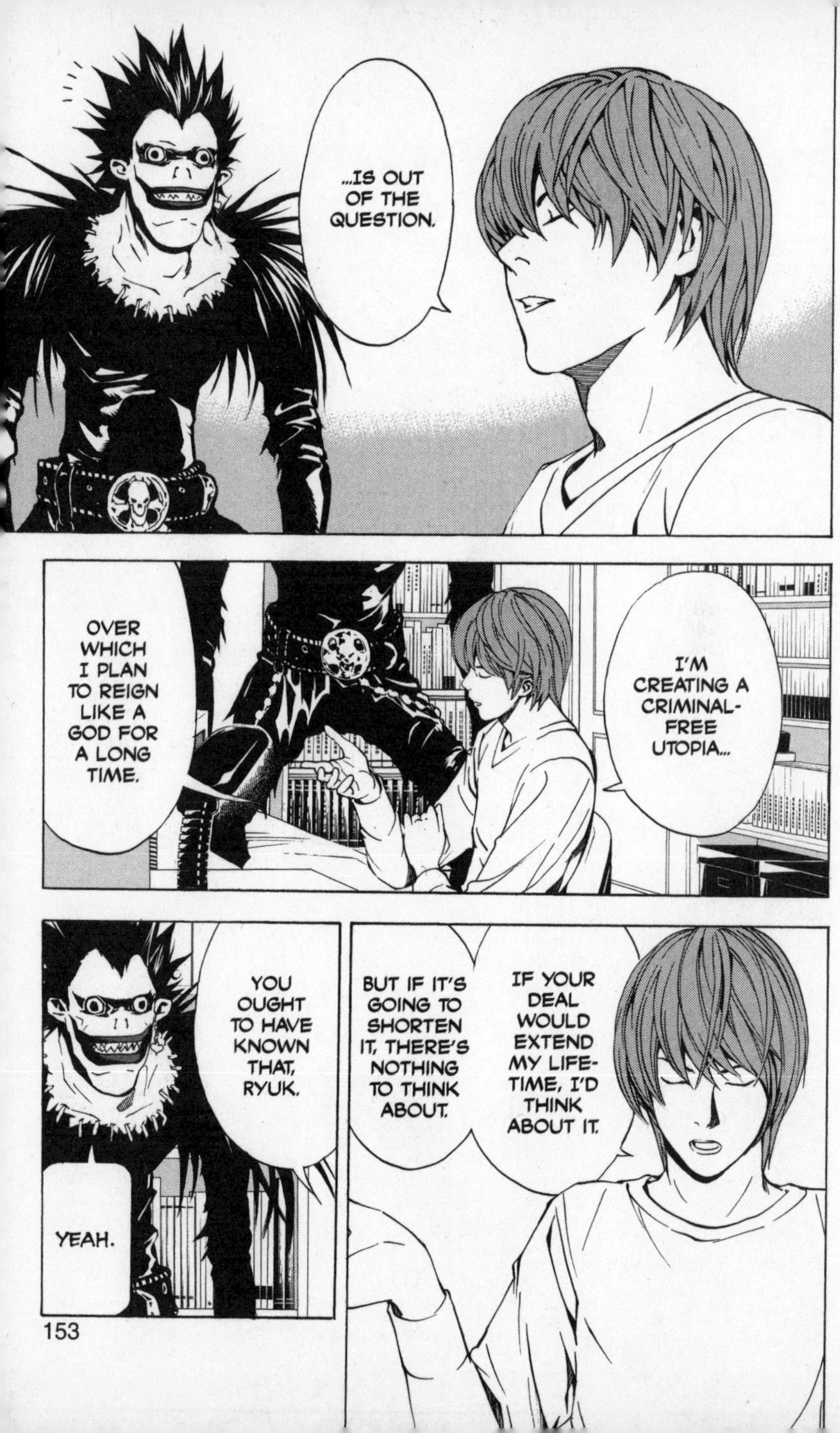
...IS OUT OF THE QUESTION.
I'M CREATING A CRIMINAL-FREE UTOPIA...
OVER WHICH I PLAN TO REIGN LIKE A GOD FOR A LONG TIME.
IF YOUR DEAL WOULD EXTEND MY LIFE-TIME, I'D THINK ABOUT IT.
BUT IF IT'S GOING TO SHORTEN IT, THERE'S NOTHING TO THINK ABOUT.
YOU OUGHT TO HAVE KNOWN THAT, RYUK.
YEAH.

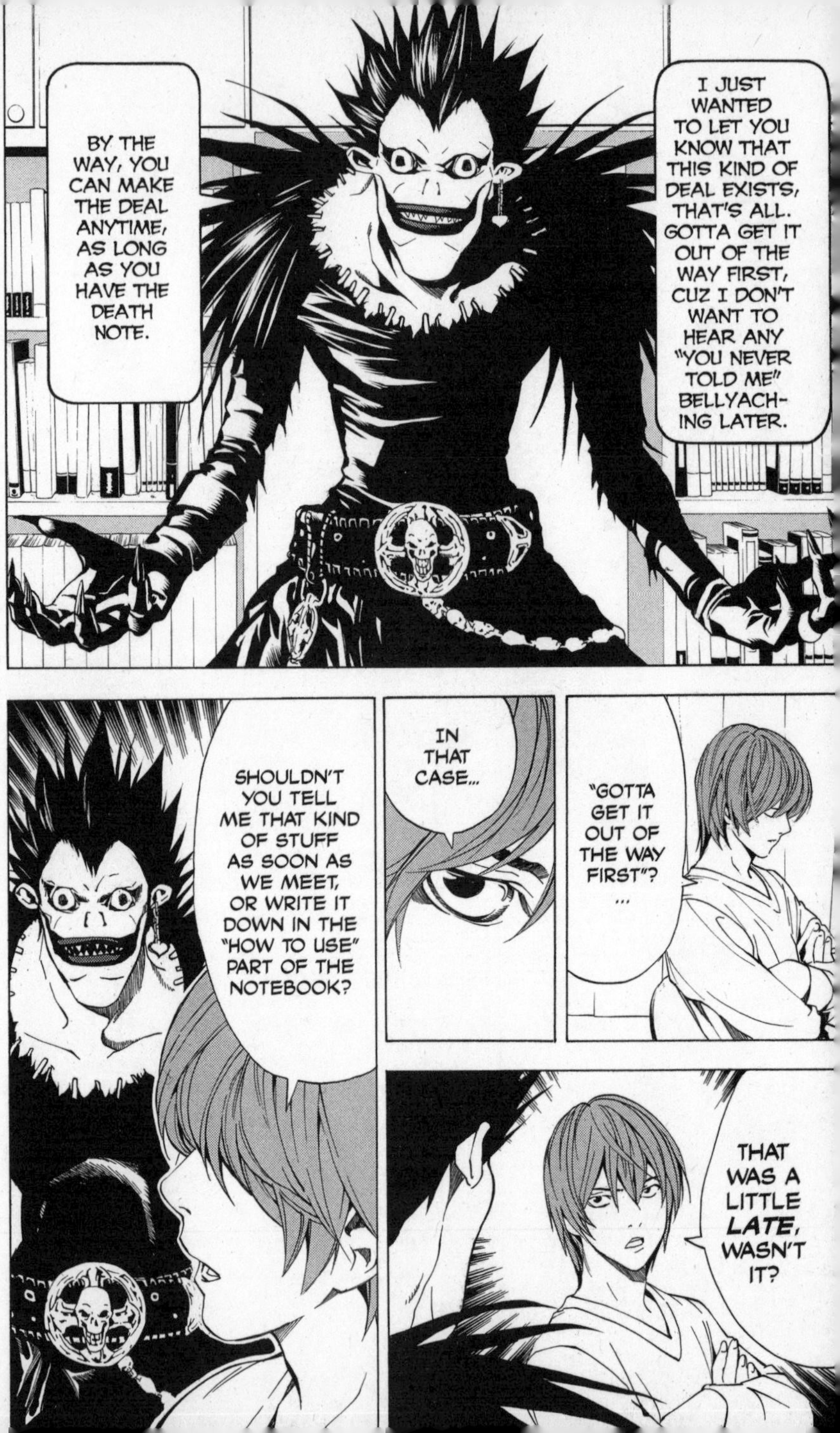
I JUST WANTED TO LET YOU KNOW THAT THIS KIND OF DEAL EXISTS, THAT'S ALL. GOTTA GET IT OUT OF THE WAY FIRST, CUZ I DON'T WANT TO HEAR ANY "YOU NEVER TOLD ME" BELLYACHING LATER.
BY THE WAY, YOU CAN MAKE THE DEAL ANYTIME, AS LONG AS YOU HAVE THE DEATH NOTE.
"GOTTA GET IT OUT OF THE WAY FIRST"? ...
IN THAT CASE...
SHOULDN'T YOU TELL ME THAT KIND OF STUFF AS SOON AS WE MEET, OR WRITE IT DOWN IN THE "HOW TO USE" PART OF THE NOTEBOOK?
THAT WAS A LITTLE *LATE*, WASN'T IT?

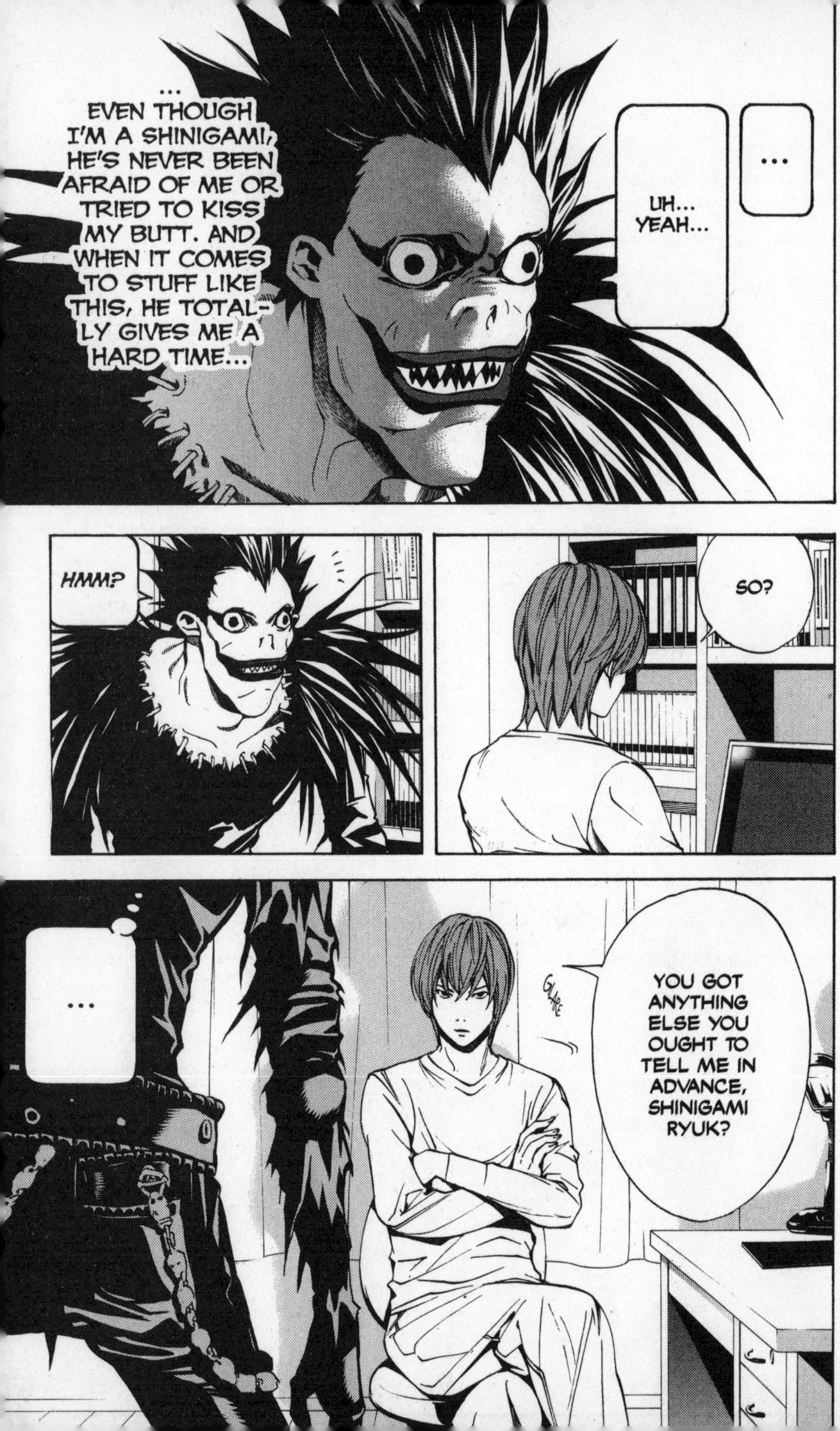
...
UH... YEAH...
... EVEN THOUGH I'M A SHINIGAMI, HE'S NEVER BEEN AFRAID OF ME OR TRIED TO KISS MY BUTT. AND WHEN IT COMES TO STUFF LIKE THIS, HE TOTALLY GIVES ME A HARD TIME...
SO?
HMM?
YOU GOT ANYTHING ELSE YOU OUGHT TO TELL ME IN ADVANCE, SHINIGAMI RYUK?
GLARE
...

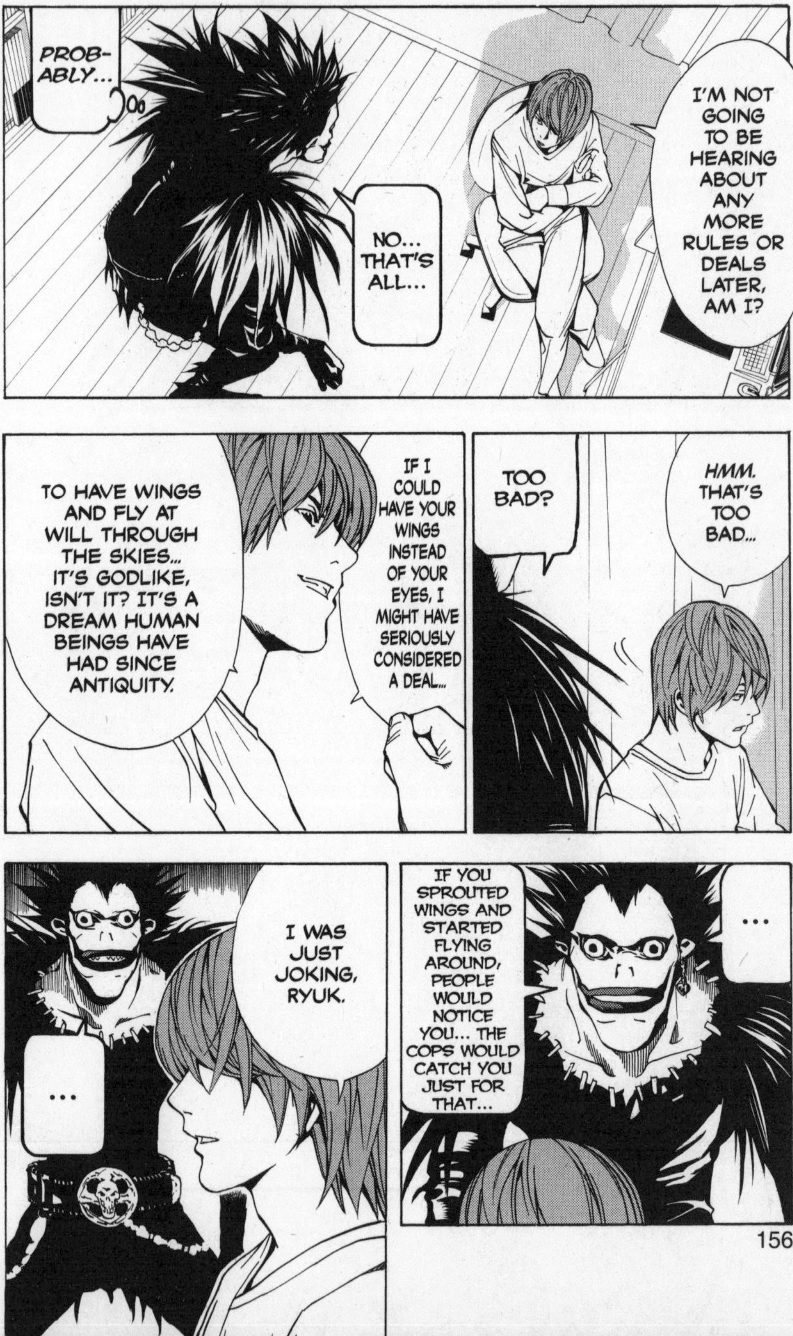
I'M NOT GOING TO BE HEARING ABOUT ANY MORE RULES OR DEALS LATER, AM I?
NO... THAT'S ALL...
PROBABLY...
HMM. THAT'S TOO BAD...
TOO BAD?
IF I COULD HAVE YOUR WINGS INSTEAD OF YOUR EYES, I MIGHT HAVE SERIOUSLY CONSIDERED A DEAL...
TO HAVE WINGS AND FLY AT WILL THROUGH THE SKIES... IT'S GODLIKE, ISN'T IT? IT'S A DREAM HUMAN BEINGS HAVE HAD SINCE ANTIQUITY.
...
IF YOU SPROUTED WINGS AND STARTED FLYING AROUND, PEOPLE WOULD NOTICE YOU... THE COPS WOULD CATCH YOU JUST FOR THAT...
I WAS JUST JOKING, RYUK.
...

READ THIS WAY

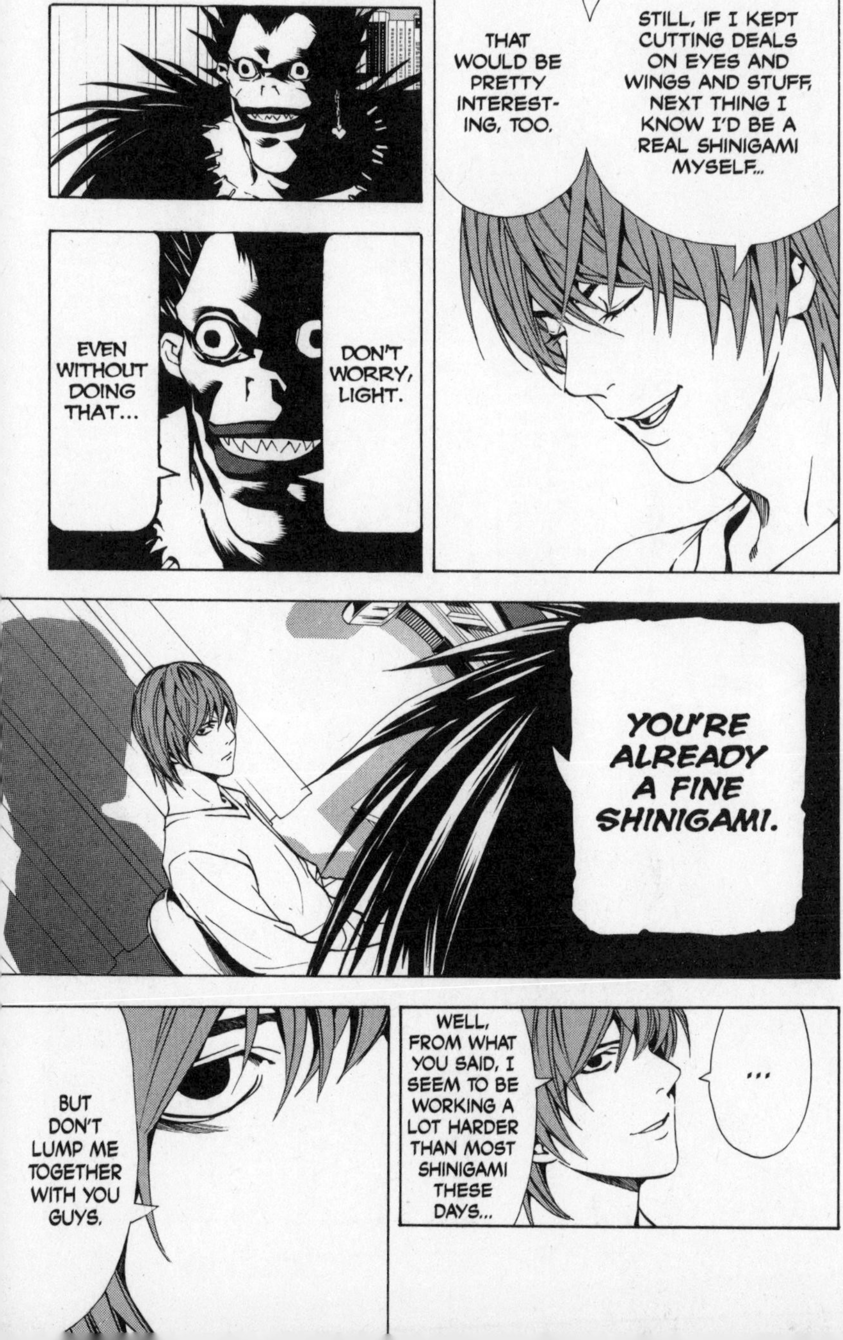

STILL, IF I KEPT CUTTING DEALS ON EYES AND WINGS AND STUFF, NEXT THING I KNOW I'D BE A REAL SHINIGAMI MYSELF...
THAT WOULD BE PRETTY INTEREST-ING, TOO.
DON'T WORRY, LIGHT.
EVEN WITHOUT DOING THAT...
YOU'RE ALREADY A FINE SHINIGAMI.
...
WELL, FROM WHAT YOU SAID, I SEEM TO BE WORKING A LOT HARDER THAN MOST SHINIGAMI THESE DAYS...
BUT DON'T LUMP ME TOGETHER WITH YOU GUYS.

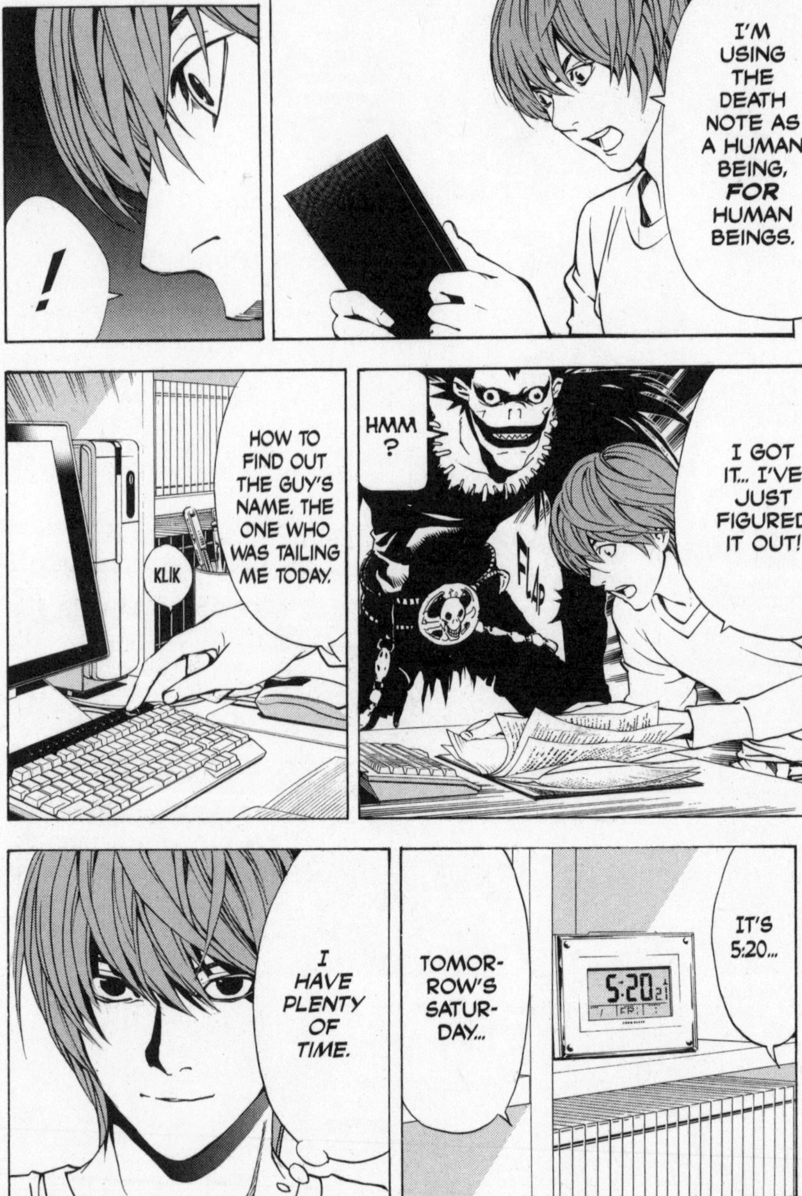
I'M USING THE DEATH NOTE AS A HUMAN BEING, **FOR** HUMAN BEINGS.
!
I GOT IT... I'VE JUST FIGURED IT OUT!
HMM ?
FLAP
HOW TO FIND OUT THE GUY'S NAME. THE ONE WHO WAS TAILING ME TODAY.
KLIK
IT'S 5:20...
TOMORROW'S SATURDAY...
I HAVE PLENTY OF TIME.

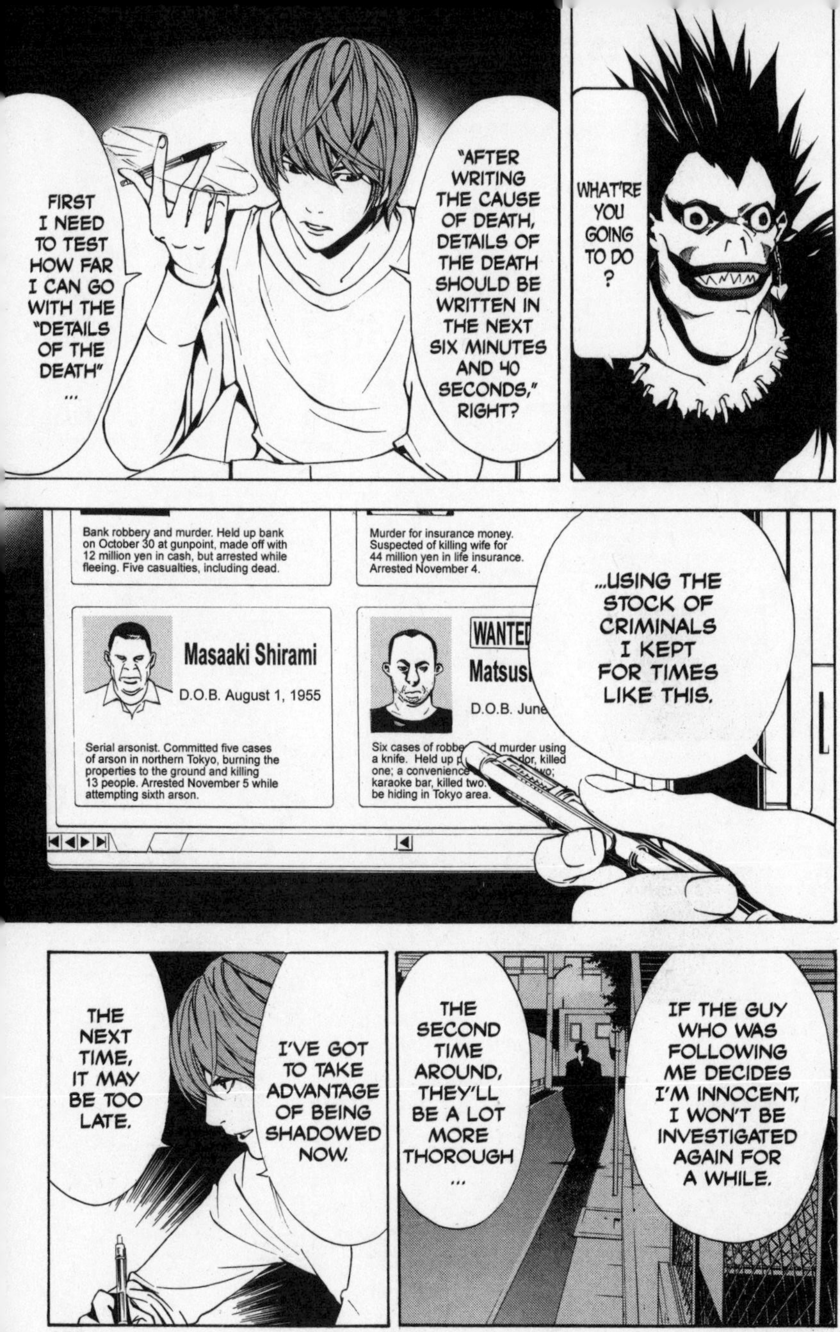
WHAT'RE YOU GOING TO DO ?
"AFTER WRITING THE CAUSE OF DEATH, DETAILS OF THE DEATH SHOULD BE WRITTEN IN THE NEXT SIX MINUTES AND 40 SECONDS," RIGHT?
FIRST I NEED TO TEST HOW FAR I CAN GO WITH THE "DETAILS OF THE DEATH" ...
...USING THE STOCK OF CRIMINALS I KEPT FOR TIMES LIKE THIS.
Murder for insurance money. Suspected of killing wife for 44 million yen in life insurance. Arrested November 4.
Bank robbery and murder. Held up bank on October 30 at gunpoint, made off with 12 million yen in cash, but arrested while fleeing. Five casualties, including dead.
Masaaki Shirami
D.O.B. August 1, 1955
Serial arsonist. Committed five cases of arson in northern Tokyo, burning the properties to the ground and killing 13 people. Arrested November 5 while attempting sixth arson.
IF THE GUY WHO WAS FOLLOWING ME DECIDES I'M INNOCENT, I WON'T BE INVESTIGATED AGAIN FOR A WHILE.
THE SECOND TIME AROUND, THEY'LL BE A LOT MORE THOROUGH ...
I'VE GOT TO TAKE ADVANTAGE OF BEING SHADOWED NOW.
THE NEXT TIME, IT MAY BE TOO LATE.

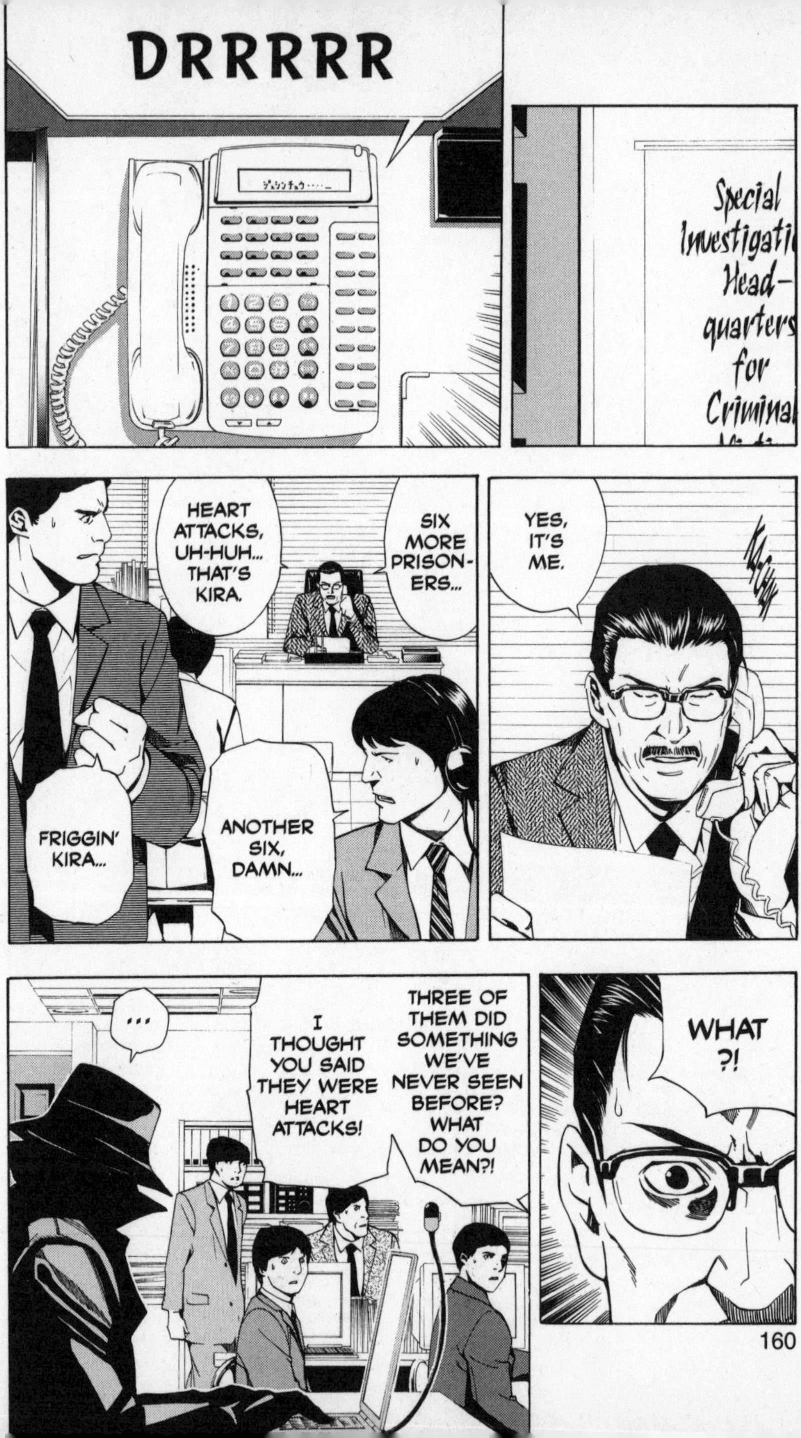
Special
Investigati
Head-
quarters
for
Criminal
DRRRRR
YES, IT'S ME.
SIX MORE PRISONERS...
HEART ATTACKS, UH-HUH... THAT'S KIRA.
ANOTHER SIX, DAMN...
FRIGGIN' KIRA...
WHAT ?!
THREE OF THEM DID SOMETHING WE'VE NEVER SEEN BEFORE? WHAT DO YOU MEAN?!
I THOUGHT YOU SAID THEY WERE HEART ATTACKS!
...

READ THIS WAY

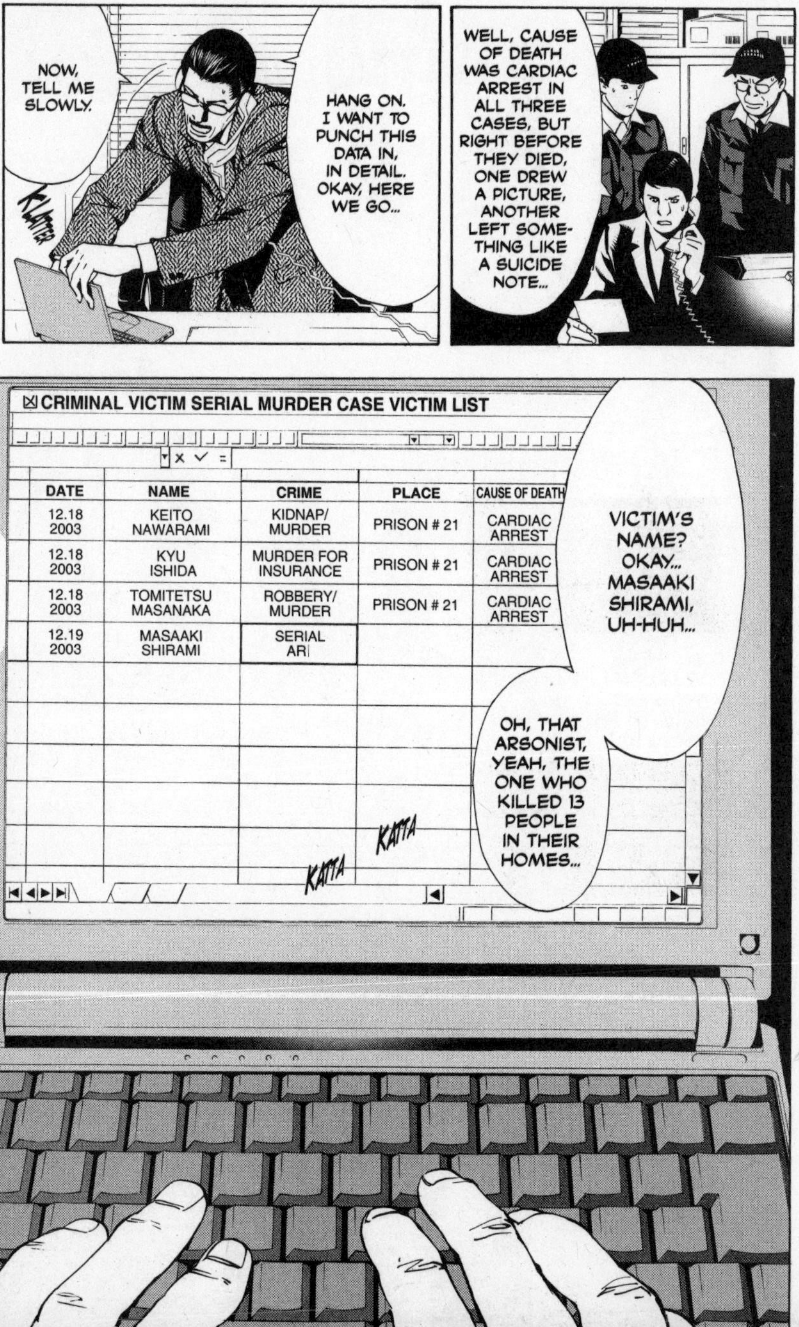
WELL, CAUSE OF DEATH WAS CARDIAC ARREST IN ALL THREE CASES, BUT RIGHT BEFORE THEY DIED, ONE DREW A PICTURE, ANOTHER LEFT SOMETHING LIKE A SUICIDE NOTE...
HANG ON. I WANT TO PUNCH THIS DATA IN, IN DETAIL. OKAY, HERE WE GO...
NOW, TELL ME SLOWLY.
KLATTER
CRIMINAL VICTIM SERIAL MURDER CASE VICTIM LIST
DATE | NAME | CRIME | PLACE | CAUSE OF DEATH
12.18 2003 | KEITO NAWARAMI | KIDNAP/ MURDER | PRISON # 21 | CARDIAC ARREST
12.18 2003 | KYU ISHIDA | MURDER FOR INSURANCE | PRISON # 21 | CARDIAC ARREST
12.18 2003 | TOMITETSU MASANAKA | ROBBERY/ MURDER | PRISON # 21 | CARDIAC ARREST
12.19 2003 | MASAAKI SHIRAMI | SERIAL AR
VICTIM'S NAME? OKAY... MASAAKI SHIRAMI, UH-HUH...
OH, THAT ARSONIST, YEAH, THE ONE WHO KILLED 13 PEOPLE IN THEIR HOMES...
KATTA
KATTA

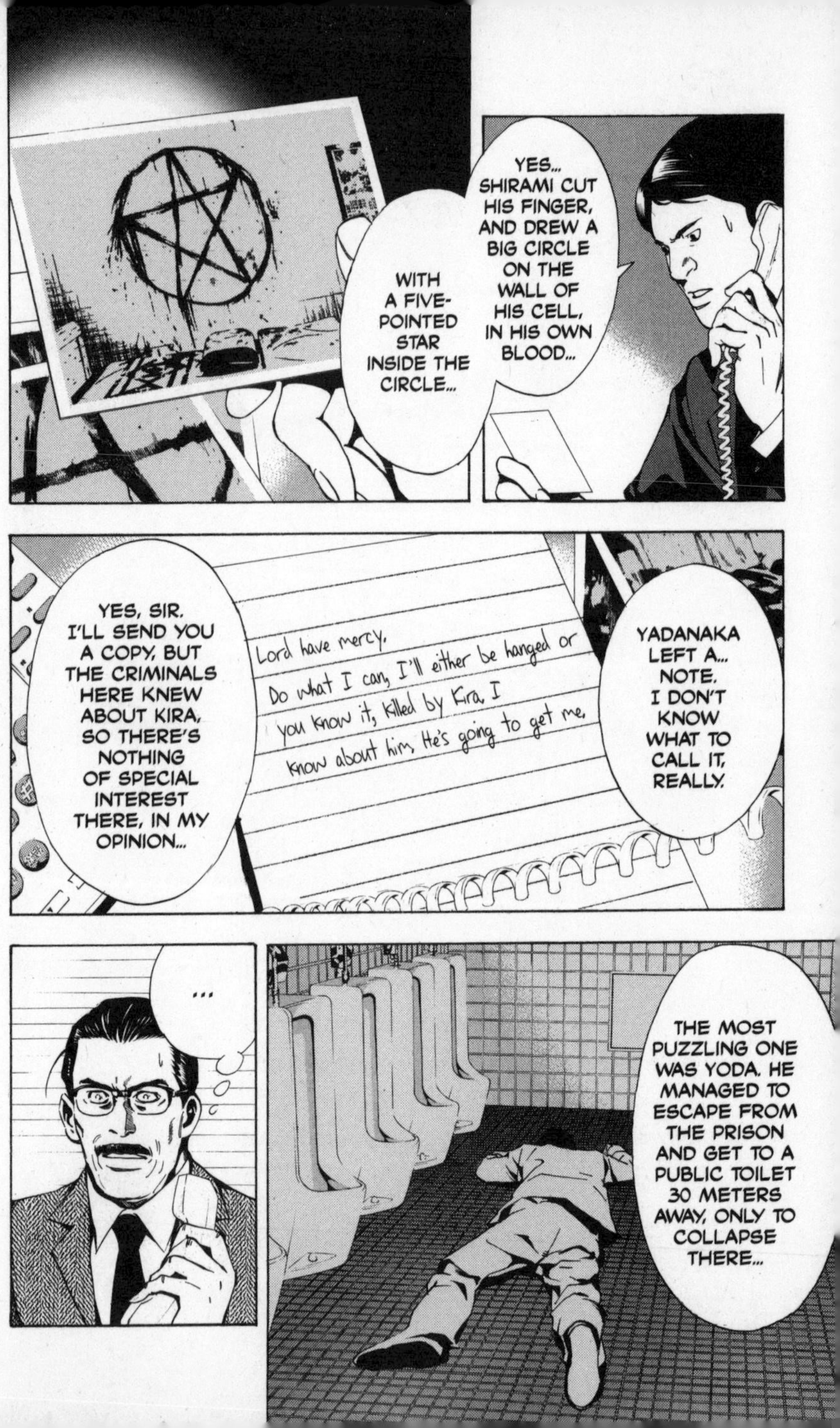
YES... SHIRAMI CUT HIS FINGER, AND DREW A BIG CIRCLE ON THE WALL OF HIS CELL, IN HIS OWN BLOOD...
WITH A FIVE-POINTED STAR INSIDE THE CIRCLE...
YADANAKA LEFT A... NOTE. I DON'T KNOW WHAT TO CALL IT, REALLY.
Lord have mercy,
Do what I can, I'll either be hanged or
you know it, killed by Kira. I
know about him. He's going to get me.
YES, SIR. I'LL SEND YOU A COPY, BUT THE CRIMINALS HERE KNEW ABOUT KIRA, SO THERE'S NOTHING OF SPECIAL INTEREST THERE, IN MY OPINION...
THE MOST PUZZLING ONE WAS YODA. HE MANAGED TO ESCAPE FROM THE PRISON AND GET TO A PUBLIC TOILET 30 METERS AWAY, ONLY TO COLLAPSE THERE...
...

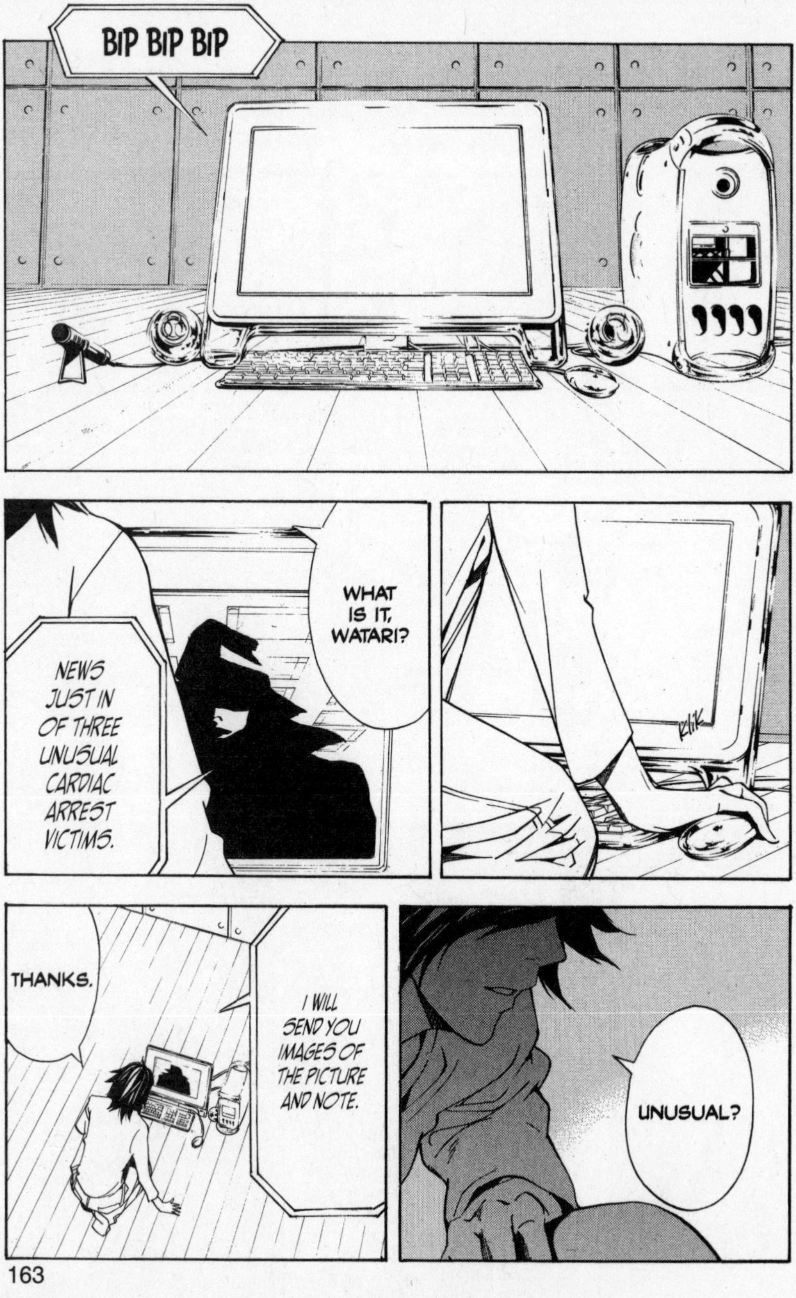
BIP BIP BIP
Klik
WHAT IS IT, WATARI?
NEWS JUST IN OF THREE UNUSUAL CARDIAC ARREST VICTIMS.
UNUSUAL?
I WILL SEND YOU IMAGES OF THE PICTURE AND NOTE.
THANKS.

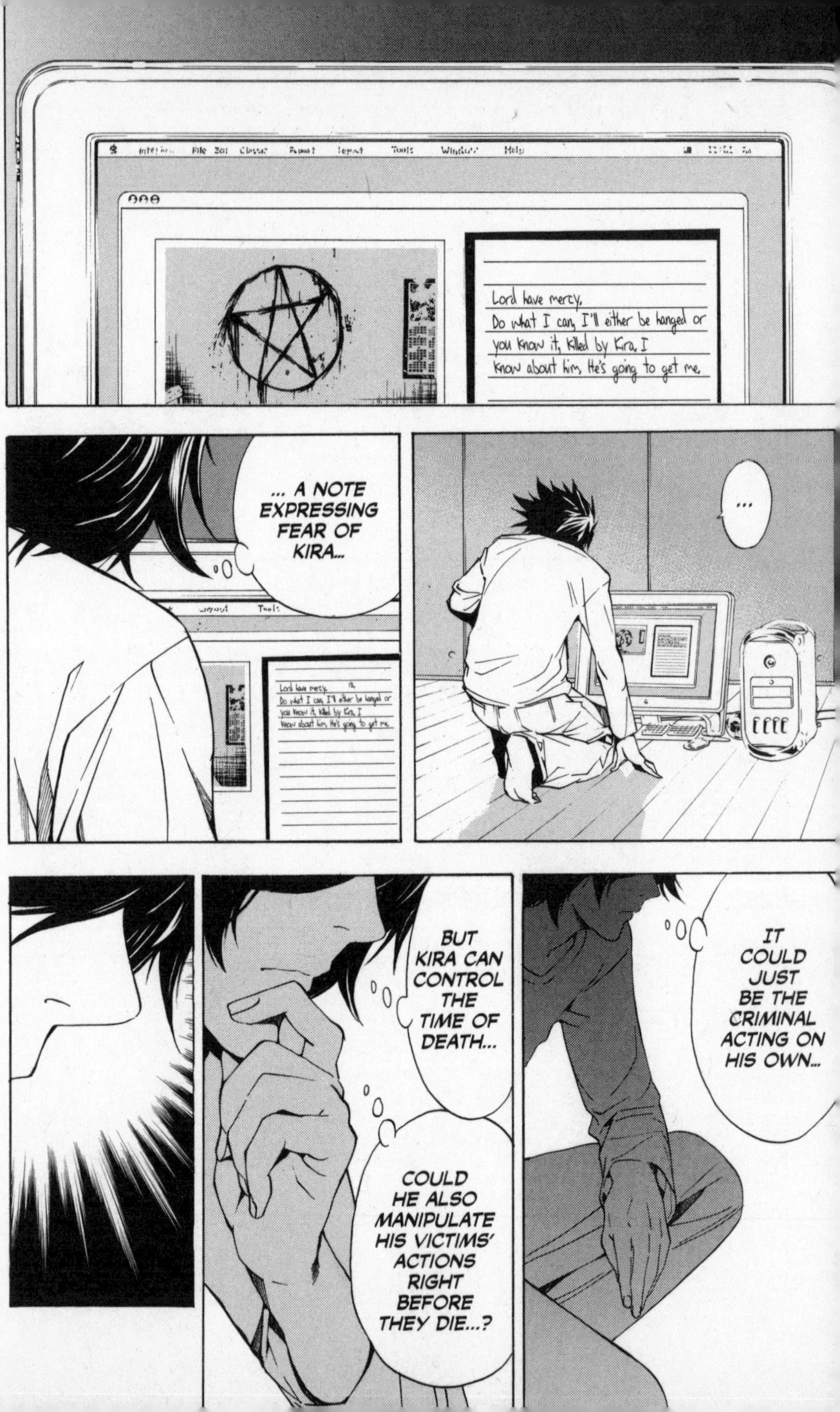
Lord have mercy.
Do what I can, I'll either be hanged or
you know it, killed by Kira. I
know about him. He's going to get me.
...
... A NOTE EXPRESSING FEAR OF KIRA...
IT COULD JUST BE THE CRIMINAL ACTING ON HIS OWN...
BUT KIRA CAN CONTROL THE TIME OF DEATH...
COULD HE ALSO MANIPULATE HIS VICTIMS' ACTIONS RIGHT BEFORE THEY DIE...?

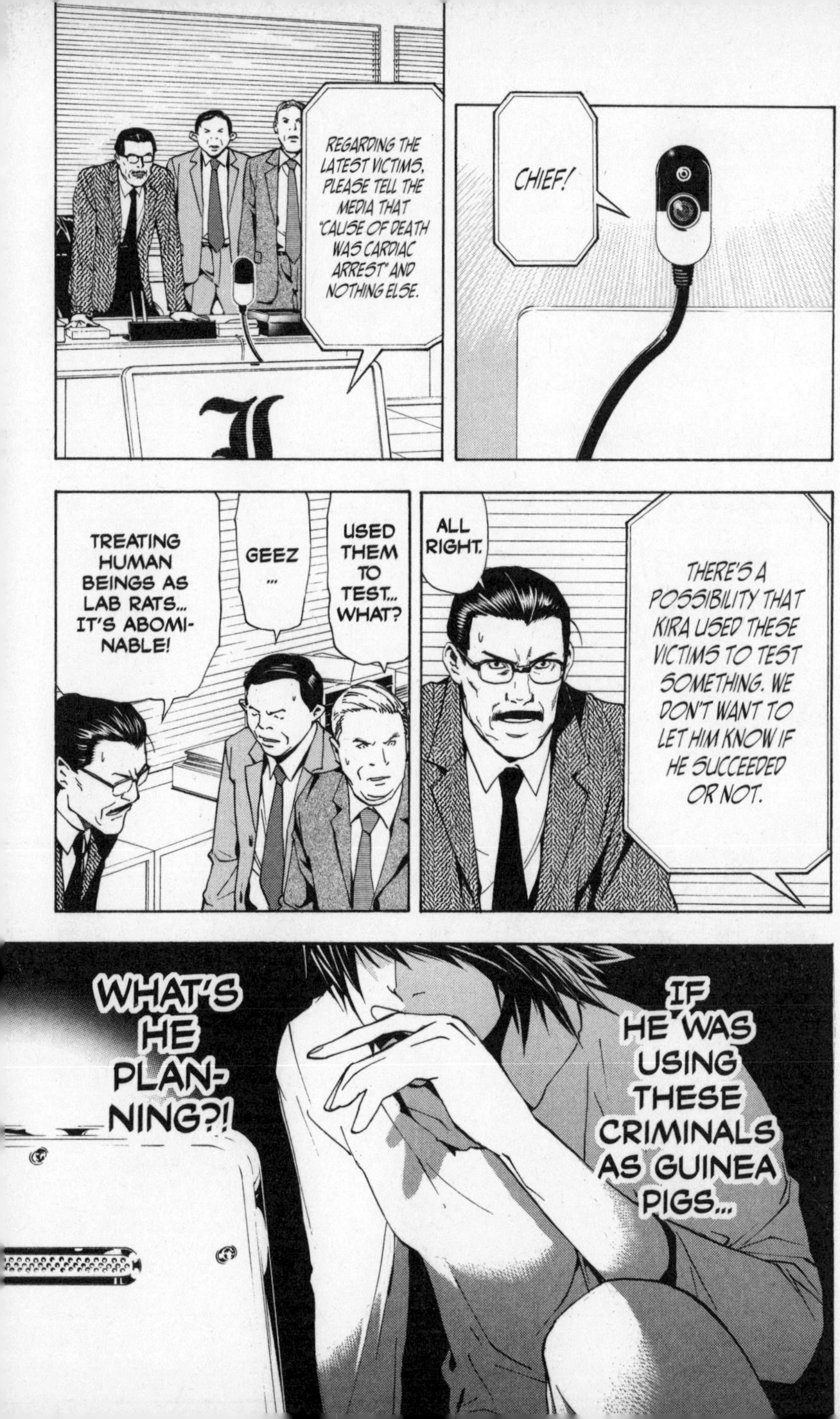
CHIEF!
REGARDING THE LATEST VICTIMS, PLEASE TELL THE MEDIA THAT "CAUSE OF DEATH WAS CARDIAC ARREST" AND NOTHING ELSE.
ALL RIGHT.
THERE'S A POSSIBILITY THAT KIRA USED THESE VICTIMS TO TEST SOMETHING. WE DON'T WANT TO LET HIM KNOW IF HE SUCCEEDED OR NOT.
USED THEM TO TEST... WHAT?
GEEZ ...
TREATING HUMAN BEINGS AS LAB RATS... IT'S ABOMINABLE!
IF HE WAS USING THESE CRIMINALS AS GUINEA PIGS...
WHAT'S HE PLANNING?!

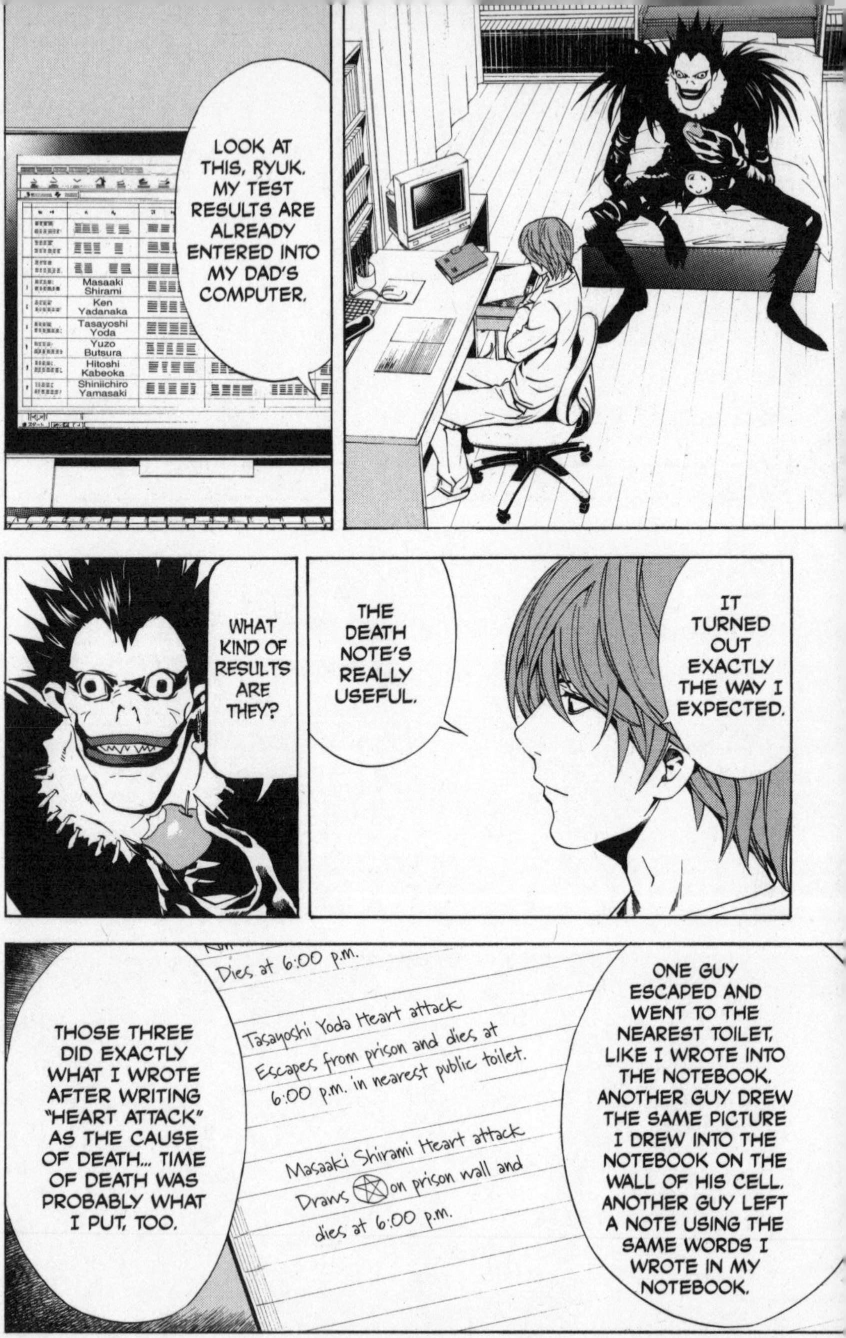
LOOK AT THIS, RYUK. MY TEST RESULTS ARE ALREADY ENTERED INTO MY DAD'S COMPUTER.
Masaaki Shirami
Ken Yadanaka
Tasayoshi Yoda
Yuzo Butsura
Hitoshi Kabeoka
Shiniichiro Yamasaki
IT TURNED OUT EXACTLY THE WAY I EXPECTED.
THE DEATH NOTE'S REALLY USEFUL.
WHAT KIND OF RESULTS ARE THEY?
ONE GUY ESCAPED AND WENT TO THE NEAREST TOILET, LIKE I WROTE INTO THE NOTEBOOK. ANOTHER GUY DREW THE SAME PICTURE I DREW INTO THE NOTEBOOK ON THE WALL OF HIS CELL. ANOTHER GUY LEFT A NOTE USING THE SAME WORDS I WROTE IN MY NOTEBOOK.
Dies at 6:00 p.m.
Tasayoshi Yoda Heart attack
Escapes from prison and dies at 6:00 p.m. in nearest public toilet.
Masaaki Shirami Heart attack
Draws on prison wall and dies at 6:00 p.m.
THOSE THREE DID EXACTLY WHAT I WROTE AFTER WRITING "HEART ATTACK" AS THE CAUSE OF DEATH... TIME OF DEATH WAS PROBABLY WHAT I PUT, TOO.

READ THIS WAY

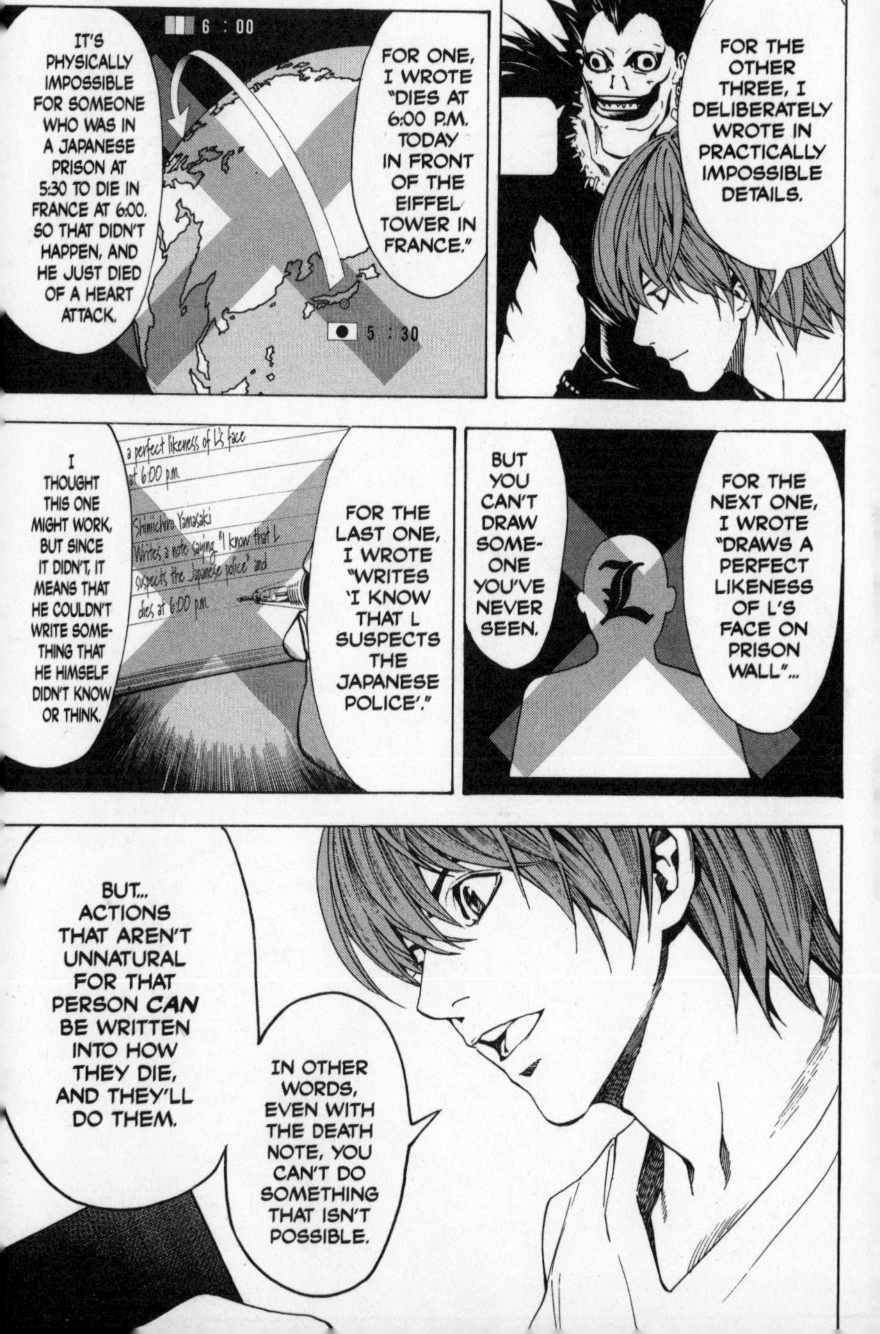
FOR THE OTHER THREE, I DELIBERATELY WROTE IN PRACTICALLY IMPOSSIBLE DETAILS.
6 : 00
FOR ONE, I WROTE "DIES AT 6:00 P.M. TODAY IN FRONT OF THE EIFFEL TOWER IN FRANCE."
IT'S PHYSICALLY IMPOSSIBLE FOR SOMEONE WHO WAS IN A JAPANESE PRISON AT 5:30 TO DIE IN FRANCE AT 6:00. SO THAT DIDN'T HAPPEN, AND HE JUST DIED OF A HEART ATTACK.
5 : 30
FOR THE NEXT ONE, I WROTE "DRAWS A PERFECT LIKENESS OF L'S FACE ON PRISON WALL"...
BUT YOU CAN'T DRAW SOME-ONE YOU'VE NEVER SEEN.
L
FOR THE LAST ONE, I WROTE "WRITES 'I KNOW THAT L SUSPECTS THE JAPANESE POLICE'."
a perfect likeness of L's face
at 6:00 p.m.
Shinichiro Yamasaki
Writes a note saying "I know that L suspects the Japanese police" and
dies at 6:00 p.m.
I THOUGHT THIS ONE MIGHT WORK, BUT SINCE IT DIDN'T, IT MEANS THAT HE COULDN'T WRITE SOME-THING THAT HE HIMSELF DIDN'T KNOW OR THINK.
BUT... ACTIONS THAT AREN'T UNNATURAL FOR THAT PERSON CAN BE WRITTEN INTO HOW THEY DIE, AND THEY'LL DO THEM.
IN OTHER WORDS, EVEN WITH THE DEATH NOTE, YOU CAN'T DO SOMETHING THAT ISN'T POSSIBLE.

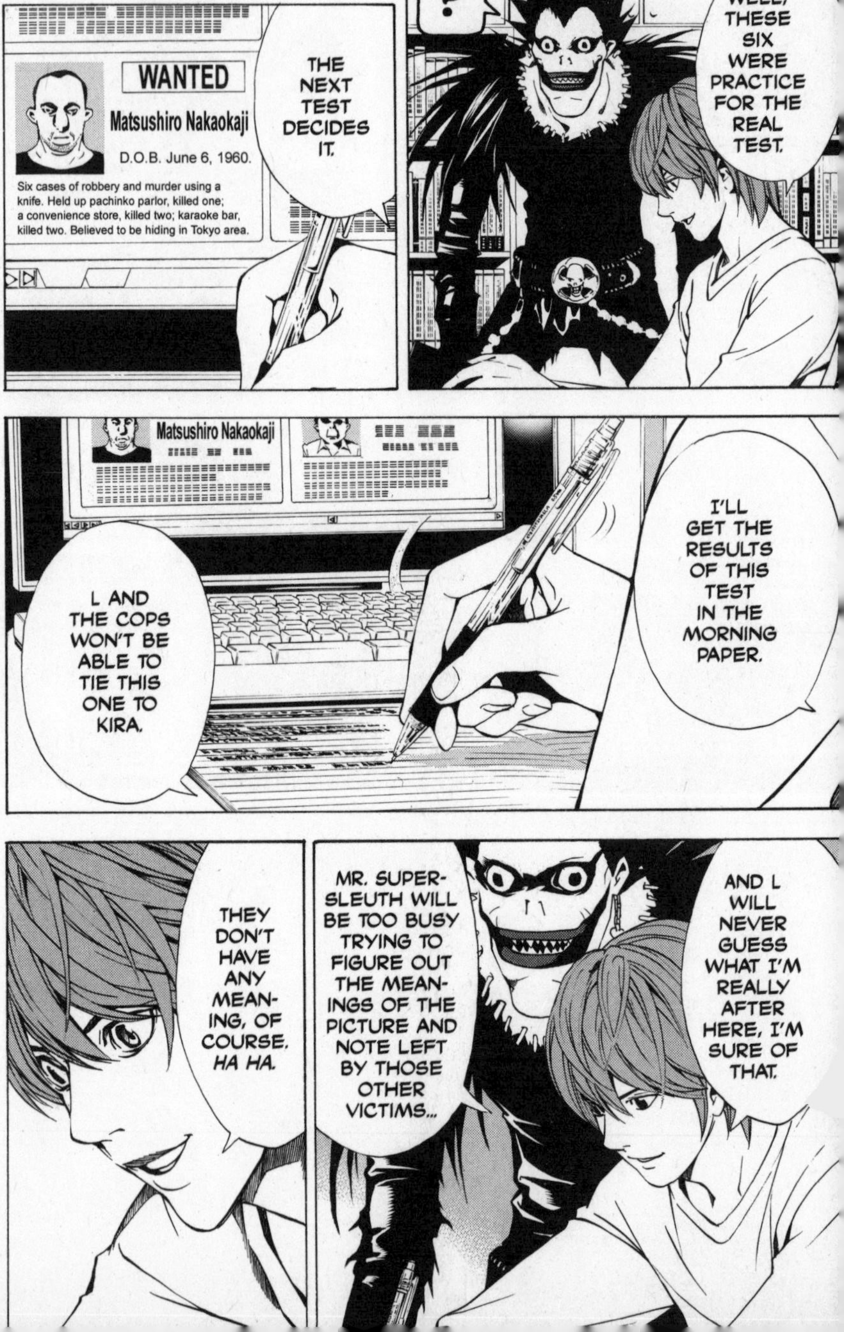
WELL, THESE SIX WERE PRACTICE FOR THE REAL TEST.
?
THE NEXT TEST DECIDES IT.
WANTED
Matsushiro Nakaokaji
D.O.B. June 6, 1960.
Six cases of robbery and murder using a knife. Held up pachinko parlor, killed one; a convenience store, killed two; karaoke bar, killed two. Believed to be hiding in Tokyo area.
I'LL GET THE RESULTS OF THIS TEST IN THE MORNING PAPER.
Matsushiro Nakaokaji
L AND THE COPS WON'T BE ABLE TO TIE THIS ONE TO KIRA.
AND L WILL NEVER GUESS WHAT I'M REALLY AFTER HERE, I'M SURE OF THAT.
MR. SUPER-SLEUTH WILL BE TOO BUSY TRYING TO FIGURE OUT THE MEANINGS OF THE PICTURE AND NOTE LEFT BY THOSE OTHER VICTIMS...
THEY DON'T HAVE ANY MEANING, OF COURSE. *HA HA.*

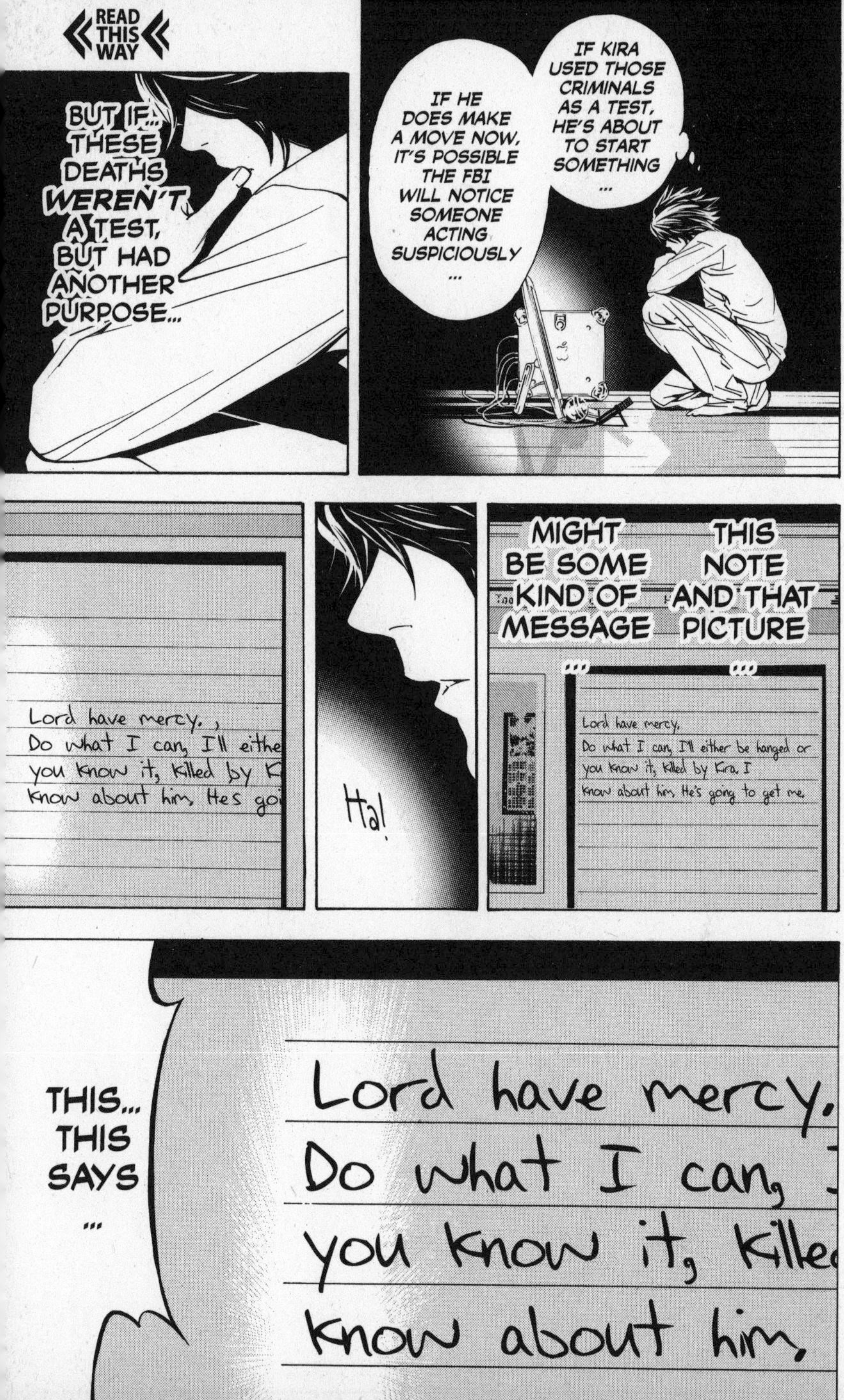
READ THIS WAY
IF KIRA USED THOSE CRIMINALS AS A TEST, HE'S ABOUT TO START SOMETHING ...
IF HE DOES MAKE A MOVE NOW, IT'S POSSIBLE THE FBI WILL NOTICE SOMEONE ACTING SUSPICIOUSLY ...
BUT IF... THESE DEATHS WEREN'T A TEST, BUT HAD ANOTHER PURPOSE...
THIS NOTE AND THAT PICTURE ...
MIGHT BE SOME KIND OF MESSAGE ...
Lord have mercy.
Do what I can, I'll either be hanged or
you know it, killed by Kira. I
know about him. He's going to get me.
Ha!
Lord have mercy.,
Do what I can, I'll eithe
you know it, killed by K
know about him. He's goi
THIS... THIS SAYS ...
Lord have mercy.
Do what I can,
you know it, kille
know about him.

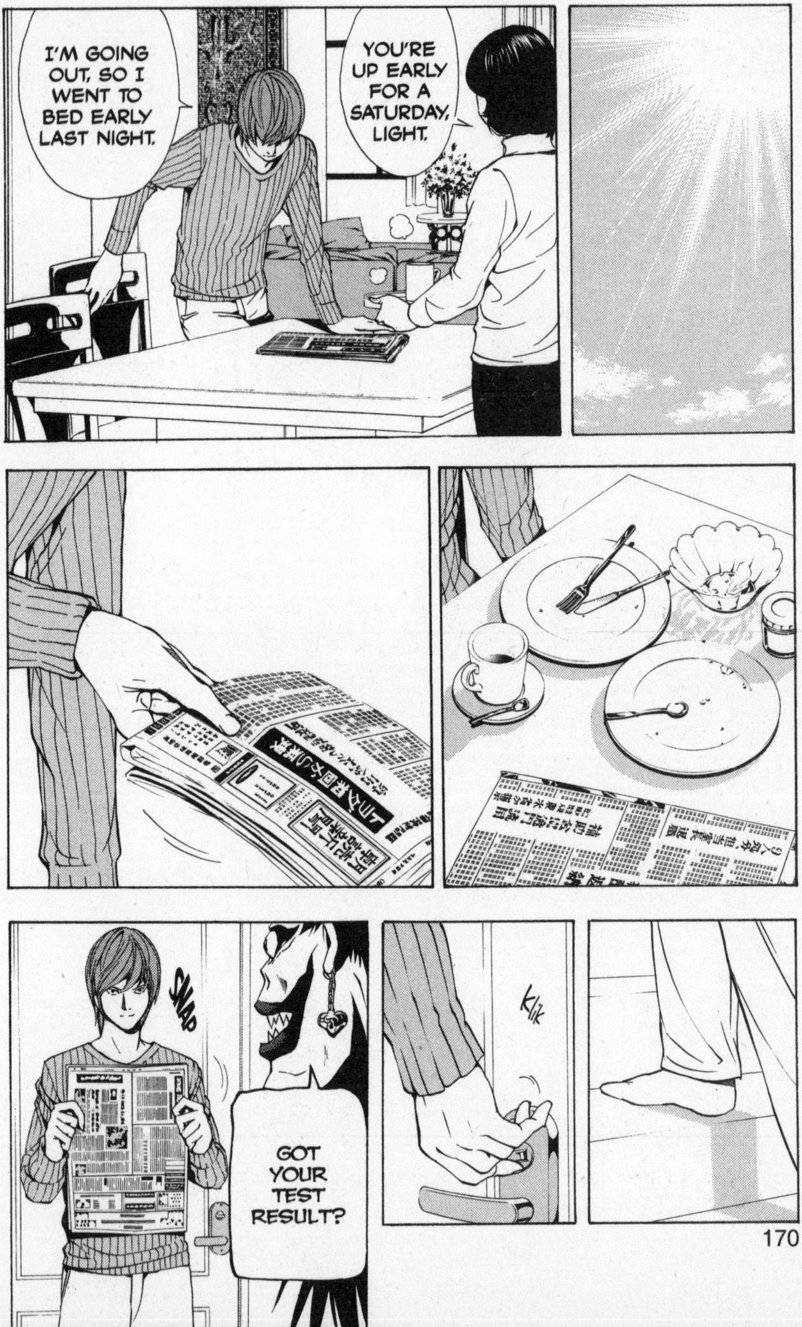
YOU'RE UP EARLY FOR A SATURDAY, LIGHT.
I'M GOING OUT, SO I WENT TO BED EARLY LAST NIGHT.
KLIK
SNAP
GOT YOUR TEST RESULT?

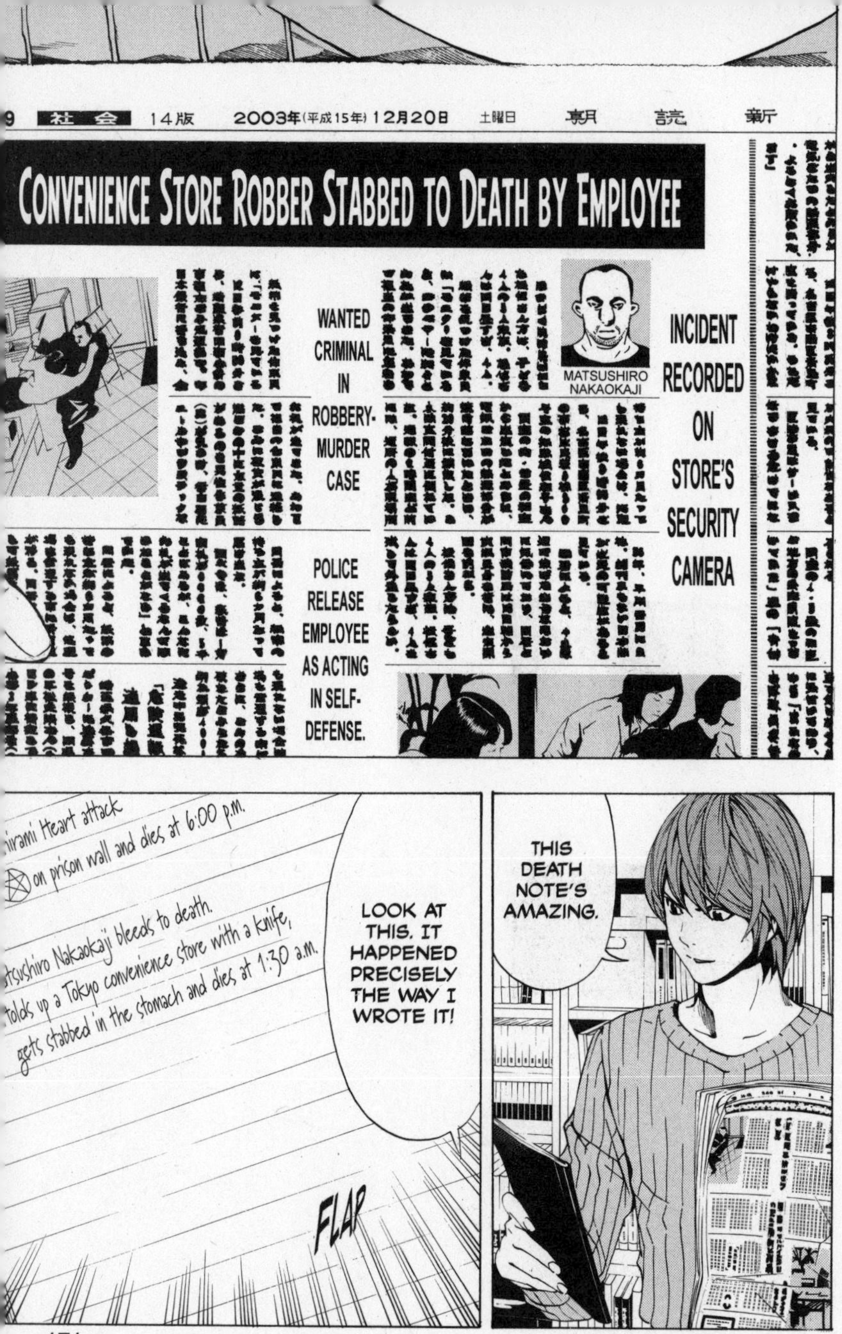
9 社会 14版 2003年(平成15年) 12月20日 土曜日 朝 読 新
CONVENIENCE STORE ROBBER STABBED TO DEATH BY EMPLOYEE
INCIDENT RECORDED ON STORE'S SECURITY CAMERA
MATSUSHIRO NAKAOKAJI
WANTED CRIMINAL IN ROBBERY-MURDER CASE
POLICE RELEASE EMPLOYEE AS ACTING IN SELF-DEFENSE.
THIS DEATH NOTE'S AMAZING.
LOOK AT THIS. IT HAPPENED PRECISELY THE WAY I WROTE IT!
irami Heart attack
on prison wall and dies at 6:00 p.m.
tsushiro Nakaokaji bleeds to death.
olds up a Tokyo convenience store with a knife,
gets stabbed in the stomach and dies at 1:30 a.m.
FLAP

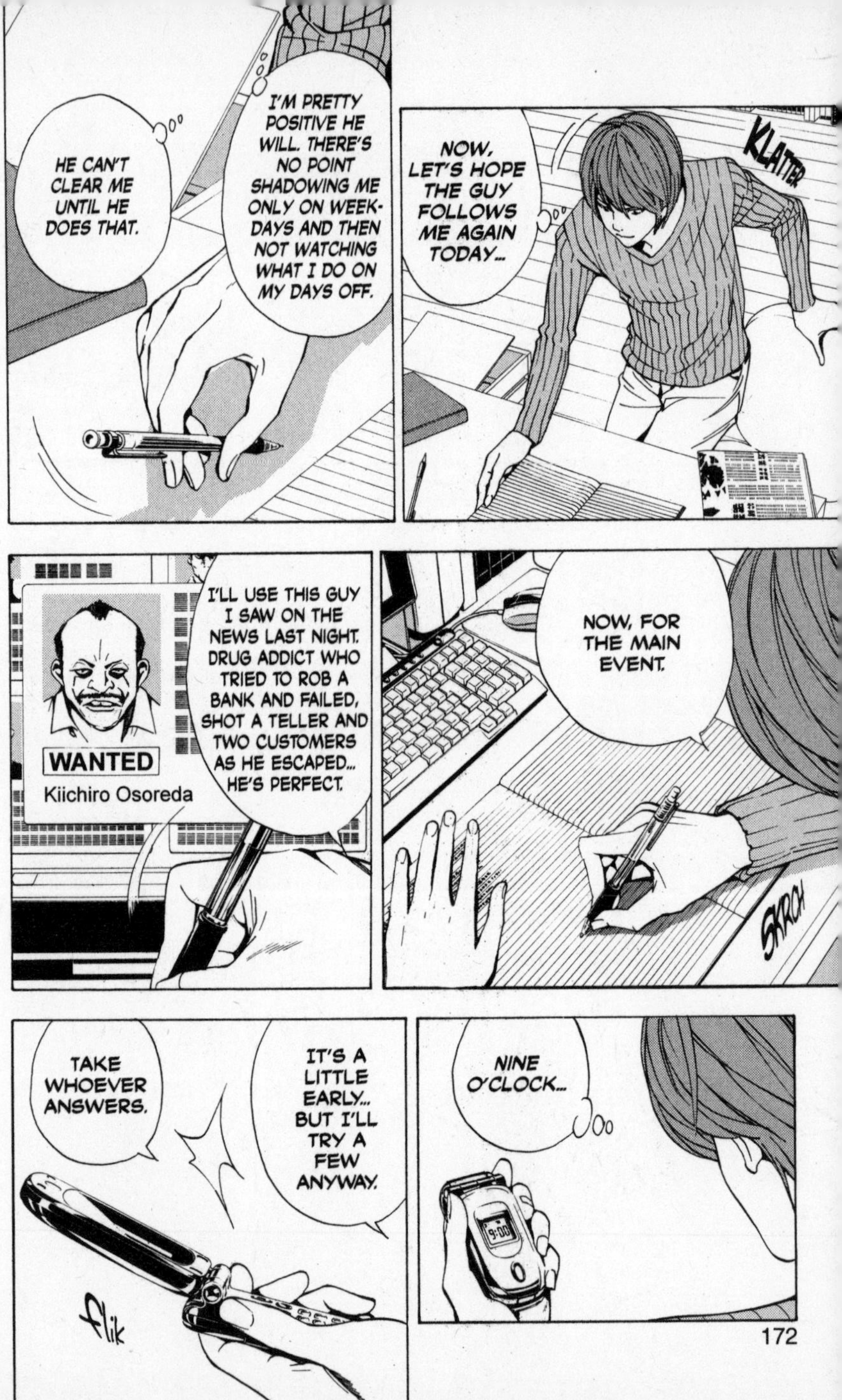
NOW, LET'S HOPE THE GUY FOLLOWS ME AGAIN TODAY...
KLATTER
I'M PRETTY POSITIVE HE WILL. THERE'S NO POINT SHADOWING ME ONLY ON WEEK-DAYS AND THEN NOT WATCHING WHAT I DO ON MY DAYS OFF.
HE CAN'T CLEAR ME UNTIL HE DOES THAT.
NOW, FOR THE MAIN EVENT.
SKRCH
I'LL USE THIS GUY I SAW ON THE NEWS LAST NIGHT. DRUG ADDICT WHO TRIED TO ROB A BANK AND FAILED, SHOT A TELLER AND TWO CUSTOMERS AS HE ESCAPED... HE'S PERFECT.
WANTED
Kiichiro Osoreda
NINE O'CLOCK...
9:00
IT'S A LITTLE EARLY... BUT I'LL TRY A FEW ANYWAY.
TAKE WHOEVER ANSWERS.
flik

READ THIS WAY

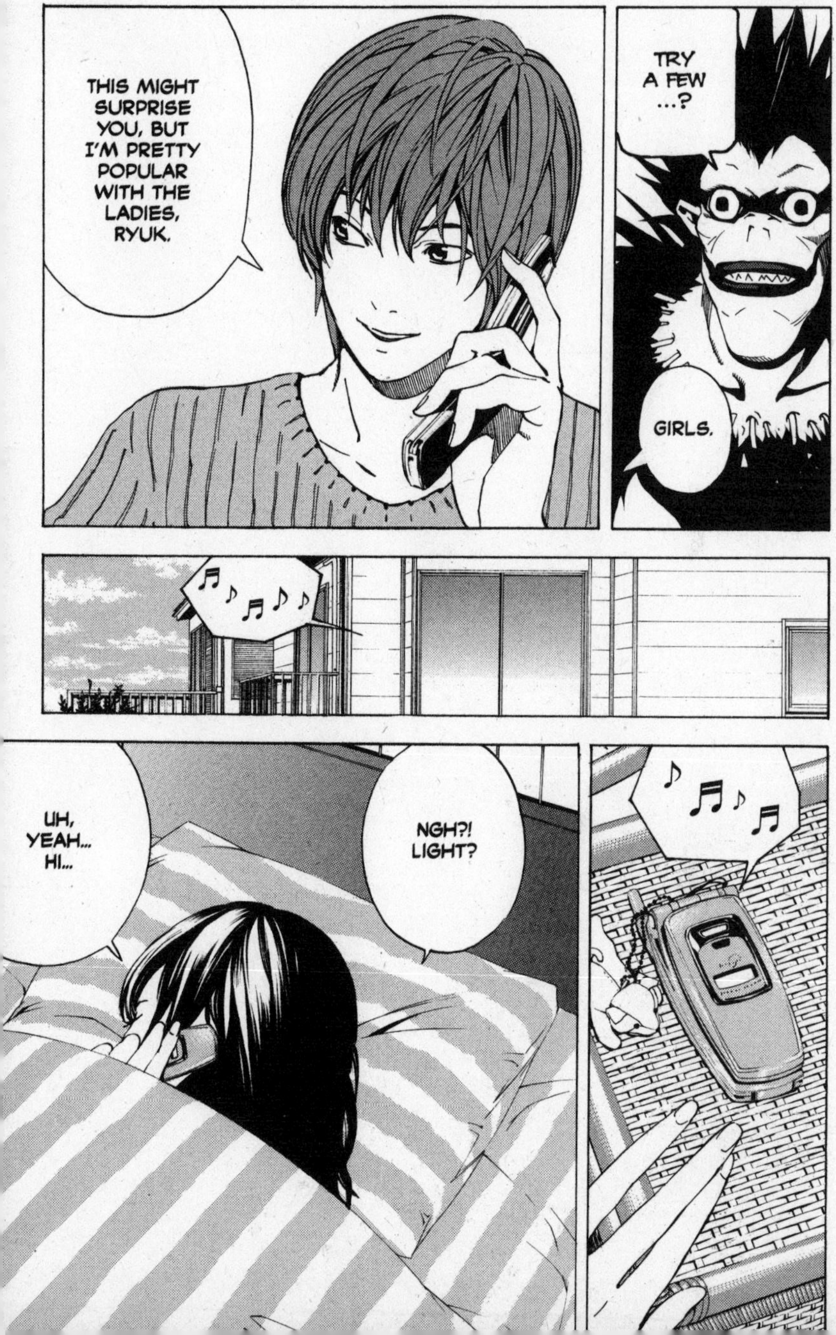
TRY A FEW ...?
GIRLS.
THIS MIGHT SURPRISE YOU, BUT I'M PRETTY POPULAR WITH THE LADIES, RYUK.
NGH?! LIGHT?
UH, YEAH... HI...

DEATH NOTE
How to use it

VI

- The conditions for death will not be realized unless it is physically possible for that human or it is reasonably assumed to be carried out by that human.

書き入れる死の状況は、その人間が物理的に可能な事、
その人間がやってもおかしくない範囲の行動でなければ実現しない。

- The specific scope of the condition for death is not known to the gods of death, either. So, you must examine and find out.

死の状況で可能になる事の詳細な範囲は死神にもわからないので、
自分で検証し明らかにしていくしかない。

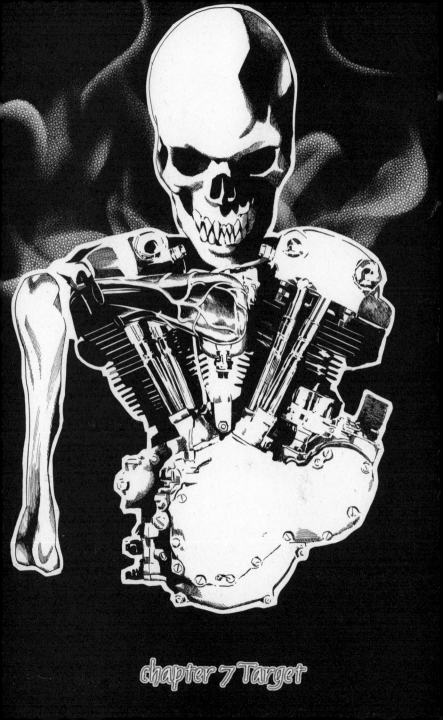

chapter 7 Target

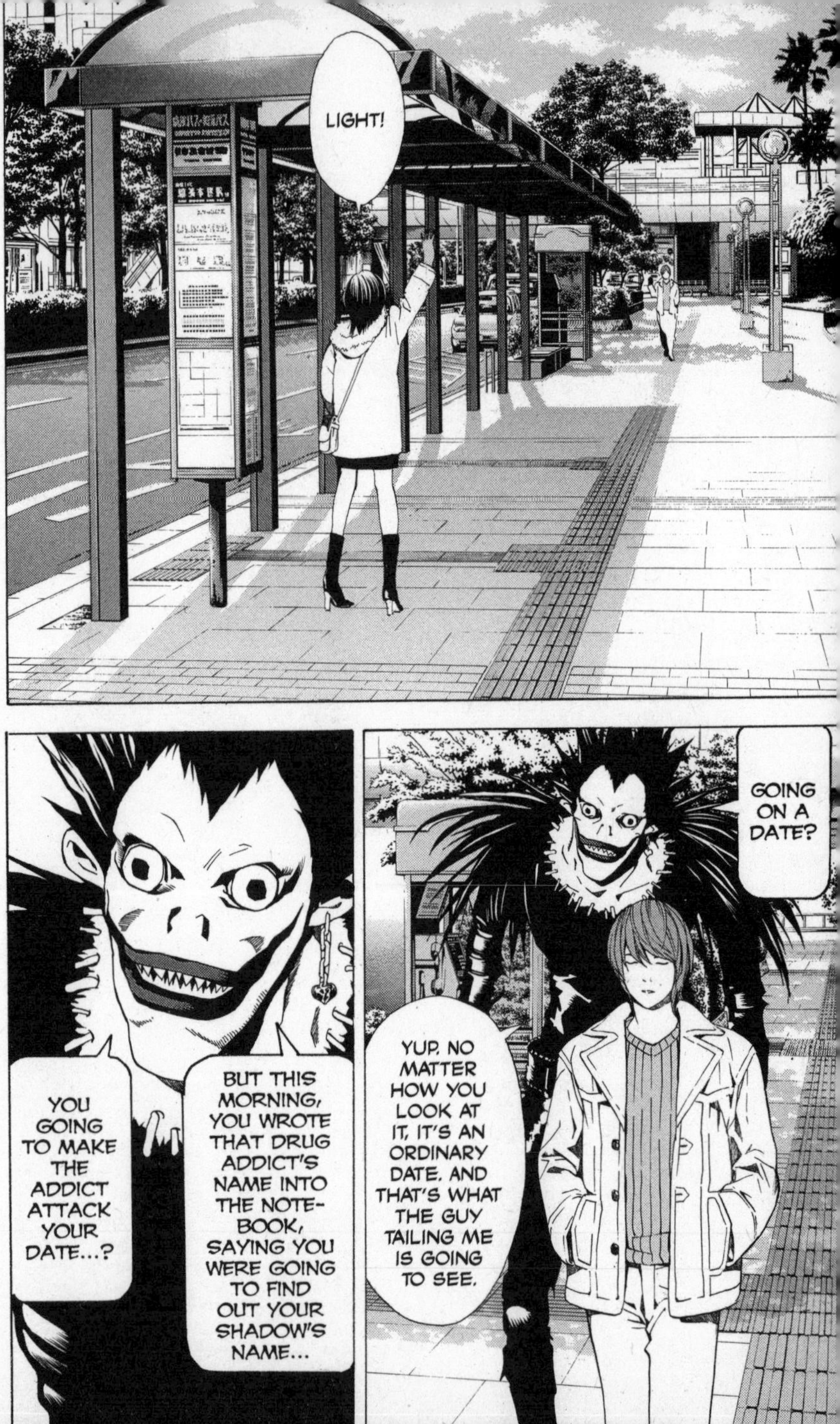
LIGHT!
GOING ON A DATE?
YUP. NO MATTER HOW YOU LOOK AT IT, IT'S AN ORDINARY DATE. AND THAT'S WHAT THE GUY TAILING ME IS GOING TO SEE.
BUT THIS MORNING, YOU WROTE THAT DRUG ADDICT'S NAME INTO THE NOTE-BOOK, SAYING YOU WERE GOING TO FIND OUT YOUR SHADOW'S NAME...
YOU GOING TO MAKE THE ADDICT ATTACK YOUR DATE...?

READ THIS WAY

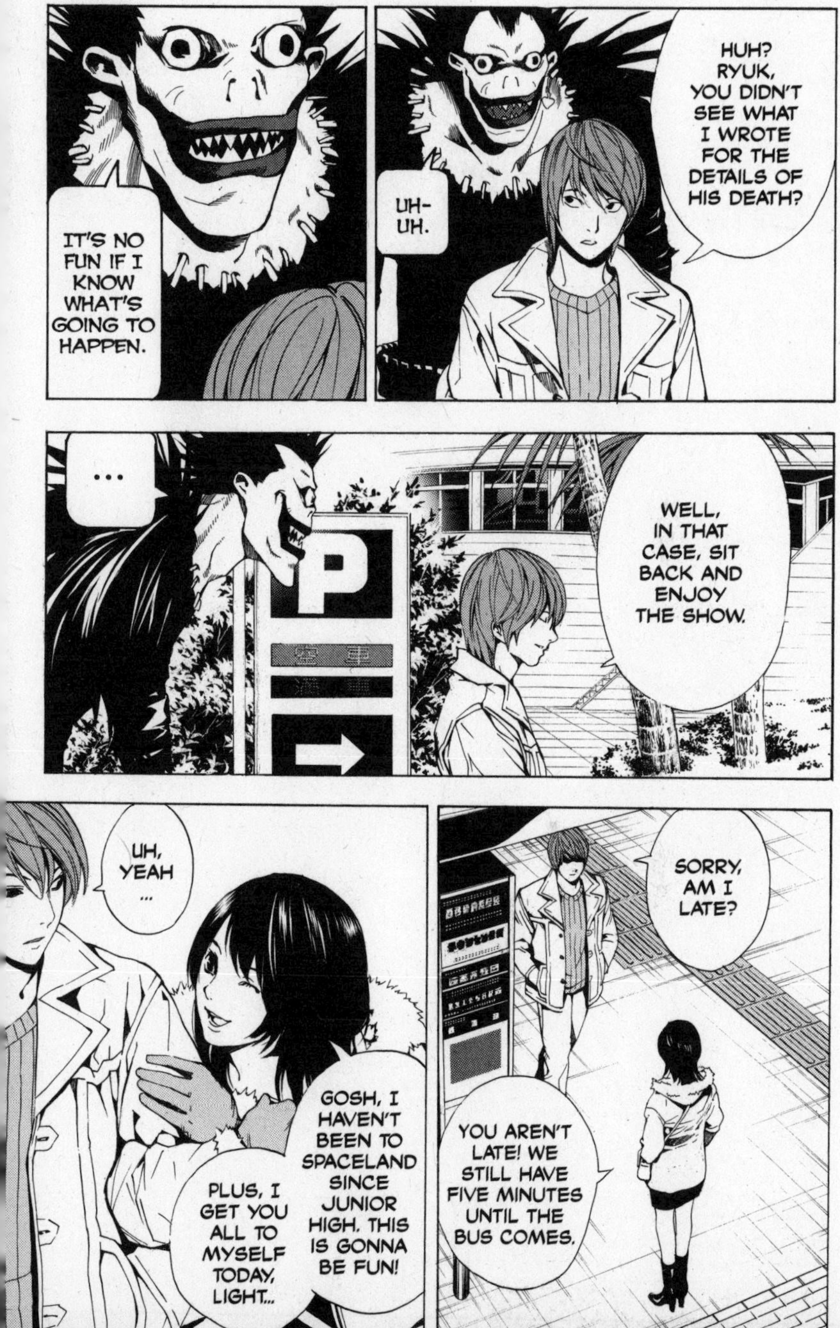

HUH? RYUK, YOU DIDN'T SEE WHAT I WROTE FOR THE DETAILS OF HIS DEATH?
UH-UH.
IT'S NO FUN IF I KNOW WHAT'S GOING TO HAPPEN.
WELL, IN THAT CASE, SIT BACK AND ENJOY THE SHOW.
...
SORRY, AM I LATE?
YOU AREN'T LATE! WE STILL HAVE FIVE MINUTES UNTIL THE BUS COMES.
GOSH, I HAVEN'T BEEN TO SPACELAND SINCE JUNIOR HIGH. THIS IS GONNA BE FUN!
PLUS, I GET YOU ALL TO MYSELF TODAY, LIGHT...
UH, YEAH ...

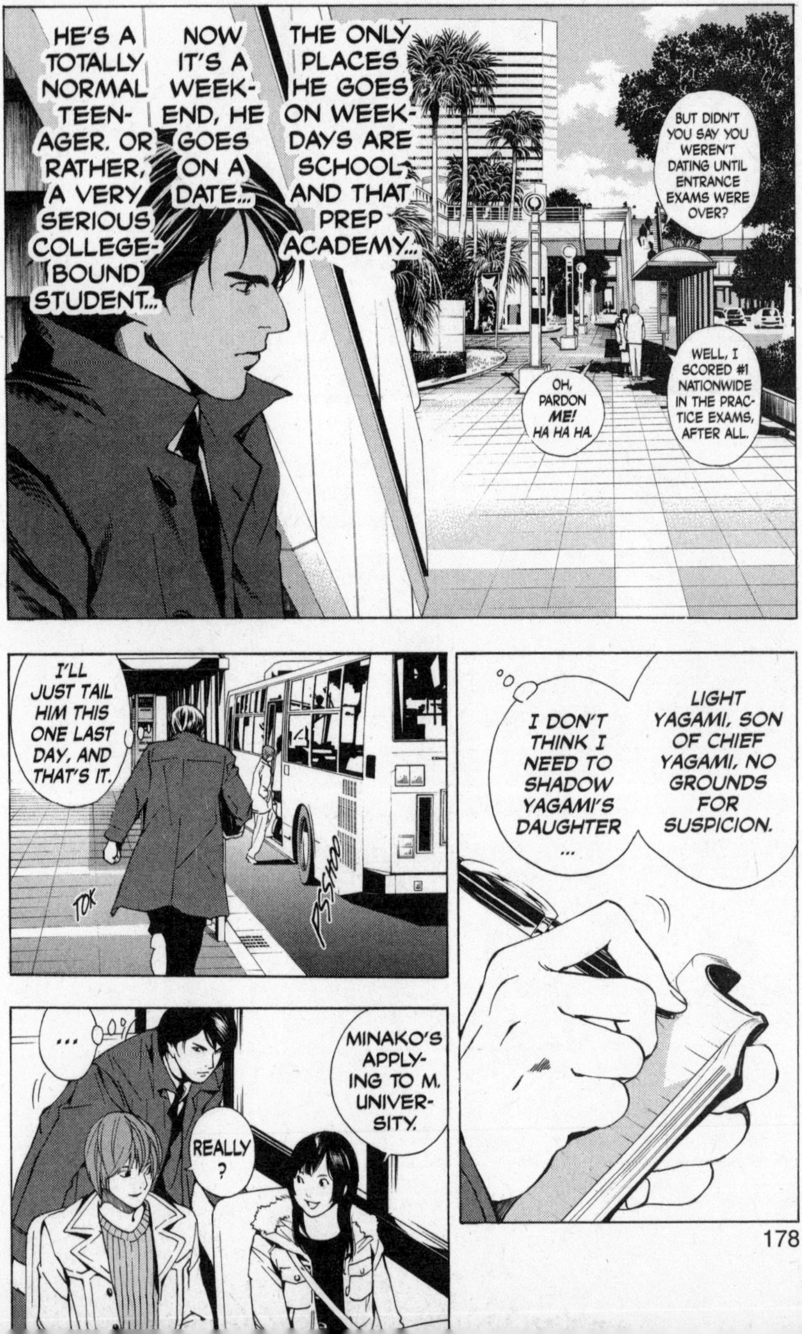
BUT DIDN'T YOU SAY YOU WEREN'T DATING UNTIL ENTRANCE EXAMS WERE OVER?
WELL, I SCORED #1 NATIONWIDE IN THE PRACTICE EXAMS, AFTER ALL.
OH, PARDON ME! HA HA HA.
THE ONLY PLACES HE GOES ON WEEKDAYS ARE SCHOOL AND THAT PREP ACADEMY...
NOW IT'S A WEEKEND, HE GOES ON A DATE...
HE'S A TOTALLY NORMAL TEENAGER. OR RATHER, A VERY SERIOUS COLLEGE-BOUND STUDENT...
LIGHT YAGAMI, SON OF CHIEF YAGAMI, NO GROUNDS FOR SUSPICION.
I DON'T THINK I NEED TO SHADOW YAGAMI'S DAUGHTER ...
I'LL JUST TAIL HIM THIS ONE LAST DAY, AND THAT'S IT.
TOK
PSSHOO
MINAKO'S APPLYING TO M. UNIVERSITY.
REALLY ?
...

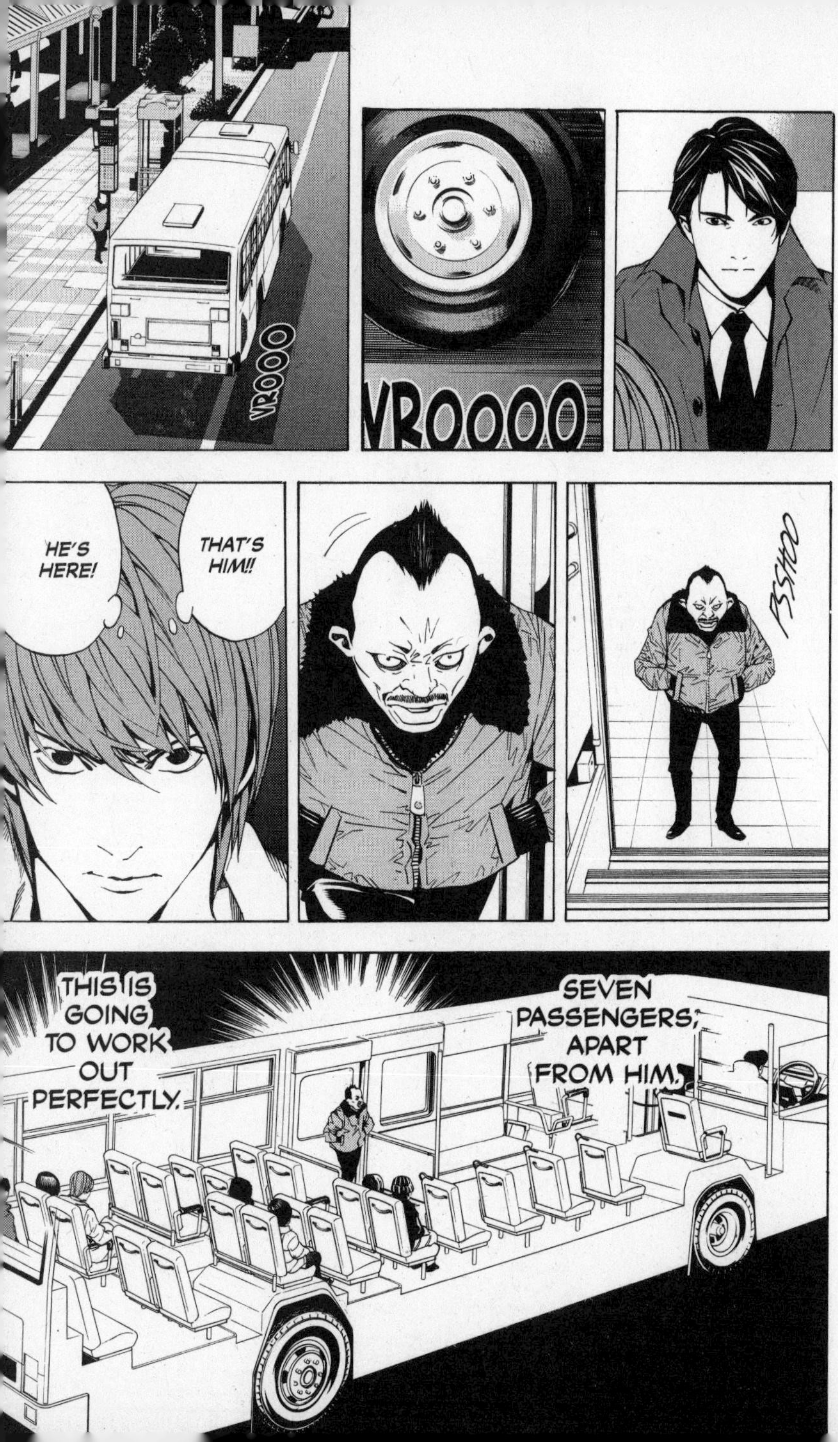
VROOOO
VROOOO
PSSHOO
THAT'S HIM!!
HE'S HERE!
SEVEN PASSENGERS, APART FROM HIM.
THIS IS GOING TO WORK OUT PERFECTLY.

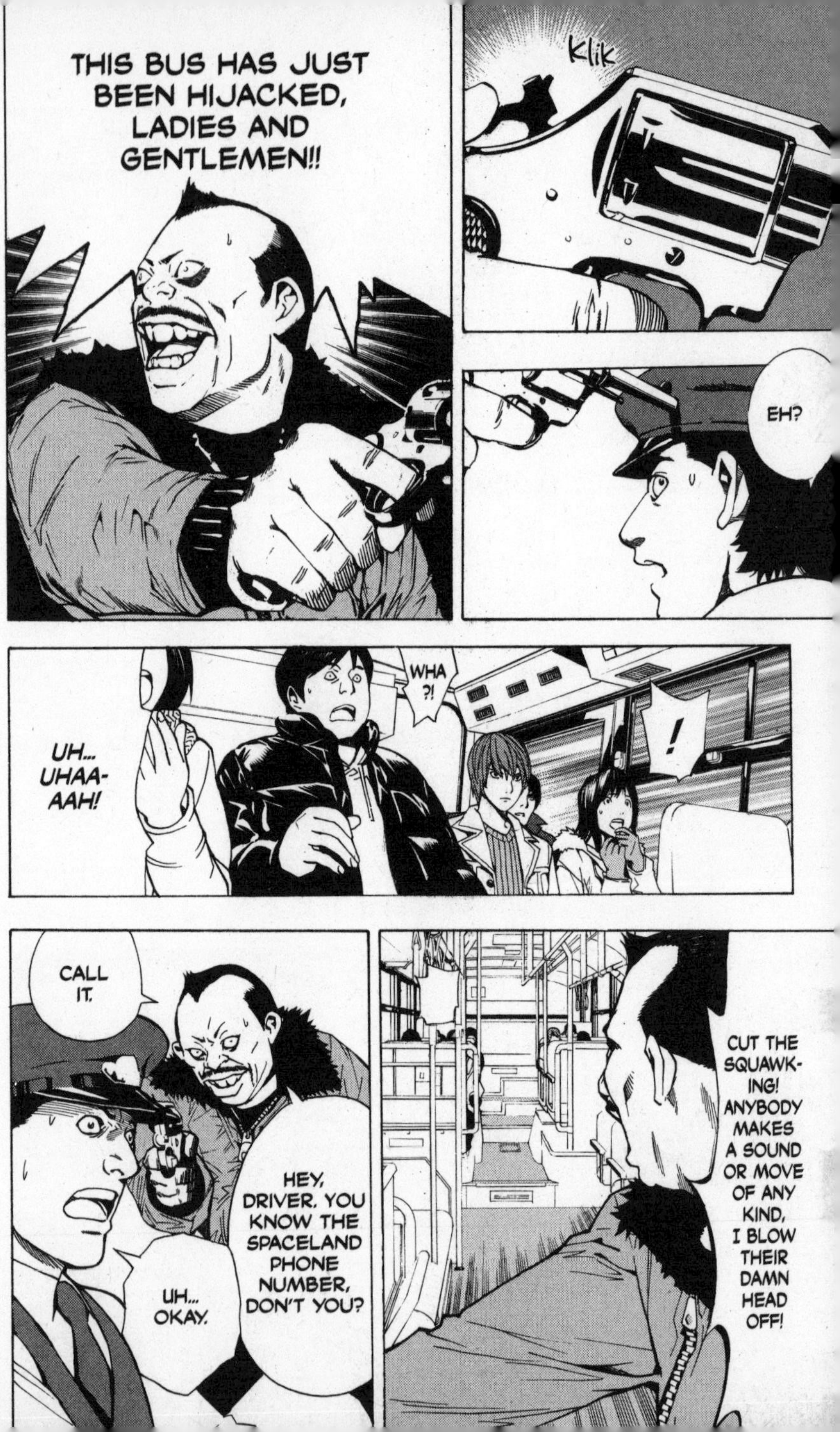
Klik
EH?
THIS BUS HAS JUST BEEN HIJACKED, LADIES AND GENTLEMEN!!
!
WHA ?!
UH... UHAA-AAH!
CUT THE SQUAWK-ING! ANYBODY MAKES A SOUND OR MOVE OF ANY KIND, I BLOW THEIR DAMN HEAD OFF!
HEY, DRIVER. YOU KNOW THE SPACELAND PHONE NUMBER, DON'T YOU?
UH... OKAY.
CALL IT.

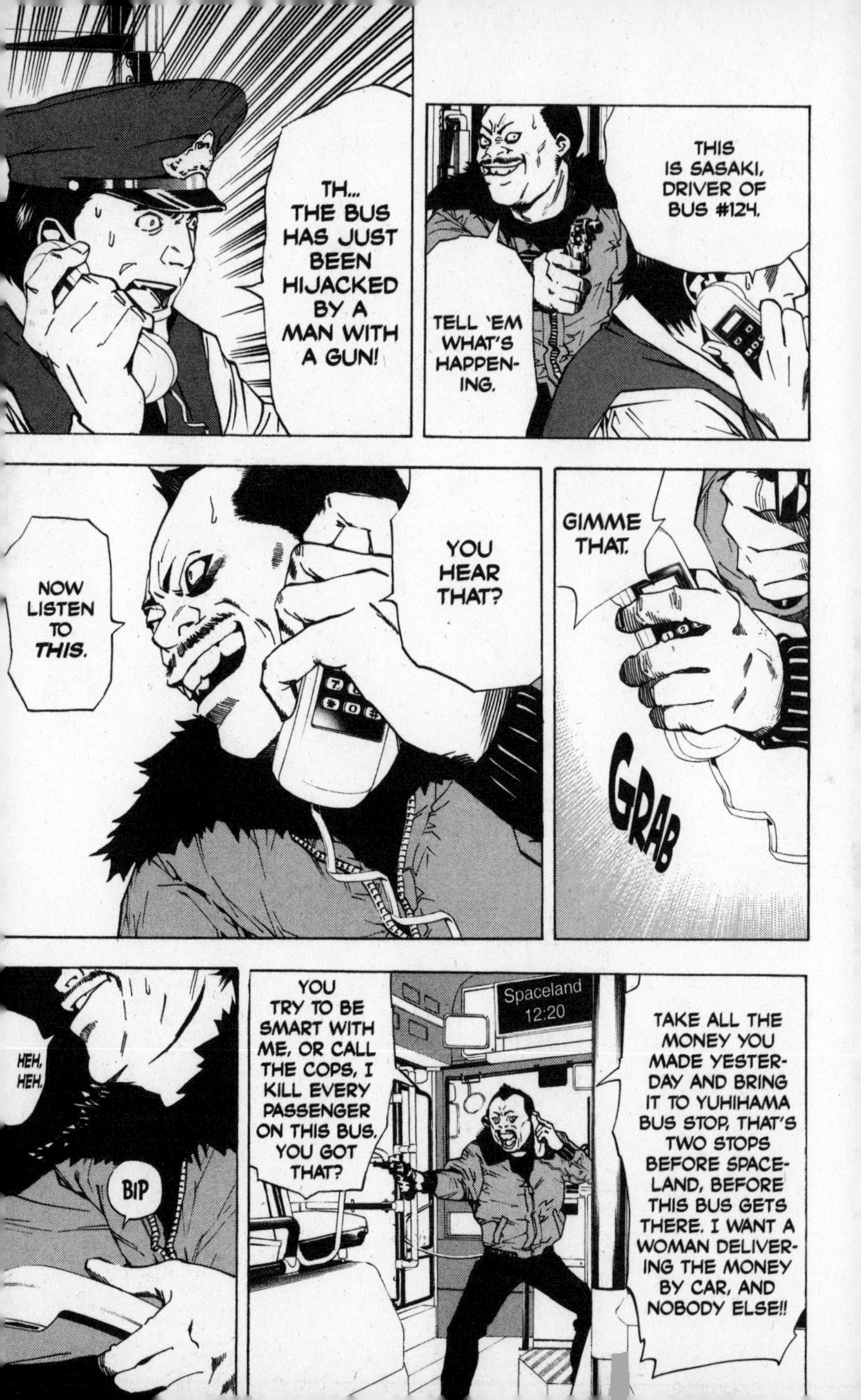
THIS IS SASAKI, DRIVER OF BUS #124.
TELL 'EM WHAT'S HAPPEN-ING.
TH... THE BUS HAS JUST BEEN HIJACKED BY A MAN WITH A GUN!
GIMME THAT.
GRAB
YOU HEAR THAT?
NOW LISTEN TO *THIS.*
Spaceland 12:20
TAKE ALL THE MONEY YOU MADE YESTER-DAY AND BRING IT TO YUHIHAMA BUS STOP, THAT'S TWO STOPS BEFORE SPACE-LAND, BEFORE THIS BUS GETS THERE. I WANT A WOMAN DELIVER-ING THE MONEY BY CAR, AND NOBODY ELSE!!
YOU TRY TO BE SMART WITH ME, OR CALL THE COPS, I KILL EVERY PASSENGER ON THIS BUS. YOU GOT THAT?
HEH, HEH.
BIP

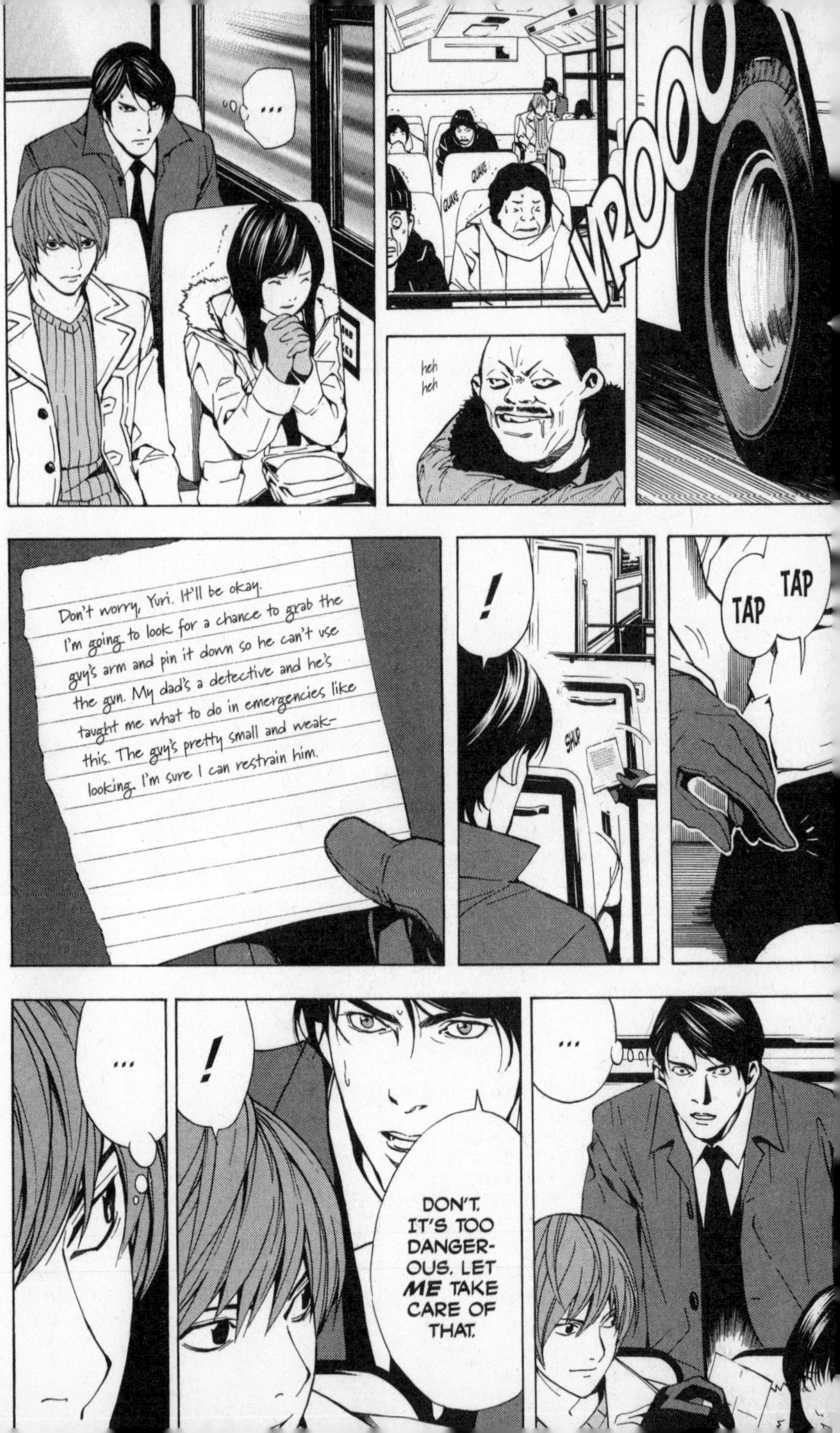
VROOOO
QUAKE
QUAKE
heh heh
...
TAP TAP
!
SHUP
Don't worry, Yuri. It'll be okay. I'm going to look for a chance to grab the guy's arm and pin it down so he can't use the gun. My dad's a detective and he's taught me what to do in emergencies like this. The guy's pretty small and weak-looking. I'm sure I can restrain him.
...
!
DON'T. IT'S TOO DANGER-OUS. LET ME TAKE CARE OF THAT.
...

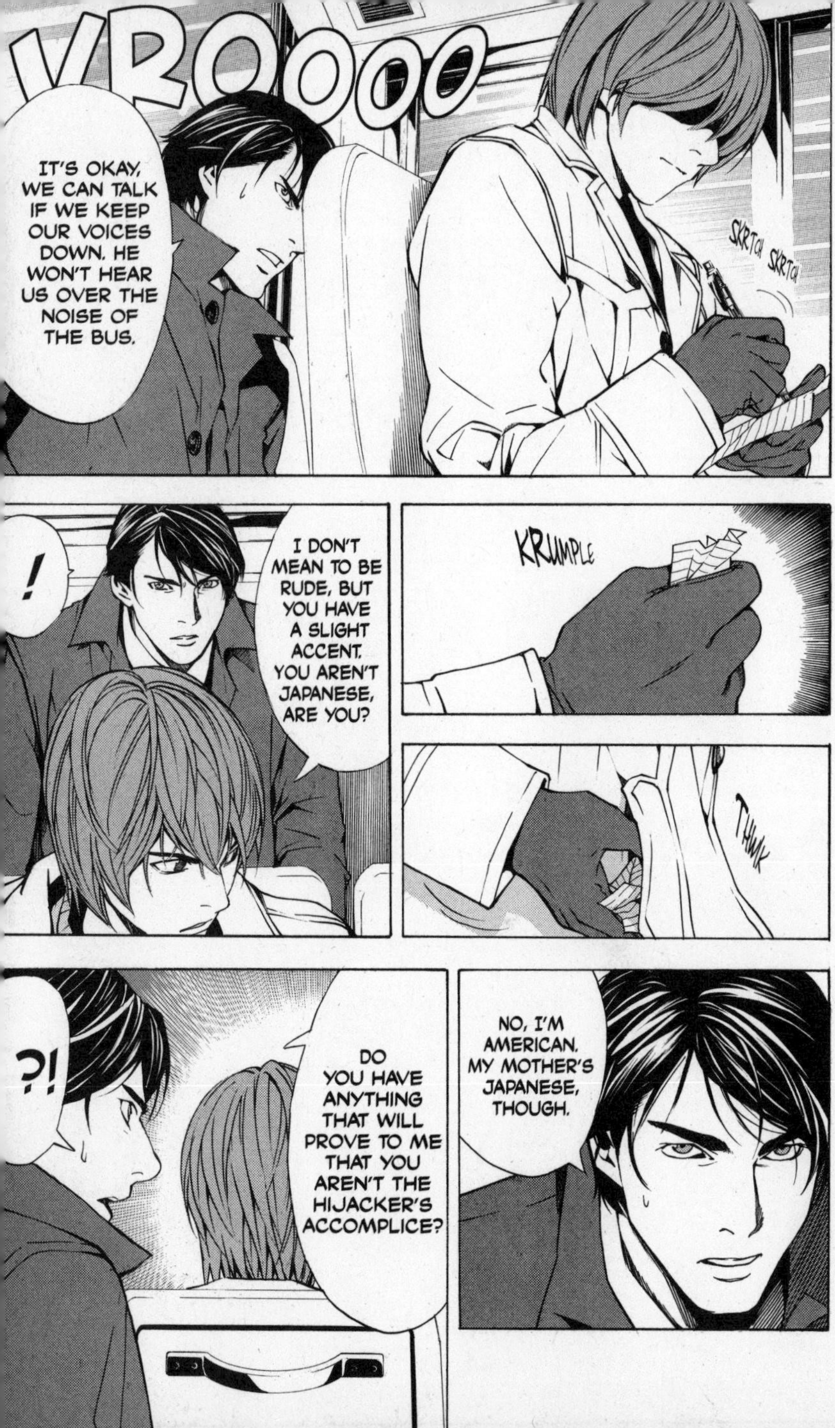
VROOOO
SKRTCH SKRTCH
IT'S OKAY, WE CAN TALK IF WE KEEP OUR VOICES DOWN. HE WON'T HEAR US OVER THE NOISE OF THE BUS.
KRUMPLE
THUNK
I DON'T MEAN TO BE RUDE, BUT YOU HAVE A SLIGHT ACCENT. YOU AREN'T JAPANESE, ARE YOU?
!
NO, I'M AMERICAN. MY MOTHER'S JAPANESE, THOUGH.
DO YOU HAVE ANYTHING THAT WILL PROVE TO ME THAT YOU AREN'T THE HIJACKER'S ACCOMPLICE?
?!

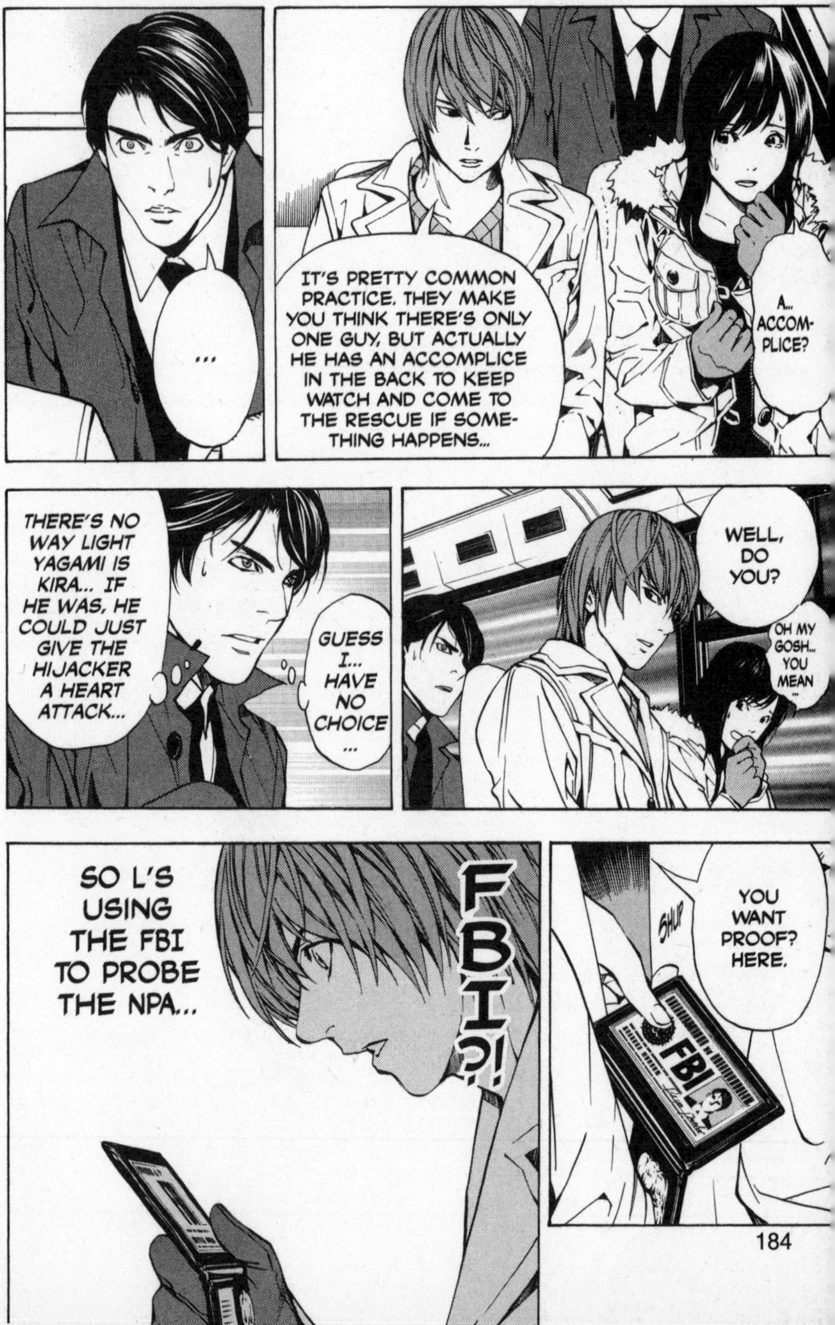
IT'S PRETTY COMMON PRACTICE. THEY MAKE YOU THINK THERE'S ONLY ONE GUY, BUT ACTUALLY HE HAS AN ACCOMPLICE IN THE BACK TO KEEP WATCH AND COME TO THE RESCUE IF SOMETHING HAPPENS...
A... ACCOMPLICE?
...
WELL, DO YOU?
OH MY GOSH... YOU MEAN ...
THERE'S NO WAY LIGHT YAGAMI IS KIRA... IF HE WAS, HE COULD JUST GIVE THE HIJACKER A HEART ATTACK...
GUESS I... HAVE NO CHOICE ...
YOU WANT PROOF? HERE.
SHUP
FBI
FBI?!
SO L'S USING THE FBI TO PROBE THE NPA...

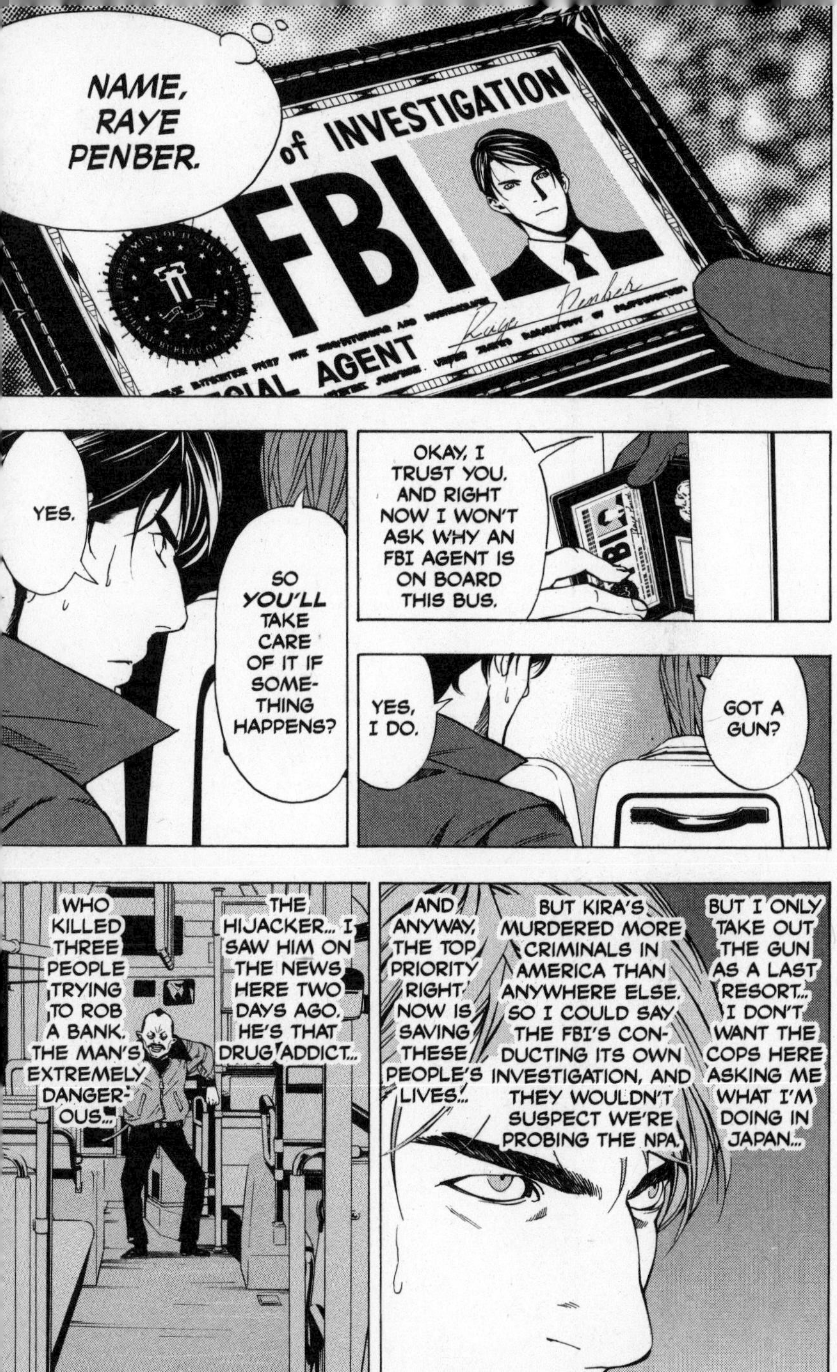
NAME, RAYE PENBER.
of INVESTIGATION
FBI
AGENT
OKAY, I TRUST YOU. AND RIGHT NOW I WON'T ASK WHY AN FBI AGENT IS ON BOARD THIS BUS.
GOT A GUN?
YES, I DO.
SO *YOU'LL* TAKE CARE OF IT IF SOMETHING HAPPENS?
YES.
BUT I ONLY TAKE OUT THE GUN AS A LAST RESORT... I DON'T WANT THE COPS HERE ASKING ME WHAT I'M DOING IN JAPAN...
BUT KIRA'S MURDERED MORE CRIMINALS IN AMERICA THAN ANYWHERE ELSE, SO I COULD SAY THE FBI'S CONDUCTING ITS OWN INVESTIGATION, AND THEY WOULDN'T SUSPECT WE'RE PROBING THE NPA.
AND ANYWAY, THE TOP PRIORITY RIGHT NOW IS SAVING THESE PEOPLE'S LIVES...
THE HIJACKER... I SAW HIM ON THE NEWS HERE TWO DAYS AGO. HE'S THAT DRUG ADDICT...
WHO KILLED THREE PEOPLE TRYING TO ROB A BANK. THE MAN'S EXTREMELY DANGEROUS...

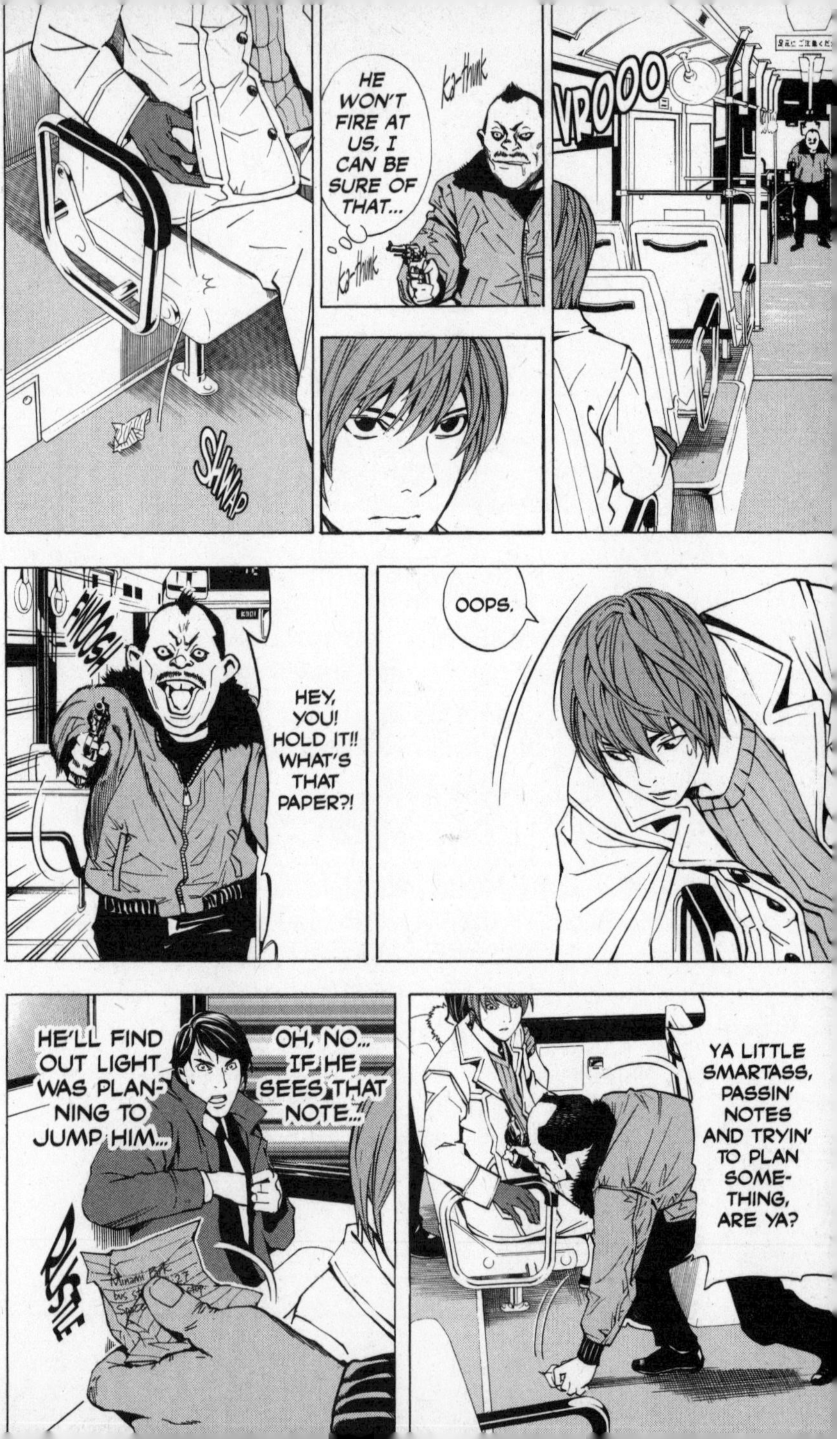

VROOO
HE WON'T FIRE AT US, I CAN BE SURE OF THAT...
ka-thunk
ka-thunk
SHWAP
OOPS.
HEY, YOU! HOLD IT!! WHAT'S THAT PAPER?!
FWOOSH
YA LITTLE SMARTASS, PASSIN' NOTES AND TRYIN' TO PLAN SOME-THING, ARE YA?
OH, NO... IF HE SEES THAT NOTE...
HE'LL FIND OUT LIGHT WAS PLAN-NING TO JUMP HIM...
RUSTLE

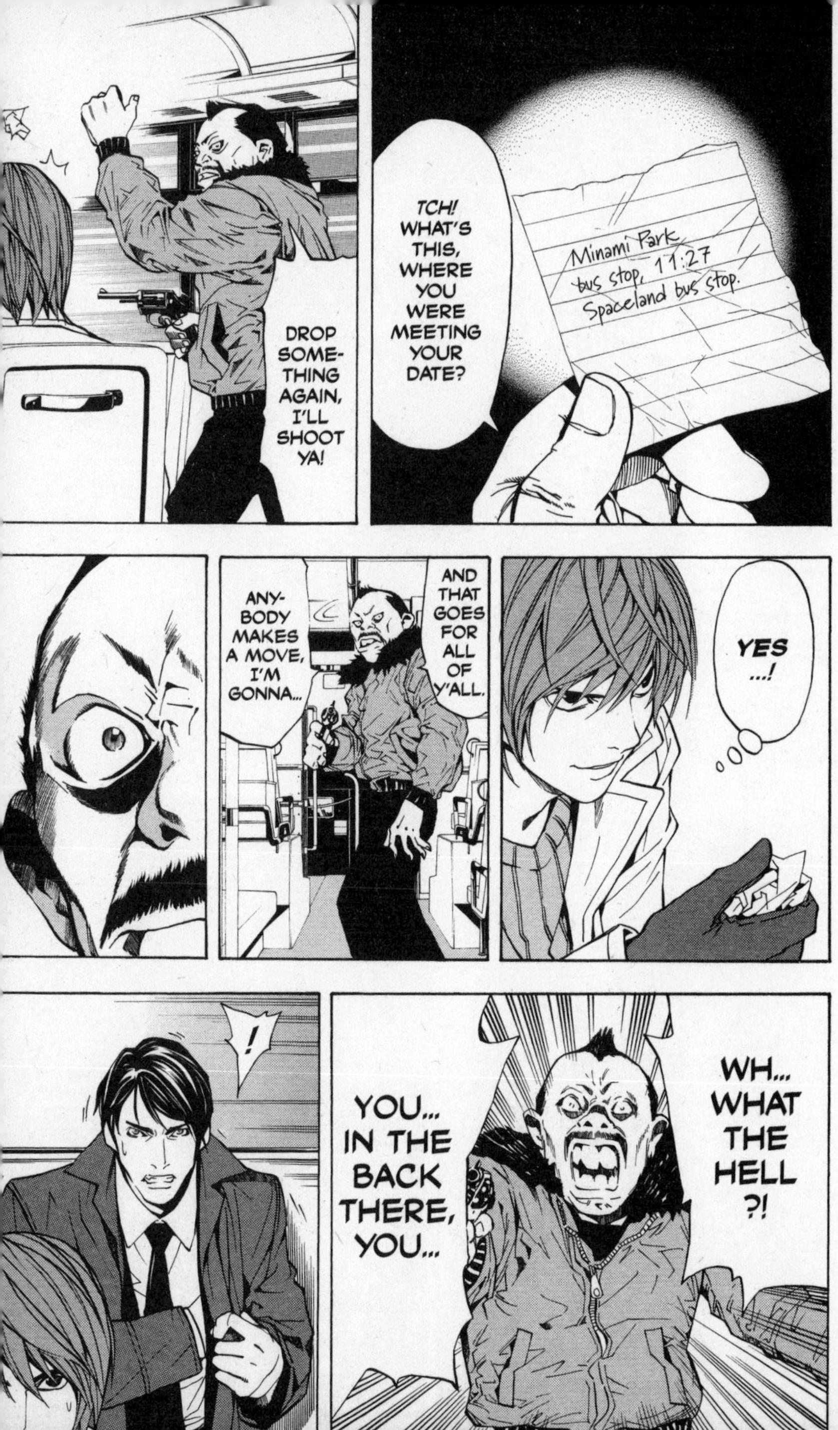
TCH! WHAT'S THIS, WHERE YOU WERE MEETING YOUR DATE?
Minami Park bus stop, 11:27 Spaceland bus stop.
DROP SOMETHING AGAIN, I'LL SHOOT YA!
YES ...!
AND THAT GOES FOR ALL OF Y'ALL.
ANYBODY MAKES A MOVE, I'M GONNA...
WH... WHAT THE HELL ?!
YOU... IN THE BACK THERE, YOU...
!

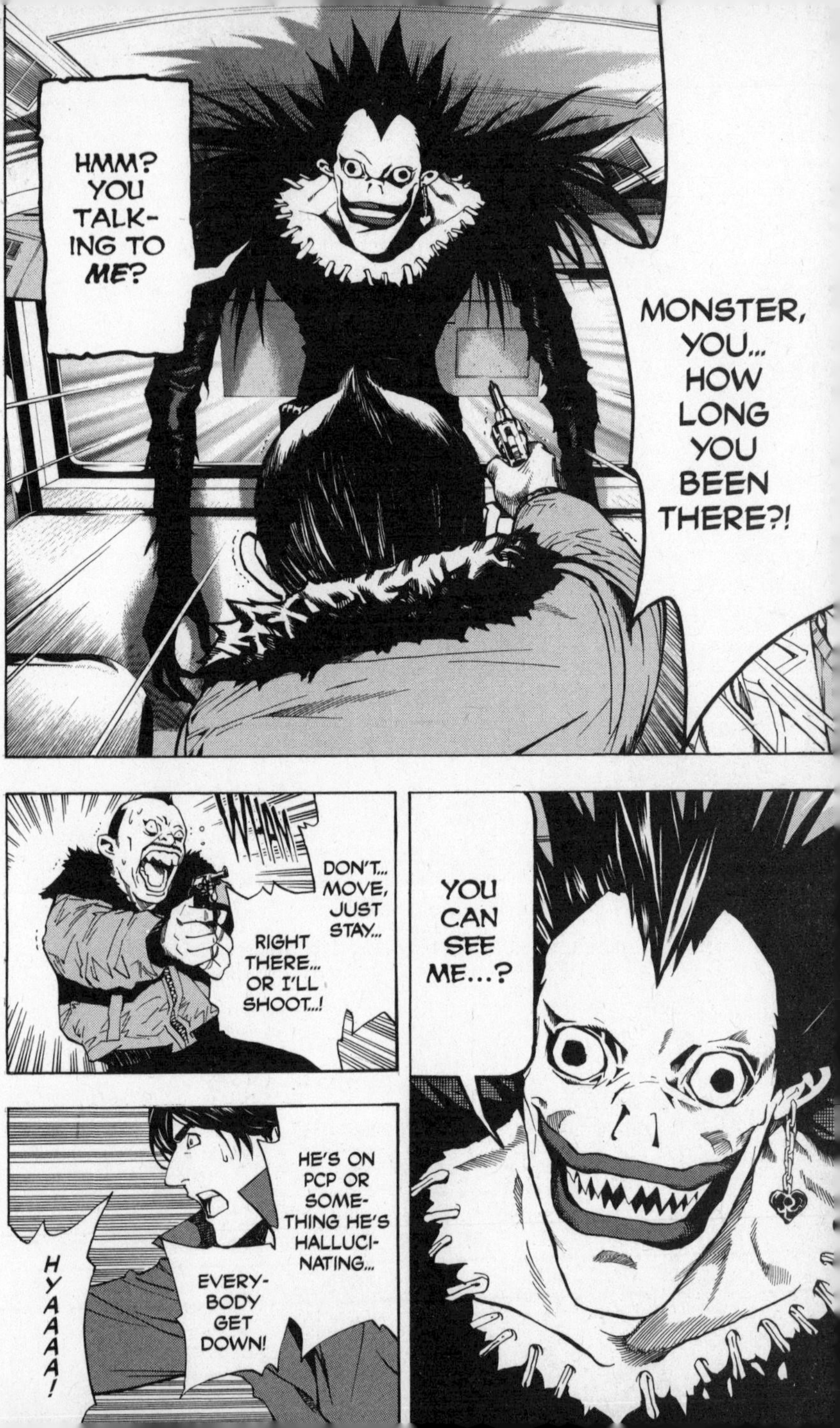
MONSTER, YOU... HOW LONG YOU BEEN THERE?!
HMM? YOU TALKING TO ME?
YOU CAN SEE ME...?
WHAM
DON'T... MOVE, JUST STAY...
RIGHT THERE... OR I'LL SHOOT...!
HE'S ON PCP OR SOMETHING HE'S HALLUCINATING...
EVERYBODY GET DOWN!
HYAAAAA!

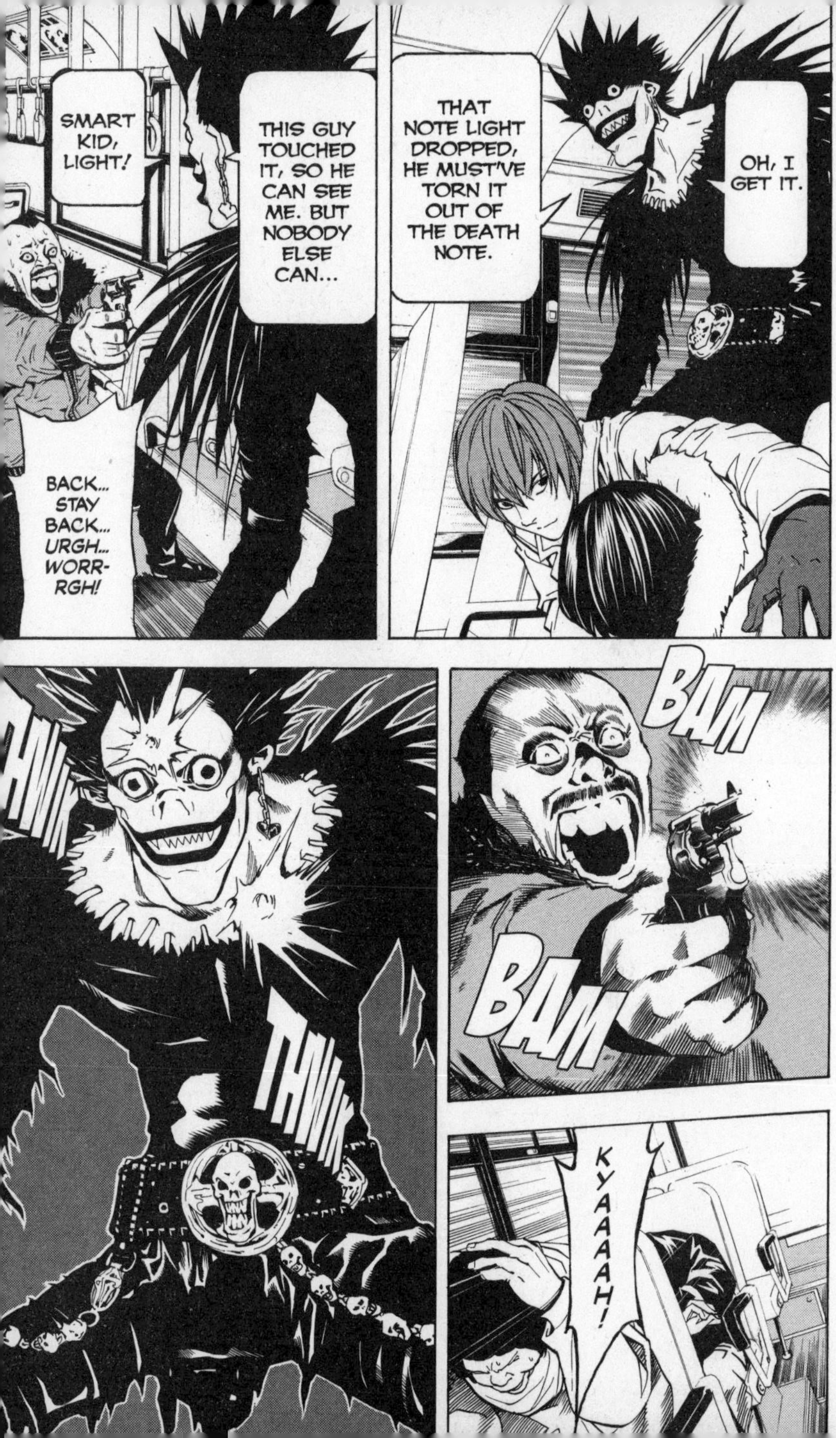
OH, I GET IT.
THAT NOTE LIGHT DROPPED, HE MUST'VE TORN IT OUT OF THE DEATH NOTE.
THIS GUY TOUCHED IT, SO HE CAN SEE ME. BUT NOBODY ELSE CAN...
SMART KID, LIGHT!
BACK... STAY BACK... URGH... WORRRGH!
BAM
BAM
KYAAAAAH!
THWIK
THWIK

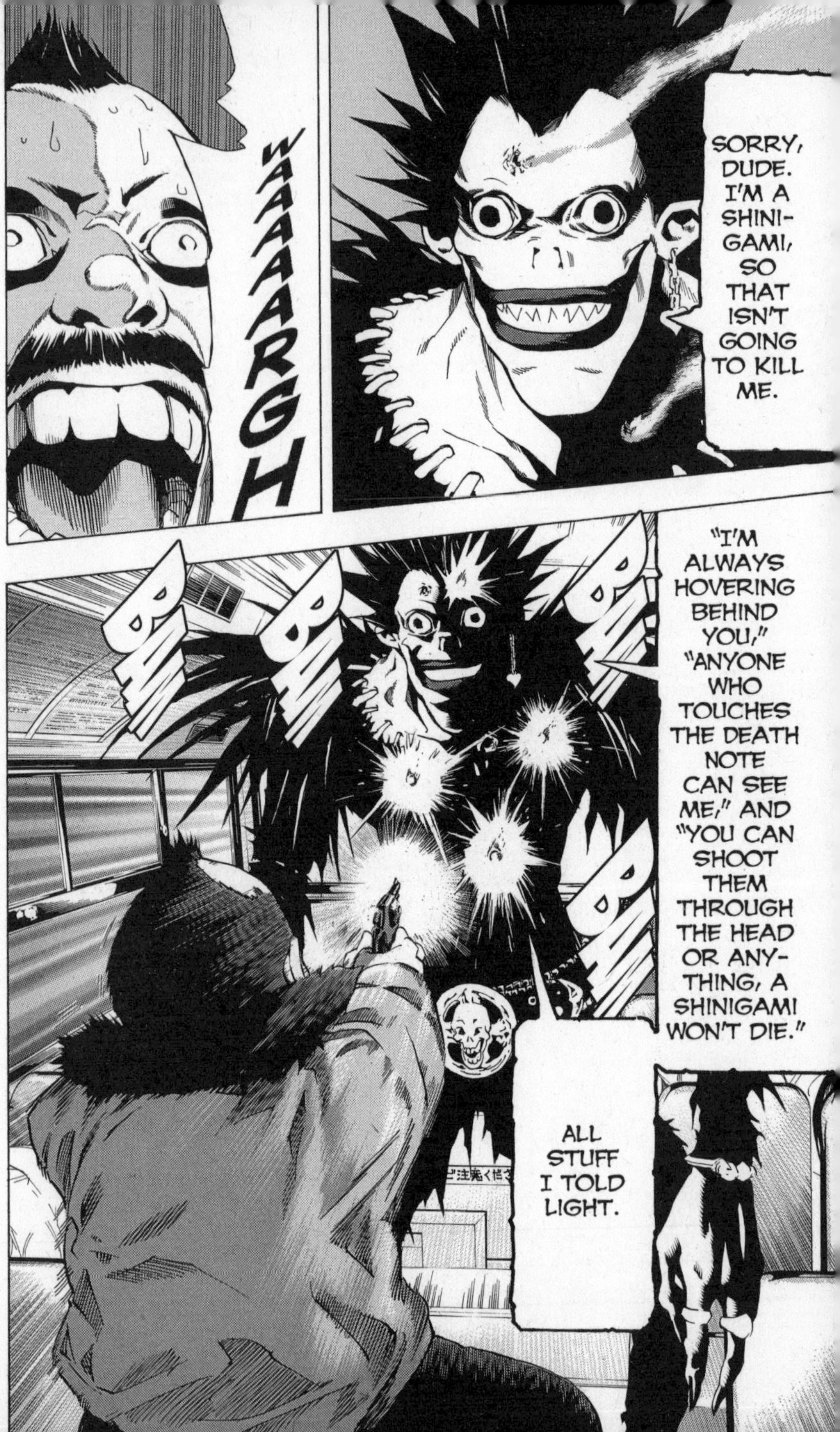
SORRY, DUDE. I'M A SHINIGAMI, SO THAT ISN'T GOING TO KILL ME.
WAAAAARGH
"I'M ALWAYS HOVERING BEHIND YOU," "ANYONE WHO TOUCHES THE DEATH NOTE CAN SEE ME," AND "YOU CAN SHOOT THEM THROUGH THE HEAD OR ANYTHING, A SHINIGAMI WON'T DIE."
BAM
BAM
BAM
BAM
ALL STUFF I TOLD LIGHT.

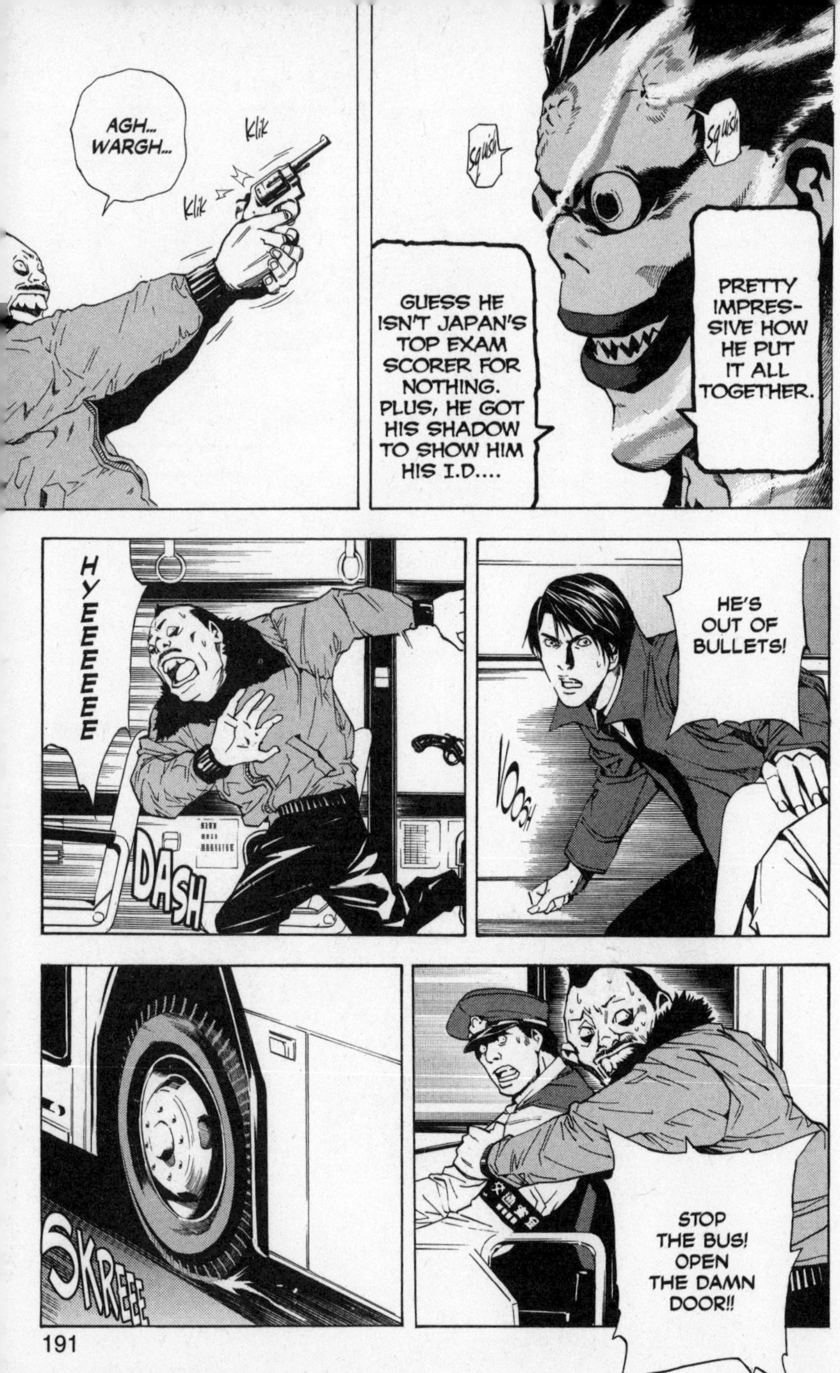
squish
squish
PRETTY IMPRESSIVE HOW HE PUT IT ALL TOGETHER.
GUESS HE ISN'T JAPAN'S TOP EXAM SCORER FOR NOTHING. PLUS, HE GOT HIS SHADOW TO SHOW HIM HIS I.D....
AGH... WARGH...
Klik
Klik
HE'S OUT OF BULLETS!
VOOSH
HYEEEEEEE
DASH
STOP THE BUS! OPEN THE DAMN DOOR!!
SKREEE

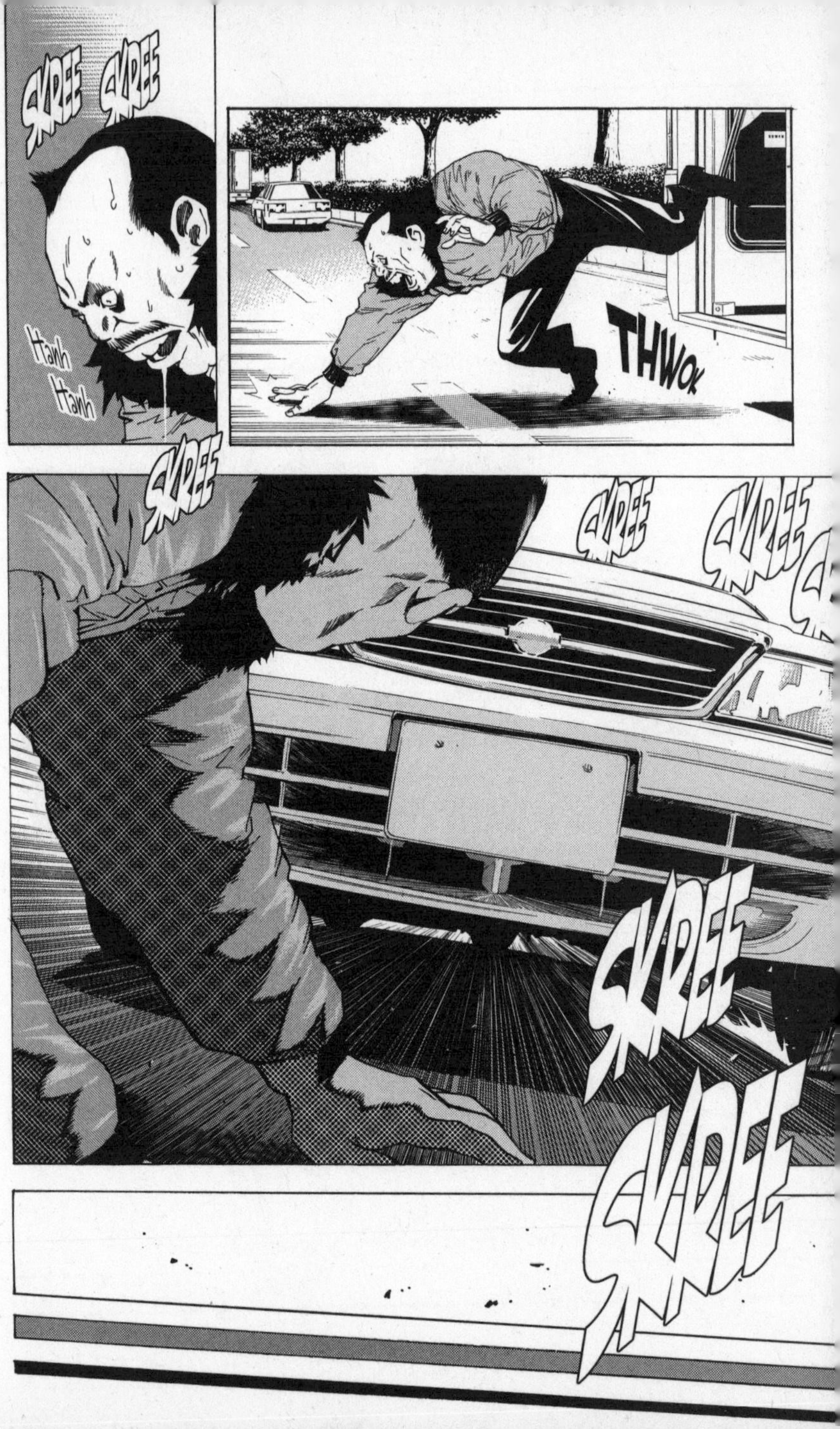
THWOK
SKREE SKREE
Hanh Hanh
SKREE
SKREE
SKREE
SKREE
SKREE

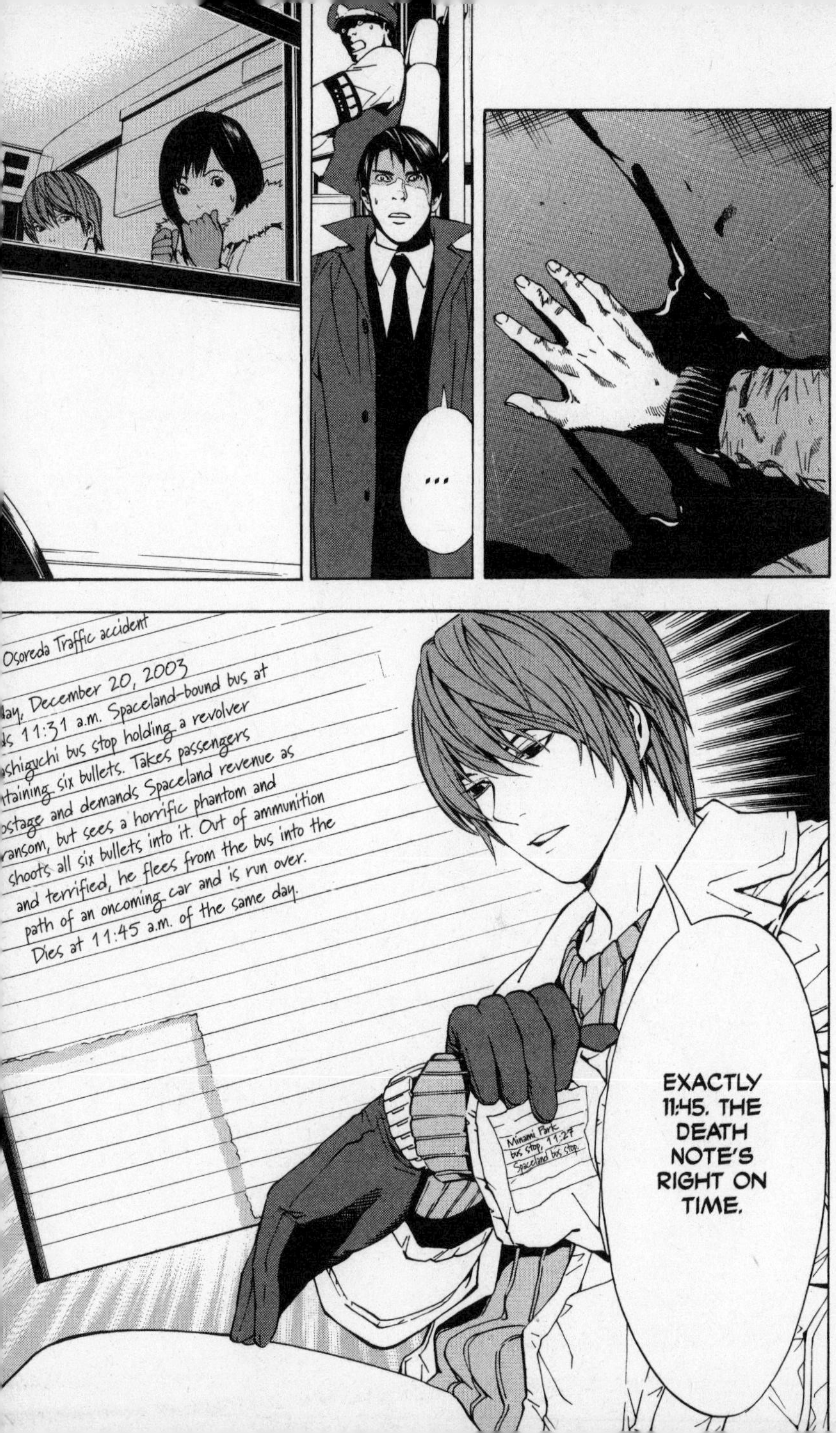
...
Osoreda Traffic accident
day, December 20, 2003
ds 11:31 a.m. Spaceland-bound bus at
ashiguchi bus stop holding a revolver
ntaining six bullets. Takes passengers
ostage and demands Spaceland revenue as
ransom, but sees a horrific phantom and
shoots all six bullets into it. Out of ammunition
and terrified, he flees from the bus into the
path of an oncoming car and is run over.
Dies at 11:45 a.m. of the same day.
Minami Park bus stop, 11:27 Spaceland bus stop.
EXACTLY 11:45. THE DEATH NOTE'S RIGHT ON TIME.

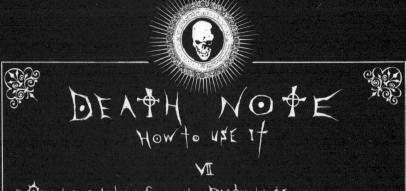

DEATH NOTE
How to Use It

VII

○ One page taken from the DEATH NOTE, or even a fragment of the page, contains the full effects of the note.

デスノートから切り取った1ページやその切れ端でも全て、デスノートの特性が有効である。

○ The instrument to write with can be anything, ((e.g. cosmetics, blood, etc)) as long as it can write directly onto the note and remains as legible letters.

文字として残る物であれば、書く道具はノートに直に書き込みさえすれば何でもよい。化粧品や血でも構わない。

○ Even the original owners of the DEATH NOTE, gods of death, do not know much about the note.

デスノートについて、わからない事は元持ち主の死神でも沢山ある。

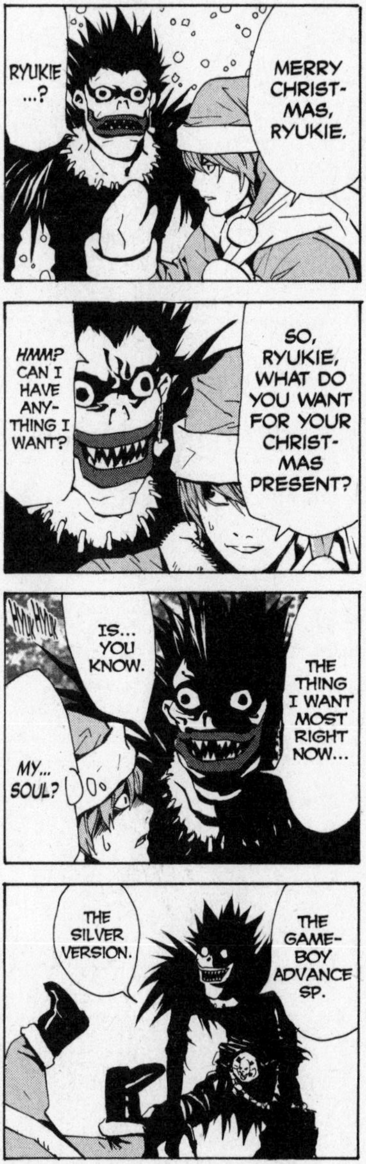
MERRY CHRIST-MAS, RYUKIE.
RYUKIE ...?
SO, RYUKIE, WHAT DO YOU WANT FOR YOUR CHRIST-MAS PRESENT?
HMM? CAN I HAVE ANY-THING I WANT?
THE THING I WANT MOST RIGHT NOW...
IS... YOU KNOW.
MY... SOUL?
THE GAME-BOY ADVANCE SP.
THE SILVER VERSION.

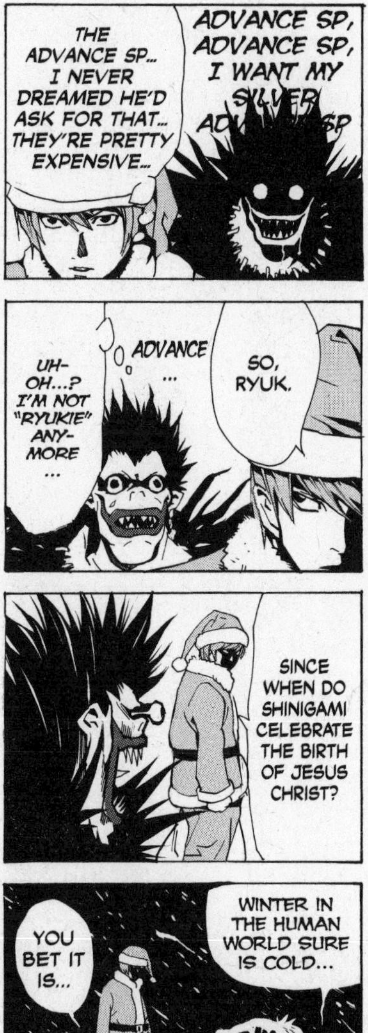
ADVANCE SP, ADVANCE SP, I WANT MY
THE ADVANCE SP... I NEVER DREAMED HE'D ASK FOR THAT... THEY'RE PRETTY EXPENSIVE...
SO, RYUK.
ADVANCE ...
UH-OH...? I'M NOT "RYUKIE" ANY-MORE ...
SINCE WHEN DO SHINIGAMI CELEBRATE THE BIRTH OF JESUS CHRIST?
WINTER IN THE HUMAN WORLD SURE IS COLD...
YOU BET IT IS...

These four-panel cartoons originally appeared in "Weekly Shonen Jump" Vol. 4-5 (double issue), 2004.

In the Next Volume

Light thinks he can end his problems with the FBI by killing off all the agents assigned to the Kira case. But even the most carefully thought-out plan leaves traces, and now Light has L, the police, and a bereaved fiancée hot on his heels!

Available Now

Hikaru no Go

Story by YUMI HOTTA
Art by TAKESHI OBATA

The breakthrough series by Takeshi Obata, the artist of *Death Note!*

Hikaru Shindo is like any sixth-grader in Japan: a pretty normal schoolboy with a penchant for antics. One day, he finds an old bloodstained Go board in his grandfather's attic. Trapped inside the Go board is Fujiwara-no-Sai, the ghost of an ancient Go master. In one fateful moment, Sai becomes a part of Hikaru's consciousness and together, through thick and thin, they make an unstoppable Go-playing team.

Will they be able to defeat Go players who have dedicated their lives to the game? And will Sai achieve the "Divine Move" so he'll finally be able to rest in peace? Find out in this *Shonen Jump* classic!

www.shonenjump.com

www.viz.com

STORY BY TSUGUMI OHBA
ART BY TAKESHI OBATA

From the creators of *Death Note*

The mystery behind manga making REVEALED!

Average student Moritaka Mashiro enjoys drawing for fun. When his classmate and aspiring writer Akito Takagi discovers his talent, he begs to team up. But what exactly does it take to make it in the manga-publishing world?

Bakuman. Vol. 1
ISBN: 978-1-4215-3513-5
$9.99 US / $12.99 CAN *

You're Reading in the Wrong Direction!!

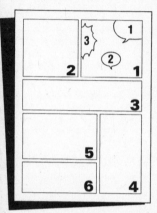

Whoops! Guess what? You're starting at the wrong end of the comic! ...It's true! In keeping with the original Japanese format, **Death Note** is meant to be read from right to left, starting in the upper-right corner.

Unlike English, which is read from left to right, Japanese is read from right to left, meaning that action, sound effects and word-balloon order are completely reversed... something which can make readers unfamiliar with Japanese feel pretty backwards themselves. For this reason, manga or Japanese comics published in the U.S. in English have sometimes been published "flopped"–that is, printed in exact reverse order, as though seen from the other side of a mirror.

By flopping pages, U.S. publishers can avoid confusing readers, but the compromise is not without its downside. For one thing, a character in a flopped manga series who once wore in the original Japanese version a T-shirt emblazoned with "M A Y" (as in "the merry month of") now wears one which reads "Y A M"! Additionally, many manga creators in Japan are themselves unhappy with the process, as some feel the mirror-imaging of their art alters their original intentions.

We are proud to bring you Tsugumi Ohba & Takeshi Obata's **Death Note** in the original unflopped format. For now, though, turn to the other side of the book and let the quest begin...!

–Editor